S0-BPO-018

THE HISTORY OF WESTERN PHILOSOPHY OF RELIGION

ref
210
OpS

THE HISTORY OF WESTERN PHILOSOPHY OF RELIGION

Edited by Graham Oppy and Nick Trakakis

VOLUME 1

ANCIENT PHILOSOPHY OF RELIGION

WITHDRAWN
LIBRARY ST. MARY'S COLLEGE

OXFORD
UNIVERSITY PRESS
2009

OXFORD
UNIVERSITY PRESS

Oxford University Press, Inc., publishes works that further
Oxford University's objective of excellence
in research, scholarship, and education.

© Editorial matter and selection, 2009 Graham Oppy and Nick Trakakis.
Individual contributions, the contributors.

Published by Oxford University Press, Inc.
198 Madison Avenue, New York, NY 10016
www.oup.com

Oxford is a registered trademark of Oxford University Press

All rights reserved. No part of this publication may be reproduced,
stored in a retrieval system, or transmitted, in any form or by any means,
electronic, mechanical, photocopying, recording, or otherwise,
without the prior permission of Oxford University Press.

Published simultaneously outside North America
by Acumen Publishing Limited.

The Library of Congress Cataloging-in-Publication Data

The history of western philosophy of religion / edited by Graham Oppy and Nick Trakakis.
p. cm.
Includes bibliographical references and index.
ISBN 978-0-19-539428-3
1. Religion--Philosophy--History. I. Oppy, Graham Robert. II. Trakakis, Nick.
BL51.H575 2009 210.9--dc22 2009011336

1 3 5 7 9 8 6 4 2

Printed in the UK by MPG Books Group

YBP 8910 03-30-10

CONTENTS

EDITORIAL INTRODUCTION

Bertrand Russell's *History of Western Philosophy* (1946; hereafter *History*) provides a model for *some* of the significant features of the present work. Like Russell's more general history, our history of Western philosophy of religion consists principally of chapters devoted to the works of individual thinkers, selected because of their "considerable importance". Of course, we do not claim to have provided coverage of all of those who have made important contributions to Western philosophy of religion. However, we think that anyone who has made a significant contribution to Western philosophy of religion has either seriously engaged with the works of philosophers who are featured in this work, or has produced work that has been a focus of serious engagement for philosophers who are featured in this work.

Like Russell, we have aimed for contributions that show how the philosophy of religion developed by a given thinker is related to that thinker's life, and that trace out connections between the views developed by a given philosopher and the views of their predecessors, contemporaries and successors. While our primary aim is to provide an account of the ideas, concepts, claims and arguments developed by each of the philosophers under consideration, we think – with Russell – that this aim is unlikely to be achieved in a work in which "each philosopher appears as in a vacuum".

Again like Russell, we have only selected philosophers or religious writers who belong to, or have exerted a significant impact on, the intellectual tradition of the West (i.e. western Europe and the Anglo-American world). We realize that this selection criterion alone excludes from our work a number of important thinkers and religious groups or traditions, such as: Asian philosophers of religion, particularly those representing such religions as Hinduism, Buddhism, Confucianism and Taoism; African philosophers of religion; and individuals, texts and traditions emanating from indigenous religions, such as those found in the native populations of Australia and the Pacific Islands. Clearly, the non-Western world has produced thinkers who have made important, and often overlooked, contributions to the philosophy of religion. We have decided, however, not to include any entries on these thinkers, and our decision is based primarily on the (admittedly not incontestable) view that the Asian, African and indigenous philosophical and religious traditions have not had a great impact on the main historical narrative of the West. It would therefore have been difficult to integrate the various non-Western thinkers into the five-volume structure of the present work. The best way to redress this omission, in our view, is to produce a separate multi-volume work that would be dedicated to the history of non-Western philosophy of religion, a project that we invite others to take up.

Where we have departed most significantly from Russell is that our work has been written by a multitude of contributors, whereas Russell's work was the product of just one person. In the preface to his *History*, Russell claimed that:

> There is … something lost when many authors co-operate. If there is any unity in the movement of history, if there is any intimate relation between what goes before and what comes later, it is necessary, for setting this forth, that earlier and later periods should be synthesized in a single mind. (1946: 5)

We think that Russell exaggerates the difficulties in, and underestimates the benefits of, having a multitude of expert contributors. On the one hand, someone who is an expert on the work of a given philosopher is bound to have expert knowledge of the relation between the work of that philosopher, what goes before and what comes after. On the other hand, and as Russell himself acknowledged, it is impossible for one person to have the expertise of a specialist across such a wide field. (Indeed, while Russell's *History* is admirable for its conception and scope, there is no doubt that it is far from a model for good historical scholarship.)

Of course, Russell's worry about a multiplicity of authors does recur at the editorial level: the editors of this work have no particular claim to expertise concerning any of the philosophers who are featured in the work. In order to alleviate this problem, we invited all of the contributors to read drafts of neighbouring contributions, acting on the assumption that someone who is an expert on a particular philosopher is likely to have reasonably good knowledge of contemporaries and near contemporaries of that philosopher. Moreover, each of the five volumes comes with an expert introduction, written by someone who is much better placed than we are to survey the time period covered in the given volume.

Obviously enough, it is also the case that the present work does not have the kind of narrative unity that is possessed by Russell's work. Our work juxtaposes contributions from experts who make very different theoretical assumptions, and who belong to diverse philosophical schools and traditions. Again, it seems to us that this represents an advantage: there are many different contemporary approaches to philosophy of religion, and each of these approaches suggests a different view about the preceding history. Even if there is "unity in the movement of history", it is clear that there is considerable disagreement about the precise nature of that unity.

Although our work is divided into five volumes – and despite the fact that we have given labels to each of these volumes – we attach no particular significance to the way in which philosophers are collected together by these volumes. The order of the chapters is determined by the dates of birth of the philosophers who are the principal subjects of those chapters. While it would not be a task for a single evening, we do think that it should be possible to read the five volumes as a single, continuous work.

* * *

Collectively, our primary debt is to the 109 people who agreed to join with us in writing the material that appears in this work. We are indebted also to Tristan Palmer, who oversaw the project on behalf of Acumen. Tristan initially searched for someone prepared to take on the task of editing a single-volume history of Western philosophy of religion, and was actively involved in the shaping of the final project. He also provided invaluable advice on the full range of editorial questions that arise in a project on this scale. Thanks, too, to the copy-editors and others at Acumen, especially Kate Williams, who played a role in the completion of this project, and to the anonymous reviewers who provided many helpful comments. We are grateful to Karen Gillen for proofreading and indexing all five volumes, and to the Helen McPherson Smith Trust, which provided financial support for this project. We also acknowledge our debt to Monash University, and to our colleagues in the School of Philosophy and Bioethics. Special thanks to Dirk Baltzly for his suggestions about potential contributors to the volume on ancient Western philosophy of religion and for his editorial help with the chapter on Pythagoras.

Apart from these collective debts, Graham Oppy acknowledges personal debts to friends and family, especially to Camille, Gilbert, Calvin and Alfie. Nick Trakakis is also grateful for the support of family and friends while working on this project, which he dedicates to his nephew and niece, Nicholas and Adrianna Trakakis: my prayer is that you will come to share the love of wisdom cultivated by the great figures in these volumes.

Graham Oppy
Nick Trakakis

CONTRIBUTORS

Dirk Baltzly is Associate Professor in the School of Philosophy and Bioethics at Monash University. He is among the team of Australians translating Proclus' *Timaeus Commentary*, 5 vols (2007–). He has also written on Proclus' ideal of assimilation to God in "The Virtues and 'Becoming Like God'" in *Oxford Studies in Ancient Philosophy* (2004).

Richard Bett is Professor of Philosophy at Johns Hopkins University. His scholarly work has focused on the ancient sceptics, Sextus Empiricus prominent among them. He is the author of *Pyrrho, His Antecedents and His Legacy* (2000), and has translated Sextus Empiricus' *Against the Ethicists* (1997) and *Against the Logicians* (2005). He is currently editing *The Cambridge Companion to Ancient Scepticism*. His next major project will be a translation of Sextus Empiricus' *Against the Physicists*, which contains Sextus' most extensive reflections on the subject of God.

George Boys-Stones is Senior Lecturer in Classics at the University of Durham. He has published on a wide range of topics in ancient philosophy, but has a special interest in the Platonist revival of the first three centuries CE, and its polemical interactions with Stoicism and early Christian philosophy. His book *Post-Hellenistic Philosophy: A Study of its Development from the Stoics to Origen* (2001) explores philosophical constructions of authority (including Christian "orthodoxy") in this context.

Tad Brennan is Professor of Philosophy at Cornell University. His work on Stoicism has appeared in articles in *Phronesis*, *Archiv für Geschichte der Philosophie* and *Oxford Studies in Ancient Philosophy*; in the *Cambridge Companion to Stoicism* (2003); and in his own monograph *The Stoic Life* (2005).

Sarah Broadie (previously Waterlow) is Professor of Moral Philosophy and Wardlaw Professor at the University of St Andrews. She specializes in ancient Greek philosophy and has mainly published on Aristotle. Her books include *Passage and Possibility* (1982), *Nature, Change and Agency in Aristotle's Physics* (1982), *Ethics with Aristotle* (1991), *Aristotle and Beyond* (2007) and a translation of, and commentary on, *Aristotle's Nicomachean Ethics* (with C. J. Rowe, 2002).

Kevin Corrigan is a Professor in the Graduate Institute for Liberal Arts at Emory University, where he conducts research in philosophy, classics, religion, patristics, literature and theory. He is the author of several books, including: *Plotinus' Theory of Matter-Evil and the Question of Substance* (1996), *Reading Plotinus* (2002) and *Fourth Century Views of Soul* (2004). He has also published an annotated translation of Gregory of Nyssa's *The Life of Macrina* (1987).

John Dillon is Regius Professor of Greek (Emeritus) at Trinity College Dublin, and Director of the Centre for the Study of the Platonic Tradition. His main works include *The Middle Platonists* (1977, 2nd edn 1996), an edition of Alcinous' *The Handbook of Platonism* (1993) and *The Heirs of Plato* (2003), as well as two collections of essays, *The Golden Chain* (1990) and *The Great Tradition* (1997).

Mark J. Edwards has been University Lecturer in Patristics at the University of Oxford, and Tutor in Theology at Christ Church, Oxford, since 1993. His publications include an annotated translation of *Philoponus on Aristotle, Physics 3* (1994), *Neoplatonic Saints* (2000), *Origen against Plato* (2002) and *Culture and Philosophy in the Age of Plotinus* (2006). He has also written articles on Gnosticism, Numenius and Porphyry, is contributing a chapter on Numenius to *The Cambridge History of Late Antique and Early Mediaeval Philosophy* and was co-editor of *Approaching Late Antiquity* (with Simon Swain, 2004).

Lloyd P. Gerson is Professor of Philosophy at the University of Toronto. He is the author of *God and Greek Philosophy* (1990) and *Plotinus* (1994); editor of *The Cambridge Companion to Plotinus* (1996); translator and editor with John Dillon of *Neoplatonic Philosophy* (2004); and author of numerous articles on various aspects of Plotinus' philosophy.

Margaret Graver is Professor of Classical Studies at Dartmouth College, where she regularly offers courses in ethical thought in antiquity, Plato, Aristotle, Latin and Greek language, and Latin literature including Lucretius, Cicero and Seneca. She is the author of *Stoicism and Emotion* (2007) and *Cicero on the Emotions* (2002), as well as numerous articles on the ethical psychology of the Stoics and Epicureans. She is currently collaborating with A. A. Long on a complete annotated translation of Seneca's *Moral Epistles*.

Michael Harrington is Assistant Professor of Philosophy at Duquesne University. He is the author of *A Thirteenth-Century Textbook of Mystical Theology at the University of Paris* (2004), as well as *Sacred Place in Early Medieval Neoplatonism* (2004). He is also the author of several articles on Dionysius, including, most recently, "Recent Attempts to Define a Dionysian Political Theory", to appear in the *American Catholic Philosophical Quarterly*.

Jeffrey Hause is Associate Professor of Philosophy and of Classical and Near Eastern Studies at Creighton University. He is the author of several articles on the history of ancient and medieval philosophy, including a number of papers on Aquinas and Abelard, and is co-editor of the Hackett Aquinas Series. He is currently working on a translation of Aquinas' *Disputed Questions on the Virtues* with Claudia Eisen Murphy, to which he will also contribute a philosophical commentary.

James H. Lesher is Professor of Philosophy at the University of North Carolina at Chapel Hill. He is the author of *Xenophanes of Colophon* (1992, 2nd edn 2002), *The Greek Philosophers* (1998), *Plato's Symposium* (edited with Debra Nails and Frisbee Sheffield, 2006), and more than fifty articles on topics relating to ancient Greek philosophy.

Constantinos Macris is a member of the Laboratoire d'Études sur les Monothéismes at Centre National de la Recherche Scientifique (CNRS) in Paris. After the publication of a commentary on Porphyry's *Life of Pythagoras* (2001) and a doctoral dissertation on Iamblichus' *Pythagorean Way of Life* (2004), he is currently engaged in a research project on the Pythagorean tradition. His publications include the entry on "Pythagoras" and some forty entries on minor Pythagoreans for the *Dictionnaire des philosophes antiques* (1989–2005). Works in progress include *Under the Shadow of Pythagoras* (2009, in French) and *Pythagoras and Pythagoreanism (1850–2010).*

Gareth B. Matthews is Professor of Philosophy (Emeritus) at the University of Massachusetts at Amherst. He is the author of many articles and three books on ancient, medieval and early modern philosophy: *Thought's Ego in Augustine and Descartes* (1992), *Socratic Perplexity and the Nature of Philosophy* (1999) and *Augustine* (2005). He is also the editor of *The Augustinian Tradition* (1999).

Mark McPherran is Professor of Philosophy at Simon Fraser University. He is the author of *The Religion of Socrates* (1996), and numerous articles, including: "Socratic Religion", in *The Cambridge Companion to Socrates* (forthcoming); "Medicine, Magic, and Religion in Plato's *Symposium*", in *Plato's Symposium: Issues in Interpretation and Reception* (2006); "Platonic Religion", in *A Companion to Plato* (2006); "The Piety and Gods of Plato's *Republic*", in *The Blackwell Guide to Plato's Republic* (2006); and "Socratic Piety in the *Euthyphro*" (1985). He is also the Director of the Annual Arizona Colloquium in Ancient Philosophy.

Anthony Meredith S.J. is Lecturer in Early Christian Doctrine at Heythrop College, University of London. He is the author of *The Cappadocians* (1995) and *Gregory of Nyssa* (1999), and has contributed the chapter on "Patristic Spirituality" for the *Companion Encyclopedia of Theology* (1995).

Eric Osborn held the position of Professor of New Testament and Early Church History at the United Faculty of Theology (formerly Queen's College), Melbourne, from 1958 to 1987, and was Honorary Professor in the Department of History at La Trobe University from 1987 to 2007. He wrote eight monographs on major theologians and theological themes in the second century, including *The Philosophy of Clement of Alexandria* (1957), *Justin Martyr* (1973), *The Beginning of Christian Philosophy* (1981), *Tertullian* (1997), *Irenaeus of Lyons* (2001) and his final work, *Clement of Alexandria* (2005). He died in May 2007, shortly after writing his contribution to this volume.

John Penwill is head of the arts programme at the Bendigo campus of La Trobe University and President of the Australasian Society for Classical Studies. He has published numerous articles on Epicurus and Lucretius and the impact of Epicureanism in the intellectual milieu of the Roman Empire. He is Associate Editor of *Ramus: Critical Studies in Greek and Roman Literature* and one of the founding editors of *Eye of the Heart*, a new online journal of traditional thought published by La Trobe University.

David T. Runia is Master of Queen's College and Professorial Fellow in the School of Historical Studies at the University of Melbourne. He has written extensively on the writings and thought of Philo of Alexandria, including *Philo of Alexandria and the "Timaeus" of Plato* (1986), *Philo in Early Christian Thought* (1993), and *Philo of Alexandria on the Creation of the Cosmos according to Moses* (2001). He has been editor of the *Studia Philonica Annual* since 1989 and is convenor of the International Philo Bibliography Project.

Stanley K. Stowers is Professor of Religious Studies at Brown University. He is the author of *A Rereading of Romans* (1994), *Letter Writing in Greco-Roman Antiquity* (1986), *The Diatribe and Paul's Letter to the Romans* (1981) and more than fifty articles in books and peer-reviewed journals. He has been president of the New England Region of the Society of Biblical Literature and a founding member and on the steering board of the following Society of Biblical Literature units: Hellenistic Moral Philosophy and Early Christianity, Ancient Myths and Modern Theories of Christian Origins, and Rhetorical Criticism of the New Testament.

1

ANCIENT PHILOSOPHY OF RELIGION: AN INTRODUCTION

George Boys-Stones

The 'philosophy of religion' is unusual as a branch of philosophy in foregrounding the question of whether it has a legitimate object of study to start with.[1] At the same time, this question makes it programmatic for philosophy as a whole. Either philosophy will be, in the end, *opposed* to religion, and defined in some measure by that opposition (as a rational or scientific outlook is opposed to, and defined by its opposition to, fideism, perhaps), or else it will turn out that religion is what frames and gives meaning to the human pursuit of knowledge.

Both of these outlooks have their adherents; and (what is evidence for the programmatic force of the question) on each is built a foundation myth for philosophy as a whole. The most potent and influential is surely the version based in the essential antagonism of religion and philosophy. According to this view, 'philosophy' finds its origins in a historical movement premised precisely on the rejection of 'religious' ways of thinking, a rejection traced to sixth-century Ionia and the revolutionary figure of Thales.

There is no denying the powerful appeal this narrative makes to the imagination. But it is by no means obviously right. An equally strong body of opinion holds that one can see far greater continuity between 'religious' thought and the origins of 'philosophical' thought: that the philosophical tradition never set out to construct itself in opposition to religion at all. Indeed, in some versions of this view, the very idea that it might have done so is unintelligible; 'religion' was not then, even if it is now, the kind of thing to which philosophy could have objected. If this second kind of view is right (as I shall go on to argue), then instead of asking from the beginning about the tools developed by philosophy to handle religious claims, the first question a study of the philosophy of religion in antiquity has to address is how philosophy ever came to have a critical interest in religion at

1. My thanks to Barbara Graziosi for invaluable comments on earlier drafts of this chapter, which was also improved in the light of comments from two anonymous readers.

all. *This*, I shall argue, is the question that provides the context for discussing the development of the particular themes, arguments and strategies that have come to characterize the subject.

PHILOSOPHY VERSUS RELIGION?

One of the main reasons for doubting that philosophy was born in the rejection of religious belief is the well-established fact that pre-Christian religion was not defined in terms of belief to begin with. Religion was constituted for its participants not by dogma, but by involvement in rituals and customs (and these were prescribed more by time and place than by personal or tribal affiliation): by a life lived within certain systems of imagery and iconography. Ancient religion has been aptly described, then, rather as a language of sorts than as a creed (e.g. Gould 1985; cf. Burkert 1985: 54): a way of referring to the world (or some aspect of the world, or the world under some particular description), not of specifying in terms that could be translated into secular language what one has to think about it. This is not to deny that particular views about how the world operated could be associated, more or less commonly, with particular aspects of religious behaviour (although Most [2003: 303] does deny it; cf. by way of contrast Harrison [2008]). But it is to deny that the panoply of ancient religion included any mechanism to determine such associations. The ancient world knew no scriptural revelation, no line of prophets, no Congregation for the Doctrine of the Faith. Priests, whose function was largely confined to the performance of ritual, claimed no authority as intermediaries for the divine; while Oracles, which did, were careful to avoid any comment on 'theological' questions such as what 'gods' were, or how they were to be conceived (cf. evidence in Fontenrose [1978]). Homer and Hesiod achieved wide currency in Greece as reference points for the subsequent mythological tradition, and were even credited with establishing the standard Greek pantheon, along with the genealogy and iconography of its members (Herodotus, *Histories* 2.53; cf. Burkert 1985: 120–22). But if they were important sources of imagery, they were not taken to be 'biblical' authorities for its use. In any case, the continued existence and tolerance of variant accounts ensured that people were quite capable of making the distinction between what one *had* to think about the gods and what Homer or Hesiod said about them.

None of this is, as it happens, especially controversial for historians of religion. Its consequences, however, are uncomfortable for many historians of philosophy. For if Greek religion does not determine the beliefs of its participants, then it is hardly meaningful to talk (as, recently, did e.g. Hussey [2006]; cf. Roochnik 2004: 12–17) about religious 'patterns of thought' or 'patterns of belief' put to bed by the philosophical revolution conventionally associated with Thales in the sixth century BCE. Thales and his successors might have developed new models of analysis, and attempted to explore more critically the basis for received assumptions; they might have used these approaches and models to suggest new explanations for phenomena previously thought inexplicable. One might – one *should* – consider their work foundational for philosophical methodology. (This is, as I mean it, a trivial truth: for it is only to rehearse the fact that it is in this work that the self-consciously philosophical tradition of later centuries identified its intellectual roots.) But to see them as rejecting a specifically 'religious' outlook is to project back onto them a debate that no one had any thought – or motive – to formulate.

It might be objected at this point that my original characterization of the difference between ancient and modern religious belief suggests too sharp a division: that, just as the average modern Christian is less bound by conciliar edict, so the average ancient Greek was more heavily influenced by Homer than I have suggested. Even if I am right to say that we should not talk of ancient religious belief as something sanctioned and defined, according to such an objection, it is enough to allow that particular views were more or less commonly associated with particular religious expression (as I have done) to make it legitimate to talk about a religious 'way of thinking'. It is this that people have in mind when they talk about a worldview that is inherently 'chaotic' (in the manner apparently envisaged by Hussey [2006: 12]) or unstable (cf. discussion in Rowe [1983]), or which surrenders the world to irrational forces (e.g. Vlastos 1975: ch. 1). It is this that is challenged by the work of Thales and his successors.

As a matter of anthropology, the nuance is welcome. But the objection misses its mark if the 'religious way of thinking' identified by it fails to attain normative status in the culture. As long as it remains merely *a* way of thinking with the language of religion, there will be (and it will be understood that there is) clear distance between what one says of the *thought* and what one says of *religion*, considered as the language that happens to be used for the expression of that thought. And we know that the supposedly 'chaotic' form of religious thinking failed to attain normative standing: we know this because the thinkers supposed (under this very theory) to be *on the attack* employ the same language without hesitation or question themselves (cf. Burkert 1985: 306). Until the atomists, all of the early cosmologists used such language to characterize the principles of a world that remained for them, as it famously was for Thales, "full of gods" (11 A 22 DK [= Diels & Kranz 1951–2]).[2] Nor is there anything to suggest that their use of this language is ironic or polemical, for its use is untempered by anything that could seriously be taken as criticism of the religious context from which it is drawn. Occasionally, it is true, reservations are expressed about *particular religious practices*; but even these presuppose the perspective of the religious insider. Far from attacking religion, they question activities and attitudes that risk bringing it into disrepute.

My claim can be mostly clearly illustrated by considering two figures who might seem to be the most obvious counter-examples to it: Xenophanes and Heraclitus.

2. All translations are my own.

These thinkers are often characterized in the literature as *critics*, at least of traditional Greek piety, and perhaps of religion in general. But a closer look will show that such a stance can only be found in them by systematic application of the prejudicial assumption that 'religion' (or anyway Greek religion) is incompatible with rational thought about the world. That this *is* a prejudicial assumption in the case of Heraclitus at least is clear from the fact that the evidence is amenable to a precisely contrary interpretation. Adomėnas (1999), for example, has argued that, so far from setting himself up as a critic of traditional religion, Heraclitus actually sees it offering support to his own metaphysics. What is certainly true is that we should not confuse Heraclitus' negative attitude towards the views held by the ignorant in their approach to religion with his attitude towards religion itself. For it is precisely personal attitude, not religious practice, that Heraclitus most often has in his sights: "They pray to these statues: one might as well converse with houses, as long as one knows nothing about the gods and heroes" (22 B 5 DK [part]; cf. 27, 86, 128). What is under attack here is not prayer to statues, but ignorance. The thought is exactly paralleled by B 107, where Heraclitus speaks of eyes and ears as things that are similarly said to be *no good* without intelligence, which is, of course, not an invitation to think that Heraclitus disapproved of eyes and ears in general.

Heraclitus does occasionally – but very occasionally – address particular religious practices: "If it was not for Dionysus that they held their procession and sang in praise of the genitals, it would be a most shameless thing" (22 B 15 DK; cf. 5, 127; perhaps 14). But the qualification here is all-important: *if it was not done for Dionysus*. Sardonic remarks about how bizarre we would consider such practices in any other than their proper context cannot be taken as a criticism of them when performed in the appropriate time and place. If they could, then, again, by parity of reasoning we should have to conclude from B 58 that Heraclitus disapproved of the medical art *tout court* as well: for it is perverse, as he says there, to pay physicians for cautery and surgery when we would normally do anything to avoid getting burned or cut.

Finally, it needs to be acknowledged that Heraclitus is capable of expressing himself in terms of conventional piety, with which he obviously feels completely at home (e.g. B 24, 79, 83, 92, 93). Indeed, what might really strike us about even the so-called 'critical' pronouncements is the religious justification he gives for the criticism (esp. e.g. B 14, 27, 86).

The same can be said for Xenophanes. His negative remarks are far fewer than one would believe from the attention they have attracted, and far more carefully circumscribed. Like most of the supposedly 'critical' fragments of Heraclitus, they attack individuals, not their religion (21 B 1, 11, 12 DK, with Graziosi 2002: 60); like all of them, they are themselves concerned with upholding standards of piety. Xenophanes' famous remarks on the cultural relativity of religious iconography, which are frequently adduced as damning indictments of traditional religion, are in fact perfectly neutral in tone: "If oxen or horses or lions had hands, if they could draw and make things with their hands as men do, horses would make images of gods like horses, oxen like oxen. They would fashion for them the bodies that they themselves had" (B 15 DK; cf. 14, 16). Such fragments do no more than point out that other peoples do, and other species might, depict their gods in other ways. They no more imply a criticism of traditional religion than if they had observed that the Greeks talk about the gods in Greek while Thracians and Ethiopians (who figure in B 16) use different languages for the purpose, namely their own. (If horses and oxen had the power of speech they would, of course, talk of them in Horse and Ox.) Commentators can turn these fragments into criticism only on the back of an assumption that the Greeks allowed no gap between the nature of divinity and the possibilities for its artistic representation. This would in any case be a bold assumption. The fluidity of the gods' representation within the Greek tradition makes it wholly untenable.

In general, then, there is no evidence at all that philosophy began with a movement opposed to 'religious' ways of thinking: none that it was, at least through the sixth and fifth centuries BCE, even an option. The continuity of language, on the other hand – and, one might add, of topic (the Milesians thematized the 'origin', *archē*, of things and their *generation* just as much as Hesiod or the Orphic cosmogonies; cf. West 1983: chs 3–4; Clay 2003: 2–3) – suggests that there might be a way of understanding the new cosmology as a *development* of religious expression.

But this, now, might seem an odd claim to make, even on my own account. For I have been careful to divorce religious forms, conceived as a kind of language, from opinions that might or might not have been associated with them in the minds of religious practitioners. The language of cosmology, on the other hand, more clearly does express particular views about the cosmos. What sense does it make, then, to connect the latter with the former? To answer this question, I take my cue from Plato and Aristotle, to whom we owe the self-conscious construction of philosophy as a distinct intellectual tradition. For they ask a pertinent question when they ask why it is that human beings engaged in (what they are defining as) 'philosophy' to begin with. It was not because there was any compelling *need* for it: "That it is not a productive art is clear right from the first philosophers. For then as now men began to do philosophy from a sense of *wonder* ..." (Aristotle, *Metaphysics* A.2, 982b11–12; cf. Plato, *Theaetetus* 155d, with Snell 1953: 38). Both Plato and Aristotle do, as a matter of fact, believe in the practical benefits of philosophy, which both make essential to happiness. But neither traces his intellectual roots to the early students of human well-being (Solon, for example, or Theognis). Both rather trace them to the 'physicists', the students of nature; both explain the characteristically philosophical impulse as a response to the *wonder* of the universe.[3] And what is really striking about the word that both

3. Natural philosophy might be turned to use as well, of course. The story is told, for example, of Thales predicting a bumper harvest and establishing a profitable monopoly on the olive presses. But it is told precisely to dissociate philosophy from the utilitarian considerations

use in this context – *thauma* – is its conventional association precisely with religious experience.[4]

It seems to me entirely credible, and much more consistent with the evidence than any alternative, that archaic Greek religion had a role to play as a 'language', not least because, whatever else it expressed for the individuals who engaged with it, it expressed a sense of 'wonder' at the world, a sense (of 'awe'?) not captured for its users in the quotidian language of opinion and practicality. Similarly it seems that Plato and Aristotle are fundamentally right to think that philosophy (i.e. what they themselves define as such) is an extension of this response: a version of it that becomes doctrinal in seeking to pin down *what* the 'wonder' consists in, how the cosmos conceived as 'wonderful' operates. This is why philosophy retained at its core the language particular to that sense of wonder: the language, that is, of 'divinity'. It is also why the very idea of an attack on 'traditional religion' – or, indeed, a defence of it – could only arise *within* a relatively well-developed philosophical system. For such an attack must be premised, not on the idea that traditional religion is a stumbling block to rational understanding, but on the reflective conclusion that it is *superfluous*: that the 'wonder' of the cosmos is not 'out there' to express at all.

CONSENSUS AND 'EXPERIENCE': CLASSICAL ORIGINS

The centrality of 'religious' language to cosmology remained quite unquestioned until the fifth century BCE, and the emergence of a raft of thinkers of whom we can take Protagoras and perhaps Democritus to be representative.[5] Democritus, as it happens, recognized the existence of "gods", or anyway of entities that explain why people think there are gods (68 A 74–9 DK). To this extent, he accepts the validity of religious language. But Democritus goes against the consensus of preceding

that *might have been*, but *were not*, its inspiration. See Aristotle, *Politics* 1.11, 1259a5–18 (= 11 A 10 DK).

4. Cf. *Homeric Hymn to Demeter* 240–41; *Homeric Hymn to Aphrodite* 84–90, 205; Pythagoras 58 C 6.30–31 DK ("Disbelieve nothing wonderful [*thaumaston*] about the gods, or doctrines concerning the gods"). Likewise of nature conceived as divinely ordered: e.g. Empedocles 31 B 35.17 DK; Galen, *On the Usefulness of the Parts of the Body* iv, 358 Kühn (= Arnim 1903–5 [hereafter *SVF*] 2.1151); Philo, *On Rewards and Punishments* 33 (*SVF* 2.1171). Likewise too in arguments from design: Sextus Empiricus, *Against the Professors* 9.99, 115. The association between *wonder* and religion is recognized even by atheists: see Euhemerus, quoted at Sextus Empiricus, *Against the Professors* 9.17.
5. Gerson (1990: 27) suggests that there is no theology in Parmenides, since he identifies reality with thought. But Parmenides certainly uses the language of religion (28 A 20, 30–31, 33, 37 DK; B 1, 12–13) and Kingsley (1999) is right to remind us that Parmenides was himself a priest. (Kingsley is able, in fact, to read his poem as precisely a record of religious experience.)

generations in refusing to use this language to describe the originative material that forms the bedrock of his cosmology. Democritean atoms are, in fact, perhaps the first example of a material principle not so described. The 'gods' of which he speaks exist at a level of the universe whose reality is secondary and derivative (cf. B 9, 125), which in Democritus' terms means not really *real* at all. So, while there is room to think that the language of deity has some residual role to play in describing the human experience of the cosmos, it is for the first time possible to conduct scientific cosmology without it. This is a significant development. To present a cosmology without religious language is not to say plainly what others had said metaphorically. It is to deny something that others asserted or assumed about the cosmos.

One can see more explicitly a similar development in the work of Democritus' older contemporary Protagoras, who began his provocative book *On the Gods* with these words: "About the gods I have no way of knowing that they exist or do not exist, or what they look like. There are many things that prevent me from knowing: the obscurity of the subject, and the brevity of human life" (80 B 4 DK). This is not, of course, atheism, although some in antiquity took it to be so (Sextus Empiricus, *Against the Professors* 9.55–6). Protagoras does not *deny* the existence of the gods. But it would be ingenuous to see this programmatic statement as merely cautious agnosticism. The philosopher who began another of his books with the famous claim that "Man is the measure of all things" here too suggests that the existence of the gods makes no difference to one's experience of the world. So there is a denial here: a denial that religious language *adds* anything at all, that it *has* meaningful content of its own. The universe will end up looking the same whether one calls its originative matter or structuring forces 'divine' or not.

It is against this background that we need to understand the first arguments adduced in favour of the existence of god. For these arguments, I suppose, are not intended *only* as vindications of belief, but, just as importantly, are meant to establish to an audience who could conceive of a world without it that 'god-talk' has purpose and content that are not covered by other areas of the language. One of our earliest pieces of evidence for the form taken by these arguments comes from a dialogue by Plato, and looks back, perhaps, precisely to the time of Democritus and Protagoras a generation before him. In the course of a discussion of the importance of religious belief, one of the participants in the dialogue, Clinias, offers what must have been the stock theistic response to the threat of atheism:

> CLINIAS: Well, my friend, it seems fairly easy to show that people who say that there are gods are telling the truth, doesn't it?
>
> ATHENIAN: How?
>
> CLINIAS: First there is the earth and sun and stars and everything, and the seasons that are so well arranged and divided into years and months. Then there is the fact that everyone, both Greeks and non-Greeks, reckon that there are gods. (*Laws* 885e–886a)

Clinias' two arguments resonate through much of the subsequent history of the philosophy of religion. The first of these is a simple form of the so-called 'argument from experience'. Clinias' claim seems to be that there is *obviously* something about the heavenly bodies that justifies the use of religious language about them. The second, an argument from consensus, is presumably meant to undermine the idea (which is in fact identified as the central plank of the atheistic thesis at 889e) that since religious *language* is merely conventional, the very gods it describes must be human fictions as well. (Such an argument is attested for Critias [88 B 25 DK].) It does this by showing that religious language cuts across all cultural boundaries by which the merely conventional is normally identified.

The reply of the Athenian (who is unnamed, but often assumed to represent Plato himself) is instructive for us in the weaknesses it identifies in these arguments. He denies first of all that universal consensus (in Clinias' form of it) bears much weight. This is partly because the consensus would have to take account of the immorality associated with divinity by some of the most influential voices of his own tradition (*Laws* 886b–d; at the front of his mind are Homer and Hesiod, of course). But it is also because the Athenian himself explicitly recognizes that the *use of religious language* is not in itself any guide to the beliefs underlying it. The fact that people use the language of religion is not proof that they need it, that they have in mind something for which they could not have used other words. In fact the Athenian's response at this point converges with his objection to the argument from experience. For all that argument does is identify items in the cosmos that the atheists already know about. Applying religious language to them cannot elevate their status:

> You and I, when we talk about proof that there are gods, adduce these very things, the sun, moon, the stars, the earth, as themselves gods and divine entities. But anyone who listens to these wise men [i.e. the atheists] will say that they are just earth and stones, incapable of any interest in human affairs, however we dress them up with persuasive language. (886d–e)

In Plato's assessment, it seems, these first forays into the definition of deity through argument are not really equal to the threat of the determined materialist. Nevertheless, it is possible for us to glean something important from what Clinias has tried, and some confirmation of the idea that the philosophical reception of religious language answers to a sense of *wonder* in the face of the world. Clinias' argument from experience asserts his sense that there is just something about the world that elicits more in response from us than mere earth and stones would. 'God' is not displacing nature here, but apparently naming some aspect of it. Indeed, this is Clinias' problem: challenged by the atheist, he has nothing new to show. A useful analogy is with the 'other minds' problem. Confronted with other human beings, one feels that one can *know* (experience, sense) the presence of minds and selves that are qualitatively comparable with one's own. Yet if one were asked to *demonstrate* that that there is a mind there, that things would look and feel very different if the person were an insentient machine, that would be very difficult. Wherever one points, it seems to be the machine one finds.

The analogy that exists between the 'other minds' problem and Clinias' sense of god did not elude Plato, for it is in effect the basis for his own improved demonstration of the existence of god. To cut short what is in the exposition a rather long argument, and one that purports to show rather more than this by the end, Plato argues (891e–899e) that corporeal entities in general, although capable of transmitting motion, are not capable of initiating it, unless they are endowed with that *self*-moving principle we call 'soul'. In the case of the cosmos too, then, its motion must be due to the presence of incorporeal, self-moving soul. (In fact this is especially true of the cosmos as a whole, since there is no other, corporeal entity to which it could conceivably owe its motion.) The cosmos, in other words, manifests the attribute of *life* – and, Plato adds, for its orderly nature, rational life at that (cf. 898c).

This argument builds on Clinias' sense that there is something (something 'wonderful'?) about the world that is not explained by a list of its material parts, and it does so by identifying a plausible candidate for the *something else* that is needed to explain it. That 'something' is, he suggests, qualitatively identical to the principle of 'life' that we identify in living creatures within the cosmos (895c). No wonder, then, that most people recognize the existence of 'gods'. (It turns out at 887c–888a that the Athenian is not altogether above an appeal to consensus after all.) The activity of the divine is *evident*, at least to perception informed by reason.

This debate marks an important moment for philosophy, as well as for the philosophy of religion. For an argument over whether the language of deity is a proper part of philosophy ultimately opens the way for philosophy to develop as a tradition *distinct from* religious discourse in a way that might bring the two into conflict. So it was, no doubt, part of Plato's own intention, in defining philosophy as a skill with its proximate roots in the work of the early Ionians, to steal a march on the atheistic tendencies to which that work had latterly given rise by insisting on its inherently *religious* character. Plato's Socrates, poster-boy of subsequent philosophical enquiry, traces his beginning in philosophy to an encounter with the divine (*Apology* 21b), and sees his philosophy as divine service (cf. *Phaedo* 60e–61b; *Euthyphro* 13d) and himself as divine intermediary (*Symposium* 203a; cf. 219c; Hunter 2004: 84; Bussanich 2006). The end of his work is variously conceived in terms of 'purification' (e.g. *Phaedo* 66b–67c), afterlife (*Apology* 40e–41c) or assimilation to god (*Theaetetus* 176a–b). This language is no accident: Plato quite deliberately shapes his philosophy as a religious pursuit, a way of celebrating the gods (cf. esp. Nightingale [2004] on Plato's appropriation of the word 'theory', *theoria*, from the context of participation in religious festivals). I have discussed above already how he, and after him Aristotle, orient it towards the *wonder* of the universe. Philosophy might be distinguishable now from religion, but in Plato's terms it is its heir, not its other.

CONSENSUS AND EXPERIENCE IN HELLENISTIC PHILOSOPHY

Plato's approach to divinity plays down the consensus argument in favour of a strengthened version of the argument from experience, which asks us to see the incorporeal conditions of order within the perceptible world. This, of course, is all of a piece with his wider belief in an incorporeal realm by which the world of the senses is structured. But one did not have to believe in such a realm to believe in the reality of the divine, as we can see from Plato's empiricist successors in the Hellenistic era: the schools of Epicurus and the Stoics. Both of these schools, though, found it necessary to strike a different balance between the descendents of Clinias' two arguments (the argument from experience and the consensus argument). Both were committed to the view that any real entity is corporeal and so, in principle at least, perceptible; both, then, steered away from the road on which Plato started towards private *inference* as a way of shoring up the experience of the divine, and towards a greater emphasis on the argument from universal consensus.

The more extreme of the two schools in this sense is the Epicurean, which privileges the consensus argument absolutely over any consideration drawn from private speculation about the cosmos:

> Epicurus alone saw, first, that there must be gods because nature itself impresses an idea of them in the minds of all. There is no people, no race of men, that lacks some untutored "preconception" of the gods – what Epicurus calls a *prolēpsis* … If everyone's nature agrees on something, it is necessarily true; so we must admit that there are gods. And since there is almost unanimous agreement on this, among the uneducated as well as philosophers, we say that it is also agreed that this preconception … is such that we think the gods blessed and immortal. (Cicero, *On the Nature of the Gods* 1.43–5)

It will be observed that this version of the consensus argument differs from that of Clinias in one significant respect. While Clinias argues that Greek and non-Greek alike believe in the existence of gods, that is, *that there are gods*, Epicurus' claim is that there is universal consensus *both* that gods exist *and* that they are blessed and immortal. Epicurus, in other words, does not invoke a second strand of argument to explore *what the gods are like*: the kind of consideration that Clinias' argument from experience was supposed to provide. It is possible to doubt that this is the safest way of developing the argument from consensus: the more one claims consensus about, the more likely it is that the consensus does not really exist (cf. Plutarch, *On the Contradictions of the Stoics* 38). In fact, it has even been suggested, with some plausibility, that Epicurus himself did not think that consensus *actually existed*: only that it *would* do in an ideal world (Obbink 1992). But if this is the claim, why make anything hang on it at all?

Epicurus' position is an unusual one, for it will turn out that, whatever he thinks the gods are, he is sure that they have no role to play in a cosmology. (In fact he thinks that the slapdash organization of the cosmos amounts to something like an argument *against* the cosmological involvement of any intelligent being; Lucretius, *On the Nature of Things* 2.167–82, 5.195–234.) Yet unlike Protagoras, for example, he takes seriously the phenomenology of religious 'experience'. He has a good reason to do so: as an empiricist, he will find the fact that people have a *sense* of deity all the more striking precisely because there is reason to believe that the gods are not active in the world.

Epicurus, then, has to provide an account of god that gives empirical content to religious experience without deriving that content from humanity's immediate cosmic environment. This, surely, is why he insists that a full characterization of god can be given by the consensus argument without further appeal to our experience of the natural world. It may also be why he insists on the idea that the experience of deity is of something tranquil and immortal: after all, nothing in our experience of the natural world is immortal; and nothing tranquil would want any part in it (*Letter to Herodotus* 76–7).

His conclusion is that, *if the experience of god is real*, then it must be direct: *parallel to*, not *derived from*, our experience of the world. His distinctive epistemology comes in very handy at this point to explain how this might work. According to Epicurus, absolutely *any* thought, whether based in sensory perception or dreams or imagination, involves the interaction of the atoms that constitute our minds with delicate 'films' (*eidōla*) of atoms thrown off by real objects in uncountable number. The idea is that in ordinary waking life our experience is dominated by more substantial films from relatively close objects that come through the sense organs. But if we shut this 'noise' out, and especially when we are asleep, we become sensitive to the much finer films from more distant objects that do not need the grosser portals of the senses. (In principle, we become open to films from objects all over the universe: they move very quickly, and are too fine to meet effective obstruction; and this is how we can experience images of anything we care to imagine.) Clearly, Epicurus argues, if we have a concept of god it is because there are films representing gods that we perceive (in sleep or imagination), and objects producing these films. Because we perceive them directly in this way, they need not be integral parts of our cosmos, but might (as Epicurus in fact thinks) be outside it.[6]

Whether Epicurus' position carries any water is a moot question. Indeed, it has been a moot question since antiquity whether it was even offered in good faith: many have supposed that the argument was a sop to conventional piety

6. We are, of course, capable of imagining fictions: this happens, according to Epicurus, when we encounter a confusion of films, as when those of a man and a horse strike us as a 'centaur'. But such confusions do not force themselves on people's minds in all parts of the world as films of tranquil and immortal beings do. Consensus heads off the objection.

from an atheist pure and simple. What is certainly true is that the Epicureans were an irritation to conventional theists. Even if their belief in god was genuine, their justification for it paradoxically (and, no doubt, infuriatingly) *removed* god from relevance to philosophical enquiry (cf. perhaps Sextus Empiricus, *Against the Professors* 9.58). The Stoics, by contrast, brought the argument from experience back to bear on the question and, by blending it in their own way with the consensus argument, hoped to provide an account of god that would vindicate his active role in the cosmos even while satisfying the demands of strict empiricism.

The way the Stoics went about this was to start their version of the consensus argument without the claim that there is consensus over the existence of god, let alone over his nature. In fact they explicitly deny that there is consensus at this point (Sextus Empiricus, *Against the Professors* 9.61; Cicero, *On the Nature of the Gods* 2.12–13). They start their version of the argument, rather, with the observation that everyone has a *concept* of god. In other words, the Stoics address not a shared belief as evidence for shared experience of something real in the world, but a shared concept.[7] Furthermore, the Stoics claim that the concept they are talking of is *simple*, somewhat in the way that the concepts of 'red' or 'hard' or 'good' might be thought to be simple. The concept of god is not, for example, a concept of 'god as good'. One might think of it as something like an irreducible concept of the 'numinous', or the *wonderful*, perhaps. In any case, this radical simplicity guarantees that the concept cannot be the product of imagination: that is, the combination or manipulation of pre-existing concepts. One could no more invent *this* concept in imagination than one could think up a new primary colour.

But how did we acquire this concept if we have never had a sensory encounter with god? The answer to this takes us back to the argument from experience, which the Stoics use to suggest that we *have* had direct sensory experience of god; in fact we are perceiving god all the time as we encounter the natural world:

> Cleanthes, of our school, said that four causes explain the formation of concepts of gods in the souls of men. The first cause, he said … arose with foreknowledge of the future; a second we derived from the wealth of benefits that can be seen in the moderation of the climate, the fertility of the earth, and in an abundance of other benefits; the third lies in things that strike terror into our souls: lightning and tempest, rainstorm, snow, hail, devastation, pestilence, the movement and groaning of the earth; showers of stones and showers as if of blood; landslides and crevices that suddenly open up in the ground; unnatural prodigies,

7. This position is not uncontroversial, since our evidence (Cicero and Sextus as cited) also characterizes the argument as one from agreement *in the existence of god*. But my view is that it is easier to explain this as a loose characterization of the argument in what is after all, in both cases, a polemical context, than to explain by any other means the insistence apparent in both passages on the role of the *concept* in the argument.

> human and animal, lights in the sky, and those stars that the Greeks call 'comets' ... The fourth and most important cause is the regularity of the movement and revolution of the heavens, the orderliness of the sun, moon and stars. It is enough to see it to know that it is not accidental.
>
> (Cicero, *On the Nature of the Gods* 2.13–15; cf. also *SVF* 2.1009–10; Sextus Empiricus, *Against the Professors* 9.60)

As a matter of Stoic doctrine, *the whole world* is pervaded by god in a way that means that god is directly perceptible in all of it; but at times, when faced with moments of natural beauty, or awe, or power, or orderliness, we need to use terms that go beyond the impersonal vocabulary of agriculture or spectrum analysis. Again, we see here 'god' being used of that aspect of the world corresponding to our sense of *wonder*. And, not to make too much of this too quickly, it is not absurd to assimilate this sense to the idea that the world possesses something like a personality. Certainly the Stoics go on to argue that 'god' is an intelligent and benevolent force. Indeed, they apparently claimed that god's philanthropic benevolence is *as* nearly inseparable from our concept of him as any other quality (Plutarch, *On the Contradictions of the Stoics* 1051D–E, 1052B).

But the further away we now get from the bare concept, the more justification these claims for his character will need. Later I shall turn to one way in which the Stoics among others tried to provide it, and a form of argument that became increasingly central to theological development. First, though, with some sense of 'god' as a personality emerging from our cosmological work, it is worth pausing to consider the implications this had for ancient ethical thinking.

ETHICS AND ESCHATOLOGY

I have described the roots of ancient 'philosophy' as a sort of development of ancient religion, not its nemesis: an extension of the attempt to use religious language and imagery that is understood to be 'conventional' (that is, culturally specific) in elucidating the underlying nature of things. I infer some extra support for this way of looking at things from the fact, to which I alluded earlier, that the thinkers identified within the later tradition as pioneers of philosophy, the Ionian cosmologists, were not known for their interest in *ethics*. This is striking because one area on which it is clear that religion in the pre-philosophical world was widely understood to have some bearing was precisely the area of human conduct. The gods were everywhere invoked to exact revenge, to guarantee oaths, to reward the beneficent, to purify and forgive the venial. There is, furthermore, a wealth of evidence for reflective interest in issues of justice and morality among writers of the archaic period, Hesiod not least among them. A tradition founded on the rejection of 'religious' or 'mythological' patterns of thought would surely be forced to confront the implications for human life of such a revolution. Yet it is not really until Empedocles that we find the development of 'ethical' themes within a clear theoretical framework as part of the cosmological tradition; and the first major cosmological thinker who also wrote systematically on the subject was Democritus, who, as we have seen, actually went further than any of his predecessors (and most of his successors) in marginalizing the relevance of religious language. If the Ionians were 'rejecting' religion, in short, they ought to have had more to say about ethics. Their silence on the matter suggests their acceptance of both ethical conventions and associated religious language. The question for us, again, becomes why the tradition ever came round to subject it to analysis at all.

The answer to this question must presumably be that the enquiry into nature (into the world conceived as *wonderful* and intriguing) at some point stumbles on ways of thinking about the world that throw light back on to the enquirer; human beings encounter *in the world* something that 'mirrors' or comments on their nature in a way that causes reflection on the adequacy of conventional social obligations. This might be by the discovery that cultural convention has no underpinning in nature whatsoever (such an extreme conventionalist position might be thought to lie behind the speculation of Democritus); but it might, conversely, be by uncovering something in one's investigation of the cosmos suggesting that nature itself supplies a normative basis for action that supplements or even contradicts local convention. One can see how this might happen as the divine forces that animate the cosmos become increasingly clearly understood (and not merely depicted) as *persons* of a sort, with 'intentions' for the way the world should be. In this case, it becomes increasingly natural to ask where we stand on their activity: how we ourselves would like the cosmos to be, and what we might be able to do about it. This may be something we can see in Empedocles. Empedocles' cosmos is constituted by four elements, themselves designated as gods (namely, Zeus, Hera, Aidoneus and Nestis; 31 B 6 DK), which are organized by the additional forces of Love and Strife. Love and Strife represent very different 'intentions' for the world: Love aims to unify the disparate elements; Strife aims to tear them apart (B 17). Oddly enough, *both* are ruinous to the cosmic order when they predominate: Love makes the cosmos a homogeneous sphere; in Strife the elements are separated beyond fruitful interaction. Nevertheless, Empedocles is clear that our preference should be for the actions of Love. His thought, perhaps, is that Love as the force that keeps elements in combination is reflected in the force (or *daimōn* as he calls it) by which we are united and maintain what integrity we have as living, organic creatures. What is clear, in any case, is that this partisan affinity with Love is at the centre of our being (in one fragment, B 128, we are told that Aphrodite is the only divinity recognized by early human beings) and has normative implications for us. We are particularly to avoid behaviour associated with the destructive work of Strife, and to adopt certain rituals and taboos that will allow the 'purification' of our *daimōn*, its release from this world, and reunion with the divine principle from which it derives (B 115, 139–41).

The belief in an immortal principle, inherited by Empedocles from the Pythagorean tradition, is taken up from the same background by Plato and made the focus, at times, of a terrifying eschatology. A soul that falters on the path to 'purification' might, for example, expect punishment (*Phaedo* 113d–155a; *Gorgias* 523a–526d; *Republic* 10, 614c–616b) or at best reincarnation (*Phaedo* 71d–e, 81d–82b; *Republic* 10, 617d–621b; *Timaeus* 42b–c, 91d–92c; *Laws* 904c–905d). Indeed Plato has been criticized since antiquity for appealing to our *fear of the gods* in this way as a motive for virtue (Chrysippus, as reported by Plutarch, *On the Contradictions of the Stoics* 1040A–B). But this stands as a criticism of Plato in particular not least because his official position seems to be based in a more positive vision of virtue as self-fulfilment through *identification* with god, a view that one way or another was to become extremely influential. This idea relates closely to two themes we have already seen, namely the argument from experience and the idea associated with it that *what* is experienced has the character of a *person* of sorts. For not only does this vindicate a sense of our *obligation* towards god – that is, as a person, and a member of the cosmic community (cf. e.g. *Gorgias* 507e–508a; also *Euthyphro* for the idea that piety is a form of justice) – but it also establishes god as a role model for us. His perfect thought, by which the cosmos is moved and governed, is an ideal for our philosophical aspirations and, since thought is not, in itself, spatially limited as we embodied creatures are, it gives us the possibility of finding our identity in a form of uncircumscribed perfection. This latter idea is found in Plato's famous definition of virtue as "becoming like god, as far as possible" (*Theaetetus* 176a–b).

It is scarcely an exaggeration to say that these two notions – that we should relate to god in a particular way, and that we should become as like him as possible – set the pattern for mainstream ethics in the subsequent tradition, from Aristotle (*Nicomachean Ethics* X.7–8, esp. 1177b26–1178a2, 1178b21–3), through the Stoics (cf. Plutarch, *On Common Conceptions* 1076A) and Epicurus (*Vatican Sayings* 33; *Letter to Menoecus* 135), to the Platonist revival (Alcinous, *Didaskalikos* 28.3, 181.43–5 Hermann), including Jewish and Christian Platonists, where it found a ready-made niche as a gloss on the notion that we were made in God's image (Philo, *On Flight and Finding* 63; Clement, *Stromata* 2.19, 2.22, 5.14.94.4–95.2). But it would be hasty to think that all of these thinkers have the same vision of human perfection. For in the meantime, ideas of god were developing, and with it the idea of what it would be like to be like god.

DESIGN AND TRANSCENDENCE

I have so far been addressing the way in which religious language found a place within the philosophical tradition as part of a complete characterization of the world, indeed as a central part of it, since it aims at the heart of the *wonder* in which, I have argued, philosophy finds its roots. As such, the arguments I have been tracing (versions of the arguments from consensus and from experience) have been about resisting the reductionist tendencies of atheism by trying to specify the nature of god *as encountered*. But such arguments necessarily have their limits. There is, as we have seen, a gap between demonstrations *that* religious language has a role, and specifications of the role it has. The Stoic proof of god from consensus, for example, is effective in inverse proportion to the amount it says about *what god is*. An opponent might say that it vindicates the category of the divine only in so far as it empties it of content.

It is at this point, then, that a second level of argumentation is introduced, to supplement experience with *inference*. If god's presence is supposed to make a difference to the cosmos, we need to establish exactly what difference he makes; and then, from the effects that god has, to infer his nature and (if he should turn out to be that sort of thing) his intentions. Absolutely central to this enterprise are two types of argument we have not yet seen, although they have a certain affinity to the argument from experience: the 'cosmological' argument, and the argument from design.

Plato's argument in *Laws* book 10 might be thought to start us on the way to an argument from design, to the extent that it relied on inferring something about god's nature (as the world's soul) from his effects. Yet the inference did not really take us away from the senses: it educated us about what we were seeing (not just movement, but *life*) rather than pointing to an unseen hand that made it possible in the first place. But then the *Laws* passage had the specific intention of addressing the divine *in so far as* it was active within the world. Things are slightly different in Plato's cosmological work, the *Timaeus*:

> We must consider in the case of the cosmos what one must consider at the beginning of an investigation into anything, whether it always existed, coming to be from no origin, or whether it came to be, starting from some origin. It came to be – for it is visible and tangible and corporeal, and all such things are perceptible, and perceptible things are grasped by opinion with perception, and are in a process of coming to be and are generated. And for things that come to be we say that there must be some cause of their coming to be. It is a job to find the maker and father of this universe, and if found impossible to talk of him to everyone. (28b–c)

It was quickly to become a matter of controversy in antiquity whether Plato meant that the world had a literal, temporal origin, or whether he is here using the language of temporal creation metaphorically, to communicate a different sort of priority, the *causal* priority of the creative principle. But what is important for now is the fact that we can see here a very different sort of claim from the one made in the *Laws*. Here it is said that what is observable – which turns out as the dialogue proceeds to *include* the soul that informs and shapes the material world (34b–36d)

–relies on a divine principle, which we either *cannot* or mostly *do not* encounter at all: a creator-god who exists a step beyond our experience; not the thing that is 'wonderful' about the world, but its cause.

One might be unclear what sense it makes to apply the language of 'god' to a principle so abstract and removed from experience, at least, given the association of 'personhood' with divinity that we have see so far. Why not think of this transcendent principle merely as the prior state of, or *condition for*, the genesis of god? (It is not adequate to say that the 'divine' is, perhaps by definition, whatever comes first. After all, even the earliest of Hesiod's gods *came to be*, and Chaos, which came to be before everything else, was not a god; Hesiod, *Theogony* 116.) Plato's view about this, then, seems to be that the principle that we infer must, if it is to do its job of explanation, still have personality of a sort. At least, it must have or embody *reason* or *intention*. Matter is given in Plato's universe as a 'brute fact'; what this cosmological argument does is to show that there is something *else* that organizes it; and organization requires planning. The creator's thought might not be quite like our thought (this is another topic for discussion among his followers); but it surely *thinks* and *intends* in some relevant, non-metaphorical sense. This is how Plato comes to designate him a 'craftsman' (*Timaeus* 28a). At the same time, of course, it must be possible to attribute 'life' to him, so that when his creation has life as well (see 30b) it makes sense to think of him as a 'father'.

One thing to note about Plato is that, although he thinks that the cosmos is designed, his argument is a 'cosmological argument' *rather than* an argument from design. (Similarly, at *Phaedo* 97c it is the hypothesis of teleological agency that leads us to seek out design, not design that leads us to teleology.) The reason for this may be that Plato does not think that the cosmos is *absolutely* well ordered, only *as well organized as possible*, given, that is, the constraints placed on god by the intractability of matter. The world shows traces of chaos as well as of order. For a true argument *from* design we have to look elsewhere (e.g. Xenophon, *Memorabilia* 1.4.2–19, with Sedley 2007: 75–86; Aristotle and the Stoics in the report of Cicero, *On the Nature of the Gods* 2.87–97). But what both cosmological and design arguments share is the *distance* they open up between god and what we directly experience: between 'god' and our immediate sense of wonder. Even for the Stoics, whose god never *can* be very far away from us, such arguments take us to an understanding *about* god that is not part of our experience *of* him. But if the argument is supposed to take us to a designer who stands outside the world – as is the case with Plato and Aristotle – new difficulties as well as new vistas are encountered.

The new opportunities that arise with the conclusion in this case (the case where we infer the existence of a god who transcends the cosmos) include the fact that this transcendent god will function as a new and superior terminus for philosophical enquiry and fulfilment of our religious impulse. Prominent among the new difficulties is the correlative fact that we, as embodied human beings, embedded in the cosmos, are designed in the first place for thinking about *it*, not beings above it: to associate with or become like this higher god will be a difficult matter (cf. Alcinous, *Didaskalikos* 28.3, 181.43–5 Hermann). A transcendent god, as *pure* intellect, is uncomplicated, but also then unrevealed, by the familiar attributes of spatial extension and organic articulation. Plato had already said that his creator-god was ineffable (*Timaeus* 28c, quoted above), and the claim is taken very seriously by his followers in the Platonist revival of the post-Hellenistic era. By the time Alcinous was writing (perhaps in the first or second century CE – we have no clear indication) a number of strategies had been developed by which philosophers could elevate their own thought to meet the god whose existence was demanded by reason, all of them to become stock-in-trade for the later philosophy of religion. They include versions of the *via negativa*, an approach to god through contemplation of the limited categories by which he is *not* bound, and the *via eminentiae*, by which we extrapolate from the good things of our experience to a god greater than any of them (Alcinous, *Didaskalikos* 10.4–6, with Mansfeld 1988).

The trouble is that there is something inflationary about the whole process. The argument from design removes god from our experience; these measures allow us to approach him again. But the closer we come to understanding this higher god and his creative activity, the closer we approach a reapplication of the question that provoked our original use of such arguments as the design and cosmological arguments. *What explains this god in his turn?* The Platonist Numenius, writing in the generation before Plotinus (on whom he was an important influence), imagines Plato upbraiding those of his contemporaries, Alcinous perhaps among them, who were content to end their enquiries with the creator intellect, ineffable or no: "The intellect which you humans conjecture to be the first," he says, "is not. There is another intellect prior to it, more ancient and divine" (*Fragments* 17.6–8 Places).

This inflationary tendency is not new with Numenius. In fact we find it as early as Philo, the Jewish philosopher of first-century Alexandria and one of our earliest witnesses to the Platonist revival. Philo addresses his god as (*inter alia*) the world's creator and architect (*On the Creation of the World* 16), its father and guardian (*That God is Unchanging* 29–32; *On the Creation of the World* 10; cf. *On Providence* fr. 2); but, for all this, places him *above* the level of creative intellect, well off the front line of duty. He is above even the principle of goodness and unity (*Contemplative Life* 2; *Questions on Exodus* 2.68); he is nameless and unknowable (*Change of Names* 11), revealed to us only indirectly in the powers that manifest themselves as his immediate effects in the universe (*Questions on Genesis* 4.8; also *Who is the Heir?* 111, *Change of Names* 15). As if in competition with the trend, early Christians vary the thought only to place God still further away from the approach of reason. The deliberate care with which they locate their own god *above* that of any Greek system is set out in dramatic terms by the apologist Justin, who imagines the approach to god as a journey through, but then finally beyond, the Hellenic schools (*Dialogue* 2, 6.6–10). Beginning with the Stoics, whose theology is rooted in the natural world, he progresses to Aristotle's school, and then to a neo-Pythagoreanism, which raises its vision as far as the realm of mathematical abstraction. Finally, he comes to Platonism and here, he says, one might have expected to "catch a glimpse of god: for this is the end of Platonic philosophy". But it turns out that the journey is not yet complete. For the Christian will show you that God, the true God, is so *unlike* the human mind that he resides beyond its grasp. Justin's God is literally *beyond the realm of rational inference.*

One of the consequences of god's recession from view in this way is a renewed interest in the early centuries of our era in *intermediary* deities, notably in those creatures who mark the space between the realms of god and humanity, known as *daimones*. Serious philosophical interest in them was traced in antiquity to Plato's early school. The Stoic Chrysippus was also well known for his interest in the subject, perhaps because he believed that a global teleology needed to operate through a network of local micro-systems (rather as we think of the global ecology as a balance of myriad eco-systems). In any case, the one place where they make a distinctive contribution to our evidence for Chrysippus is in his suggestion that minor lapses on the part of these *daimones* might be responsible for some of the phenomena we allege as part of the problem of evil (Plutarch, *On the Contradictions of the Stoics* 1051c). But the later Platonist interest in *daimones*, associated especially with Apuleius and Plutarch (cf. Kidd 1995; Brenk 1998) surely goes beyond this. It addresses the metaphysical question of how an increasingly distant god interacts, practically speaking, with the world. One of the principal roles fulfilled by *daimones*, then, was to bridge the ontological gaps opened up by the design argument, in a way that would ultimately lead to the baroque celestial hierarchies developed in Proclus and Pseudo-Dionysius. But it also addresses the phenomenological question of how we *encounter* deity across these ontological divides. Our immediate point of religious contact is with *daimones* (and the World Soul too): it is through them that we can be said to encounter god (cf. Plutarch, *On Isis and Osiris* 360D–F; Finamore 2006).

REVELATION AND THE PHILOSOPHY OF RELIGION

Christians accept the idea that the *scala naturae* is fuller than is immediately obvious (e.g. Clement, *Stromata* 6.17.157.4–5, 161.2; Origen, *On First Principles* 1.8.1; Pseudo-Dionysius, *Celestial Hierarchy* esp. 3.2, 4.3), and are delighted to take over the notion that the gods of Greek religious experience are really mere *daimones* (Athenagoras, *Plea* 23; Justin, *II Apology* 5; Origen, *Exhortation to Martyrdom* 45; Augustine, *City of God* 18.14). But there are further intermediaries crucial to the identity of Christianity as a movement as well: the Hebrew prophets, first of all, read in the light of the belief that Jesus was the Christ they foresaw; and then, of course, Christ himself as the incarnate 'word' (cf. esp. Augustine, *City of God* 8.18–21). These additional entities have a very particular importance for Christianity. I noted a little earlier that Justin positions Christianity as the perfection of philosophy by locating God one step beyond the reach of inference. In doing so, he finds a radical way of limiting the inferential sequence begun by the argument from design. But if we can neither experience God directly nor infer his nature, how can we possibly know he exists at all or have any regard for him? The answer lies in these extra intermediaries: for one of the things that they bring is direct knowledge of God's intentions: divine revelation.

It has been suggested that one of the things that makes Plotinus such an important figure for subsequent Hellenic (i.e. non-Christian) Platonism is that he found a way of bringing a conclusive end to the search for a first principle, by locating it *above being*, at a place beyond which there is nowhere for enquiry to go (Gerson 1990). Justin, I have suggested, found a different terminus for philosophy, in a first principle that exists *beyond rational inference*. One advantage to Justin's way of doing things is that it is easier for him to retain a sense that the first principle is a *person* of sorts: an entity, that is, to which religious language remains applicable. To be sure, Platonists were also keen to retain this sense (as Gerson [1990: 217] stresses); but it is only now in a very attenuated sense that one can talk of the will or creative thought or even providence of the divine. This in turn matters for philosophical, and not just for sentimental, reasons, because it relates to the problem of evil, a problem that was always going to be found lurking behind attempts to establish a philosophical account of the cosmos based on an appeal to its good order or evident design. Briefly put, it will be easier to excuse and explain apparent disruption to cosmic order if we can explain it in the light of some form of personal relationship that we, as human beings, can have with god.

My point is perhaps most clearly made by starting with the alternative recourse adopted by Platonists. For most Platonists (exceptions include those, such as Plutarch and his contemporary Atticus, who were dualists; cf. Armstrong 1992), evil was understood to be principally a metaphysical rather than a moral issue. In Plotinus, for example, the price paid for the increase and diffusion of *being* is that in order for some things to *be* at all, they must be imperfect (*Enneads* 1.8). The trouble is that it is *human beings* who bring consciousness to the level where this imperfection is most manifest. The cosmos benefits from the expansion of being, but it is human beings who suffer the consequences. Ideally, we would like to be able to appeal to an additional principle that justifies the allocation of this burden. But where the Christian can talk of God's *intentions* and *concerns* for us as human beings to provide a context and, at last, a justification for our suffering, it scarcely makes sense to attribute "concerns" and "intentions" to the Platonist One. Instead of offering a justification of human suffering, then, Platonists will suggest that philosophy offers us the means to rise *above* the evil, and approach the goodness definitively embodied in god. But we can only do this by rising above our humanity, our rootedness in the cosmos. It is, in the end, as if the problem of evil is circumnavigated by rejecting the relevance of human suffering. After all, as Celsus put it with unusual bluntness (although perfect orthodoxy; with Origen, *Against Celsus* 4.75–99, see Plato, *Laws* 903b–c), humanity is for the world, not vice versa.

Celsus' views are expressed thus bluntly in an anti-Christian work, and this is significant, for Christians in general adopt a much more anthropocentric view of the world. It is, in fact, part of the Christian recognition of the fact that the world is the work of something properly designated a 'god' that it is, in the relevant sense, *for* humanity. In his reply to Celsus, and in setting out his own cosmology, Origen, for example, develops the idea that human beings are entirely responsible for their own woes, which come to them through the misuse of free will, with which they were originally created. The natural world, he argues, is nothing less than a systematic *response* to this, a reformatory designed by God for the purpose (cf. esp. Koch 1932).

An explanation like this of the world's purpose might satisfy Christian theodicy, then, by retaining a sense of God's relationship with us as persons; but, as I noted, it is bought at the price of his elevation beyond the reach of rational inference. Justin asserts it as fact: Origen explains why it must happen. If the world is created for human beings, he says, and not only this but, more specifically, for the reform of creatures whose natures have been perverted by the exercise of their own free will, there is a very real sense in which the world *could have been different.* (It *must* have been different if just one individual had chosen a different path, as its reformatory prescription must be tailored to its inmates.) And if the world could have been different, if it is a contingent system, then it is not such a straightforward task to infer, from the way it is organized, the nature of the principles responsible for its order. This, for Origen at least, is a large part of the reason why Platonists go wrong. Platonists assume as a matter of methodology that the world is an inevitable outpouring of the first principle, and this assumption allows them to infer causes from their effects. Origen argues that it is a contingent *response* to choices unknowable in their totality to human beings. This puts a limit on what can be inferred about God as its creator.

But God has thought of this too; and in order to restore the possibility of our approach to him, he has built *revelation* into the scheme of things. The Oracles of the Greeks, as I noted, say nothing about the nature of god; the Hebrew prophets say everything. If commentary is needed, everything is clarified for the Christian by Christ, the incarnation of God's reasoning, the principle *through which* the world was made in the first place. For a Christian, then, Scripture is a very different kind of thing to the religious narratives of the Greeks. Christian Scripture has an importance at least equal in philosophical relevance to the data of the senses and the inferences of logicians. The alliance of faith and Scripture in this way offers a new perspective on the world, a perspective that really is distinct from, and to some degree in competition with, that of philosophical reason.

***

In the generation before Plotinus, Numenius described the programme a philosopher ought to follow. One should, he says, first of all apply reason to the question in hand; then confirm the results by appealing to philosophers one has a reason to trust, namely Plato and Pythagoras; and last of all, one can look at where and how this truth is expressed in the religious traditions of the world (all in *Fragments* 1). Very different is the approach set out by Plotinus' contemporary, Origen. In his metaphysical magnum opus *On First Principles*, Origen puts faith at the beginning of the process when he issues his invitation to "those who have believed and been convinced" in the opening words of the book. In the course of the work he will take them *from* their belief *into* the philosophical frameworks within which it is to be organized. This rethinking of the relationship between faith and philosophy completes the divorce of the two in a way that makes the former available as a clearly defined object of study for the latter. The 'philosophy of religion' is built from arguments that have roots as ancient as philosophy itself; it is with Christianity that it acquires its identity as a distinct discipline.

2

PYTHAGORAS

Constantinos Macris

Pythagoras of Samos (*floruit c.*530 BCE) is one of the most famous thinkers of ancient Greece, and his influence and imprint are still felt in Eastern and Western philosophical and religious thought. Already considered the father of 'philosophy' a generation after Plato (Riedweg 2005: 90–97), this famous inventor or, rather, 'importer' into Greece of the mathematical theorem that bears his name (cf. Zhmud 1989) was much honoured in the ancient Academy, and especially in the philosophically predominant Neoplatonic circles of both late antiquity (O'Meara 1989) and the Italian Renaissance (Riedweg 2005: 129ff.).

SOURCE PROBLEMS: THE 'PYTHAGOREAN QUESTION'

The factual and textual ground on which this spectacular and monumental edifice built by tradition stands is, by contrast, extremely insecure for the modern scholar. First, there are no fragments of Pythagoras' writings. Very much like Socrates, Buddha and Jesus, the Samian sage was – principally, if not exclusively – a master of orality who left no written texts behind him: neither poems nor treatises in prose (see Riedweg [1997] for the possibility that Pythagoras committed something to writing). Secondly, even if he had written something, the mystery-inspired secrecy practised in the circle of followers gravitating around him (Brisson 1987; Bremmer 1995: 63–70; Petit 1997; *contra* Zhmud 1997: 85–91) had as a consequence that, apparently, no writings were in public circulation outside the sect-like early Pythagorean communities before Philolaus of Croton (*c.*470–after 399 BCE). Thirdly, no direct disciple of Pythagoras is known to have recorded the master's voice or written his biography, as for example Xenophon and Plato did for Socrates and Porphyry for Plotinus. So, quite disappointingly – and in the absence of any other direct literary, epigraphic or archaeological evidence – we are definitively deprived of first-hand access to the historical Pythagoras and his teachings. Only a few dozen of his supposed oral sayings (*akousmata*) and some sparse indirect testimonies of the late sixth and early fifth centuries that seem reliable have survived, all transmitted by later sources, and most of those testimonies are usually polemical or at least ambiguous (Burkert 1972: 166–92, esp. 170–73; Riedweg 2005: 48–58, 63–77; Macris 2009). All of these points convergingly show the degree to which our information about Pythagoras and early Pythagoreanism relies, and in fact depends, on oral tradition.

This tradition also has a legendary side, whose aim was to celebrate the much respected master of old by relating and propagating miracle stories illustrating his alleged extraordinary gifts and super-human status (Macris 2003). Pythagoras' legend grew considerably as time passed, so the overwhelming majority of the biographical data concerning him are preserved in an undifferentiated, cumulative way by quite late and often biased sources. More precisely, of the three main surviving biographies of Pythagoras – the ones by Diogenes Laertius, Porphyry and Iamblichus, all dating from the third and early fourth centuries CE – the last two are written by sympathizing Neoplatonists, while the last one, in addition, takes the shape of a 'hagiographical' discourse.[1]

Moreover, if we are to believe Iamblichus (1991: §§158, 198; but see Zhmud [1997: 91–2]), in the continuous flow of the Pythagorean tradition, the doctrines going back to the founder are even more difficult to isolate because the aura of his authority seems to have prompted (many of) his disciples as well as later Pythagoreans to attribute the paternity of their novel ideas to him, in order to honour him but also, we might assume, in order to give their own ideas a more respectable pedigree.

On the philosophical level, we must contend with the absence of preserved primary, authentic sources emerging directly from Pythagorean circles earlier than Philolaus. In addition, from Plato we have only few references and cryptic allusions regarding the Pythagorean tradition that he had known personally both in Athens and during his journeys in Magna Graecia. Similarly, there is a reticence in Aristotle, in his surviving corpus, to attribute specifically to Pythagoras or to any of the latter's disciples or epigones the doctrines he discusses in various places anonymously under the collective and vaguely generic label 'Pythagorean' (a label that he sometimes also uses for designating the views of his Pythagoreanizing comrades in the Academy; see McKirahan forthcoming). As a result, we shall never know with certainty which Pythagorean tenets go back to Pythagoras himself,[2] nor the extent to which Plato was influenced by them and has creatively reshaped them, either in his written dialogues or in his unwritten doctrines (*agrapha dogmata*) (Boyancé 1966b; Meinwald 2002; Périllié 2008).

The situation is further complicated by the fact that in the enthusiastically Pythagoreanizing milieu of Plato's successors in the early Academy, thinkers

1. For annotated translations, see Diogenes Laertius (1972); Porphyry (1965, 2001); Iamblichus (1991).
2. For a serious and optimistic attempt in this direction, see Kahn (2001: 49–62).

such as Speusippus and Xenocrates attempted a profound fusion of Platonic and Pythagorean ideas that obfuscates any clear distinction between the two (cf. Dillon 2003), a fusion that was destined to become canonical from Imperial times onwards. So the pendulum of modern scholarship is condemned to move eternally back and forth between (i) a more or less slavish acceptance of the numerous doctrines traced back to Pythagoras (to the detriment of other philosophers, such as other Presocratics or Plato) by a doxographic tradition ultimately influenced by the early Academy and Aristotle's pupil Theophrastus, and (ii) a completely distrustful reaction to this kind of information: a hyper-critical attitude that goes hand in hand with a tendency to minimize Plato's debt to the Pythagoreans of his time and, symmetrically, to (over)emphasize his originality as a thinker.[3]

In the domain of religion, the originality of Pythagoras' and the Pythagoreans' contribution depends on the acceptance (or not) of the priority of the Orphic literature, and on his/their debt to it. But in the present state of our knowledge, the establishment of a precise or even approximate relative chronology of the Orphic and Pythagorean movements seems a desperate undertaking: within the existing literary corpus (and supposed continuum) of the Orphic tradition we cannot easily distinguish between early and late Orphic poems, whereas, given the essentially oral character of the early Pythagorean tradition, the latter's eventual influence on the *Orphica* remains difficult to detect and almost impossible to prove.

Given the complicated situation described above, ancient Pythagoreanism seems to be 'sandwiched' between the supposed Orphic origins and background of its religious tenets on the one side, and the artful and insightful literary and philosophical elaboration of its doctrines in written form by Plato on the other side. It is perhaps not a coincidence that, despite some essential disparities, in both cases the Pythagorean oral tradition had to compete with extraordinarily prolific literary *corpora*: the Orphics' famous 'hubbub of books', or Plato's dialogues. So the archaic preference of Pythagoras and his disciples for orality seems to have been defeated by the growing literacy of the classical period.

All these difficulties amount to the notoriously controversial 'Pythagorean question', which is no less complex than the 'Homeric' one. Taking into account the particularities of the sources that inform us about the Pythagorean tradition, in my account of Pythagoras' contribution to Western philosophy of religion I shall employ three methods: (i) identifying the elements of the tradition that could most reliably be considered to be part of the master's original religious insights; (ii) examining the relevant doctrines attributed to the early Pythagoreans as a group,

3. For a balanced account of this delicate and complex question, see Burkert's magisterial *Lore and Science in Ancient Pythagoreanism* (1972), as well as the more recent monographs of Huffman (1993, 2005). Huffman (1999) and Kahn (2001) are excellent introductory syntheses of the matter. The sharply opposed but well-founded and skilfully argued views of Kingsley (1995) and Zhmud (1997) show how fragile the otherwise admirable interpretative equilibrium obtained by Burkert can be.

as well as the fragments of, and testimonies about, individual sixth- and fifth-century Pythagoreans such as Philolaus (or even Empedocles); and (iii) reviewing Pythagorean ideas probably echoed in Plato. By this multiple approach I hope to obtain a more complete and comprehensive picture of the diversity of views that were in circulation, already at an early stage, in circles whose point of reference and source of inspiration was Pythagoras himself.

PRELIMINARY HISTORICAL AND METHODOLOGICAL CONSIDERATIONS AND SOME QUALIFICATIONS

Pythagoras' religious insights are well known. They are mainly two: the theory of the immortality and transmigration of the soul, and the conception of the world as a harmonious order (*kosmos*) structured according to numerical proportions. As Walter Burkert (1972) has shown, they do not suffice to make of him a philosopher *stricto sensu*. Our understanding of him would be more accurate if we think of him rather as a wise man or sage, a 'charismatic master of wisdom'[4] perceived by his contemporaries as possessing and revealing to humanity divine truths, and consequently endowed with a dogmatic authority (Macris 2009). So in Pythagoras' case we are still situated in the 'pre-history', or perhaps 'proto-history', of the philosophy of religion.

Consequently, among the remains that most authentically reflect Pythagoras' thought we shall look in vain for the dialectical approaches and the detailed, systematic argumentations we would have expected, and to which we are nowadays accustomed. These are characteristic of the later generations of Pythagoreans, and especially of those among them who were called *mathematikoi*, namely 'the learned ones', or 'the ones engaged in (the mathematical) sciences (of the *quadriuium*)', as opposed to the more traditionalist and ritualistic branch of the sect, the *akousmatikoi*, who stick to Pythagoras' oral sayings, the *akousmata*.[5] Pythagoras' own aphoristic formulations were taken as oracular pronouncements, authoritatively ordained, (quasi-) divine prescriptions. His followers used to refer to them by the phrase, "He has said so" (*autos epha*, *ipse dixit*) – and there ended the discussion.

However, somehow unexpectedly in our eyes, Pythagoras' authoritative teachings do not seem to have functioned as fixed, immovable dogmas for a long time. Orality, after all, gave fluidity and plasticity to the early Pythagorean tradition. Within the latter (even putting aside the '*acusmatici* versus *mathematici*' divide, which may be dated to the middle of the fifth century), we can hear a plurality of voices, often reported collectively and anonymously (e.g. in Aristotle's accounts of the opinions of

4. See Macris (2003) (with extensive bibliography), where I argue for the use of this designation, instead of the more widespread category of 'shaman'.
5. For the two branches that are attested among the early Pythagoreans, see Burkert (1972: 192–208).

different Pythagorean groups), but also, in some cases, explicitly attributed to individual thinkers (especially after Philolaus' publication of his book *On Nature* under his own name). Predictably enough, up to the time of Plato this plurality and variety became even more pronounced, owing to the internal 'dynamics of evolution' of the living tradition, as well as to external influences or syncretistic phenomena, but especially thanks to the Pythagoreans' ability to interact in a creative way with the trends of their times: by updating their vocabulary and methodological approaches, by adapting their discourse to the new intellectual needs and philosophical questions, and by engaging in a fertile dialogue with other schools of thought or religious movements of the rapidly changing Greek world of the fifth century BCE.

This complex situation makes it even more difficult for us to reconstruct properly the unwritten, orally transmitted doctrines of Pythagoras himself out of their kaleidoscopic reflections in later, undoubtedly more sophisticated developments. However, given the archaic context out of which Pythagoras emerges, it could be interesting for our purposes not to restrict ourselves solely to the argumentatively mute insights of the master himself but to also take into consideration the arguments elaborated later by other representatives of the Pythagorean movement, in their effort to explain, clarify, consolidate and/or (eventually) defend more effectively the doctrines of their own tradition against the attacks of later critics. What is important, I would suggest, is to reconstruct *the general train of thought* followed diachronically by the (anonymous and eponymous) early Pythagorean thinkers in the *longue durée*, especially in so far as they were in continuity and in consonance with their master's voice, and to identify *the main lines of argumentation* adopted by them on some fundamental issues in the philosophy of religion.

Taking into consideration the aforementioned necessary qualifications, as well as the historical and cultural context out of which Pythagoras and the tradition deriving from his teachings emerge, the general thesis of this chapter will be that there *is* a proper contribution that Pythagoras and the early Pythagorean thinkers made to the history of the philosophy of religion, and that this contribution is not only important, original and multifarious, but also influential and long lasting.

THE PYTHAGOREAN CONTRIBUTION TO THE PHILOSOPHY OF RELIGION: AN OUTLINE

As has been amply demonstrated by Pierre Hadot in *What Is Ancient Philosophy?* (2002) and previously in his *Philosophy as a Way of Life* (1995), ancient philosophy consisted not only of thinking supported by reasoned argument and productive of more or less coherent worldviews and doctrines, but also in a way of life that had to be lived according to the principles deriving from these views, and which was an exercise in self-discipline and a process of self-transformation. The perfect marriage of the theoretical and the practical aspect of philosophy is achieved for the first time, and in a remarkable way, in the ancient Pythagorean tradition.

Accordingly, in our overview of the Pythagorean contribution to the philosophy of religion it is apt to distinguish between 'theology' and 'bios'. In the domain of theology, understood in the ancient sense of *theo-logia*, we shall look for reflection and discourse (*logos*) on gods and the divine: their essence, and their relation to the cosmos in general and to man in particular. In the domain of bios, or of what we could more precisely call religious 'praxeology', we shall look for reflection and discourse on humanity's attitude towards the divine. Two kinds of practical concerns are involved here: *ritualism* and *morality*.

The ancients conveniently distinguished three types of theology: mythical, physical and civic.[6] The first, illustrated by the poets (and mythographers), spoke of the gods in terms of mythical tales and narratives about their life and activities. The second, practised by the philosophers, attempted to give a reasonable account of the gods' identity, origin and nature (*physis*), and of our capacity to apprehend these cognitively. The third is confined to priestly knowledge or the citizens' understanding of the practices (rituals, sacrifices, initiations, etc.) surrounding the worship of the gods in the context of civic religion. Useful though it may be, this distinction is somewhat artificial. The three types of theology it identifies are to a great extent complementary and interdependent, and this is even more the case with the quite undifferentiated fusion of poetry, philosophy and religion that is characteristic of the archaic period (but also of a figure like Empedocles, some decades later). But still, in our investigation of the early Pythagorean contribution to the philosophy of religion, the above-mentioned distinction could serve as a reminder that we should examine not only the Pythagoreans' opinions on the gods of the Greek pantheon, their speculations about the relationship between numbers and gods and their natural theology, but also their use and reinterpretation of myth – be it Homeric, Hesiodic, Orphic or Eleusinian – and their reformative attitude towards the cult and rituals of the Greek *polis*.

In a stimulating essay, Glenn Most (2003: 307–10) has recently suggested that in the ancient Greek world the role of philosophy in its relationship with religion was to reinforce religiosity either by supplementing religion in the domains of cosmology, eschatology and morality, or by undertaking "to correct and improve it, by systematizing its intuitions, by reinforcing its justifications, by generalizing its applicabilities" (*ibid.*: 310). This applies perfectly to ancient Pythagoreanism, which produced physical–animistic as well as number-oriented cosmogonies and cosmologies, eschatological doctrines centred on the soul's immortality, metempsychosis and astral afterlife and, last but not least, a rationally structured and coherent model of reformed piety, a bios combining ritualistic and moral prescriptions and aiming at purification and, through it, at eternal blessings beyond the grave. To Most's scheme we could add another important domain, that of (reli-

6. See Aëtius, *On the Opinions of the Philosophers* = Ps.-Plutarch 1.6.9 (in Diels 1965: 295); Varro, *Antiquities of Human and Divine Things* (in Varro 1976), frs 7–9.

gious) 'anthropo-logy', understood as reflection and discourse about man's place in the cosmos, his mortality and the degree of his affinity (*syggeneia*) to the divine. This domain deserves special attention, given the Pythagoreans' (alleged?) propensity to speak about 'divine men' and *daimones*, their invitation to 'follow god' and to be assimilated to the divine in this life, and their theories about post-mortem divinization.

For each of the fields mentioned in this brief overview a detailed analysis of the evidence is needed, and such an approach would have certainly brought us beyond the limits prescribed for this modest chapter. Given the repeated and exhaustive treatment in modern scholarship of the Pythagorean way of life and of the theory of immortality and transmigration of the soul, the following pages will focus on the Pythagorean contribution to the domain of theology, taken in the broadest possible sense.

EARLY PYTHAGOREAN VIEWS ON GODS AND THE DIVINE

Let us start with the gods. In a typically Greek way, Pythagoras and the Pythagoreans must have taken the traditional gods of the Homeric–Hesiodic pantheon as their starting-point for discussion on the matter, without developing any criticism of a Xenophanian type. Early Pythagoreanism, which used Homer and Hesiod as sources for both moral exemplars and magical incantations for cathartic-healing purposes, is often associated with an allegorical understanding of Homer (attested for the first time by Theagenes of Rhegium, in southern Italy, toward the end of the sixth century BCE). But we do not have any traces of speculation about the gods specifically, neither in physical nor in moral allegories, and it is far from certain that the mystical allegorization of Homer that later Platonists so often attribute retrospectively to the early Pythagorean tradition has in fact archaic roots (Lamberton 1986: 31–43).

If we turn to the Hesiodic poems things seem quite different. In a series of identifications handed down by Aristotle and considered as deriving from authentic Pythagorean *akousmata* originally formulated in a question-and-answer form, the sea is called "the tears of Kronos", the Great and Little Bear (i.e. the constellations Ursa Major and Ursa Minor) "the hands of [the goddess] Rhea", the Pleiades "the lyre of the Muses", and the planets "Persephone's dogs" (fr. 196 Rose, in Aristotle 1984: vol. 2 [= Porphyry 1965: 120]). The list could be extended in order to include the explanation of thunderbolts as Zeus' threat to the inhabitants of Tartarus, in order to frighten them, of Iris (i.e. the rainbow) as the gleam of the sun, of earthquakes as the result of a concourse of the dead in the underworld, of the echo as the voice of mightier beings (*kreittones*), of the fourfold *tetractys* as "the harmony in which the Sirens sing" and so on (cf. 58 C 1–2 DK [= Diels & Kranz 1951–2]). Here we find an original and intriguing use of mythical elements familiar from traditional Greek mythology, especially from

Hesiod, for the allegorical–symbolical designation of astronomical realities and natural phenomena that order the world. On the mythical level we can glimpse intimations of the Hesiodic myth according to which Kronos and Rhea were the ruling couple of the ancestors of the gods preceding Zeus and Hera (Riedweg 2005: 75). In this context we can suppose that Kronos weeps because he has been dispossessed of power by Zeus, that Rhea's hands refer to the means by which she protected Zeus from being swallowed up by Kronos by taking him far away from his father and hiding him in a cave on Crete, and that Zeus' thunderbolts are destined to threaten Kronos, who, once overthrown by his son, has become an inhabitant of the Tartarus together with his siblings, the Titans. And we may recall that Iris, one of Zeus' favorite messengers, is mentioned by Hesiod primarily in connection with the description of Tartarus and its inhabitants (*ibid.*: 75–6). On the level of natural philosophy, on the other side, we are in the presence of a quite coherent picture of the physical world, including some recasting of the nomenclature of the constellations. Riedweg proposed to see here a Pythagorean doctrine of nature developed out of the allegorical, naturalistic explanation of Orphic poems, on the basis of the fact that the Kronos–Rhea myth was also adopted in Orphic theogonies. But it is safer to say that this systematic rationalizing interpretation of myth arose out of the exegesis of the *Theogony* by Hesiod (whose *Works and Days* also contains many parallels with the more ritualistic Pythagorean *akousmata*). In the resulting rather bizarre synthesis, "mythical personages and events are construed as features of the natural world about us, yet of a world conceived not really as nature but as a theatre populated by unseen spiritual beings engaged in a drama of life and death", and the whole is clearly "worked out largely in the service of a distinctive eschatology" (Kirk *et al.* 1983: 236).

Despite the obvious prominence of the Hesiodic background in the identifications examined above, it is true that already during the sixth century BCE the Homeric–Hesiodic monopoly in the domain of *theologia* had been abolished. At that time, new and quite different theogonies in verse began to circulate in southern Italy under the name of the mythical poet Orpheus (and the closely associated Mousaeus and Linus), supplemented by cosmogonical, anthropogonical and eschatological myths. If we accept as historically accurate the evidence provided by Ion of Chios (36 B 2 DK) and by a certain Epigenes, we are faced with the fact that some early Pythagoreans such as Bro(n)tinos and Zopyros, and even Pythagoras himself, contributed actively to the production of this religious literature, whose aim was to compete with Hesiod's *Theogony* and to propose alternative versions of the latter's narratives (West 1983: 7–15; Kingsley 1995: 133–48, 159ff.). It is in these texts that we could have possibly detected traces of a Pythagorean, or more precisely Orphic–Pythagorean, theogony and theology, but these texts are now lost, and what remains are only their titles.

Two of the titles attested for the early Pythagorean *Orphica* (*Mixing Bowl*, *Net*) show their authors' mythological conception of the process of cosmogony, which is likened to the mixture of material elements in a mixing bowl or to the knitting of a net, both of cosmic dimensions, whereas the third, *Robe* (i.e. Persephone's robe), symbolizes the surface of the earth and its seasonal recovery by means of crops, flowers and other vegetation. A fourth title, *Sacred Discourse* (*Hieros Logos*), "should be a narrative about the gods, or at least a theological exposition of some kind, giving a basis for religious observances" (West 1983: 13). Given the Orphic and poetic character of this work, a *theologia* of a mythical rather than a physical type should be supposed here, leading up to a corresponding cultic *theopraxia* within the limits of the civic religion, but the fifth (unfortunately too general) title, *Physics* (*Physika*), leaves open the possibility that there also existed a more philosophical account of the nature (*physis*) of both the gods and the cosmos, perhaps comparable to Presocratic natural theology.

What emerges with absolute certainty about the Pythagorean tradition of theology is that the deity most honoured within it, already from its founder's own time, is Apollo the purifier (*kathartēs*), in his aspects of prophet of Delphi (Pythian), healer (especially by means of music, Paian), begetter (*genētōr*, in Delos, receiving only vegetal offerings) and Hyperborean (coming from the uppermost north). Pythagoras himself was unequivocally assimilated to him in an oral saying, and perhaps also, more enigmatically, in the reported story that made him a reincarnation of Euphorbus, a hero of the *Iliad* with Apollonian features. Apollo was also revered in his quality of *Mousagetēs*, that is, patron of the Muses, and the latter, as daughters of Mnemosyne, had a place of honour within the early Pythagorean pantheon; they were not only accorded importance in memory training and recollection (initially in order to preserve the memory of one's previous incarnations) but were also believed to preside over the arts and sciences, especially astronomy and music (Boyancé 1972). It has been argued by Boyancé (1966a) that Apollo's identification with Helios, the sun, which is attested from the fifth century BCE and is echoed by Oenopides of Chios, is due to the Pythagoreans.[7] If this proved to be true, it could be one more important testimony for the practice of natural allegory among them (perhaps strengthened by etymological speculations of a Cratylian type), comparable to the one found some time later in the commentary of an Orphic poem composed by the unknown author of the Derveni papyrus (Betegh 2004).

The 'Orphic connection', as well as the religious trends in Magna Graecia in general, can explain the central place occupied by Demeter and Persephone in the Pythagorean pantheon. We have already met Persephone in one of the 'astronomical' oral sayings and, in an allusive way, in the title of one of the Orphic texts composed by the Pythagoreans. But there is more. In fact, some elements, such as Pythagoras' legendary or ritually enacted descent (*katabasis*) into Hades and his return to earth bringing commands "of the mother", or the transformation

7. This is accepted by Seaford (2005: 605–6), who refers also to Schefer's recent studies (see Schefer 1996), where it is argued that Plato was profoundly influenced by the Apollonian mysticism of the Pythagoreans.

of his house into a temple of Demeter (*telestērion*) after his death, can be interpreted as signs that he presented himself as a kind of hierophant in the chthonic mysteries of Demeter (assimilated to the Great Mother) (Burkert 1972: 155–9). It was only natural that from the fifth century BCE onwards the close connection of Pythagoras to "the goddesses" came to be more specifically associated with the Eleusinian mysteries, owing to the growing popularity of these local, properly Athenian mysteries of Demeter and Persephone on a Panhellenic level. But the connection with the chthonic mysteries in general was there from the beginning.

Aristoxenus' reports about the Pythagoreans of the fourth century BCE (Wehrli 1945: frs 33–4), as well as the opening lines of the Pythagorean *Golden Verses*, a late document of disputed dating, show that the Pythagoreans were interested, perhaps already from Pythagoras' time, not only in gods but also in all kinds of divine beings (*kreittones*), especially *daimones*, heroes and the (divinized) souls of the dead, which are set in a hierarchical order. This distinction of separate 'classes' of the divine had obvious consequences for the establishment of a 'protocol of worship' within the context of a civic theology. On a more philosophical level the Pythagoreans seem to have done more than just uncritically accept, systematize and order pre-existing traditional categories and hierarchies of the so-called popular religion of their times. We can suppose that some theological reflection on the various *genera* of the divine (the *kreittones*) as well as some ethical reflection on the attribution of honours are implied in the background, and what emerges as the organizing principle of the resulting hierarchies is the principle of *presbyteron kreitton* or *seniores priores*, namely, the idea that what precedes in time (and what is older) is more honourable than what follows (Thom 1995: 104–6). Given their claimed special knowledge of *daimones* (and, eventually, their original contribution to the discussion about them as a special divine class[8]), their emphasis on heroes and the attention they paid to the world of the deceased (whose souls were omnipresent and visible even in sunbeams), the Pythagoreans probably influenced Socrates in his conception of the personal *daimonion* and certainly paved the way for later developments in Plato (especially in the *Symposium*) and the ancient Academy (especially Xenocrates) concerning the importance of the divine classes that occupy a position between gods and human beings, so that they can function as intermediaries (*metaxy*) between the two.

We cannot tell with certainty if the Pythagoreans believed that the founder of their sect had himself been a *daimōn*, but the testimony of Aristotle's "writings on the Pythagorean philosophy" (Iamblichus 1991: §31) orients us toward this direction when Aristotle states that the Pythagoreans kept among their greatest secrets (*pany aporrheta*) a division according to which there are three kinds of rational, living beings: "one kind is divine, another human, and another such as Pythagoras" (*ibid.*). However interpreted, this statement (in contrast with the *akousma* identi-

8. See Detienne (1963); Burkert (1964; 1972: 73ff., 171 n.34, 185ff.); Brenk (1986: 2094–8).

fying Pythagoras with the Hyperborean Apollo) sees Pythagoras as a super-human being, in the literal sense of the word, and if we are not supposed to recognize in him a *daimōn*, then we have to see him at least as a divine man (*theios anēr*).

To return to demonology proper, early Pythagoreans seem to have believed that the *daimones* inhabit the moon, that the air is full of them (as well as of souls of heroes), that they send dreams, signs and diseases to human beings and beasts, and that their number within a certain region remains constant (Brenk 1986: 2095). Current research on Empedocles, whose close relationship with Pythagoreanism is known at least as well as the original and idiosyncratic philosophical system he developed out of Pythagorean premises, is still attempting to elucidate the exact meaning of his own *daimones* and their place and function in the natural and civic theology developed in his two separate but interrelated poems, *On Nature* and *Purifications*. Future Empedoclean studies could shed much light on the evolution of early Pythagorean views on *daimones* (and heroes). Meanwhile, what is certain is that these views are clearly connected to the "general superstitious aura surrounding the dead" (*ibid.*: 2098) in the death-oriented Pythagorean *Weltanschauung*, and at the same time that "somewhere within the development of Pythagoreanism a sublimation took place in which the folk beliefs received philosophical elevation" (*ibid.*: 2096). We could isolate two main directions in this development. The first one arises from the Hesiodic myth about the Isles of the Blest and from the notion that "the men of the Golden Age, when their race died out, were transformed by the will of Zeus into *daimones*, guardians over mortals" (Burkert 1985: 180). This first direction is connected to the transposition of the Isles of the Blest from the mythical edge of the Ocean to the sun and moon, within the physical universe (a transposition implying astral immortality in the afterlife), as well as to speculations according to which great and powerful figures can be honoured after death as *daimones*. The second direction, explicitly formulated in Plato but stemming from earlier traditions clearly indebted to the Pythagoreans, concerns the conception of the *daimōn* as a special being who has obtained the person at his birth by lot, and who watches over each individual (*ibid.*: 181). Heraclitus' paradoxical saying that "character is for man his *daimōn*" (22 B 119 DK) is already directed against such a view, and it would not come as a surprise if the target of his criticism here is Pythagoras, who in another fragment of the Ephesian is accused for the supposed emptiness of his "much learning and artful knavery" (B 129).

In what we may call a Pythagorean 'theology of the intermediaries' (between god and man), or the dynamics of man's immortalization, the heroes also occupy a place of honour. Having died (as the existence of their graves bore witness) they could not have been gods, but because of their origin (i.e. as the product of the union between a god or goddess and a human being) or extraordinary abilities they were clearly more than human. They are soon recognized as semi-divine beings and are connected with the gods; together they constituted the sphere of the sacred. Heroes formed a link in the chain between the immortal gods and mortal men trying to regain their immortality, since heroes occupied a privileged position in the world of the dead (Thom 1995: 110–12). So their souls should not be disturbed, and this belief explains the religious silence, *hēsychia* or *euphēmia*, in which the Pythagoreans went past the funeral monuments (*hērōia*) built for the heroes. More importantly, Heracles and the Dioskouroi, heroes whose presence in southern Italy was preponderant anyway, easily became Pythagorean heroes. Heracles has broken the terrors of death and thanks to his ascension to heaven and his apotheosis through immolation was considered the paradigm *par excellence* for the crossing of boundaries between the human and the divine spheres. At the same time, because of his fundamental choice of the way of virtue instead of that of vice, according to an old legend, he was also invested with moral values, incarnating the paragon of virtue and labour (*ponos*). Combining the two, he became "a model for the common man who may hope that after a life of drudgery, and through that very life, he too may enter into the company of the gods" (Burkert 1985: 211). As for the Dioskouroi, literally 'the youths of Zeus', they were above all "rescuers from personal distress, especially from danger at sea", and more generally saviours, *sōtēres*, and they "were seen as guiding lights for those hoping to break out of the mortal sphere into the realm of gods" (*ibid.*: 213). A late testimony recorded by Iamblichus (1991: §155) possibly echoes the early Pythagorean propensity for natural allegory we met earlier in connection with the gods when it sees in Heracles the power of nature and in the Dioskouroi the harmony of all things, and this seems to extend the applicability of the naturalizing principle to more than one class of *kreittones*.

It is not easy to decipher the philosophical meaning lying behind another theologizing tendency of the early Pythagoreans, namely, number theology, according to which attributes of numbers correspond to attributes of gods and vice versa. The ground is particularly slippery here because an age-old tradition starting with Speusippus and the early Academy and going down to Iamblichus, Proclus and even Psellus, regularly but mistakenly attributes 'arithmetical *theologoumena*' to early Pythagoreans, especially to (Pseudo-)Philolaus. The attribution concerns both equations of numbers with gods and speculations supporting them.[9] However, Aristotle's testimony (fr. 203 Rose, in Aristotle 1984: vol. 2, 2443–4) supports the view that this trend has its roots in ancient Pythagoreanism in light of the statement, attributed by Aristotle to the Pythagoreans, that the number seven is to be equated with the virgin goddess Athena on the ground that it is, like her, 'motherless' (in the sense that it cannot be generated by other numbers). The pre-Platonic character of the testimonies concerning the other numbers of the 'decad' is more uncertain and therefore debatable, but it is difficult to accept that

9. In this Academic and late Platonic tradition we also find geometrical *theologoumena*, that is, associations between gods and geometrical figures, and especially the idea of dedicating angles of triangles, squares and so on to various gods, not only in a speculative way but also in worship; see Huffman (1993: 381–91); Steel (2007).

this kind of theologizing speculation was not extended and generalized in order to embrace all of the first ten numbers. In their Academic, reworked form, the remaining equations resemble the following ones: the number one is mystically called Apollo, because he is apart from the many (*apō tōn pollōn*), that is alone; the number two is equated to the consort of Kronos, that is, the goddess Rhea, because of the association of the dyad-mother of the flowing being (*rheustē ousia*) to time (*chronos*) as the cause of destruction; and so on (Philolaus fr. 20–20a, in DK; cf. Huffman 1993: 334–9, 350–52).

Number theology brings us most naturally to another important and influential aspect of ancient Pythagorean thought, namely its scientific-mathematical conceptions and theologico-metaphysical speculations, perhaps mystical in nature, that go beyond the pantheon of civic religion or the gods of the mystery cults, and find in numbers the divine *archē* of the world or the first principle(s) of things (cf. Drozdek 2007: 53–70). In a famous passage from the *Metaphysics*, Aristotle states that the Pythagoreans identified the principles of mathematics (that is, number and its principles odd and even, limit and unlimited) with the principles of all things, and that:

> since … all other things in the whole of nature seemed to be modelled after numbers, and numbers seemed to be the first things in the whole of nature, they supposed the elements of numbers to be the elements of all things, and the whole heaven to be an attunement (*harmonia*) and a number. (*Metaphysics* A.5, 985b23ff. = 58 B 4 DK; trans. in Kirk *et al.* 1983: 329)

"The point of the doctrine as a whole is surely to teach that the cosmos – and everything that happens in it – exhibits a wholly intelligible order" (Kirk *et al.* 1983: 332), and that it is fitted harmoniously thanks to the musical ratios. This aspect of Pythagoreanism is well known, and it would be beyond the scope of this brief overview to present it in detail here. What we can do instead is to underline its antiquity and to focus on its importance for the philosophy of religion.

In what seems to be an ancient and authentic oath going back to the first generations of Pythagoreans, Pythagoras is revered as the revealer of "the *tetraktys* [= 'fourthness'] which contains the fount (*paga*) and root (*rhizoma*) of eternal/ever-flowing/ever-growing nature (*aenaou physeos*)" (B 15 DK = Aëtius, *Opinions* 1.3.8). So, everything in nature is supposed to flow or grow out of this mysterious *tetraktys*, which is the true source of all things, but its precise content is not revealed to the uninitiated. In an oral teaching attributed to the master himself, *tetraktys* is even said to be identical to the Delphic Oracle: the wisdom contained in it is as profound as the Pythian Apollo's, but its meaning is not at all obvious and needs interpretation in the same way as Apollo's oracles do. However, an intimation of its meaning is given: the *tetraktys* is equated to "the harmony in which the Sirens are" (Iamblichus 1991: §82).

With the help of other parallel texts we can safely conclude that the *tetraktys* encapsulates number as the basic principle of the universe. The reasoning runs as follows. The *tetraktys* (literally meaning 'group of four different things') contains in it the first four natural numbers: 1, 2, 3 and 4. What is amazing about them is, first, that their sum is 10, the complete and perfect number, the basis for counting in the decimal system of the Greeks, and the receiver (*dechad*) of the unlimited according to Philolaus (fr. 20b, in Huffman 1993: 352). All other numbers can be generated out of the numbers 1–9 contained in the decad. So all the possible numbers (with the exception of the irrational ones, of course, which were not yet discovered at the time of Pythagoras) are potentially contained in the "pregnant" decad-*tetraktys*. Out of these numbers are harmonized all the ratios, proportions or numerical formulas (*logoi*) that lie behind the ordered constitution of every single thing in the natural world, some of which are called by Philolaus "stronger (*kreittous*) than we are" (fr. 16, in Huffman 1993: 333), either because "we are not able to grasp all the ways in which they govern our world" or because "they control the world independent of our wishes" (Huffman 1993: 334). In either case some kind of invisible, divine power of the *logoi* is meant, especially if we take into consideration that the adjective *kreittones* in the plural was used to designate the 'mightier', superior beings.

The second aspect of the marvellous nature of the first four numbers is that the principal harmonic intervals or concords known to ancient Greek musicians and musicologists can be represented as ratios of them (fourth – 4:3; fifth – 3:2; octave – 2:1; later also the double octave – 4:1). These harmonic ratios are also considered responsible for the cosmic 'attunement', as we can glimpse from the reference to the Sirens, whose song Plato identifies in the *Republic* (616b–617e) with the "music of the spheres" in which the heavenly bodies move.[10] So by the very fact that it encompasses the basic harmonic ratios the *tetraktys* can reasonably be said to contain the clue to the invisible mysteries of the universe, and at the same time a mystic promise that the latter exhibits a harmonious order and rationality.[11] These 'proto-structuralist' considerations make extremely plausible the often doubted doxographic attribution of the paternity of the term *kosmos* (in the sense of 'world-order') to Pythagoras (Zhmud 1997: 292–5). At the same time they show how close we are to the formulation of the classical teleological argument from design, which is one of the most important theistic proofs in the history of the Western philosophy of religion. In our sources for early Pythagoreanism the perfection of the world is not explicitly connected to its divine origin or causation, let alone to its creation by a divine Demiurge, and this is in tune with the general tendency of Presocratic thinkers to limit themselves to an *assumption* that the world is governed by a divine power (Sedley 2007: 2). But

10. This is explicitly stated later by Sextus Empiricus, *Against the Mathematicians* 7.94–5.

11. For my discussion on the *tetraktys* I have drawn freely from Kirk *et al.* (1983: 232–4) and Thom (1995: 174–7).

it cannot be ruled out that some steps towards a first conception of the idea of a creator-god working with numerical ratios and applying the principle of harmony were already made by the Pythagoreans, if we take into consideration that the eponymous speaker of Plato's *Timaeus*, who is clearly the proponent of cosmic teleology, is probably – whether real or fictional – a Sicilian Pythagorean (*ibid.*: 94 n.4).

It is also number that will later constitute one of the two basic and pervasive principles that not only underlie the constitution of everything in the world, but also serve as a link between the human and the divine spheres, because they are shared by both, the other such principle being breath or soul. According to later Pythagorean texts reproduced by Iamblichus (1991: §146), it is the "eternal essence" of number that forms the basis not only of the material world, but of the divine sphere as well (gods and *daimones*), a notion that is absent from our evidence concerning early Pythagoreanism, unless we consider that it is somehow implied in the number theology discussed above. Sextus Empiricus, by contrast, speaks of breath or soul as the principle of the kinship of all living beings, from animals to gods:

> Now [the followers of] Pythagoras and Empedocles, and the rest of the Italian company declare that there is a certain community (*koinōnia*) [uniting us] not only with each other and with the gods but even with the irrational animals. There is in fact one breath (*pneuma*) pervading, like a soul (*psychēs tropon*), the whole universe, [the same breath] which also makes us one (*henoun*) with them.
>
> (*Against the Mathematicians* 9.127)

This seems to combine in a quite convincing way three closely interrelated early Pythagorean doctrines: (i) the immortality of the soul, which brings mortal man close to the immortal gods; (ii) the kinship between human beings and animals, on the principle that they are both animate beings (*empsycha*) possessing a soul and breathing; and (iii) the rather materialistic–animistic cosmogonic doctrine attested by Aristotle (*Physics* V.6, 213b22, and fr. 201 Rose [= 58 B 30 DK]), and shared also with the Orphics, according to which the world as a whole is a living, breathing being receiving, or rather 'drawing', its respiration, like the human embryo, from the unlimited outside it. To be sure, no god and nothing divine is mentioned in Aristotle's testimony, but soul, associated with breath, is a divine principle and, interestingly enough, breath and number are interrelated there: by breathing in (time and) the air or the void that separates and distinguishes the natures of things, the undivided universe – the One – becomes divided (and temporal), and it is this very distinction that is also the origin of numbers.

Out of these elements W. K. C. Guthrie tentatively reconstructed the rationale for the Pythagorean belief in the immortality of the soul in the following way:

> [I]f the world was a living, eternal and divine creature, and lived by breathing in air or breath from the infinite around it; and if man too got his life by breathing (which was evidence that the human soul itself was air): then the natural kinship between man and the universe, microcosm and macrocosm, must be close. The universe was one, eternal and divine. Men were many and divided, and they were mortal. But the essential part of man, his soul, was not mortal, and it owed its immortality to this circumstance, that it was neither more nor less than a small fragment or spark of the divine and universal soul, cut off and imprisoned in a perishable body. (1962: 201)

Another way to apprehend the relationship between man, god and the cosmos is found in a famous passage of Plato's *Gorgias*, which contains also an interesting hint at the notion of cosmic justice (Kouloumentas 2009: 146–66) and where the reference to the Pythagoreans is unmistakable:

> And wise men (*hoi sophoi*) tell us, Callicles, that heaven and earth and gods and men are held together by communion (*koinōnia*) and friendship (*philia*), by orderliness (*kosmiotēs*), temperance (*sōphrosyne*), and justice; and that is the reason, my friend, why they call the whole of this world by the name of order (*kosmos*), not of disorder or dissoluteness. Now you, as it seems to me, do not give proper attention to this, for all your cleverness, but have failed to observe the great power of geometrical equality amongst both gods and men.
> (*Gorgias* 507e–508a, in Plato 1925: 469–71)

However conceived of or argued, the relationship between god and man presupposes a likeness in being, and for the Pythagoreans this *syggeneia* resides in the existence of a divine parcel in man's body, namely, his soul. The attribution of a double nature to man, one bodily and mortal and the other spiritual and immortal, and its corollary, the radical body–soul dualism that goes hand-in-hand with the depreciation of the body and the symmetrical upgrading of the soul, is something completely new, which represents a radical reversal of the traditional Homeric conceptions. In the Homeric poems it is the body that represents the real self of the person, and it is celebrated as the seat of life: when it perishes at death the soul that goes down beneath the earth to the realm of Hades is little more than a bloodless shadowy image that resembles its bodily form but has no strength or real life. With Pythagoras' (and the Orphics') emphasis on the divine origin of man's soul and its immortality and survival after death we can truly speak of a religious revolution, of a 'shift of paradigm'. Further, this 'good news' or 'gospel' of salvation, which rendered the prospect of dying quite appealing by promising a happy afterlife into eternity for the souls of the good and righteous men and women, was accompanied by belief in the transmigration of the soul, reincarnation or metempsychosis, and *palingenesia* through successive rebirths, a belief that was unheard of in the Greek world before Pythagoras' time (cf. Vernant 1991). But this is another (fascinating) story.

FURTHER READING

Bremmer, J. 1999. "Rationalization and Disenchantment in Ancient Greece: Max Weber Among the Pythagoreans and Orphics?". In *From Myth to Reason? Studies in the Development of Greek Thought*, R. Buxton (ed.), 71–83. Oxford: Oxford University Press.

Bremmer, J. 2002. *The Rise and Fall of the Afterlife*. London: Routledge.

Burkert, W. 2006. *Kleine Schriften*, 3: *Mystica, Orphica, Pythagorica*, F. Graf (ed.). Göttingen: Vandenhoeck & Ruprecht.

Casadesús, F. 2008. "Orfismo y pitagorismo". In *Orfeo y la tradición órfica: Un reencuentro*, A. Bernabé & F. Casadesús (eds). Madrid: Akal.

Delatte, A. 1915. *Études sur la littérature pythagoricienne*. Paris: Champion.

Kahn, C. 2001. *Pythagoras and the Pythagoreans: A Brief History*. Indianapolis, IN: Hackett.

Kingsley, P. 1995. *Ancient Philosophy, Mystery, and Magic: Empedocles and Pythagorean Tradition*. Oxford: Clarendon Press.

Parker, R. 1983. *Miasma: Pollution and Purification in Early Greek Religion*. Oxford: Clarendon Press.

Thesleff, H. 1965. *The Pythagorean Texts of the Hellenistic Period*. Åbo: Åbo Akademi.

Tortorelli Ghidini, M., A. Storchi Marino & A. Visconti (eds) 2000. *Tra Orfeo e Pitagora: Origini e incontri di culture nell'antichità* (Atti dei seminari napoletani, 1996–98). Naples: Bibliopolis.

Zuntz, G. 1971. *Persephone: Three Essays on Religion and Thought in Magna Graecia*. Oxford: Clarendon Press.

On the IMMORTAL SOUL see also Ch. 4; Vol. 2, Chs 12, 16; Vol. 3, Chs 10, 19. On MYTH see also Vol. 4, Chs 5, 15. On VICE see also Ch. 7. On VIRTUE see also Chs 11, 14, 15; Vol. 3, Chs 20, 21.

3

XENOPHANES

James H. Lesher

Xenophanes was a poet and singer of epic verse who lived in various parts of the Greek world during the late sixth and early fifth centuries BCE. A number of the surviving fragments of his poetry touch on the usual subjects of Greek sympotic verse: on proper conduct at symposia (21 B 1, 5, 22 DK [= Diels & Kranz 1951–2]), the measures of personal excellence (B 2, 3) and aspects of his life and interactions with various notable individuals (B 6–8, 10, 19–21, 45). But in seven other fragments (B 27–33) Xenophanes follows the lead of the Milesian philosopher-scientists in describing a number of natural phenomena as products of a set of basic physical substances and processes. And in a series of remarks concerning the stories about the gods told by Homer and Hesiod (B 11–12), the true nature of the divine (B 23–6), and the tendency of believers to conceive of the gods as like themselves (B 14–16), Xenophanes explored, so far as we know for the first time, questions central to the philosophy of religion.

While a definitive interpretation of all aspects of Xenophanes' thinking may lie beyond reach, we can hope to develop plausible answers to at least four basic questions: (i) did Xenophanes espouse monotheism; (ii) on what basis did he repudiate anthropomorphism in religion, and did his own positive account of the divine avoid the errors he decried in the views of others; (iii) on what basis did he deny the possibility of knowledge concerning divine matters, and how in the light of that pessimistic assessment should we view his own account of the divine nature; and (iv) how did he understand the relationship between god and the cosmos?

XENOPHANES' MONOTHEISM

The case for crediting Xenophanes with monotheism comprises three main bodies of evidence and reasoning: (i) the view of the divine he presented in fragments B 23–6; (ii) the views about god and nature expressed or implied in his other poems; and (iii) the series of ancient testimonials that credit him with the view that 'god is one'. Determining the probative value of these materials requires an assessment of the relevant evidence as well as some specification of the kind of monotheism being considered.[1]

In fragment B 23 (on one common translation) Xenophanes speaks of: "One god, greatest (*heis theos ... megistos*) among gods and human beings, / Not at all like mortals in either body or thought ...". This characterization of the divine as unlike mortals in bodily form squares with the (apparently critical) sentiment expressed in B 14 – "But mortals suppose that gods are born, / Wear their own clothes, and have a voice and a body" – while the claim that god is unlike mortals in thought squares with the contents of B 24 – "Whole he sees, whole he thinks, and whole he hears" – as well as with the striking description of a telekinetic deity in B 25: "But completely without toil he shakes all things by the thought of his mind". The attributes of a single, special god also appear to be the subject of B 26: "... always he abides in the same place, not moving at all, / Nor is it seemly for him to travel to different places at different times". These remarks at least suggest that Xenophanes, perhaps uniquely among his contemporaries, affirmed the existence of a god who was in some sense 'greatest', capable of perceiving and thinking without the benefit of bodily organs, and able to effect change on a cosmic scale simply through the exercise of his mind. But should we conclude that Xenophanes was an 'exclusive monotheist', that is, that he held *both that one god exists and that there are no other gods of any kind or description*? Fragments B 23–6 clearly warrant crediting Xenophanes with a belief in the existence of one god who is in several respects the *greatest* of all, but they do not in any obvious way rule out the existence of other gods.

We might attempt to gain support for such a conclusion from other Xenophanean comments concerning the gods and various natural phenomena long regarded as rich in religious significance. A remark preserved in Eusebius' *Preparation for the Gospel,* attributed (incorrectly) to Plutarch, says of Xenophanes that: "He declares also that there is no one of the gods in single command over them, for it would be impious for any of the gods to be mastered; and not one is in any way in need of any of them" (Ps.-Plutarch, *Miscellanies* 4). The Pseudo-Aristotelian treatise, *On Melissus, Xenophanes, Gorgias*, also dating from the beginning of the Common Era, similarly asserts: "And if god is the strongest of all things, he says that it is fitting for god to be one. For if there were two or more, he would no longer be the strongest and best of all things ... for this is what god and god's nature is: to master and not to be mastered" (3.6.3). And while he does not mention Xenophanes by name, Euripides, 'the philosopher of the stage', may well have been following Xenophanes' lead when he wrote in the *Heracles*: "But I do not think ... that one god is master over another. For god, if indeed he is truly a god, lacks nothing" (1341–6). These passages point back towards an original remark that might have run: "God, if he is truly god, cannot be mastered by

1. Except where noted, all translations of the Greek texts are my own.

another, nor can he be in need". And if we can imagine neither a hierarchy of gods nor a god whose existence depends on that of any other being, then we might wish to regard this as, in effect, the expression of an exclusive monotheism. In addition, in a series of fragments (B 30–32 DK) and testimonia (A 38–46) Xenophanes offers (or is reported to have offered) a set of entirely naturalistic explanations of phenomena long thought of as divinities, or the work of divinities (e.g. the sun, moon, stars, ocean, rainbows, meteors, lightning, St Elmo's fire, etc.). While these observations may not completely preclude a belief in subordinate deities of some description, they do appear to dispense with the usual subordinate deities of Greek popular religion.

A number of ancient writers, moreover, showed no reluctance in crediting Xenophanes with a belief in the existence of a single supreme being of some description. The character in Plato's *Sophist* known as 'The Eleatic Stranger' depicts Xenophanes as a pioneering 'monist' (one who holds that essentially only one thing exists): "our Eleatic tribe, which harkens back to Xenophanes as well as even earlier, relates its stories on the assumption that what are called 'all things' are really one" (242d). And Aristotle similarly reports:

> But Xenophanes, the first of these to have been a 'one-ifier' (*henisas*) – for Parmenides is said to have been his pupil – made nothing completely clear, nor does he seem to have touched on the nature of these [attributes or causes], but with regard to the whole universe, he says that the one is the god [alternatively but less likely: that the god is the one – *to hen einai phēsi ton theon*]. (*Metaphysics* A.5, 986b21–5)

A number of later summaries of the views held by earlier thinkers are similar:

> For this is what [he says] god is: one and the whole universe. (Simplicius, A 31 DK)

> He says also that god is eternal and one ... (Hippolytus, A 33)

> [Xenophanes said that] all things are one, and this is unchanging, and is god ... (Cicero, A 34)

> Xenophanes [believed] only that all things were one and that this was god ... (Pseudo-Galen, A 35)

It would not be completely unwarranted to view Parmenidean monism as the end product of a process of thought that had its beginnings in a Xenophanean belief in the existence of one and only one god.

Yet there is another side to the story: in B 23 Xenophanes did not unambiguously affirm the existence of only one god; elsewhere in his poetry he did not speak of god as a exclusive monotheist might be expected to speak; and a number of considerations serve to *distance* Xenophanes' 'one god' from the Parmenidean 'One' rather than to unite them.

To begin with, while the crucial phrase *heis theos ... megistos* may be translated as "one god, greatest ...", thereby celebrating god's singularity as well as his greatness, it may with equal justice be translated as "one god is greatest" (with *heis* serving to strengthen the superlative, as in "*heis oiōnos aristos*", "one bird [of omen] is best" [*Iliad* 12.243]), thereby celebrating god's greatness, but *not* his singularity. And the reference to 'gods' in the plural (*theōn*) – in this very sentence ("greatest among gods and human beings") – is, at the least, surprising. We might be able to discount the significance of this reference to plural gods as an instance of the 'polar' style of expression characteristic of early Greek writers (meaning essentially "greatest among all sorts of beings"), or as a classic instance of a philosopher who was willing to 'speak with the vulgar' while simultaneously adopting a contrasting philosophical point of view. Yet we must still ask, as Michael Stokes (following Freudenthal) put it, "whether a convinced monotheist in an unreceptive polytheistic society would cloud the issue by a mention of plural gods which is at best ambiguous, in the very context where he is firmly stating his revolutionary view" (Stokes 1971: 76). The appearances of the plural form *theōn* in Xenophanes' B 1 and B 34 are also problematic, especially when in B 1 Xenophanes concludes his account of a high-spirited symposium with the sober reminder that "It is good always to hold the gods (*theōn*) in high regard". Unless we can somehow relegate this remark to a pre-monotheistic stage of Xenophanes' life and thought (which we have no basis for doing), we must acknowledge that the case for viewing Xenophanes as an exclusive monotheist, based on the fragments of his poetry that have come down to us, is more suggestive than definitive.

One might more plausibly hold that Xenophanes expressed the rudiments of a monotheistic view, or made a partial advance toward monotheism, or that one might be able to construct an exclusive monotheism by drawing out one or more logical consequences of the remarks he is reported to have made. Among these might be the lost verses ascribing maximal power and self-sufficiency to the divine, as well as the surviving fragments (B 30–32) and testimonia (A 38–46) that dispense with the various minor deities of Greek popular religion. Yet when we attempt to go beyond a claim of 'rudiments' or 'partial advance' we risk committing what Richard Robinson once called "misinterpretation by inference" (1953: 2): claiming that in so far as an author affirmed that *p*, and *p* implies that *q* (or *r* or *s* ...), then our author must also have believed that *q* (or *r* or *s* ...). No author, and no person for that matter, is properly credited with believing every proposition implied by the other things he or she believes.

A similar difficulty faces those who would seek to credit Xenophanes with an exclusive monotheism on the basis of an assumed historic Xenophanes–Parmenides connection. It is true, as many early writers noticed, that Xenophanes employed a form of the adjective 'one' (*heis*) in speaking of god, just as Parmenides employed a form of the adjective 'one' (*hen*) in speaking of *to eon* or 'what is' (B 8.6). Xenophanes also spoke of god as 'unmoving' (*kinoumenos ouden*; B 26) just as Parmenides spoke of 'what is' as 'changeless' (*akinēton*; B 8.26, 8.38). Xenophanes, moreover, spoke of some 'whole' being (*oulos*; B 24) who sees, hears and thinks, just as Parmenides spoke of 'what is' as a 'whole' or 'entire' being (*oulon*; B 8.38). Yet Xenophanes spoke specifically about 'god' (*theos*) rather than about 'what is' (*to eon*). So far as we can tell, he simply affirmed his view of the divine rather than attempting to establish its truth by evidence or argument, as Parmenides famously did; and while it is clear that Xenophanes called for decent conduct and a respectful attitude towards the gods, Parmenides did neither of these in connection with 'what is'. So while one can understand how the idea of a Xenophanes–Parmenides (or monotheism–monism) connection gained wide support among early historians of Greek thought, there are significant dissimilarities at various points.

One might plausibly speak of Xenophanes as a 'henotheist' or 'kathenotheist' in so far as he commented on the attributes of *one* special god while appearing to acknowledge the existence of other gods. He might also be regarded as an 'inclusive monotheist' (in so far as he might have considered other deities aspects of, or elements within, a single divine being), although we have no way telling how the gods he spoke of in the plural related to the 'one greatest god' he spoke of in B 23. It would be problematic, however, to view Xenophanes as a 'pluriform monotheist' (i.e. one who regards other gods as phases, subsequent stages or manifestations of a single divine substance) in so far as two fragments (B 25, 26) appear to place god (or at the least 'the greatest god') beyond the possibility of all motion and change.

XENOPHANES' CRITIQUE OF ANTHROPOMORPHISM IN RELIGION

As we have seen, in fragment B 14, Xenophanes speaks of mortals who believe, apparently incorrectly, that "gods are born, wear their own clothes, and have a voice and body". Although we are nowhere told that mortals are mistaken in so believing, the fragment's opening word 'But' (*alla*, which appears frequently in the surviving fragments) at least suggests that this belief contrasted with the view that Xenophanes himself held. (Our source for B 14, the late-second- and third-century Christian apologist Clement of Alexandria, placed B 14 after B 23, which affirmed the existence of the "one greatest god … not at all like mortals in body or thought".)

In another famous remark, Xenophanes comes very close to criticizing the tendency of believers to think of the gods as like themselves: "Ethiopians <say that their gods are> snub-nosed and black; / Thracians <say that their gods are> blue-eyed and red-haired" (B 16). While it has often been thought that these lines contain an element of ridicule, it is not obvious precisely where and how that ridicule is expressed. Taken just by themselves these lines impute no patent absurdity to either the Ethiopians or the Thracians. That there would have been nothing inherently ridiculous, at least to the ancient Greek mind, in the idea of a god possessing a particular bodily feature is evident from the frequent references in early Greek poetry to gods such as 'grey-eyed Athena', 'blond-haired Apollo' and 'dark-haired Poseidon'. And since the bodily features mentioned in B 16 are all different (nose shape and skin colour in the case of the Ethiopians, eye colour and hair colour for the Thracians), technically speaking, no inconsistency is being imputed to any mortal believer or believers. Yet there is at least the suggestion of a suspicious degree of coincidence in this set of beliefs: the gods turn out to have the very same features their human believers typically possess. So B 16 at least implicitly raises the possibility that human beings have created the gods in their own image, rather than the other way around. And when we bear in mind that for the ancient Greeks Ethiopia represented the southernmost civilization in the world, while Thrace was located in the far north, we can read Xenophanes' remark not as a characterization of practices in two individual cultures, but rather as a generalization of literally global dimensions: if all human beings (in effect, 'all people from pole to pole') depict the gods as like themselves, we may reasonably conclude that believers credit the gods with having certain features *because those are the features the believers themselves happen to possess.*

Aristotle expressed just such a thesis in a passage in his *Politics* (which may itself be a reminiscence of an earlier Xenophanean remark) concerning the notion of 'a king of the gods': "Wherefore people say that the gods have a king because they themselves either are or were in ancient times under the rule of a king. For they imagine not only the forms of the gods but also their ways of life to be like their own" (1252b23–36). The same message is conveyed in Xenophanes' striking (perhaps even jocular) analysis of the manner in which other kinds of living creatures might depict their gods if they had the physical means of doing so:

> But if oxen and horses or lions had hands,
> Or could draw with their hands and accomplish such works as men,
> Horses would draw the figures of the gods as similar to horses,
> And the oxen as similar to oxen,
> And they would make the bodies of the sort which each of them had.
> (B 16 DK)

We may conclude that Xenophanes put forward a genetic explanation of at least one central aspect of religious belief: the manner in which believers conceive of or depict the divine. As such, Xenophanes was an ancient forerunner to modern thinkers such as Feuerbach and Freud who found the root causes of religious belief in certain features of the human psyche. And in so far as the divine traits Xenophanes had in mind were all identifiably human, we may also credit him with a pioneering critique of anthropomorphism in religion.

It is not yet clear, however, whether Xenophanes was led on the basis of his analysis to *repudiate as erroneous* all anthropomorphic aspects of religion: that is, whether he held that in so far as religious believers have acquired their conceptions of the divine as they have, they were wrong to do so. To make such a claim, of course, would be to commit a solecism. To reject a view as false or mistaken on the grounds that it was adopted on the basis of factors or conditions that have nothing to do with its truth would be to commit the genetic fallacy. Even a belief adopted on the basis of entirely irrelevant considerations may still enshrine the truth. It is, moreover, not essential that a finding of anthropomorphic tendencies among religious believers be regarded as inherently problematic; one might find reason to regard anthropomorphism as a benign, perhaps even positive aspect of religious belief (cf. Allport 1960).

In any case, we are under no compulsion to saddle Xenophanes with the indefensible thesis that in so far as mortals have fashioned their views of the gods on the basis of irrelevant considerations, those views are all in error. In his reflections on the nature of the distinction between knowledge and true belief (B 34), Xenophanes allows that a person may "happen to speak truly concerning what is brought to pass" but not possess the kind of experience that would warrant the attribution of knowledge. Thus the notion of the 'lucky guess' or 'accidental truth' lay well within his reach. It is also clear that the positive account of the nature of the divine (or perhaps the 'one greatest god') provided Xenophanes with all the foundation he needed in order to repudiate popular conceptions of the divine. Fragments B 23–6 may be read as maintaining that there are specific features the divine must possess or lack in light of what is 'seemly' or 'fitting' to its nature (cf. the phrase *min epiprepei*, "seemly for him", in B 26). Once Xenophanes developed this account, he would have been fully justified in repudiating popular conceptions of the gods at odds with the truth, irrespective of the aetiology of those conceptions.

Some readers, however, have been troubled by the way in which Xenophanes appears to want to have it both ways: on the one hand criticizing the attribution of *some* human attributes to the divine (namely, being born and having a human body, voice and clothing) while simultaneously ascribing *other* human attributes (seeing, thinking, hearing, having a mind, and, at least implicitly, moral perfection). However, what Xenophanes specifically criticized, on several occasions, was the tendency of human beings to think of the gods as *like* themselves. In B 16 he reflects on the possibility that horses and oxen had the capacity to depict their gods as being of "the same sort as themselves" (*toiath' hoionper*), while by contrast B 23 speaks of the one god as "not at all (*outi* … *omoiios*) like mortals in body or thought". What Xenophanes specifically rejected, then, was a view of god, or the gods, as *like* mortals in various respects. Nothing he states in any of the surviving fragments prevents him from employing terms that apply to both human beings and gods, so long as he is careful not to use those expressions to affirm a significant degree of likeness between the two. He may consistently think of the divine as possessing a body of some (extremely unusual) sort, or a mind of some (extraordinary) kind, as well as a will of some (superlative degree of) goodness.

XENOPHANES' DENIAL OF KNOWLEDGE CONCERNING THE GODS

In fragment B 34 Xenophanes offers a rather somber assessment of the prospects for human knowledge:

> And indeed no man has been nor will there be one
> Who knows the sure truth (*to saphes*)
> Concerning such things as I say about the gods and all things.
> And even if at best he succeeded in speaking of what is brought to pass
> Still he himself would not know. Yet opinion is fashioned for all.

The 'sceptical' character of these remarks has been a matter of debate ever since they were quoted, and thereby preserved for posterity, by Plutarch and Sextus Empiricus, but recent discussions have served to narrow the range of plausible alternative readings. The mention in line three of "such things as I say about the gods and all things" indicates that these remarks date from a time in Xenophanes' life when he had already developed a set of views of the divine nature and the make-up of the physical universe. As a result, we can make use of our understanding of those aspects of Xenophanes' thought in order to grasp the rationale that may have lain behind these pioneering observations concerning the limits of human knowledge.

But first a brief comment about *to saphes*: 'the sure truth' that represents the focus of Xenophanes' concern here in B 34. Forms of *saphēs* appear throughout Greek literature of the archaic and classical periods, often in connection with knowing and saying. Quite commonly those who know 'the sure truth' do so on the basis of their direct or personal experience of the relevant circumstances. Thus when in B 34 Xenophanes denied that anyone has known or ever will know *to saphes*, what he probably meant was that no mortal being has been or ever will be in a position to gain a sure grasp of the truth *based on his or her direct experience of the relevant circumstances*. This reading makes good sense in this context in so far as nothing could be at a greater remove from the personal experiences of mortal beings than the actions of the gods and the totality of events that take place throughout the cosmos.

When we turn to consider which of Xenophanes' teachings might have lent some support to the thesis that mortals live far removed from those who dwell in a divine realm, we find many relevant remarks. As we have seen, fragments B 23–6 describe a supreme being unlike mortals in either body or thought, which is able to effect change throughout the cosmos by the exercise of its mind, while remaining always in the same place. Nowhere does Xenophanes indicate precisely why the divine must of necessity possess these attributes, but if by 'greatest' Xenophanes meant something like 'greatest in honour and power' (the usual measures of the greatness attributed to the gods in Homer; cf. *Iliad* 2.350, 2.412, 4.515; *Odyssey* 3.378, 5.4; Hesiod, *Theogony* 49, 534, 538), then the basic premise underlying his view of the divine nature would have been that *any* attribution of a physical or material attribute, process or activity would entail a degree of limitation that is strictly incompatible with the divine nature. With this conception of the divine Xenophanes undercuts at a single stroke the credibility of the countless tales of localized epiphanies and dramatic interventions found in Homer, Hesiod and other early writers.

Fragments B 14–16 serve to reinforce a view of the gods as 'wholly other' by explaining how the attributes typically assigned to the gods by mortal believers are properly regarded as projections of their own physical attributes. In addition, in fragments B 27–33 (as well as in the views reported in testimonia A 1, 32, 33, 36, 38–46) Xenophanes explains why a wide range of natural phenomena should be regarded not as signs or messages sent to humankind by the gods, but simply as clouds, earth and water that appear, disappear and change in form as a result of perfectly regular (hence understandable) physical processes. Included among these are his characterization of earth and water as the dual sources of all things (B 29, 33), the sea as the source of all clouds, winds and rain (B 30) and – perhaps most significantly – the rainbow as a purple, red and greenish-yellow kind of cloud, rather than as Iris, the messenger deity (B 32).

A view of the divine as wholly inaccessible to mortals would also serve to explain Xenophanes' rebukes of various claimants to knowledge or expertise in religious matters. These would include his ridiculing of Pythagoras for claiming to be able to recognize the soul of a departed friend in the yelping of a puppy (B 7), his comment on the practice of placing pine branches about the house, perhaps in an attempt to extract something of their 'evergreen' nature as a form of protection (B 17), his rebuke of Epimenides (A 1), as well as his blanket and emphatic (*outoi*) denial that "from the beginning, gods have intimated all things to mortals" (B 18). In addition, two ancient sources (A 52) report that Xenophanes, alone among ancient thinkers, repudiated the practice of divination (*mantikē*), the set of techniques or 'art' that ancient peoples (and some modern ones) believed enabled human beings to penetrate the obscurities of the past, present and future. A scepticism concerning divination would also serve to explain the dismissive reference in B 34 to one who may "succeed better than others in speaking of what is brought to pass (*tetelesmenon eipōn*)".

To sum up, as Xenophanes understood it, the divine cannot possibly speak to human beings in a language they can understand, nor can it vacate its heavenly abode and move about in their midst. In reality, popular conceptions of the gods tell us more about the attributes of believers than they do about the gods, and the amazing events that take place in the heavens are merely natural phenomena to be accounted for strictly in terms of natural substances and regular physical processes. As Hermann Fränkel aptly summarized Xenophanes' position: "he made the chasm between the here and the beyond unbridgeable" (1974: 130). About the gods, therefore, as about the nature of things at all times and places, no mortal being has known or ever will know the sure truth, but all may have their opinions.

Yet B 34 contains at least one unresolved puzzle: if indeed there never has been nor ever will be anyone who knows the sure truth about the gods, how are we supposed to regard Xenophanes' own understanding of the nature of the divine? The distinction between knowing and believing (or having an opinion, *dokos*) so clearly articulated in B 34 offers us an initially attractive answer: Xenophanes could easily have viewed his own account of the nature of the divine as governed by the broad pessimism he expressed in B 34, as representing his 'opinion' and nothing more. Similarly, when, in B 35, he proclaims, "let these be accepted as like the realities", we may understand this admonition to apply to his own teachings on both natural and supernatural subjects.

This manoeuvre, however, gains us consistency on one front at the price of creating new difficulties elsewhere. For if Xenophanes regarded his own view of the divine as 'merely his opinion', and if the phrase "opinion is fashioned for all" in B 34.4 means something like 'all are entitled to their own opinions' then it is difficult to see how he could have considered himself entitled to decry as erroneous the views of the gods promulgated by Homer and Hesiod, to belittle popular superstitions and to ridicule Pythagoras and Epimenides as fraudulent claimants to an expertise in divine matters. So while our first response may render B 34 internally consistent, it creates serious tensions between B 34 and remarks Xenophanes makes in a number of other fragments.

It is possible, of course, that the surviving fragments of Xenophanes' poetry date from different stages of his intellectual development. Perhaps Xenophanes, like Kant, had an earlier 'dogmatic' period in which he confidently set out his views as the sure truth while decrying all competing accounts as mistaken, and then entered a later 'critical' period in which he came to recognize that his convictions, like those of his opponents, represented *dokos* and nothing more. It might also be possible to distinguish those aspects of the divine about which we might gain sure knowledge from others about which this would not be possible. But, however one may attempt to resolve it, there is a clear tension between the pessimistic outlook Xenophanes expressed in B 34 and the many strongly worded assertions made elsewhere in his poems.

THE RELATIONSHIP BETWEEN XENOPHANES' GOD AND THE PHYSICAL UNIVERSE

As we have seen, Plato included Xenophanes among those who had held that 'all things are one'. Similarly, Aristotle stated that "with regard to (or turning his eye toward, *apoblēpsas*) the whole universe, [Xenophanes] says that the one is the god" (*Metaphysics* A.5, 986b24–5), and a series of ancient writers (A 31, 33–5) claimed that Xenophanes identified god with "the One", "the whole heaven" and "the universe". Perhaps, then, in much the same manner in which Anaximander had previously characterized his basic reality ('The Indefinite') as divine, Xenophanes identified his god (or at least 'the one greatest god') with the entire physical universe. Modern scholarly opinion on the merits of this view of Xenophanes remains sharply divided, but its defenders face two major challenges.

First, we are required to embrace a series of strained (although not completely impossible) readings. We would not be able to regard Plato's characterization of Xenophanes in the *Sophist* as yet another of his many fanciful renderings of the views of his predecessors, but as an unvarnished statement of fact. We would have to understand Aristotle's phrase *apoblēpsas to holon ouranon* along the lines of 'having turned his gaze toward the whole physical universe' rather than the more usual 'with reference to the whole physical universe'. We would have to read each of Xenophanes' various statements about 'god' or 'the one greatest god' as a characterization of the entire physical universe (rather than of a special supernatural being). Somewhere in Xenophanes' poems (perhaps in the *oulon* of B 24 or in the unmoving – hence in equipoise – god of B 26?) we would have to find an implicit reference to god's spherical nature. And if we are to trace this idea back to Parmenides we would have to believe that when Parmenides likened 'what is' to "the bulk of a well-rounded sphere" (B 8.43) what he meant was not that 'what is' is *in some way* 'like the bulk of a sphere' (e.g. fully developed in every respect), but rather that 'what is' is quite literally spherical.

The second challenge to this reading is that the two comments Xenophanes actually makes about the cosmos and its relationship to the divine tend to count against the traditional view. Fragment B 25 states that "completely without toil he shakes all things by the thought of his mind" thereby suggesting that in so far as god shakes the cosmos he is not identical with it. And B 28 holds that "This upper limit of the earth is seen here at our feet, pushing up against the air, but that below goes on without limit", suggesting that Xenophanes did not believe that the cosmos was shaped like a sphere. But here, as elsewhere in the interpretation of Xenophanes' teachings, our conclusions will reflect not only what we take to be his *ipsissima verba* but also the standards for credibility with which we choose to operate. Those who insist on finding clear and convincing evidence before accepting the traditional view will almost certainly demur. Yet others, perhaps of a more adventurous nature, will recognize the gaps in the evidence, acknowledge the possibility of error, yet conclude that, almost certainly, Xenophanes identified god with the cosmos.

FURTHER READING

Baarda, T., R. van den Broek & J. Mansfeld (eds) 1988. *Knowledge of God in the Graeco-Roman World*. Leiden: Brill.

Babut, D. 1974. "Sur la théologie de Xénophane". *Revue Philosophique de la France et de l'Etranger* **164**: 401–40.

Babut, D. 1974. "Xénophane critique des poètes". *L'Antiquité classique* **43**: 83–117.

Babut, D. 1977. "L'idée de progrès et la relativité du savoir humain selon Xénophane (Fragments 18 et 38 D-K)". *Revue de Philologie, de Littérature et d'Histoire Ancienne* **51**: 217–28.

Drechsler, W. & R. Kattel 2004. "Mensch und Gott bei Xenophanes". In *Gott und Mensch im Dialog: Festschrift für Otto Kaiser zum 80. Geburtstag*, M. Witte (ed.), 111–29. Berlin: Walter de Gruyter.

Drozdek, A. 2007. "Xenophanes and One God". In *Greek Philosophers as Theologians: The Divine Arche*, A. Drozdek, 15–25. Aldershot: Ashgate.

Finkelberg, A. 1990. "Studies in Xenophanes". *Harvard Studies in Classical Philology* **93**: 104–67.

Guthrie, W. K. C. 1962. *A History of Greek Philosophy: Vol. 1, The Earlier Presocratics and the Pythagoreans*. Cambridge: Cambridge University Press.

Heitsch, E. 1983. *Xenophanes: Die Fragmente*. Munich: Artemis Verlag.

Heitsch, E. 1994. *Xenophanes und die Anfänge kritischen Denkens*. Mainz: Akademie der Wissenschaften und der Literatur.

Kaiser, O. 2003. "Der eine Gott und die Götter der Welt". In his *Zwischen Athen und Jerusalem: Studien zur griechischen und biblischen Theologie, ihrer Eigenart und ihrem Verhältnis*, 135–52. Berlin: Walter de Gruyter.

Lebedev, A. 2000. "Xenophanes on the Immutability of God: A Neglected Fragment in Philo Alexandrinus". *Hermes* **128**: 385–91.

Jaeger, W. 1947. *The Theology of the Early Greek Philosophers*. Oxford: Oxford University Press.

Mogyorodi, E. 2002. "Xenophanes as a Philosopher: Theology and Theodicy". In *Qu'est-ce que la philosophie présocratique?*, A. Laks & C. Louguet (eds), 253–86. Villeneuve d'Ascq: Presses Universitaires du Septentrion.

Palmer, J. 1998. "Xenophanes' Ouranian God in the Fourth Century". *Oxford Studies in Ancient Philosophy* **16**: 1–18.

On DIVINATION see also Chs 7, 8. On MONOTHEISM see also Ch. 4. On THE ONE see also Chs 11, 14, 16, 19; Vol. 4, Ch. 9; Vol. 5, Ch. 15.

4

SOCRATES AND PLATO

Mark McPherran

Socrates (469–399 BCE) of Athens was the son of Sophroniscus (father) and Phaenarete (mother), and husband of Xanthippe, with whom he had three sons. Although Socrates never wrote anything, his many years of philosophical discussion established him as the founder of Western moral theory. The main sources for his views are the *Clouds* by Aristophanes (a parody), the dialogues of Plato, various works by Xenophon and passages in Aristotle; since these sources offer differing perspectives, the task of determining Socrates' actual views is daunting.

Plato depicts Socrates as a man who disavows possessing any real wisdom himself (except the mere human wisdom of understanding that lack) and who pursues a divinely ordained philosophical mission that requires him to question those who profess moral wisdom to see if they actually possess it. This questioning – the famous Socratic method – involves asking interlocutors to define one of the canonical virtues – piety, justice, courage, moderation, wisdom – and then eliciting various other statements from them that then turn out to be mutually inconsistent, thus showing their lack of knowledge of the relevant virtue. Socrates' own 'intellectualist' moral theory holds that: (1) every kind of creature desires/aims to achieve that kind's particular good; (2) thus, every person aims to achieve the human good (everyone desires to be an *agathōs*, a good, successful person); (3) the human good is *eudaimonia* ('happiness', human flourishing) (and a person is not a body, but is, rather, a soul, a *psuchē*); (4) the means to this end are the virtues (*aretai*, 'excellences'); (5) the virtues are a kind of craft-knowledge; (6) knowledge is best obtained by means of philosophizing; (7) thus, the happiest (and most pleasurable) life belongs to the philosopher. Some odd consequences of this view (the 'Socratic paradoxes') are that no one does wrong knowingly or voluntarily and that it is always better to suffer an injustice than to do it.

Socrates was indicted for impiety on the grounds that he corrupted the young by teaching them to recognize not the gods of the state but new divinities instead. He was sentenced to die by hemlock poisoning, and although given a chance to flee (as depicted in the *Crito*), he obeyed the order. His death was a model of noble self-control (made paradigmatic by Jacques-Louis David's famous painting of the scene); his last words are reported to have been: "Crito, we owe a cock to Asclepius: please pay the debt and do not forget" (*Phaedo* 118a7–8).

Plato (429–347 BCE) of Athens, or Aristocles (Plato is a nickname), was the son of Ariston (father) and Perictione (mother). He was a student of Socrates, the teacher of Aristotle and established the first formal philosophical school in Athens, the Academy. Plato's approximately twenty-six dialogues are masterpieces of Western literature, covering everything from epistemology, metaphysics and ethics, to philosophy of education, aesthetics and political science; they are generally regarded as having established the central agenda of the Western philosophical enterprise.

Plato's early Socratic dialogues (e.g. the *Euthyphro*) offer us a fictionalized portrait of Socrates that arguably captures the style and substance of the historical Socrates. Plato's later, more constructive works (e.g. the *Republic*, *Sophist*), outline a metaphysical theory – the theory of Forms – according to which there is, besides the world of sensible material objects and their properties, a non-spatiotemporal 'world' populated by the objects that are the perfect exemplars of those properties – Forms – and also by gods. These super-sensible Forms are the objects of our knowledge: 'Triangle-itself' is, for example, what our knowledge of Triangularity is 'of'. Since the objects of this world possess the properties they do by being in relation to the Forms – by 'participating' in them – when we correctly judge some person, say Helen, to be beautiful, we are able to recognize that instance of beauty by reference to our knowledge of Beauty-itself. Because the sensible world is constantly changing and because sensible objects have opposite properties in them, we can have warranted beliefs only and not knowledge concerning the physical world of material objects.

In contrast to Socrates' view of the soul as a rational intellect, Plato's account of the soul in several places (esp. the *Republic*) takes it to have 'parts' – the rational intellect, the spirited element (*thumos*) and the appetitive element – where the just, 'happy' soul is one whose parts are in harmony, that is, reason allied with *thumos* exerting proper control over the appetites.

Plato argues in several dialogues (e.g. the *Phaedo*, *Republic* and *Phaedrus*) that our souls are immortal, that they are able to apprehend the Forms in the afterlife, are rewarded or punished there and are then reborn for a new round of learning. The universe is governed by a single deity, the *dēmiourgos*, who looks to the Forms as to blueprints in his maintenance of the world-order.

Plato's dialogues and the characters they portray continually invoke the realm of divinity by using the religious vocabulary of their own time and place. Sometimes these allusions to gods, prayers and so on are merely figures of speech, but typically Plato has his characters speak of the divine in an unmistakably serious fashion in order to make points that are simultaneously philosophical and religious in nature. So prominent is this feature of Plato's work that the ancient world took it for granted that the chief goal of those who follow the Platonic line was to "become as much like god as is possible" (Sedley 1997: 329). Although this aspect of first Socratic and then Platonic thought has been underplayed in modern scholarship, it should not surprise us: both Socrates and Plato were born into a culture that took the existence of divinities for granted. More importantly, Plato was a discerning student of Socrates, a thinker who was himself not only a rational philosopher of the first rank but a profoundly religious figure as well. These commitments were, however, not those of a small town polytheist but of a sophisticated religious reformer whose innovations appear to have led to his trial and execution on a charge of impiety (see Beckman 1979; Vlastos 1991: ch. 6; McPherran 1996: ch. 3). Plato should be understood, then, to have followed the path laid down by his teacher by appropriating, reshaping and extending the religious conventions of his own time in the service of establishing the new enterprise of philosophy. The results were far-reaching, impacting his intellectual heirs (e.g. Aristotle, Plotinus) and with them Jewish, Christian and Islamic thought. Within the limits within which I must work, I shall trace out here the main threads of the religious dimension of first Socrates' and then Plato's philosophy.

I think it reasonable to make a rough distinction between Plato's Socratic, aporetic dialogues and those in which Plato appears to be following out a more constructive line of thought (especially in view of the evidence that Plato developed a metaphysics and epistemology that went far beyond those claims that can be reasonably attributed to his teacher; see e.g. Aristotle *Metaphysics* M.4, 1078b9–32). This view, at any rate, accounts for the important differences between the way the notion of piety and other religious topics are treated in Socratic dialogues such as the *Euthyphro* as opposed to more explicitly theory-laden, constructive works such as the *Republic*, *Phaedrus*, *Timaeus* and *Laws*.[1]

Next, it is important to note at the outset that the distinct phenomena we designate by using terms such as 'religion' were, for Plato and his contemporaries, seamlessly integrated into everyday life. Moreover, no ancient text such as Homer's *Iliad* had the status of a Bible or Koran, and there was no organized Church, trained clergy or systematic set of doctrines enforced by them. What marked out a fifth-century BCE Greek city or individual as pious (*hosios*; *eusebēs*) – that is, as being in accord with the norms governing the relations of human beings and gods – was

1. Listed in alphabetical order, the Socratic dialogues are *Apology*, *Charmides*, *Crito*, *Euthyphro*, *Hippias Minor*, *Ion*, *Laches*, *Protagoras* and *Republic I* (with *Euthydemus*, *Gorgias*, *Hippias Major*, *Lysis*, *Menexenus*, and *Meno* serving as 'transitional dialogues'). The more constructive dialogues are *Cratylus*, *Parmenides*, *Phaedo*, *Phaedrus*, *Republic II–X*, *Symposium*, *Theaetetus*, *Critias*, *Laws*, *Philebus*, *Sophist*, *Statesman* and *Timaeus*. There is not sufficient space here to address the complex issue of whether and how we might legitimately use the testimony of Aristotle in conjunction with that of Plato's dialogues and Xenophon's work to triangulate to the views of the historical Socrates in the manner of Vlastos (1991: chs 2, 3); but see, for example, McPherran (1996: ch. 1.2).

thus not primarily a matter of belief, but rather correct observance of ancestral tradition. The most central of these activities consisted in the timely performance of prayers and sacrifices (see e.g. *Iliad* 1.446–58; *Odyssey* 3.418–72).

Even though ancient conceptions of divinity were not elaborated or enforced by an official theological body, religious education was not left to chance. The compositions attributed to Homer and Hesiod were a part of everyone's education, and both authors were recognized as having established for the Greeks a canon of tales about the great powers that rule over us. Later writers then drew from this poetic repertory, "while simultaneously endowing [these] traditional myths with a new function and meaning" (Zaidman & Pantel 1992: 144). Thus, for example, the dramas of Aeschylus and Sophocles (e.g. *Antigone*) juxtapose some present situation against the events represented in Homer's texts, extending that mythology while also calling into critical question some facet of the human condition and contemporary society's response to it. By the time of Socrates, some of this probing of the traditional stories was influenced by the speculations and scepticism of those thinkers working within the new intellectualist traditions of natural philosophy (e.g. Xenophanes) and sophistry (e.g. Protagoras). As a result, in the work of authors such as Euripides and Thucydides even the fundamental tenets of popular religion concerning the gods and the efficacy of sacrifice and prayer became targets of criticism. Socrates should be placed within this movement.

SOCRATES

Socrates' philosophical reputation has always rested on his adherence to the highest standards of rationality, one given its clearest expression in the *Crito*:

T1 "I'm not the sort of person who's just now for the first time persuaded by nothing within me except the argument that on rational reflection seems best to me; I've *always* been like that" (*Crito* 46b4–6, trans. Reeve, in Cohen *et al.* 2005).

Socratic reasoning commonly employs the Socratic method, and we are encouraged to believe that for many years Socrates subjected a wide variety of self-professed experts on the topic of virtue to this form of examination (*Apology* 20d–23c). The result of this long effort, however, appears to be not a body of knowledge, but the meagre pay-off of moral scepticism:

T2 "I'm only too aware that I've no claim to being wise in anything either great or small" (*Apology* 21b4–5), "[except that] … I'm wiser … in just this small way: that what I don't know, I don't think I know" (*Apology* 21d6–8, trans. Reeve).

This would not be so surprising an outcome were it not that Socrates represents this awareness as resulting from a quest performed at the behest of Greece's preeminent religious authority, the Delphic Oracle. For as Socrates sees it, the god Apollo, speaking through the Oracle, has stationed him in Athens as though he is a warrior, ordering him to philosophize by elenctically examining himself and others (*Apology* 28d–29a, 30e–31a). As he summarizes the matter:

T3 "I had to go to all those with any reputation for knowledge ... So even now I continue to search and to examine, in response to the god ... I come to the assistance of the god ... I've had no leisure worth talking about ... because of my service to the god" (*Apology* 21e5–23c1); "the god stationed me here ... to live practicing philosophy, examining myself and others" (*Apology* 28e4–6, trans. Reeve).

Socrates also emphasizes that his interpretation of the Delphic Apollo's pronouncement that "no one is wiser" than he as an order to philosophize has been confirmed through other extra-rational sources:

T4 "I've been ordered to do [philosophy] by the god, both in oracles and dreams, and in every other way that divine providence ever ordered any man to do anything at all" (*Apology* 33c4–7, trans. Reeve; cf. *Apology* 30a; *Crito* 43d–44b; *Phaedo* 60c–61c).

In addition, Socrates tells the jurors at his trial that ever since his childhood he has been assisted in his philosophical mission through the frequent warnings of his divine sign, the *daimonion*:

T5 "a sort of voice comes, which, whenever it does come, always holds me back from what I'm about to do but never urges me forward" (*Apology* 31d2–4, trans. Reeve).

Our texts should now prompt us to ask how it is that Socrates can also subscribe to T2: for, lacking wisdom, how can Socrates be confident that gods such as Apollo even exist, let alone be assured that Apollo always speaks the truth (21b)? Moreover, since he also endorses T1, we can expect him to justify the claims implied by these texts; but it is hard to see how the Socratic method could provide that sort of warrant (since it appears to reveal only the inconsistency of interlocutors' beliefs; hence, their lack of expert knowledge; see Benson [2000] and Scott [2002]). Texts such as T4 and T5 also make Socrates appear to be far more 'superstitious' than the average Athenian: not the sort of behaviour we expect from the paradigm of the rationally self-examined life. After all, if enlightened contemporaries such as Thucydides could stand aloof from comparable elements of popular religion, and if even traditionally minded playwrights such as Aristophanes could poke cruel fun at seers (e.g. *Birds* 521, 959–91), how could Socrates not do so as well? Worse yet, it is hard to see how the Socrates who accepts T1, T3 and T4 as he investigates the religious claims of his interlocutors can be self-consistent when he goes on to criticize such interlocutors for acting on ungrounded religious judgements:

T6 "if you [Euthyphro] didn't know with full clarity what the pious and the impious are, you'd never have ventured to prosecute your old father for murder on behalf of a day laborer. On the contrary, you wouldn't have risked acting wrongly because you'd have been afraid before the gods and ashamed before men" (*Euthyphro* 15d4–8, trans. Reeve).

Here a rational principle of morality is implied: actions that are morally ambiguous ought not to be performed in the absence of a full understanding of the relevant concepts involved. So we are then left to wonder how the epistemically modest Socrates of T2 would respond if pressed to defend his risky conduct of challenging the moral and religious views of his fellow Athenians. The mere citation of divine authority instanced by T3, T4 and T5 would appear inadequate in view of the demands of T1; such a citation would also open up to interlocutors such as Euthyphro (a self-professed diviner) the possibility of replying in kind that they too, like Socrates, have been commanded in divinations and in dreams to contest conventional norms.

The preceding texts exemplify the way that Plato presents us with a puzzling, street-preaching philosopher who is both rational and religious, and whose relationship to everyday Athenian piety is anything but clear. To begin to make sense of that relationship, and thereby resolve the tensions between these and related texts, it is useful to examine Socrates' own examination of a self-professed expert in Greek religion: Euthyphro.

The *Euthyphro*'s discussion of the virtue of piety makes it a key text for determining the religious dimension of Socratic philosophy. It also provides vivid examples of the Socratic method through its portrayal of Socrates' relentless interrogation of Euthyphro's attempted definitions of piety. Definition (1) – piety is proceeding against whomever does injustice (5d–6e) – is quickly dispensed with because it is too narrow; Euthyphro holds there to be cases of pious action that do not involve proceeding against wrongdoers (5d–e). Socrates also reminds Euthyphro that he is seeking a complete account of the *one* characteristic (*eidos*) of piety: that unique, self-same, universal quality the possession of which makes any pious action pious and which Euthyphro had earlier agreed was the object of their search (6d–e; cf. 5c–d; *Meno* 72c). Definition (2) – piety is what is loved by the gods (6e–7a) – is next rejected on the grounds that since Euthyphro's gods quarrel about the rightness of actions, a god-loved and hence pious action could also be a god-hated and hence impious action; thus, definition (2) fails to specify the real nature of pious actions (7a–9d). Note, however, that by presupposing without restriction in his definitional search that the definition of piety must apply to *every* pious action – and given his apparent rejection of divine enmity and violence (6a–d, 7b–9c) – Socrates is committed to the claim (i) that there is but one universal moral canon for all beings, gods and human beings alike, and thus must reject the tradition of a divine double standard of morality (cf. e.g. *Republic* 378b). Socrates' examination also suggests that his gods (ii) are perfectly just and good, and so (iii) experience no moral disagreements among themselves.

Socrates' rebuttal of Euthyphro's third attempt at definition (3) – piety is what is loved by all the gods (9e) – constitutes the most logically complex section of the *Euthyphro* (9e–11b).[2] Socrates' apparent rejection of this definition comes at the end of a long and complex passage (10e–11b) where he first drives home his conclusion that Euthyphro's various concessions undercut this third definition of piety and then explains the apparent source of Euthyphro's confusion; namely, given Euthyphro's claim that something is god-loved because it is pious, his purported definition 'god-loved' appears to designate only a non-essential property of piety rather than specifying piety's essential nature. With this Socrates makes it evident that he is no divine command theorist: that is, unlike gods modelled after Homeric royalty, his gods do not issue morality-*establishing* commands such that a pious action is pious simply because it is god-loved; rather, it seems, his gods love things that are independently pious because they themselves are by nature wise, virtue-loving beings. By tacitly allowing that the gods are *of one mind* on the topic of virtue, Socrates here lays the groundwork for the view that there is ultimately only one divinity (see below).

---

2. For analysis of this argument, see Cohen (1971) and Benson (2000: 59–62). McPherran (1996: 43 n.43), provides a bare-bones version:

> Euthyphro agrees that (1a) the pious is loved by the gods because it is pious and that (1b) it's not that the pious is pious because it is loved by the gods. He also agrees that – as with the examples of seer and seen thing, carrier and carried thing, lover and loved thing – (2) a god-loved thing is god-loved because the gods love it, and (3) it's not that the gods love a god-loved thing because it is god-loved. But if D3 [his third definition: piety is what is loved by all the gods] were true (viz., that the pious = the god-loved), then by substitution from D3 into (1a), it would be true that (4) the god-loved is loved by the gods because it is god-loved, and by substitution from D3 into (2) it would be true that (5) a pious thing is pious because the gods love it. However, (4) contradicts (3), and (5) contradicts (1b). Thus, (1a), (1b), (2), and (3) cannot be jointly affirmed while also affirming D3 (resulting in D3's rejection).

To conclude, "the god-loved is not what's pious … nor is the pious what's god-loved, as you claim, but one differs from the other" (*Euthyphro* 10d12–14, trans. Reeve; cf. 10e2–11a6).

It should be noted that although Socrates takes himself to have established that D3 is inconsistent with Euthyphro's other commitments (to e.g. [1a]), he need not be taken to also conclude that D3 is false; see Benson (2000: 59–61).

Socrates assists Euthyphro in producing a fourth definition of piety by confronting him with the question of piety's relation to generic justice: are all the just pious, or is justice broader than piety such that piety is then a part of justice (11e–12e)? Subsequent to his adoption of the part-of-justice view, Euthyphro attempts to differentiate pious justice from the remainder ('human justice') by stipulating that piety involves the *therapeutic tendance* of gods (*therapeia theōn*) (12e6–9). This differentia, however, is rejected by reference to a craft analogy comparing those who would tend the gods in this fashion to those who tend horses, dogs and cattle (13a–d). Such therapists possess the sort of expert knowledge that includes the capacity to benefit their particular kind of subjects substantially by restoring or maintaining their health, or by otherwise meeting their essential needs and improving the way in which they function. Obviously, then, since mere mortals cannot benefit gods in these ways, the virtue of piety cannot be a form of therapy (13c–e). By contrast, *skilful service* (*hupēretikē*) along the lines of assistants to craftspeople contributes to an acceptable differentia of generic justice; assistants to a shipwright, for example, serve the shipwright by satisfying his or her desire to receive assistance in building ships but do not restore or improve on the shipwright's own nature or functioning. Socrates has thus brought Euthyphro to the point of agreeing that:

P Piety is that part of justice that is a service of humans to gods, assisting the gods in their primary task to produce their most beautiful product (12e–14a).

Within the constraints of this account, Euthyphro is then asked to specify precisely the nature of that most beautiful product of the gods' chief work in whose production the gods might employ our assistance (13e–14a). Euthyphro, however, tenaciously avoids answering this question (13d–14a), citing instead a fifth definitional attempt: (5) piety is knowledge of sacrificing and praying (14b–15c). To this Socrates emphatically responds that Euthyphro is abdicating their search just at the point where a *brief* answer might have finally given Socrates all the information that he really needed to have about piety (14b–c). Many scholars have found this good evidence for ascribing something like P to Socrates. The question then becomes how Socrates would have answered the question of the identity of the gods' beautiful, chief product.

First, we can expect Socrates to maintain that although we human beings cannot have a complete account of the gods' work, since the gods are wholly good, their chief project and product must be superlatively good. But what reasons, *per* the rationality principle (T1), does Socrates have for holding that the gods are entirely good? His thinking would seem to run roughly as follows. Since gods are perfectly knowledgeable, they must be entirely wise (*Apology* 23a–b; *Hippias Major* 289b3–6); but because wisdom and virtue are mutually entailing, it would follow that a god must be at least as good as a good person; but then since the latter can only do good, never evil (*Crito* 49c; *Republic* 335a–d), the same goes for the former (cf. *Republic* 379a–391e) (see Vlastos 1991: 162–5; McPherran 1996: chs 2.2.2–6, 3.2).

Socrates' moral reformation of the gods indicates that his gods cannot be fully identified with those of tradition. For Greek popular thought assumed, as a fundamental principle from Homer onwards, that justice consists in reciprocation, in repayment in kind: a gift for a gift, an evil for an evil (the *lex talionis*). Even among the gods the principle of *lex talionis* is assumed as basic (e.g. Zeus suggests that Hera might allow him to destroy one of her favorite cities in return for abandoning Troy [*Iliad* 4.31–69]; cf. Sophocles *Ajax* 79). In respect of this venerable principle, Socrates must be ranked a self-conscious moral revolutionary (*Crito* 49b–d): as he sees it, since we should never do injustice, we should never do evil, and from that it follows that we should never do an evil in return for even an evil done to us (*Crito* 48b–49d, 54c; cf. *Gorgias* 468e–474b; *Republic* 335a–d). For Socrates, then, not even Zeus can return one injury for another.[3]

Next, the Socratic view that the only or most important good is virtue/wisdom (e.g. *Apology* 30a–b; *Crito* 47e–48b; *Gorgias* 512a–b; *Euthydemus* 281d–e) makes it likely that the only or most important component of the gods' chief product is virtue/wisdom. But then, since piety as a virtue must be a craft-knowledge of how to produce goodness (e.g. *Laches* 194e–196d, 199c–e; *Euthydemus* 280b–281e), *our* primary service to the gods would appear to be to help the gods produce goodness in the universe *via* the protection and improvement of the human mind/soul. Because philosophical examination of oneself and others is for Socrates the key activity that helps to achieve this goal *via* the improvement of moral-belief consistency and the deflation of human presumptions to divine wisdom (e.g. *Apology* 22d–23b), philosophizing is a pre-eminently pious activity (see McPherran 1996: chs 2.2, 4.2).

Finally, Socrates' treatment of Euthyphro's fifth definition – (5) piety is knowledge of sacrificing and praying – makes evident that he rejects the idea that piety consists in traditional prayer and sacrifice motivated by hopes of a material payoff (*Euthyphro* 14c–15c).

This appropriation and reconception of piety as demanding of us philosophical self-examination would, however, seem to be a direct threat to everyday piety. For now it would appear that for Socrates time spent on prayer and sacrifice is simply time stolen from the more demanding, truly pious task of rational self-examination *per* T1. More threatening still, Socrates' theology of entirely just, relentlessly beneficent gods in conjunction with his moral theory would seem to make sacrifice and prayer (and especially curses) entirely useless. To what extent, then, is Socrates at odds with the ritual bedrock of Greek religion (see McPherran 2000)?

---

3. Cf. Xenophanes, who testifies that "Homer and Hesiod have ascribed to the gods all deeds which among men are a reproach and a disgrace: thieving, adultery, and deceiving one another" (Sextus Empiricus, *Against the Professors* 9.193, trans. McKirahan).

I think it is clear that Socrates rejects not conventional religious practices *in general*, but only the narrowly self-interested motives underlying their common observance. Xenophon, for example, portrays him as "the most visible of men" in cult-service to the gods (*Memorabilia* 1.2.64) and has him testify that he often sacrificed at the public altars (*Apology* 10–12; cf. *Memorabilia* 1.1.1–2, 4.8.11). It seems unlikely that Xenophon would offer as a defence a portrait of Socrates that simply no Athenian could take seriously. There is, in addition, some corroborating Platonic evidence on this point.[4] Although it would not seem that Socrates could consider prayers or sacrifices alone to be *essentially* connected to the virtue of piety, their performance is nonetheless compatible with the demands of piety reconceived as philosophizing. After all, since Socrates embraces the positive side of the *talio* – the return of one good for another – we should reciprocate as best we can the gods' many good gifts (see e.g. *Euthyphro* 14e–15a) by honouring the gods in fitting ways by performing acts with the inner intention to thank and honour them (*Memorabilia* 1.4.10, 18; 4.3.17). While, again, serving the gods *via* philosophical self-examination has pride of place in providing such honours, there is no reason why such actions cannot include prayers and sacrifices (cf. *Memorabilia* 4.3.13, 16). Socrates may well hold that prayers and sacrifices that aim to honour or thank the gods, or that request moral assistance from them, serve both ourselves and the gods: they help to induce our souls to follow the path of justice (thus producing god-desired good in the universe) by habituating us to return good for good. These actions also help to foster and maintain a general belief in the existence of good and helpful gods and an awareness of our inferior status in respect of wisdom and power, something that Socrates is clearly interested in promoting (see e.g. *Memorabilia* 1.4.1–19, 4.3.1–17; *Apology* 21d–23c).

It appears, then, that with the perfectly wise and just deities of Socrates we have few specific, materially rewarding imprecations to make; beyond the sincere, general prayer that one be aided in pursuing virtue, there are few requests or sacrifices to which all-wise deities can be counted on to respond. This implication of Socrates' moral theory cuts straight to the heart of everyday self-interested motivations underlying many cult practices. But if Socrates rejected the efficacy of improperly motivated requests, then he was a threat to popular piety. After all, to many Athenians the assistance of a Heracles would have meant, above all, help against the non-human forces bearing down on them (e.g. plague), and for most of them this meant material help against oppressive *other deities*. By taking away the enmity of the gods and conceiving of them as fully beneficent, the need for and the efficacy of *this* Heracles is also removed.

4. For example, Plato is willing to put twelve prayers into the mouth of his Socrates (see Jackson 1971; *Euthydemus* 275d; *Phaedo* 117c; *Symposium* 220d; *Phaedrus* 237a–b, 257a–b, 278b, 279b–c; *Republic* 327a–b, 432c, 545d–e; *Philebus* 25b, 61b–c). Note too the stage-setting of the start of the *Republic* (327a), where Socrates has travelled down to the Piraeus in order to pray to the goddess Bendis and observe her festival.

It seems clear that those jurors able to recognize the implications of Socrates' views for sacrificial cult would have seen him as threatening the stability of the state, for if you take away the conflicts of the deities and the expectations of particular material rewards and physical protections in cult, you disconnect the religion of everyday life and the state from its practical roots. To those not already focused on the development of their inner lives, the substitute of the difficult, pain-producing activity of philosophical self-examination would seem to offer little solace in the face of life's immediate, everyday difficulties. Socrates, therefore, raised the stakes for living a life of piety considerably by making its final measure the state of one's philosophically purified soul.

As T3, T4 and T5 demonstrate, Socrates is portrayed as a man who gives clear credence to the alleged god-given messages and forecasts found in dreams, divinations, oracles and other such traditionally accepted incursions by divinity.[5] But the degree of trust Socrates places in such sources appears to put him at odds with T1 and T2: what is the rational justification for heeding them and, by doing so, are they not regarded as sources of wisdom? The natural response is, I think, to hold that while Socrates accepts the everyday notion that the gods provide us with extra-rational signs and so does not pursue a form of the intellectualist rejection of divination's efficacy,[6] he also does not take the operations of traditional divinatory practices at face value. Rather, he insists in accord with T1 that conventional methods of oracular interpretation must give way to a rational method for evaluating such phenomena. These extra-rational sources, however, do not supply Socrates with general, theoretical claims constitutive of the expert moral knowledge he seeks and disavows having obtained *per* T2. Rather, they yield items of what we might call non-expert moral knowledge (e.g. that his death is good; *Apology* 40a–c).[7] Let us consider a few examples.

Early in his defence speech, Socrates explains that his reputation for wisdom can be best understood by attending to the testimony provided by the god who speaks through the Delphic Oracle, Apollo (*Apology* 20d–23b). As Socrates relates the tale, his friend Chaerephon travelled to Delphi to ask the Oracle if anyone was wiser than Socrates, and the response was "No one is wiser" (21a5–7). This report, however, was at odds with Socrates' own conviction that he possessed no real

5. During Socrates' lifetime, divination (*mantikē*) was widely employed by both states and individuals, and appeared in roughly three forms: (i) divination by lots; (ii) interpretation of signs, such as thunder; and (iii) the production and interpretation of oral oracles by a seer (*mantis*) (recorded and interpreted by 'oracle-mongers' [*chrēsmologoi*]). See e.g. Zaidman & Pantel (1992: 121–8).
6. For example, in the manner of the characters of Euripides, who challenge both the abilities and honesty of traditional seers (e.g. *Philoctetes* fr. 795) and the existence of the gods who allegedly provide foreknowledge (*Bellerophon* fr. 286; *The Trojan Women* 884–7; fr. 480; Sextus Empiricus, *Against the Professors* 9.54).
7. For discussion of how Socrates can endorse T2 but also know (or justifiably believe) things, see Brickhouse & Smith (1994: ch. 2) and Vlastos (1994).

wisdom, and so – given that "it is not lawful for the god to speak falsely" (21b5–7) – he was provoked to discover an interpretation that would preserve Apollo's veracity. He does this by going from one self-professed expert to another in hope of finding someone wiser than himself so as to refute the apparent meaning of the oracular pronouncement (and so uncover its real meaning). After continually failing to find such a person, Socrates concludes that what the god actually meant is that Socrates is wisest by best grasping his own lack of real wisdom (this is 'human wisdom'). This, in turn, is taken to mean that Apollo has stationed Socrates in Athens ordering him to philosophize and *examine* himself and others (28d–29a). Thus, since one ought always to obey the command of a god at all costs, Socrates is obliged to philosophize regardless of any dangers (29d). His jurors, therefore, should understand that the Oracle's pronouncement marked a turning point in his life so profound that he now philosophizes under a unique and divine mandate (T4 and 29c–30b). Socrates also continually interrogates others because he has come to believe that the god is using him as a *paradigm* to deliver the virtue-inducing message that that person is wisest, who – like Socrates – becomes most cognizant of how little real wisdom he or she possesses (23b).[8]

This account, despite its complexity, suggests that Socrates takes it to be obligatory to subject extra-rational signs to rational interpretation and confirmation whenever possible, and especially if they urge him to act in ways that appear to run counter to tradition or prudential considerations. That postulate dissolves two of our initial puzzles. First, the conflict between reason *per* T1 and revelation *per* T3, T4 and T5 is mitigated by noting how Socrates allows *rationally* interpreted and tested revelations to count *as reasons* in the sense of T1 (see below). The second tension between revelation and T6 is dissolved as well: this principle can be understood to claim that actions traditionally held to be unjust ought to be refrained from in the absence of compelling rational or *rationally* interpreted and tested divinatory evidence to the contrary. To confirm this account of Socrates' treatment of extra-rational indicators, let us consider his reliance on his divine sign, the *daimonion*.

Socrates' *daimonion*, we are told, is an internal, private admonitory "sign" (*sēmeion*; *Apology* 40b1, c3; *Euthydemus* 272e4; *Phaedrus* 242b9; *Republic* 496c4; *Memorabilia* 1.1.3–5) and "voice" (*phonē*; *Apology* 31d1; *Phaedrus* 242c2; Xenophon, *Apology* 12) caused to appear within the horizon of consciousness by a god. It has occurred to few or none before Socrates (*Republic* 496c) and it has been his companion since childhood (*Apology* 31d). The *daimonion*'s intervention in his affairs is frequent and pertains to matters both momentous and trivial (*Apology* 40a). That Socrates receives and obeys these monitions is well-known in Athens (*Apology* 31c–d; *Euthyphro* 3b), and they are understood to be apotreptic signs that warn him *not* to pursue a course of action that he is in the process of

8. See Brickhouse & Smith (1983); Stokes (1992: 29–33); Vlastos (1989: 229–30; 1991: 166–73).

initiating (*Apology* 31d; *Phaedrus* 242b–3; *Theages* 128–131a). These interventions are regarded as unfailingly correct in whatever they indicate (*Memorabilia* 1.1.4–5), just as we would expect the gift of an unfailingly good divinity to be. The *daimonion*'s generosity even extends to warning Socrates of the inadvisability of the actions intended by others (*Theaetetus* 150c–151b; cf. *Theages* 128d–131a; *Memorabilia* 1.1.4; *Apology* 13), but in no case does it provide him with general, theoretical claims constitutive of the expert moral knowledge he seeks and disavows having obtained *per* T2. Nor does it provide him with ready-made explanations of its opposition. Rather, its occurrences yield instances of non-expert moral knowledge of the inadvisability of pursuing particular actions because those actions are disadvantageous to Socrates and others: for example, the knowledge that it would not be beneficial to let a certain student resume study with him (see e.g. Xenophon, *Symposium* 8.5; *Theaetetus* 150c–151b; *Alcibiades I* 103a–106a). Finally, these divine "signs" always target *future* unbeneficial outcomes, and especially those whose reasonable prediction lies beyond the power of human reason (*Apology* 31d; *Euthydemus* 272e–273a; *Memorabilia* 1.1.6–9, 4.3.12). It is, in short, a species of the faculty of divination, true to Socrates' description of it as his 'customary divination' (*Apology* 40a4) and himself as a seer (*mantis*; *Phaedo* 85b4–6; cf. *Phaedrus* 242c4).

One important example that displays Socrates' reliance on and rational confirmation of a daemonic warning is found at *Apology* 31c–32a, where Socrates notes his obedience to the *daimonion*'s resistance to his entering public partisan politics (cf. *Republic* 496b–c) and then offers an explanation for its warnings: namely, that such political activity would have brought him a premature death, thus curtailing his vastly beneficial mission to the Athenians (cf. *Phaedrus* 242b–243a; *Alcibiades I* 103a–106a). Another instance of daemonic activity is found at *Euthydemus* 272e–273a. There we find that Socrates had formed the intention to leave his seat but, just as he was getting up, the *daimonion* opposed him, and so he remained. In this case, Socrates exhibits no doubt that its warning is utterly reliable; rather, Socrates implicitly trusts the *daimonion*, although *how* or *why* it is that the result of his obedience will be good-producing is opaque to reasoned calculation (*Theaetetus* 150c–151b; *Memorabilia* 4.3.12, 1.1.8–9). But this trust is in no way *ir*rational – and so does not contradict T1 – for it may be rationally confirmed in its wisdom and so given credence on an inductive basis, since (i) in Socrates' long experience of the *daimonion*, it has never been shown not to be a reliable warning system (Xenophon, *Apology* 13; *Apology* 40a–c), and (ii) the reliability of its alarms has been confirmed by the good results that flow from heeding it.

Given the above account, the *daimonion* appears to be compatible with Socrates' profession of T1 and T2: if, during or after a process of deliberation, the *daimonion* should oppose his action, then, given the prior rationally established reliability of the *daimonion*, it would seem that an occurrence of the *daimonion* would count in a perfectly straightforward way *as a reason* for not performing that act. For if one had very frequently in the past always obeyed the promptings of an internal warning that one has reason to believe comes from all-wise gods, and this had always been judged to have resulted in the best outcome, then one has good reason for letting this internal warning trump one's merely human judgement.

Socrates' claims to receive guidance from the gods bring us to our last puzzle: how can Socrates satisfy the rational demands of T1, the sceptical restraint marked by T2, and yet affirm that gods exist and that they have characteristics such as wisdom (*Apology* 41c–d; *Euthyphro* 14e–15a; *Gorgias* 508a; *Hippias Major* 289b; *Memorabilia* 4.4.25)? Unfortunately, Plato's texts show Socrates simply assuming and never proving the existence of gods. However, in Xenophon we are given an innovative teleological cosmology and theodicy grounded on an argument for the existence of an omniscient, omnipresent god: the maker of an orderly and beautiful universe, a deity who also now governs it in a fashion analogous to the way in which *our* minds govern *our* bodies (1.4.1–19; 4.3.1–18; cf. Sextus Empiricus, *Against the Professors* 9.92–4; see McPherran 1996: ch. 5).

The relation between this omniscient, omnipresent deity and the other gods is left entirely obscure. Socrates speaks at one moment of that singular deity as responsible for our creation and aid and, in the next breath, depicts the plural gods as doing the same (e.g. 1.4.10–11, 13–14, 18). Next, he distinguishes this one deity *from* the other gods by characterizing it as that particular god who "coordinates and holds together the entire cosmos" (4.3.13) but also treats that deity as fulfilling *all* the functions of the gods. To reconcile such oddities with what evidence there is that Socrates would affirm a belief in Delphic Apollo and plural Greek gods, we might credit him with being a henotheist; that is, he may understand the maker-god to be a supreme deity overseeing a community of lesser deities in the manner of Xenophanes' "greatest one god" (21 B23 DK). Alternatively, it is also possible that Socrates shared the not-uncommon view that understood the gods to be manifestations of a singular supreme spirit (Guthrie 1971: 156). In any event, we may expect that Socrates holds that his reasons for affirming the existence and nature of his maker-god do not constitute the sort of complete and certain account that would give him the kind of theological wisdom he disclaims in T2.

In any event, in view of the preceding outline of Socratic religion, we should not be surprised that Socrates' defence against the charge of impiety laid against him failed. In the end, the prejudices and allegations against Socrates proved so numerous and wide-ranging that he was in effect put on trial for the conduct of his entire life. His strange, provocative, street-preaching conduct, purportedly commanded by a divinity and exemplifying the new intellectualist conception of piety that Socrates had forged, proved all too prone to misrepresentation before an undiscerning crowd. From outside the circle of Socratic philosophy, that revised piety looked all too similar to the newfangled impiety Aristophanes had lampooned in his *Clouds* long before (423 BCE), an impiety that Socrates himself would have condemned (*Apology* 19c–d).

In sum, Socrates should be understood to have appropriated the principles of traditional Apollonian religion that emphasized the gap separating the human from the divine in terms of wisdom and power by connecting those principles with the new enterprise of philosophical self-examination (see e.g. *Iliad* 5.440–42).[9] But as we shall now see, Plato proved much more philosophically ambitious and optimistic about our natural capacities for knowledge and wisdom. Influenced on the one hand by Socrates' new intellectualist conception of piety as elenctic 'caring of the soul' and the success of the methods of the mathematicians of his day, which he took to overcome the limitations of Socrates' elenctic method, and on the other by the aim at human-initiated divine status as expressed by some of the newer, post-Hesiodic religious forms that had entered into Greece, Plato's philosophical theology offered the un-Socratic hope of an afterlife of intimate Form-contemplation in the realm of divinity. Self-knowledge on Plato's scheme leads not so much to an appreciation of limits, then, as to the realization that we are ourselves divinities in some sense: immortal intellects that already have within them all the knowledge there is to be had (*Meno* 81c–d; *Phaedo* 72e–77e; *Symposium* 210a–211b). In such a scheme there is little room for Socratic piety, since now the central task of human existence becomes less a matter of assisting gods and more a matter of becoming as much like them as one can (e.g. *Theaetetus* 172b–177c).

PLATO[10]

Plato's most explicit statement of the way in which he intends to both retain and transform traditional religious forms is to be found in his *Republic* and *Laws* (here I focus on the *Republic*). The *Republic* contains over a hundred references to 'god' or 'gods', with most occurring within the outline of the educational reforms advanced in books 2 and 3. The traditional gods are first brought into the conversation in their guise as enforcers of morality by Glaucon and his brother Adeimantus (357a–367e). These gods are rumoured to repay injustice with frightful post-mortem punishments, but ambitious people can create a facade of illusory virtue that will allow them to lead profitable lives here and in the afterlife (364b–365a; cf. *Laws* 909a–b).[11] For (i) if the gods do not exist or (ii) if they are

9. He also uses the terminology of ecstatic cults such as the Corybantes to distinguish poetry and sophistry from philosophy (e.g. *Ion* 533d–536d; *Euthydemus* 277d–e), and that of shamanic medicine to recommend the methods of philosophy as an effective, rational revisioning of their healing and salvational rites (e.g. *Charmides* 156d–157c; Morgan 1990: ch. 1).

10. Parts of this section closely follow my "Platonic Religion", in *A Companion to Plato*, H. Benson (ed.), 244–60 (Oxford: Blackwell, 2006).

11. Adeimantus alludes to begging priests and soothsayers who hold that through sacrifices, incantations and initiations found in books by Musaeus and Orpheus divine punishment of injustice can be averted (364b–365a; cf. *Laws* 909a–b). Plato is in general a harsh critic of everyday prophets and priests; rather, the true priest must now be a philosopher (e.g. *Phaedrus* 248d–e).

indifferent to human misconduct, we need not fear their punishments; and (iii) even if they are concerned with us, given "all we know about them from the laws and poets" (365e2–3) they can be persuaded to give us not penalties but goods (365c–366b, 399b; cf. *Laws* 885b). No wonder, then, that in the view of the many "no one is just willingly" but only through some infirmity (366d). As a result, the challenge that Socrates must now meet by constructing the perfectly just state Kallipolis is to demonstrate the superiority of justice to injustice independently of any external consequences (366d–369b). Then, when at last Kallipolis is established, he must outline the educational system necessary for producing the character traits its rulers will require (374d–376c).

Socrates asserts that it would be hard to find a system of education better than the traditional one of offering physical training for the body and music and poetry for the soul, but he quickly finds fault with its substance. This form of education moulds the character of the young by using stories to shape the form of their aspirations and desires in ways conformable to the development of their rational intelligence. However, although such stories are false, some approximate the truth better than others and some are more conducive to the development of good character than others (377a, 377d–e, 382c–d). Plato assumes that the most accurate representations of the gods and heroes will also be the most beneficial, but the converse is also true, and this means that there will have to be strict supervision of the poets and storytellers of Kallipolis. Moreover, much of the old literature will have to be cast aside because of its lack of verisimilitude and its debilitating effects on character-formation.

First on the chopping block is Hesiod's *Theogony*, with its deceitful, harmful tale of Cronos castrating Ouranos at the urgings of his vengeful mother Gaia, then unjustly swallowing his own children to prevent his overthrow by Zeus (377e–378b). Poetic lies of this sort that suggest that gods or heroes are unjust or disagree or retaliate against each other must be suppressed. To specify with precision which myths are to be counted false in their essentials, Socrates offers the educators of Kallipolis an 'outline of theology' in two parts, establishing a pair of laws that will ensure a sufficiently accurate depiction of divinity (379a7–9) (L1, L2a, L2b below):

(1) All gods are [entirely] good beings (379b1–2).
(2) No [entirely] good beings are harmful (379b3–4).
(3) All non-harmful things do no harm (379b5–8).
(4) Things that do no harm do no evil, and so are not the causes of evil (379b9–10).
(5) Good beings benefit other things, and so are the causes of good (379b11–14).
(6) Thus, good beings are not the causes of all things, but only of good things and not evil things (379b15–379c1).
(7) Therefore, the gods are not the causes of everything – as most people believe – but their actions produce the few good things and never the many bad things there are (379c2–8; 380b6–c3).

L1 God is not the cause (*aitia*) of all things, but only of the good things; whatever it is that causes bad things, that cause is not divine (380c6–10; 391e1–2; cf. *Laws* 636c, 672b, 899b, 900d, 941b).

The argument for conclusion (7) is a reasonably cogent inference, but we are bound to ask how Plato can simply presuppose the truth of the non-Homeric premise (1), which, once granted, drives the rest of the argument. He can do so, I think, because of his inheritance of Socratic piety: the gods are good because they are wise, and they are wise because of their very nature. That said, however, we are left wondering how the new poetry is to depict the causes of evil, what those causes might be and how they could coexist within a cosmos ruled by omnibenevolent gods. Plato himself addresses this issue in his other, later work (see below). Here, at any rate, the practical upshot of L1 is clear: stories of the gods' injustices such as those at *Iliad* 4.73–126 and 24.527–32 must be purged. If the poets insist, they may continue to speak of the gods' punishments, but only so long as they make it clear that these are either merited or therapeutic (380a–b; cf. *Gorgias* 525b–c).

Next up for elimination are those tales that portray the gods as changing shape or otherwise deceiving us. By means of two further arguments Socrates establishes a law with two parts:

L2a No gods change (381e8–9); and
L2b The gods do not try to mislead us with falsehoods (383a2–6).

This second law will allow Kallipolis to purge traditional literature of all variety of mythological themes, ranging from the shape-shifting antics of Proteus (381c–e) to the deceptive dreams sent by Zeus (e.g. *Iliad* 2.1–34) (383a–b). Book 3 continues with further applications of Laws 1 and 2 to popular poetry, and by its end the gods of that poetry have been demoted to the status of harmful fabrications (Plato retains this view into his *Laws*; e.g. 636c, 672b, 941b). Although the revisionary theology that results puts Plato at striking variance with the attitudes of many of his fellow Athenians, there is nothing in his theology that directly undermines the three axioms of Greek religion (a–c) to which Adeimantus alluded earlier (365d–e): the gods exist, they concern themselves with human affairs and there is reciprocity of some kind between human beings and gods. Moreover, it would have been no great shock for Plato's audience to find his Socrates denying the poets' tales of divine capriciousness, enmity, immorality and response to ill-motivated sacrifice. As mentioned earlier, they had for years been exposed to such criticisms by thinkers such as Xenophanes and Euripides, and Hesiod himself had admitted that poets tell lies (*Theogony* 26–8).

Although Plato, like Socrates, vigorously rejects the idea that gods can be magically influenced to benefit us, it is clear that he retains a role for traditional-appearing religious practices (McPherran 2000). There will still be sacrifices (419a) and hymns to the gods (607a), along with a form of civic religion that features temples, prayers, festivals, priests and so on (427b–c; Burkert 1985: 334). Plato also expects the children of Kallipolis to be shaped "by the rites and prayers which the priestesses and priests and the whole community pray at each wedding festival" (461a6–8). The *Republic* is lamentably terse on the details of all this, but that is because its Socrates is unwilling to entrust the authority of establishing these institutions to his guardians or to speculative reason (427b8–9). Rather, the foundational laws governing these matters will be introduced and maintained by "the ancestral guide on these matters for all people" (427c3–4): Delphic Apollo (427a–c; cf. 424c–425a, 461e, 540b–c). (Plato assigns the same function to Delphi in his *Laws* [738b–d, 759a–e, 828a] and pays better attention there to the details [e.g. 759a–760a, 771a–772d, 778c–d, 799a–803b, 828a–829e, 848c–e].) This fact alone suggests that the ritual life of Kallipolis will be very hard to distinguish from that of Plato's Athens. Confirmation of this occurs when we are told that the citizens of Kallipolis will "join all other Greeks in their common holy rites" (470e10–11; cf. *Laws* 848d).

Plato holds that worship is a form of education that should begin in childhood, where it can take root in the feelings; thus, he finds charming tales, impressive festivals, seeing one's parents at prayer and so on to be effective ways of impressing on the affective parts of the soul a habit of mind whose rational confirmation can only be arrived at in maturity (401d–402b; cf. *Laws* 887d–888a). Most citizens of Kallipolis, however, will be non-philosophers who are unable to achieve such confirmation, but who will still profit from the habitual practice of these rites in so far as they promote the retention of their own sort of psychic justice. For philosophers, however, such pious activity is quite secondary to the inwardly directed activity that it supports; this is their quest for wisdom – an activity that focuses directly on making oneself "as much like a god as a human can" (613a–b). The education given to these future philosopher-kings of Kallipolis will thus take them far beyond the limitations imposed by the anti-hubristic tenets of Socratic piety. For by coming to know the ultimate Form, the Good-itself, they will no longer be regarded as servile assistants of the gods, but will serve Kallipolis as the gods' local representatives (540a–b).

It should be clear by this point that the inner religious life of Plato's philosophers will be vastly different from that of the ordinary citizens of Kallipolis. Thus, we might reasonably expect to learn more about the purified gods of *Republic* books 2 and 3 in the later metaphysical books' account of their heavenly abode: the realm of Forms (books 5, 6, 7). However, despite this section's discussion of these immaterial and divine objects of knowledge, the gods hardly appear at all (e.g. 492a). This fact, in concert with Plato's confessions of the difficulty of adequately conceiving of god/gods (e.g. *Phaedrus* 246c), can create the impression that although Plato is willing to retain morally uplifting talk of all-good gods for the children and non-philosophers of his Kallipolis, when he turns to the serious business of educating his philosophers he reveals that the only true divinities are the Forms. Nevertheless, justice-enforcing gods are redeployed as real features of the cosmos in book 10 (612e; cf. *Laws* 901a). Secondly, Plato frequently alludes to genuine gods in dialogues contemporaneous with, and later than, the *Republic* (e.g. *Phaedrus*, *Parmenides*, *Laws*). Hence, the most plausible stance is that Plato affirms the existence of both gods and Forms.

Probably the clearest expression of the relationship between the middle-dialogue Forms and gods occurs in the second half of the Greatest *Aporia* of the *Parmenides* (133a–134e), where we find an argument purporting to establish the impossibility that the gods could either know or rule over sensible particulars such as ourselves. This argument is founded on the account of sensibles and Forms we find in the *Phaedo* and *Republic*, with the clear implication being that the Form-realm is also the heavenly home of gods who govern us as masters govern slaves and whose business it is to apprehend all of the Forms, including Knowledge-itself (134a–e). This brief glimpse of gods and Forms corresponds with the account of the gods offered first in the *Phaedo*, and then in the more complex portrait of the *Phaedrus*. In the course of the *Phaedo*'s affinity argument for the soul's immortality (78b–84b), for example, we are told that our souls are most like the divine in being deathless, intelligible and invisible beings that are inclined to govern mortal subjects (e.g. our bodies) (see below). When the philosophically purified soul leaves its body, then, it joins good and wise gods and the Forms (80d–81a). The sorts of activities they carry on together is left unclear, but since this section and others parallel the *Parmenides*' attribution of mastery to the gods (62c–63c, 84e–85b), we can expect that these gods are likewise able to rule wisely because of their apprehension of the Forms.

The *Phaedrus* also features souls and gods who know Forms and who have the capacity to rule, and by detailing their relations in his outline of "the life of the gods" (248a1) Plato gives us a partial solution to the identity of the gods of the *Republic* and other middle dialogues. As part of his palinode (242b–257b), Socrates first offers a proof that the self-moving souls of both gods and human beings are immortal (245c–e), and then turns to a description of their natures (246a–248a). It is, he says, too lengthy a task to describe accurately the soul's structure in a literal fashion: a god could do it, but not a mortal; but we can at least say what the soul resembles (246a3–6; cf. 247c3–6). Dismissing the common conception of the Olympian deities as composites of soul and body (246c5–d5), Socrates offers his famous simile, comparing every soul to "the natural union of a team of [two] winged horses and their charioteer" (246a6–7), whose ruling part is Reason and whose horses correspond to the spirited and appetitive parts of the soul described in the *Republic* (book 4) Hackforth (1952: 72).[12] Unlike the mixed team with which mortal drivers must contend, however, the souls of gods and *daimones*

12. Plato's appropriation of the immortal horses of the gods (the *hippoi athanatoi*, offspring of the four Wind-Gods who draw the chariot of Zeus; *Iliad* 5.352–69) is typical of his entire approach to the myths of Greek religion: he retains the traditional ambrosia and nectar as food and drink for the lower, horsey parts of the soul (247e), but has the philosophical Intellect feed on the new, true ambrosia of the immortal Forms.

have horses and charioteer-rulers that are entirely good. The most important of these gods are to be identified with the twelve traditional Olympians: their "great commander" is Zeus, who is then trailed by Hera, Poseidon, Demeter, Apollo, Artemis, Ares, Aphrodite, Hermes, Athena and Hephaestus, while Hestia remains at home. Being entirely good, these gods roam the roads of heaven, guiding souls, and then travel up to heaven's highest rim (247a–e). From these heights each driver – each god's Intelligence – is nourished and made happy by gazing upon the invisible, fully real objects of knowledge to which he or she is akin: Forms such as Justice and Beauty themselves. Even Knowledge-itself is here, "not the knowledge that is close to change and that becomes different as it knows the different things that we consider real down here", but "the knowledge of what really is what it is" (247d7–e2). This account should recall both the *Parmenides*' characterization of the two kinds of knowledge there are – the Knowledge-itself that ruling gods possess and the knowledge-among-us that we possess (cf. *Theaetetus* 146e) – and the *Republic*'s declaration in L1 that the gods are the causes of only good. Moreover, this *Phaedrus* myth parallels the *Republic* in so far as the latter alludes to the knowledge possessed by those guardians who are able to rule by virtue of the wisdom they have come to possess (428c–d) and whose intellects are nourished and made happy by their intercourse with the Forms (490a–b). (Both texts also possess parallel psychologies and eschatological myths that contain Olympian post-mortem rewards and punishments [*Phaedrus* 256a–c; *Republic* 621c–d] and reincarnation into a variety of lives [*Phaedrus* 247c–249d; *Republic* 614b–621d]).

In view of such parallels, it is reasonable to suppose that the deities sanctioned by the *Phaedrus* would also be those of the *Republic*, and this seems especially true when we consider the conservative streak Plato displayed by putting Delphic Apollo in charge of the establishment of temples and sacrifices; hence, the instalment of the specific deities the city will honour at *Republic* 427b–c (and note that the *Phaedrus* similarly credits Delphi with the ability to offer sound guidance to both individuals and cities; 244a–b). Thus, when Socrates acknowledges the Apollo of Delphi at 427a–b and Zeus at 583b and 391c, and defends the reputations of Hera, Ares, Aphrodite, Hephaestus and Poseidon at 390c and 391c, he is affirming the existence of distinct deities with distinct functions who may still be credited with distinctive personalities, each one resembling the kind of human soul it will lead up to the nourishment of the Form realm (248a–e). The series of cosmological etymologies concerning the names of the gods provided by the *Philebus* (395e–410e) reinforces this account.

What, then, is the relation of that super-ordinate Form, the Good-itself (*Republic* 504d–534d), to these gods? It was a commonplace in antiquity that the Good is god (cf. e.g. Sextus Empiricus, *Against the Professors* 11.70), a view that still finds some favour. If that were right, we could then postulate that the image of the Great Commander Zeus is one of Plato's ways of conceptualizing the Good in order to make it a subject of honorific ritual. In fact, we are encouraged to think of the Good as a god in several ways: the Good is said to be (a) the *archē*

– the cause of the being – of the Forms (509b6–8) and everything else (511b, 517b–c); (b) a ruler over the intelligible world in the way the sun, a god, rules over the visible realm (509b–d); (c) analogous to the maker (*dēmiourgos*) of our senses (507c7), the sun, one of the gods of heaven (508a–c [which is an offspring of the Good; 508b, 506e–507a]). This identification can then (d) explain book 10's odd and unique claim that the Form of Bed is created by a craftsman-god, who is – in a sense – the creator of all things (596a–598c). Finally, if the Good were not a god, then (i) the gods of the *Republic* would apparently be the offspring of a non-god (the Good), (ii) the Good would be subordinate to these gods or (iii) the gods would exist in independence from the Good; but none of these possibilities seem to make sense in light of (a–d) (Adam [1908] 1965: 442). Despite all this, however, the characterization of the Good as being beyond all being in dignity and power (509b8–10) means that it cannot be a mind, a *nous*, that knows anything; rather, it is that which makes knowledge possible (508b–509b). Thus, since for Plato a necessary condition for something's being a god is that it be a mind/soul possessing intelligence, the Good cannot be a god.

Plato's maker-god, the Demiurge, marks another of Plato's debts to his teacher. As we saw earlier, Xenophon's Socrates argued that since individual beings in the universe are either the product of intelligent design or mere dumb luck, and since human beings are clearly the products of intelligent design, we ought to be persuaded that there exists a vastly knowledgeable god, a god who is moreover "a wise and loving Maker (*dēmiourgos*)" (1.4.2–7; cf. 4.3.1–18). Plato's mature expression of this idea in the *Timaeus* and elsewhere goes well beyond this Socratic inheritance by incorporating his theory of Forms in a conscious attempt to rebut materialists who deny the priority of soul over body (27d–29b; cf. *Philebus* 30c–d; *Laws* 889b–c, 891e–899d). The "likely account" (29b–d) Plato puts forward there is, in brief, that:[13]

(1) The cosmos is an ordered, perceptible thing.
(2) All ordered perceptibles are things that come to be.
(3) Thus, the cosmos is not eternal but came to be.
(4) Every ordered thing that comes to be has a craftsman as the cause of its coming to be.
(5) Thus, the cosmos has a craftsman as the cause of its coming to be.
(6) The craftsman-cause of the cosmos patterned the cosmos after one of two kinds of model: (a) a changeless model grasped by reasoned understanding or (b) a changing model grasped by opinion involving sense-perception.
(7) If the cosmos is beautiful and its craftsman is good, then its craftsman used (a) a changeless model grasped by reasoned understanding.

13. The account is only likely because "to find the maker and father of this universe is hard enough" and impossible to describe to everyone (28c4–5; cf. *Cratylus* 400d–401a).

(8) The cosmos is beautiful and its craftsman is good.
(9) Thus, the cosmos "is a work of craft, modeled after that which is changeless and is grasped by a rational account, that is, by wisdom" (29a6–b1, trans. Zeyl).

The claim that the craftsman is good in premise (8) appears to come out of thin air, but is perhaps to be inferred from the evident beauty and order of the cosmos, and its providential, human-serving design (cf. *Memorabilia* 1.4.10–19; cf. 4.3.2–14). In any event, from that goodness it is then supposed to follow that the Demiurge was free of jealousy prior to the creation, and hence, he desired that everything that exists be as much like himself as possible, and thus, as good as possible. This desire then led the Demiurge to bring order to the recalcitrant, disorderly motion of visible material by making it as intelligent as possible. This required that he put intelligence into a World Soul, placing that soul into the body of the cosmos, thereby making it a living being "endowed with soul and intelligence" (30b6–c1), modelling it after the generic Form of Living Thing (29d–31a; a Form that contains at least all the Forms of living things, if not all Forms).

In Plato's middle-dialogue account of physical change in the *Phaedo* (99c–107b), the Forms are treated as having the ability to act as both the formal and efficient causes of a subject's possession of properties, somehow radiating instances of themselves into sensible individuals (so that, say, Simmias comes to be tall by coming to possess an immanent character instance of Tallness-itself; *Phaedo* 100b–105c). The *Timaeus* retains this same ontology of immanent characters and Forms and appears to give the job of implanting immanent characters to god (*Timaeus* 48d–53c). Then, in place of the plural sensible subjects of participation, Plato posits a single particular subject that is the receptacle, nurse and mother of all becoming (49b, 50d): like a plastic substance such as gold (50a–c), it provides a place or space (52a–b) for Form-instances to manifest themselves in those various locations that we call by individual subject names.

Apart from the Demiurge, the created cosmos and the stars, there is little mention of the activities of other, more traditional gods. Although these gods seem to be invoked generically at the outset of the creation story (27c–d), and the Muses receive a mention (47d–e), the only other significant mention of gods at 40d6–e4 (cf. *Laws* 948b) appears to undermine their having any genuine existence in this scheme. Here it is hard to resist the impression that the old gods have become little more than noble lies that philosophers offer to children and non-philosophers in order to train and keep in check their unruly souls.[14]

14. Cf. *Phaedrus* 229c–230a, where Plato has his Socrates disclaim the scepticism concerning stories about lesser deities such as Boreas and Orithyia advocated by the men of science. This is because, he says, he has no time for the investigation of such issues in view of the priority of his mission of self-examination conducted on behalf of Apollo. Consequently, he merely accepts the current beliefs about them.

Nevertheless, gods bearing the names of the Olympians make a prominent appearance in the *Laws* from its outset, as its discussants make their way from Cnossus to Zeus' birthplace and shrine on Mount Ida (625b). There are, for example, close to two hundred references to god or gods. Moreover, when it comes time to address the inhabitants of his new Cretan city, the Athenian Stranger tells them that they must "resolve to belong to those who follow in the company of god" (716b8–9) and so model themselves after god. The most effective way to do this, he tells them, is to pray and sacrifice to the gods, and this means the gods of the underworld, the Olympians, the patron deities of the state, and *daimones* and heroes (716b–717b; see Burkert [1985: chs 3.3.5, 4] on *daimones* and heroes). Later, as he mounts his case against atheism, the Athenian makes it clear that he and his companions' memories of seeing their parents earnestly addressing the Olympian gods with an assured belief in their actual existence are not to be undermined by scepticism (887c–888a; cf. 904e). Finally, the argument for there being a craftsman-god of the cosmos includes the existence of lesser gods spoken of in the plural (893b-907b): this maker and supervisor of the universe has established these gods as rulers (*archontes*) over various parts of the universe (903b–c). We found similar gods in the *Phaedrus* – and such beings appear elsewhere (*Politicus* 271d, 272e; *Timaeus* 41a–d, 42d–e) – and thus it seems that Plato consistently understood his maker-god to be a supreme deity who may be called Zeus (e.g. *Philebus* 30d; *Phaedrus* 246e) overseeing a community of lesser deities (Morrow 1966: 131) who may still be called by the names of the Olympians.

At the end of the *Apology* Socrates expresses confidence that death is a good thing, but it is an ambivalent confidence grounded in his dilemma that death is either like being nothing or is like a journey from here to another place where – if certain tales are true – our souls will have the supreme happiness of philosophizing with great judges, poets and heroes (40c–41c) (McPherran 1996: ch. 5.1). Plato, however, solves the dilemma in favour of this second optimistic horn by advancing a variety of arguments for the immortality of the soul; we find four in the *Phaedo* (the cyclical argument [69e–72e]; the recollection argument [72e–77e]; the affinity argument [78b–82b]; and the final argument [102a–107b]), a rather different one in the *Republic* (608d–611c), and then another in the *Phaedrus* (245c–246a). There is not sufficient space here, however, to assess the structure and cogency of these arguments.

In a number of places Plato attempts to characterize the soul's immortality in terms of post-mortem rewards and punishments, followed by reincarnation (*Phaedo* 107c–115a [cf. 63e–64a]; *Republic* 612c–621d; *Phaedrus* 246a–257b; *Timaeus* 91d–92c; cf. *Gorgias* 522b–527e). These accounts are cast in the traditionally authoritative language of poetry, and incorporate many of the motifs and patterns of action of various traditional myths of descent, death and judgement (e.g. *Iliad* 23.65–107; Hesiod, *Works and Days* 178–94; Pindar, *Olympian* 2.57–60, 63–73). The idea of reincarnation is itself called an "old legend" by Socrates (*Phaedo* 70c5–6); it turns up before Plato in the works of Pindar and Empedocles, and was allegedly introduced into Greece by Pythagoras (Porphyry, *Life of Pythagoras* 19). We are also led to believe that these myths are approximations of the truth (*Phaedo* 114d; *Republic* 618b–d, 621b–d; cf. *Gorgias* 523a), although we are given little help in determining which of their elements come closer to the truth than others (see Edmonds 2004: ch. 1).

The *Republic*, for example, ends with a consideration of the previously dismissed question of the rewards of justice by first proving the soul's immortality (608c–612a) and then arguing for the superiority of the just life in consequentialistic terms. Plato first affirms Adeimantus' earlier story (362d–363e) that the gods reward the just person and punish the unjust during the course of their lives (612a–614a), but then offers the Myth of Er to show how they also do the same in the afterlife (614a–621a). This story is similar in theme and detail to Plato's other main eschatological myths that display a willingness to use the prospects of pain and pleasure as inducements to virtuous behaviour for those of us as yet unready to pursue virtue for its own sake.[15] Nevertheless, its complex portrait of the long-term rewards for striving after justice is often found to be depressing, not reassuring (e.g. Annas 1981: 350–53). For although there are tenfold rewards for the just and tenfold punishments for the unjust, there are also non-redeeming, everlasting tortures for those who, because of impiety and murder, have become morally incurable (615c–616b; cf. *Gorgias* 525b–526b). Moreover, unlike the eschatologies of the *Phaedo* and *Phaedrus*, Plato rules out there being any final liberation from the cycle of incarnations (Annas 1982: 136). True to L1, however, Plato explicitly relieves the gods of all responsibility for the future suffering we will experience in our next incarnation by means of a lottery (617e, 619c).[16] As he constructs it, a soul's choice of a happy life of justice will depend both on the random result of that lottery and that soul's ability to choose wisely. But it is unclear if the lottery is rigged by Necessity and a soul's degree of practical wisdom is constrained by its prior experiences, experiences that were in turn the result of prior ignorant choices. This means that those who have lived lives of justice – through habit and without philosophy – and so arrive at the lottery after experiencing the rewards of heaven will, by having forgotten their earlier sufferings, make bad choices and suffer further (617d–621b). Finally, aside from the chancy work of the lottery, Plato has never adumbrated the many sources of evil

15. It is hard to know how to view this particular fiction in light of Plato's earlier categorical denigration of all mimetic writing (*Republic* 595a–608b).
16. In the *Phaedo*, a failure to purify oneself sufficiently of one's ties to bodily desires by having lived an irrational, bestial life automatically entails rebirth into an animal form appropriate to one's ruling passion; for example, the gluttonous become donkeys and the merely habitually virtuous become bees (81e–82b; cf. *Phaedrus* 249b–c). Thus, here reincarnation is always a punishment for some fault, with final liberation from the wheel of incarnation the reward for a life of philosophical virtue; cf. *Phaedrus* 248e–249c.

mentioned in book 2, against which even the gods are powerless.[17] So although the last lines of the *Republic* encourage us to race after justice so that we may collect our Olympian rewards (621b–d), given their uncertainly and lack of finality some will find Thrasymachean short cuts a better gamble.

There is no sure way to determine how Plato meant for us to read this and other such myths; perhaps modern readers are right to find its details of coloured whorls and lotteries to be only entertaining bits of window dressing, not to be taken as contributing to a philosophically coherent eschatology (cf. Annas 1981: 351–3). This is poetry, after all, and it is composed within the framework of a dialogue that consistently disdains poetry. On the other hand, it is possible to read Er's tale of reincarnation as alluding to the beneficial initiations of Eleusis, but now connected to the true initiation and conversion of the soul provided by philosophical dialectic (Morgan 1990: 150). There are also reasons to suppose that the display of whorls, Sirens and Necessity are symbolic of the metaphysical elements of the *Republic*'s middle books, and are thus meant to impress on each soul prior to its next choice of life and its drink from the River of Unheeding (620e–621c) the message of those books: that the happiest life is the life of justice and the good, and so ought to be chosen for that reason alone (Johnson 1999).

The message that does come through in all of Plato's eschatological myths, however, is that no god or *daimōn* can be blamed for whatever fix we may happen to find ourselves in when we put down Plato's texts. Moreover, the many complications of these stories and the way in which they put our future judgement in the hands of gods and fate seem intended to undermine our using that future state as a source of motivation and choice-making in the here and now; perhaps we are being encouraged to dismiss the cheap motivations of carrot and stick that drive the vulgar many so that we might recall the truly pious aspirations of philosophy developed in the preceding main body of Plato's text (cf. *Phaedo* 114d–115a; Annas 1982). At the same time, however, Plato appears to be using "traditional mythic material ... to ground his advocacy of the philosophical life in the authority of the [mythic] tradition" (Edmonds 2004: 161), giving that life motivational substance by persuasively picturing the unseen noetic realm that is the goal of every true philosopher. These myths, then, can be read as returning us to both the stern, early

17. The role of chance here, though, suggests that Plato may have had his later *Timaeus* view of the causes of evil in mind, causes that he locates in the disorderly motions of matter (see Cherniss 1971; cf. *Phaedrus* 248c–d; *Statesman* 273c–e). The *Republic* does at least make clear that human evil is a consequence of our having souls that are maimed by their association "with the body and other evils" (611c1–2; cf. 611b–d, 353e; *Phaedo* 78b–84b; *Theaetetus* 176a–b; *Laws* 896c–897c); for example, not even the *Republic*'s rulers are infallible in their judgements of particulars, and so Kallipolis will fail owing to the inability of the guardians to make infallibly good marriages (given their need to use perception; *Republic* 546b–c). Such imperfection is, however, a necessary condition of human beings having been created in the first place, a creation that Plato clearly thought was a good thing, all things considered.

Socrates of *Republic*, book 1 (and elsewhere; e.g. the Socrates of *Crito* 48a–49e), who urges us to choose the path of justice *simpliciter*, and the hopeful Socrates of the *Phaedo*, who foresees a return to the friendly divinities and Formal delights of heaven (*Phaedo* 63c, 81a; *Phaedrus* 247c). Through all this and more, Plato laid the groundwork for the flowering of Western religious thought.

FURTHER READING

Beckman, J. 1979. *The Religious Dimension of Socrates' Thought*. Waterloo: Wilfrid Laurier University Press.

Brickhouse, T. & N. Smith (eds) 2002. *The Trial and Execution of Socrates: Sources and Controversies*. Oxford: Oxford University Press.

Burkert, W. 1985. *Greek Religion*. Cambridge, MA: Harvard University Press.

Despland, M. 1985. *The Education of Desire: Plato and the Philosophy of Religion*. Toronto: University of Toronto Press.

Destrée, P. & N. Smith (eds) 2005. *Socrates' Divine Sign: Religion, Practice, and Value in Socratic Philosophy*. Kelowna: Academic Printing & Publishing.

Feibleman, J. 1971. *Religious Platonism: The Influence of Religion on Plato and the Influence of Plato on Religion*. Westport, CT: Greenwood Press.

More, P. 1921. *The Religion of Plato*. Princeton, NJ: Princeton University Press.

Morgan, M. 1990. *Platonic Piety*. New Haven, CT: Yale University Press.

Morgan, M. 1992. "Plato and Greek Religion". In *The Cambridge Companion to Plato*, R. Kraut (ed.), 227–47. Cambridge: Cambridge University Press.

Parker, R. 1996. *Athenian Religion: A History*. Oxford: Oxford University Press.

Smith, N. & P. Woodruff (eds) 2000. *Reason and Religion in Socratic Philosophy*. Oxford: Oxford University Press

Solmsen, F. 1942. *Plato's Theology*. Ithaca, NY: Cornell University Press.

Vlastos, G. 1989. "Socratic Piety". In *Proceedings of the Boston Area Colloquium in Ancient Philosophy*, vol. 5, J. Cleary & D. Shartin (eds), 213–38. Lanham, MD: University Press of America.

On FORMS/IDEAS see also Chs 11, 13; Vol. 2, Ch. 15. On HENOTHEISM see also Ch. 7. On IMMORTALITY OF THE SOUL see also Ch. 4; Vol. 2, Chs 12, 16; Vol. 4, Chs 10, 19. On INTELLIGENT DESIGN see also Ch. 8; Vol. 3, Ch. 23; Vol. 4, Chs 11, 12. On MONOTHEISM see also Ch. 3. On PIETY see also Chs 5, 6, 12.

5

ARISTOTLE

Sarah Broadie

Aristotle (384–322 BCE) was a native of the Macedonian city of Stagira, now in northern Greece. His father, Nicomachus, was a physician at the Macedonian court. In 367, at the age of seventeen, Aristotle went to Athens, where he was attached to Plato's school, the Academy, until Plato's death in 347. Aristotle then moved to Assos on the coast of Asia Minor; he married Pythias, niece of Hermeias, ruler of Assos, and had by her a daughter, Pythias. (After his wife's death Aristotle formed a liaison with Herpyllis, with whom he had a son, Nicomachus.)

Further moves took Aristotle to the Aegean island of Lesbos, and then back to Macedon, where he acted as tutor to Alexander the Great. In 334 Aristotle returned to Athens where he founded his school, the Lyceum. Despite his long periods of residence in the city, Aristotle was not an Athenian citizen. When, because of the politics of the moment, anti-Macedonian feeling ran high in Athens, Aristotle's links with the Macedonian court were a liability for him. In this atmosphere in 323 it became prudent for him to leave Athens again, this time for Chalcis in the nearby island of Euboea. Aristotle died there the following year.

By some estimates the works of Aristotle's surviving corpus represent about half of his actual output. These works lie at the foundation of almost every branch of Western philosophy and science apart from mathematical theory. Their hallmarks are close argumentation, rigorous analysis, systematic coverage of previous problems and theories and a style that is usually plain and terse.

AN ARISTOTELIAN ARGUMENT FOR THEISM

Aristotle has bequeathed us a number of concepts and arguments important in philosophy of religion. Some, located in works now lost, we know of only from fragments and ancient reports. One of the most interesting, from Aristotle's lost dialogue *On Philosophy*,[1] has been preserved by Cicero:

> Thus Aristotle brilliantly remarks: "Suppose there were men who had always lived underground, in good and well-lighted dwellings, adorned with statues and pictures, and furnished with everything in which those who are thought happy abound. Suppose, however, that they had never gone above ground, but had learned by report and hearsay that there was a divine spirit and power. Suppose that then, at some time, the jaws of the earth opened, and they were able to escape and make their way from those hidden dwellings into these regions which we inhabit.
>
> When they suddenly saw earth and seas and skies, when they learned the grandeur of clouds and the power of winds, when they saw the sun and realized not only its grandeur and beauty but also its power, by which it fills the sky with light and makes the day; when, again, night darkened the lands and they saw the whole sky picked out and adorned with stars, and the varying light of the moon as it waxes and wanes, and the risings and settings of all these bodies, and their courses settled and immutable to all eternity; when they saw those things, most certainly would they have judged both that there are gods and that these great works are the works of gods."
>
> (Aristotle, fr. 12 Rose = Cicero, *On the Nature of the Gods* 2.37.95, in Aristotle 1984: vol. 2, 2392)[2]

At first sight the passage seems concerned not directly with god or gods, but with human belief in gods. Other reports of lost material suggest that Aristotle entertained speculations on the origin of religion, and linked it to human observation of the motions of the sun, moon and stars: "They came to think that there was a god who is the cause of such movement and order" (Aristotle, fr. 10 Rose = Sextus Empiricus, *Against the Mathematicians* 9.23, in Aristotle 1984: vol. 2, 2392). However, the longer passage just quoted is strange if meant as a piece of anthropology: it directs attention not to actual human responses but to those people in the fictitious situation described hypothetically in the first three sentences. What could such imagined responses teach about the origins of actual human religious attitudes? In fact, we should surely see the story as a variant of the argument from design: it is meant to lead *us* to affirm that the cosmic system is the work of gods. That is how Cicero understood it. The hypothetical conditions of the first three sentences are intended to eliminate certain objections, or to get us to place ourselves in the shoes of judges free of limitations that distort our actual judgements. First, if

1. Since the work was a dialogue, one can always question whether a passage of it represents Aristotle's own position at the time of writing.
2. Quotations from Aristotle are from the *Complete Works* (Aristotle 1984).

the cosmic phenomena are such good evidence of a divine cause, why does everyone not embrace this belief already? The answer is that many of us take them for granted; through familiarity we have lost all sense of their wondrousness and grandeur; but if we could see them through really fresh eyes, we would draw the conclusion drawn by the people in the story. Secondly, if actual people regard the cosmic phenomena as the work of gods, is it not because the humble nature of their own surroundings tricks them into being over-impressed by the luminous patterns of sun, moon and stars? Is it not simply the contrast with the mess and drabness of our own world that creates the belief that the cosmic phenomena manifest an awesome type of causation not found among things down here? The answer here is that even if there were people who had the luxury of living all their lives enclosed in surroundings ordered and beautified by the skill of consummate human artists, and who were thus thorough connoisseurs of order and immune from being bowled over disproportionately, even they, when they suddenly emerged under the real sky, would be struck by beauties and regularities so majestic that they would see them as the works of a super-human intelligence.

Thus, even if Aristotle did mean to explain religious belief as arising from the spectacle of sun, moon and stars, the passage preserved by Cicero shows no sign of any inclination to 'explain it away' in the way that some philosophers would find both obvious and attractive, that is, by drawing the conclusion that religious belief can be accounted for psychologically, without postulating gods. In fact, according to Aristotle's general methodology, what most people at all times and places regard as true deserves to be treated as true; hence he himself presumably endorsed the passage's theistic conclusion.

DIVINITY AND THE NATURAL WORLD: ARISTOTLE'S TWO-TIERED PHYSICS AND THE CONTRAST WITH PLATO

The context in Cicero suggests that the argument above from *On Philosophy* is a theistic response to the atheistic cosmology of the atomists. And Aristotle's surviving works, particularly the *Physics* and the *Metaphysics*, contain versions of a Prime Mover argument which later theologians used as a source for demonstrating the truth of theism. But in general Aristotle seems wholly untroubled by any need to defend belief in gods. In the *Physics* and the *Metaphysics* the Prime Mover argumentation serves a very different purpose. The reasoning starts from some presumed fact about the natural world, but the aim is not to prove that god or gods exist, but rather to explain something about the world of nature. Divinity comes into the picture not as an object of independent interest demanding investigation in its own right: it figures, rather, as an element implicit in a correct account of nature or some aspect of nature (cf. Frede 2000: 52).

We shall illustrate this generalization by looking at Aristotle's theory of the physical heavens, and of the perpetuity of the universe. To set the stage we must take stock of a fundamental difference between his account (in the extant corpus) of the natural world and that put forward by Plato in the *Timaeus*.

Both philosophers hold that this cosmos or physical world order is unique in the whole of reality; that it consists of a single spherical system of astronomical bodies in geocentric orbit, together with the regions and their contents within this system; and that the system, its operations and the mortal kinds that exist within it will last for ever. Notoriously, Plato couched his account in the form of a 'myth' in which, 'in the beginning', a supremely intelligent and good incorporeal divinity founded the cosmos we have today by building it from pre-existent ingredients according to an intellectually articulated plan. The supreme divinity himself constructed the imperishable, all-encompassing, cosmic system. This entire system, for Plato, is in fact a single living, intelligent, being, and Plato does not stop short of calling it a god. Within this whole there is the specifically astronomical system, likewise immortal: its movements express the intellection of the great cosmic god, and the celestial bodies and earth also count as divine. Certain created divinities received the task of constructing the *mortal* kinds so as to complete the cosmos according to the supreme god's plan. We are shown these divine agents constructing what in effect are the prototypes of the mortal species. In their design of anatomy and choice of materials the divine makers provide for functions such as sense-perception, nutrition and respiration, and they also provide for biological reproduction. Thus, once the mortal species have been divinely launched, they take care of their own continuation by natural means, just as they do in the biblical Genesis story. Even so, the naturally born posterity carries in each case the stamp of its divine incorporeal origin, since in it is reproduced the divinely planned prototype-form. In Plato's universe, the naturally born members of the mortal species should take our minds back to the very same divine mind that constructed the mighty and immortal astronomical system.

Here Aristotle parts company. On various grounds he argues that the present order of the cosmos is necessarily everlasting in *both* temporal directions. Hence there never could have been a beginning of the unique, immortal, astronomical system with its regular rotations, and likewise there could not have been a first generation of the kinds of mortal creatures. Different interpretations of this result are possible, but Aristotle insists that every generation of mortal beings must have come into existence by purely natural processes. (In the case of practically every species, this means by reproduction from parents of the same kind.) These natural generative processes are end-directed and craftlike: Aristotle constantly compares the workings of organisms to the workings of a craftsman. But this is for illustration only. He is perfectly clear that these natural workings are not real examples of craft. For one thing, unlike the operations of human craftsmen and Plato's divine craft-workers, they are not governed by mind or by any intellectually articulated plan. The natures of Aristotelian mortal natural substances – the biological natures by which parents reproduce and offspring grow and nourish themselves – are imbued with non-mental purposefulness. They are blind, not in the sense of impaired or lacking orientation, but of not needing *cognitive* guidance to achieve complex biological ends. For another thing, these operations are not controlled by an agency that is *external* in the way human craftsmen generally are to the materials they organize, or in the analogous way that Plato's divine agents are clearly not themselves embodied in the materials they use to fashion the prototype mortals. No, the Aristotelian biological operations express powers that the mortal creatures and their like-natured parents possess simply through *being the creatures they themselves* are. The agency here is essentially internal to the individual organisms themselves, and it is naturalistic through and through.[3]

So given this new Aristotelian perspective, we cannot survey the domain of mortal living beings and see everywhere the stamp of a divine intellect: the same intellect that framed the immortal heavens. To the scientist, the domain of mortal kinds is still wondrous, and teleological explanation is still in order; but the wonders have been naturalized, and the explanatory ends are not what a god has posited on behalf of organisms, but what the organisms themselves characteristically seek just in virtue of their own inherited natures. Consider how the shift to this perspective might alter one's picture of the cosmos in general. Think first of an alteration that might have occurred with some thinkers, but is alien to Aristotle. This would have been a change towards viewing the heavenly bodies in a straightforwardly naturalistic light along with the sublunary substances: a change towards disconnecting the former from theistic causation as thoroughly as Aristotle has disconnected the latter. This is not Aristotle's path. Although his astronomy departs in important ways from Plato's, he never abandons the assumption that in the spectacle of the physical heavens with their everlasting regular movements we perceive the operations of divinities, or at any rate operations that immediately express the living activity of divine perfection. It is not that Aristotle (any more than Plato) is refusing to 'be scientific' about the heavens. On the contrary, Aristotle's carefully reasoned conviction that the universe is necessarily everlasting in both directions (and always contains essentially the same kinds), makes absurd any notion of divine mortal prototypes; but no absurdity has emerged to force him to strip the imperishable celestial realm of its divine affiliation.

Bringing these points together we see that the shift to Aristotelianism concerning sublunary substances results in a disparity between the divine-like celestial domain and the sublunary domain of mortals that is far more radical than any in Plato's cosmology. For Aristotle, the objects in the two domains do not spring from a common divine origin; and the fact that the celestial entities were never brought into being at all, not even by some supreme god, sets them in stark

3. Thus when Aristotle says, "Nature does nothing in vain" (*On the Soul* III.12, 4334a31–2), he is iterating the fundamental maxim of teleological science, not referring literally to a super-agent. When he applies the dictum 'There are gods here too' (supposedly said by Heraclitus in a kitchen) to the domain of mortal zoology, Aristotle presumably means 'here too are marvels deserving the most respectful study' (*Parts of Animals* I.5, 645a18–21).

contrast with the mortal substances, which not only come into being but owe this to agents as humble as themselves.

Aristotle tries to address this dualism in his theory of nature. (i) He restates Plato's dictum that mortals too participate in the eternal and the divine as best they can: by reproducing and thereby maintaining the eternity of the species (*On the Soul* II.4, 415a26–b2; cf. Plato, *Symposium* 207d, 206c). (ii) Aristotle emphasizes the dependence of the eternal succession of mortal generations on recurrent conditions brought about by eternally repeated celestial movements, in particular the rotation of the fixed stars and the annual circling of the sun. The former ensures for ever the duration of the whole universe and all the kinds it contains, while the latter guarantees for ever the cycle of seasonal variations necessary for the life-cycles of perishable things (*On Generation and Corruption* II.10; *Metaphysics* Λ.6, 1072a9–19[4]). (iii) Aristotle emphasizes the generality and necessity of the propositions that for him supposedly constitute the corpus of any science (*Posterior Analytics* I.2, 71b9–72a6), whether the individuals in the science's domain are eternal or perishable.[5] The tiers of his universe have it in common that both are scientifically knowable. (One might add that since for Aristotle the human race is eternal, there always have been and will be human souls wondering at the heavens and observing them, and in different ways trying to understand them; hence there is always a cognitive line running from some mortals to the celestial imperishables.[6]) (iv) Moreover, some perishables, namely the four elements of the sublunary world, transform into one another in a cycle of interlocking stages, and Aristotle sees this roundelay as actually mimicking the spatial cyclicity of the astronomical rotations (*On Generation and Corruption* II.10, 337a1–6). (v) Aristotle brings together the two physical realms under the single category 'sensible substance', even though he immediately subdivides this into 'eternal' and 'perishable' (*Metaphysics* Λ.1, 1069a30–31). (vi) He employs the same basic concept of 'natural locomotion' in discussing both the movements of the sublunary elements and the celestial rotations (*On the Heavens* I.2).

Notwithstanding these efforts by Aristotle to represent the physical world as a fully integrated system, Theophrastus, his successor as head of the Peripatetic School, saw reason to worry that the sublunary part of the Aristotelian universe was not properly connected with the 'upper cosmos'. Theophrastus saw grounds for the complaint that the influence of the *primal* causes of the physical world (supposedly demonstrated by Aristotle's Prime Mover argumentation) stops short of the sublunary realm (Theophrastus, *Metaphysics* 9, 5b10–26; cf. 1, 4a9–17).

---

4. The most recent detailed commentaries on the individual chapters of *Metaphysics* Λ (i.e. book 12) are collected in Frede & Charles (2000).
5. Among the examples he uses to illustrate the general account of science in the *Posterior Analytics* are ones drawn from botany and astronomy.
6. In the context of astronomy Aristotle says: "The same ideas, one must believe, recur in men's minds not once or twice but again and again" (*On the Heavens* I.3, 270b18–20).

From the point of view of philosophy of religion, this complaint, given the divine affiliation of the celestial realm, expresses the anxiety that divinity and its traces are gloriously present in the outer parts of the cosmos precisely to the extent that they are drearily absent from the part around the centre.

Such a picture could adversely affect motivation to pursue the various sublunary sciences. Theoretical astronomy stood in special esteem because of the sublimity of its objects, and because of their supposed proximity to the primal causes. Aristotle himself is vividly aware that any such justification for admiring the research of astronomers could harm his cause when it came to arousing educated interest in the incipient theoretical discipline of sublunary biology: thus he goes to especially energetic lengths to promote the very different attractions of the latter (*Parts of Animals* I.5).

DIVINITY IN *ON THE HEAVENS*, THE *PHYSICS* AND THE *METAPHYSICS*

In *On the Heavens* Aristotle's starting-point is his concept of natural locomotion. As already stated, he uses this to establish a single perspective from which to view celestial and sublunary bodies alike. But the theory's specific consequences, far from creating a bridge between Aristotle's two cosmological realms, bring out the immensity of the gap. Aristotle holds that each basic type of physical matter moves through space in a manner natural to itself. The movements of the four sublunary elements are rectilinear and are defined by reference to the elements' natural places. Each moves spontaneously to its natural place where it then spontaneously comes to rest. Each is capable of motion away from its natural place or of resting in the place of one of the others, but these things happen only through continuous application of external force. The natural region of earth is immediately around the centre of the universe, and those of water, air and fire (in that order) occur in three successive layers around the earth and contained beneath the moon. The qualitative natures of the elements are different, and these differences are reflected in their irreducibly different patterns of natural locomotion. Now, Aristotle quite reasonably applies this approach to the physical material of which the celestial bodies consist. (Note that, in the context of *On the Heavens*, the *Physics* and the *Metaphysics*, the primary reference is not to the sun, moon, planets and stars as such, but to posited transparent physical spheres in which these luminous objects are supposedly embedded and by the motions of which they are carried around.) As we have seen, Aristotle holds that the celestial system and its movements are necessarily eternal. He cannot believe that a necessarily eternal motion is anything but *natural* to the body that moves. Consequently, rotation is the natural motion of the stuff of the celestial spheres, and its natural place the celestial region. It follows that this is a *sui generis* stuff: a fifth kind of physical matter intrinsically different from the four others just as they are from each other. Aristotle calls it '*aether*'. *Aether* is completely indestructible, because it is not made of any of the other four, or any combination: were it so made, *celestial rotation* could not be its natural motion. Moreover, the others are destructible just because they can cyclically transform as mentioned earlier, but the cycle contains no position for a fifth kind of matter. Nor does the theory allow portions of sublunary elements to change place with portions of celestial material, or to combine with portions of it, or to affect it in any way. Although the celestial material is genuinely located in the cosmos in relation to the various tracts and bits of the perishable materials – it *surrounds* them – the impossibility of mutual displacement means that it and they in a sense do not share the same physical space. In Aristotle's world it is as impossible that a sublunary equipage should land on one of the spheres, remove some sphere-matter, and return with it to earth as it is in Einstein's universe that anything should outstrip light. The celestial material is not only not displaceable by any sublunary material, but it is not displaceable by some other kind of celestial material, since no other kind is postulated. It is physically impossible for anything to intrude into its realm and impede its rotations (*On the Heavens* I.2–3).

Logically, that which possesses these attributes – attributes that explain how the celestial material carries on as the indestructible source of the necessarily ceaseless eternal rotation that contains and sustains the cycles of generation and destruction beneath the moon – could be an inanimate substance, as inanimate as Aristotle's four sublunary elements. But he does not consider this possibility. To him, the imperishability of the celestial bodies, and the completely effortless eternity and uniformity of their motion, spell divine immortal life. At one place in *On the Heavens*, at least according to most of our manuscripts, Aristotle first reasons in general that since god's activity is eternal life it belongs to god to be in eternal motion; and then immediately applies this to the case of the heavens (*On the Heavens* II.3, 286a7–11). Thus, on this reading, here he goes beyond treating the celestial system as godlike or close to the divine: he actually identifies it with a god or set of gods, and he may even be identifying the eternal circular motion with the divine life. We see him unconstrained by any theory according to which nothing can meaningfully be called 'god' that is not conceived of as essentially incorporeal and immutable.[7]

The attribution of circular motion to god may seem to contradict an argument in *On Philosophy* according to which god must be changeless (fr. 16 Rose). But that involved the assumption that improvement or deterioration cannot apply to god, as if these were the only possibilities of change.[8] The celestial rotation of *On the Heavens* is the uniformly perfect movement of a perfect physical system: it scarcely counts as a change in the sense relevant to the *On Philosophy* argument. However, by the time Aristotle composed the Prime Mover arguments of the *Physics* and the *Metaphysics*, he had developed positions from which it follows

7. Moreover, the *On the Heavens* account of the properties of the *aether* shows how the traditional divine attribute of impassibility need not be taken to presuppose incorporeality.
8. Plato had used this argument at *Republic* II, 381b–c.

that whatever gives rise to the eternal rotation is incorporeal, hence subject to no sort of locomotion. He now argues: (1) every motion is the effect, immediate or mediated, of a simultaneously acting first mover; (2) it is logically impossible for anything literally to move itself; hence (3) the first or 'prime' mover in a series is not identical with any in-motion member thereof: it causes motion otherwise than by being in motion itself; (4) nothing with physical magnitude can produce a necessarily eternal motion (*Physics* VII.1; VIII.4, 255b32–256a3; VIII.5–6; VIII.10; cf. *Metaphysics* Λ.7, 1073a3–14). It follows from (4) that any mover responsible for the celestial motion would be incorporeal and so not subject to any physical movement, and from (3) that this immutability is no sort of disqualification for being a mover, indeed a first mover. Notice that although Aristotle undoubtedly still takes it for granted that the source of celestial motion is divine, the inference to the mover's incorporeality is reached from physical and logico-metaphysical premises, not from any specifically theological assumption that divinity as such excludes corporeality. That non-theologically deduced incorporeality is in turn the ground for denying all physical change to the celestial first mover; the denial is not based on a conception of god as such.

Theology has Aristotle to thank for the idea of god as *pure act*: activity without any trace of potentiality. This notion was surely fed by the conceptual connections leading from *god* to *immortality*, from *immortality* to *life* and from *life* to *activity*, but it, like the Aristotelian idea of god as incorporeal, is shaped by the cosmological exigency of explaining how necessarily eternal motion is possible. It is possible because it is due to a substance whose activity is so essentially complete through and through that it harbours none of the potentiality and lack that, in Aristotle's thinking, motion and change presuppose (in effect he defines motion and change as the cancellation of lack). With a Prime Mover that was in any way merely potential there would be potential for the movement it causes to waver or cease; but the movement in question is necessarily uniform and eternal. We now have the result that the Prime Mover is necessarily free of all change whatsoever, not merely physical change.[9]

The concept of god as pure act does more than guarantee the eternity of celestial motion. Aristotle sees unimpeded activity as the core of pleasure (*Nicomachean Ethics* VII.12, 1153a13–17; X.4–5), thus he can conclude to the supreme pleasantness of the eternal activity that is the cosmic Prime Mover: "Its life is such as the

9. In *Metaphysics* E.1 Aristotle maintains that if an absolutely immutable substance exists, the study of it would be theology, and theology would be a science distinct from physics. He also assigns to this science the study of being *qua* being. It is notoriously unclear how the latter topic is supposed to relate to that of immutable substance. Interpreters try to reconstruct the connection in different ways. One possibility is that Aristotle envisaged another route to theology that would go not *via* cosmology but *via* purely ontological considerations. Another is that he saw the cosmological route as providing (in the Prime Mover) an entity whose existence answers to a requirement of systematic ontology.

best which we enjoy, and enjoy but for a short time" (*Metaphysics* Λ.7, 1072b15). For Aristotle, the one human experience that can illustrate the life of the Prime Mover is the intellection we engage in when, rather than using knowledge to bring about a practical end or to hunt for knowledge that is external to what we already know, we as it were animate and exercise what we already possess, remaining within it, so that our intellection becomes like an autonomous life that takes us over, and it is as if our whole being consists in nothing else. Since intellection necessarily has an object, this illustration forces Aristotle to confront the question 'What is the object of the divine intellection?', and his answer is that it has itself for object. For *its* object cannot be just anything: it must be what is 'most divine and precious', and changelessly so; but this is nothing other than the perfect intellection, *alias* god, itself (*Metaphysics* Λ.9).[10]

Theology also has Aristotle to thank for one version of the view that love undergirds the being of the cosmos. It is not the version whereby god causes the cosmos to exist so as to have it as an object of love (this fits Plato's account), but the less easily grasped version whereby the celestial rotation is due to god as focus of love on the part of the celestial rotator. Aristotle says that the Prime Mover moves "as an object of love" (*Metaphysics* Λ.7, 1072b3–4): that is, the circular motion is somehow a natural expression of homage by the physical heavens to the perfect divine self-thinking. This incorporeal, intellectual, activity figures as the ultimate cause of the rotation by being what the sphere and the sphere's spatial activity are 'all about'. We should not think of Aristotle's Prime Mover as causing only the movement, and not also the very being, of the heavens. Their movement is their life, and the life of the universe (*Physics* VIII.1, 250b11–15). For, as we have seen, the ongoing processes of the sublunary world depend on celestial rotation. So, directly or indirectly, it is true of the Prime Mover that "on such a principle depend the heavens and the world of nature" (*Metaphysics* Λ.7, 1072b14).

The picture of the Prime Mover as source of movement in the sphere purely through the latter's adoration of the former rests on the thought that what is beautiful and good can make a difference just in virtue of its beauty and goodness *only* by being loved for that beauty and goodness (and no doubt also for the difference that loving them makes). The god of *Metaphysics* Λ.7 does not need an attribute of power in addition to the attribute of goodness; this goodness 'rules' purely through being correctly appreciated by the physical heaven, whose appreciation somehow translates into physically perfect movement.[11]

10. One tradition of interpretation resists the possible implication that the Prime Mover of *Metaphysics* Λ thinks *only* itself; cf. de Koninck (1994), reprinted in Gerson (1999).

11. This conception of the divine causality of celestial motion seems intelligible in itself, but elsewhere, and even within *Metaphysics* Λ, Aristotle seems to think of the Prime Mover as efficient cause of movement in the *primum mobile*. For a recent detailed discussion of this problem, see Berti (2000).

I have been writing as if there is a single rotatory movement that is somehow caused by one incorporeal unmoved mover. Matters are not so simple. On any account there must be more than one necessarily eternal celestial rotation: one to guarantee the ongoing sameness of the cosmos, and another to guarantee the ongoing variation of coming to be and passing away. From a more purely astronomical standpoint there must in fact be as many rotations as are needed (given a concentric framework) to account for all the observed astronomical movements. It is for astronomical theorists to calculate the number: Eudoxus gave it as twenty-six; Callippus as thirty-three; Aristotle thinks it is fifty-five. The number may change: this is an *a posteriori* question (*Metaphysics* Λ.8). When he takes account of all the astronomical details Aristotle still clings to the general physical theory according to which the rotation of each distinct celestial sphere requires its own perfectly active incorporeal unmoved mover (causing movement, presumably, as an object of love). In this context, the title of 'Prime Mover' traditionally goes to the mover of the *primum mobile*, that is, the all-containing sphere of the fixed stars. Later tradition has had to wrestle with the fact that even if the mover of this outermost sphere has obvious primacy over all the other incorporeal unmoved movers, such primacy is not nearly absolute enough to distinguish the god of monotheism.

In summary so far, one could say that Aristotle mostly takes it for granted that there are gods, just as he takes it for granted that there is nature. His main contributions to theological thinking occur in the course of efforts to establish and make sense of the doctrine that the cosmos is necessarily eternal, and the celestial part of it necessarily in eternal motion. He develops what many theologians would regard as a correct and refined conception of god as pure act, incorporeal and changeless, but Aristotle is driven to this by cosmological, not specifically theological, considerations.

DIVINITY, HUMAN NATURE, AND PIETY

Aristotle's cosmic divinities are radically different from the mostly anthropomorphic gods of traditional ancient Greek religion. He welcomes the strand of traditional religion that sees the sky as a home of gods (*On the Heavens* I.3, II.1; cf. *Metaphysics* Λ.8, 1074b1–14), but he derides the stories of the Olympian gods at their banquets (*Metaphysics* B.4, 1000a9–18). Even so, the anthropomorphism has a function, he believes: it fosters "the persuasion of the multitude" and "legal and utilitarian expediency". It fits with this that, in the *Politics* (an essentially practical work), Aristotle indicates no scepticism about the traditional public religious practices. It is taken for granted there that the conduct of the traditional cults is an essential function of the city-state (*Politics* VI.8). And Aristotle himself in his will, which has been preserved, provides for the offering of statues to Demeter, Athena and Zeus (Aristotle 1984: 2464–5). In general, he gives the impression of having a powerful sense of the naturalness and importance of religion, and of the importance, for religion, of time-honoured beliefs and practices.

Aristotle's cosmic divinities are postulated for the sake of scientific explanation, but they are much more to him than theoretically required realities. His language about them shows reverence. In fact, it would seem that for him a certain religious solemnity is part and parcel of scientific seriousness when the scientific questions are ones about the heavens and the eternity of the world. And we are about to see that even when the questions are about the psychology, biology, physics and chemistry of perishable substances, for Aristotle something sublime is going on when the theorist investigates these things.

For he holds that reason or intellect in human beings is our most godlike element. Although it is not at all clear that he ever implies that human intellect could exist separately from the body, there is strong evidence that he regards human intellect as not a straightforwardly natural phenomenon (*On the Soul* III.4–5; *Parts of Animals* I.1, 641a17–b10). *On the Soul* III.5, arguably the most cryptic half page of the entire corpus, has sometimes been understood to convey that what is known as the 'agent intellect' in us is nothing other than divine eternal intellect. But the ambiguities of the chapter are exegetically daunting. However, even if *On the Soul* III.5 stops short of literally identifying the agent intellect in us with god or a god, it seems to ascribe to us something transcendent, using language at one point strikingly reminiscent of the *Metaphysics* Λ conception of the Prime Mover as pure activity (*On the Soul* 430a18; see also *Eudemian Ethics* VIII.3, 1249b6–25).[12]

For ethics, Aristotle surely thinks it matters more to know which things deserve to be revered and treasured as godlike than it does to know exactly how much 'godlike' commits one to metaphysically, or to puzzle about how something godlike manages to be united with the rest of human nature. Whatever the precise ontology of the human intellect, the important thing is that in valuing the sheer exercise of it in the autonomy of purely theoretical thinking we value what is highest in us. Although we are human, we ought to 'assimilate to the immortals', and in theoretical reasoning we achieve this more than in any other human activity. We thereby taste the most precious, although not the only, form of human happiness (*eudaimonia*). That it is happiness at all makes us like the gods, since gods are traditionally blessed and happy (*Nicomachean Ethics* X.7–8).

Aristotle concludes his Nicomachean discussion of happiness with this reflection:

> Now he who exercises his intellect [in the theoretical mode] and cultivates it seems to be both in the best state and most dear to the gods. For if the gods have any care for human affairs, as they are thought

12. For a particularly well argued interpretation of *On the Soul* III.5, see Burnyeat (2008).

> to have, it would be reasonable both that they should delight in what was best and most akin to them (i.e. the intellect) and that they should reward those who love and honour this most, as caring for the things that are dear to them and acting both rightly and nobly. And that all these attributes belong most of all to the [theoretically] wise person is manifest. He therefore is dearest to the gods. And he who is that will presumably be also the happiest; so that in this way too the wise man will more than any other be happy.
>
> (*Nicomachean Ethics* X.8, 1179a22–32)

The passage makes a veiled claim about the truest form of personal piety. No one familiar with Plato's *Euthyphro* can fail to remember that 'dear to the gods' and 'pious' are necessarily co-extensive (*Euthyphro* 9eff.). However, commentators on the Aristotelian passage have puzzled over who these gods are to whom human affairs are arguably of some concern,[13] and over the nature of the reward they supposedly grant the theoretical sage. The answer to this latter question is surely 'intellectual illumination'. If these gods share the nature of the Prime Mover of the *Metaphysics*, this is the gift they value most, and the one most appropriate for the human theoretical sage. But how such gods could be identified with the celestial-sphere-moving divinities of the *Metaphysics* Aristotle does not try to say. It tells us something about Aristotle that he did not think it necessary to explicate a system coordinating all his philosophical thoughts about the divine before declaring them in the various relevant contexts.

FURTHER READING

Bodéüs, R. 2000. *Aristotle and the Theology of the Living Immortals*, J. Garrett (trans.). Albany, NY: SUNY Press.

Lear, J. 1988. *Aristotle: The Desire to Understand* (esp. ch. 6). Cambridge: Cambridge University Press.

Patzig, G. 1979. "Theology and Ontology in Aristotle's *Metaphysics*". In *Articles on Aristotle*, vol. 3, J. Barnes, M. Schofield & R. Sorabji (eds), 33–49. London: Duckworth.

On PIETY see also Chs 4, 6, 12.

13. The second sentence of the last quoted passage is a conditional, but it is clear that Aristotle asserts the antecedent.

6

EPICURUS

John Penwill

Although Epicurus (341–270/71 BCE) was born and bred an Athenian citizen, he did not set up permanent residence in Athens until 306 BCE. He grew up on the island of Samos in the Aegean (then an Athenian colony) and moved to Colophon in Asia Minor after the Macedonian Perdiccas had expelled the Athenians from Samos in 321. It was in Colophon that Epicurus received his early and formative philosophical training from Nausiphanes of Teos, a philosopher who had espoused Democritean atomism and who held that the goal of the individual in life was *akataplēxia*, the ability to maintain composure. After his move to Athens Epicurus purchased a house, where he and his close associates lived, and a kitchen garden near the Academy, where he gave his lectures (whence the term 'The Garden' to denote Epicurean philosophy). As a philosophical school, Epicureanism was remarkable for including both women and slaves as members, although the chief positions were held by men. Epicurus died in 271; the school in Athens continued after his death as did other communities that had been established in various parts of the Greek-speaking world.[1]

According to one of Epicurus' ancient biographers, what impelled Epicurus towards a life of philosophy was the inability of his teachers to explain what Hesiod meant by 'Chaos'. According to another, he started out as a schoolteacher himself but turned to philosophy after coming across the works of Democritus (this presumably under the tutelage of Nausiphanes). The two are not unrelated and may well both be true. In Hesiod's *Theogony* Chaos is said to be the first entity that came into existence (*Theogony* 116), followed by Gaia, Tartaros and Eros. No reason is given for the appearance of Chaos nor is any explanation offered as to what exactly it is; Hesiod apparently expects his readers to know. What it is not is the confused mass of matter that writers such as Ovid assumed to be the original state of the universe before the creator-god set to work on it (Ovid,

1. For a fuller biography, see Rist (1972: 1–13).

Metamorphoses 1.5–31). What it is is the first stage in a process that occurs seemingly spontaneously (like the big bang of modern cosmology), from which everything else develops in a series of what Hesiod describes as matings and begettings. Democritean atomism offers a material explanation of the same process; but instead of divine mating what we get is a series of interactions between primary particles that eventually result in the formation of *kosmoi*, world-systems. Hesiod's cosmogony-cum-theogony eventually brings us to the world order familiar to all Greeks from Homer and the cults of the various city-states, one in which the world and everything in it including (and especially including) human beings are ruled by a group of gods whose behaviour is capricious and inscrutable but who nonetheless expect to be worshipped and threaten dire consequences either in this world or the next to those who offend them. Democritean atomism offered a way to write these gods out of the equation.

It is here that we come to the core of Epicurus' philosophy of religion. What Nausiphanes also imparted to Epicurus was a sense of what the ultimate end of studying philosophy should be: it is not to gain insight into cosmology, theology, physics, metaphysics, ethics, psychology or the other branches of learning that philosophy covers, but to attain peace of mind (see *LP* 85–6; *PD* 11–13).[2] Everything else is a means to this end. Epicurus' term for this happy state was *ataraxia*, the state of being unperturbed. *Tarachos*, perturbation, is the spiritual condition of most human beings; the philosopher's role is to be a spiritual healer. And in order to effect the cure one needs to identify the causes of the disease. For Epicurus this is resolved into desires and fears; we want what we do not need and cannot have and we fear what there is no reason to fear. The natural wish of everyone to achieve pleasure and avoid pain can be fulfilled by regulating our desires (see esp. *LM* 127–33; *PD* 3, 8–10; *VS* 33); and the disturbance caused by our fear of the gods and our fear of death – the two principal fears that Epicurus identifies – can be resolved by dispelling the errors perpetrated by Homer and our traditional upbringing. We need to understand that there is nothing fearful about either. And that is where religion comes in. Traditional religion, with its belief in interventionist gods and its tales about rewards and punishments in the afterlife, has led human beings seriously astray and been responsible for a significant amount of human unhappiness. It is time to set the record straight. And for having the courage thus to stand up against the tyranny of tradition, Epicurus is hailed as a hero by his followers (see esp. Lucretius, *De Rerum Natura* [On the nature of things; hereafter *DRN*] 1.62–79; 3.1–30; 5.1–12, 43–54; 6.1–41).

In determining Epicurus' views about the gods and religion, there is an obvious problem of sources. Diogenes Laertius[3] reports Epicurus as being a prolific writer,

2. The works of Epicurus are hereafter abbreviated as follows: *Letter to Herodotus* (*LH*); *Letter to Menoeceus* (*LM*); *Letter to Pythocles* (*LP*); *Principal Doctrines* (*PD*); *Vatican Sayings* (*VS*).
3. In Diogenes Laertius, *Lives of the Eminent Philosophers* (hereafter DL).

listing forty-one separate titles (including the monumental thirty-seven-book *On Nature*) and claiming that he produced enough material to fill around 300 *kylindroi*, the containers that held the papyrus rolls (DL 10.26–8). Of these there was one treatise *peri theōn* (On the gods) and one *peri hosiotētos* (On holiness); there remain four brief fragments of the former (17.1–4 Arrighetti [in Arrighetti 1973: 169–71]), five of the latter (19.1–5 Arrighetti [in *ibid.*: 172–5]), and tantalizing fragmentary citations from other works preserved in what is left of Philodemus' own *peri eusebeias* (On piety) and *peri theōn* (On the gods). The principal sources for Epicurean theology that remain are *LM* 123–4 and *PD* 4; these can be supplemented by secondary material found in later writers such as Lucretius, Philodemus, Cicero, Plutarch, Diogenes of Oenoanda, Diogenes Laertius and the Church Fathers; of these some are adulatory, others hostile, none dispassionate or neutral.

PHYSICS, COSMOLOGY AND THE SOUL

To understand Epicurean theology it is first necessary to know the basics of Epicurean physics and cosmology. The cardinal principle is that nothing comes to be from what is not (*LH* 38 *fin.*). There is no god who can magically create something out of nothing (cf. Lucretius, *DRN* 1.149–50). There is an infinite universe comprising on the one hand an infinitude of primary particles of existence-matter, which, following Democritus, Epicurus terms *atomoi ideai*, 'uncuttable shapes' or 'atoms', and an infinite emptiness or void within which the atoms move. Every material object is a compound of these primary particles. The atoms themselves are eternal; they have no beginning and cannot be destroyed. The compounds they form on the other hand are inherently unstable, since even when locked together atoms do not cease to move; they vibrate (*LH* 43). Compounds also contain void, which means they can be broken apart; the atoms themselves do not. Within the infinite universe there are an infinite number of world-systems (called *kosmoi*), each – like the compounds contained within them – subject to the cycle of coming-to-be and passing-away. The world in which we live is one of these; it came into existence as a result of a random set of collisions and combinations of atoms and it will at some time in the future be resolved again into its constituent parts. The stars, planets and galaxies we see in the sky are not other world-systems but part of our own; our knowledge of other *kosmoi* is based on reason alone (see *LP* 88–9). The whole process is material and mechanistic. It operates according to the laws of physics, which are not evidence of some grand intelligent design but simply the way things are. No god created our world, nor does any god oversee what occurs in it.

The human organism is likewise a material construct, and like the world (and for the same reason) is subject to the cycle of coming-to-be and passing-away. It comprises particles whose combinations variously make up skin, bone, hair, blood, nails, intestines and soul. It is nourished from the moment of conception by particles ingested first by its mother and then by itself. The particles that make up the soul are spherical and extremely fine (*LH* 63); they accrue in the body through the same process as particles that make up bodily parts. But because of their shape they cannot cohere as a separate entity. Thus when the organism dies body parts may retain their form for some time (since they are made up of particles that *can* cohere), but the soul simply dissipates into the air, its round particles available to be ingested into other organisms through breathing. Reason shows that this must be the nature of the soul: its particles round and volatile enough to traverse every part of the organism at great speed; in the living organism kept in place by the denser body structures but after death free simply to fall apart since there is no longer anything to keep it together. There is therefore no possibility of post-death existence for the soul; while Epicurus agrees with the mainstream of Greek thought that it is the presence of soul that differentiates between a live human (or other) organism and a corpse, he rejects the notion prevalent from Homer on and most fully articulated and passionately argued by Plato in the *Phaedo* and elsewhere that this 'life' must continue to exist somewhere.

It is this that allows us to do away with one of those two basic fears. We fear death for one of two reasons (cf. *LH* 81). One is that we worry about what might happen to us after we die: that the gods might condemn us to eons of agony for sins committed during our lifetime. Since there is no separately existing soul to suffer such punishments, that worry can be dispelled. The other is that we feel life to be so precious that we cannot bear to give it up, and the thought of total annihilation is itself a cause of terror. This, of course, is an aspect of our natural tendency to preserve life; if we are faced with a life-threatening situation, we normally seek to avoid it. The argument that Epicurus advances against this is summarized in *PD* 2: "Death is nothing to us. For what has been dissolved has no sense-experience, and what has no sense-experience is nothing to us" (1994: 32).[4] In other words what we fear is literally nothing, since when we are dead we have no consciousness of that fact. While we are alive, death is not present; and when death is present, 'we' are not there to experience it. It is thus an empty fear. (See further *LM* 124–7; Lucretius, *DRN* 3.830–1094.)

There is thus no need to engage in religious rituals in an attempt to secure a blessed life for our souls after death. Indeed, such rituals are both pointless and counter-productive; they perpetuate an erroneous view of the nature of the relationship between the human and the divine, and they are open to corruption in that they give those who operate these cults a pernicious hold over their adherents (Lucretius, *DRN* 1.102–11). The task of philosophy is to enlighten people as to the true nature of the world and their place in it, to bring them literally back to earth,

4. Unless otherwise indicated (as here), translations from Greek and Latin works are my own.

and to offer a coping mechanism that is based on reality rather than fantasy. No god will intervene to help you; there is no afterlife of bliss to which the gods are calling you; the human race is on its own in an insentient and uncaring universe. That is the truth of the matter. To believe that we have been placed here for some purpose is a product of human arrogance; ultimately life is meaningless, a drop in the bucket of an infinity of time and space. We, not god, are responsible for our spiritual well-being; and when we understand what the soul is and how it actually works we can start doing something about it.

So how does the soul work? It is, as stated above, composed of extremely fine and spherical particles. These are distributed throughout the body and it is this fact that enables both sense-perception and motion to occur. It is the soul that drives the body (corpses clearly do not have the capacity to move themselves) and, as Epicurus argues, it is absurd to suppose that what is material can be acted on by what is immaterial (*LH* 67); hence the soul too must be material. In addition, a large concentration of these particles is located in the chest cavity, and it is the interaction of these with each other that constitutes what we call thinking. This is where the mind is located; it is also the seat of the emotions (anger, love, pity and the rest). It is the motions of those particles that constitute the mind that we need to acquire the power to control; harmonious and smooth motions bring pleasure and happiness, discordant and violent motions pain and distress. The goal of *ataraxia* is thus quite a literal one: lack of perturbation means the elimination of those violent motions in favour of the smooth, untroubling ones. That is what Epicurean philosophy offers its adherents the means to attain.

GODS AND HOW WE PERCEIVE THEM

It may seem surprising given the fact that Epicurus is so insistent on eliminating the gods from any role in the creation or management of our world that gods remain very much part of his system. Why is this so? Part of the answer to this question lies in what apparently was one of the basic principles of Epicureanism, although it is not found in any of his extant writings. This is the principle of *isonomia*, which is outlined by the Epicurean spokesman, Velleius, in Cicero's dialogue *On the Nature of the Gods* (see esp. 1.50). The Greek term actually means 'equal shares', and in practice means that within the infinite universe for every instance of *x* there is an instance of anti-*x*. At the basic level this is manifested in the balance between matter on the one hand and void on the other; within the world-systems that exist in the universe, it is reflected in the fact that for every force tending towards generation and conservation there is a corresponding force tending towards dissolution and destruction. It further holds that for every compound subject to the cycle of coming-to-be and passing-away, there is a corresponding compound that is not, that is, one in which the forces of generation and dissolution are so perfectly balanced that it is both uncreated and indestructible, existing from everlasting to everlasting. This, of course, is a property of God or the gods.

That is what reason tells us. But we do not have to rely on reason. As Epicurus argues at *LM* 123 the gods must exist because we have "clear knowledge" (*enargēs ... gnōsis*) of them. This brings us to the fundamentals of Epicurean epistemology, or what was known in the school as the Canon. The first stage in our acquisition of knowledge is perception (*aisthēsis*). All perception is explained in terms of touch; given the material base of Epicurean physics and psychology this is hardly surprising, since physical contact is the only way in which the motions of soul particles that constitute perception can be set up. In the case of sight it works like this (see *LH* 46–50). One consequence of the inherent instability of atomic compounds referred to above is that a constant stream of images or surface films (called *eidōla* in Greek) is emitted from every object. These pass through the intervening space and strike our eyes, which in turn sets up particular motions in the soul particles behind the eyes. When seeing an object for the first time, the motions so set up are unfamiliar and we do not know what we are seeing; however, after a number of experiences of seeing the same class of thing a general concept (technical term *prolēpsis*) is formed in the mind, which enables us to recognize (say) the motions set up by the impact of *eidōla* from a cat and distinguish these from the motions set up by the impact of *eidōla* from a dog or an elephant. The formation of *prolēpseis* is the process of education and learning to make sense of the world.

However, we obviously do not *see* gods, so we must have acquired this knowledge of them by some other means. Just like the *kosmoi*, gods are material objects, compounds of atoms; and like all such compounds they give off *eidōla*. But gods are not like the compounds that we are familiar with in our world. For a start, they are eternal; in them there is perfect equilibrium between what they give off (images) and what they take in, so that while their component parts are constantly changing, their physical essence remains the same. (For a full discussion of the physical nature of Epicurean gods, see Penwill [2000: 25–7].) Secondly, they are composed of a substance unlike any that we know. This is indicated by what Cicero has Velleius say in *On the Nature of the Gods*: "Yet that form is not body but quasi-body, and it does not have blood but quasi-blood" (1.49). Some have interpreted this to mean that they do not have substance at all, for example A. A. Long and D. N. Sedley (1987: 139–49), who see them as "thought-constructs". But this does not accord with the basic principle of Epicurean physics, by which there are only two entities in the infinite universe: atoms and void (*LH* 39). If the gods were void, they could not be perceived at all and indeed would have no existence; they must therefore be substance. What Cicero presents is a distortion of the Epicurean viewpoint, setting up an Aunt Sally for the academician Cotta to shoot down when he comes to give his reply (*On the Nature of the Gods* 1.71). What lies behind it is the perfectly reasonable proposition that the gods have bodies that are totally unlike the bodies we encounter on earth (our own and those of our fellow human beings). And because of this, the images that they give off behave very differently from the images that impact on our eyes and enable us to see. For a start, they are the only images that can both traverse the vast distances of intercosmic space (given that the gods are located in the spaces between *kosmoi*; Penwill 2000: 31–2) and pierce the membrane surrounding our world (what Lucretius terms the *moenia mundi*, the "ramparts of the world" at *DRN* 2.1144 and elsewhere). Images of other *kosmoi* are unable to do this, which is why we can only posit their existence through the exercise of reason. It argues that this substance that the gods are made up of is so fine that it can pass through the void contained within this membrane and indeed within any other substance that it encounters on the way, behaving rather like what today we understand to be the case with cosmic rays or streams of neutrons. Again, so fine is it that it cannot impact on the coarse material substance of the eyes but passes directly through our bodies to impact directly on our souls. In fact, what it impacts on is likely to be the constituent of the material that makes up the soul that is most akin to it, the unnamed 'third element', finest of them all, of which Epicurus speaks at *LH* 63, and which by Lucretius' time had become the similarly unnamed 'fourth element' (*DRN* 3.241–57, 273–81), called "the soul of the soul" (3.280–81).

It is by means of this process that we acquire our awareness of majestic figures that exist somewhere outside ourselves and our world. The continuous impact of these images sets up a *prolēpsis* of such beings within our minds, and makes 'god' a meaningful concept. The argument advanced at *LM* 123 that such knowledge proves the existence of god/gods is no empty or frivolous one; it derives from another fundamental Epicurean principle that nothing can come from nothing. It is an observable fact that the entire human race (even professed atheists) has a concept of god, and this cannot happen unless there is some cause that has implanted this in our minds. In Cicero's *On the Nature of the Gods* (1.44), Velleius is made to suggest that the *prolēpsis* of god is somehow innate; if this is so, it could only be because the images have impacted on the soul forming in the foetus within the womb: not at all impossible, given that they pass through the body. It would seem more likely, though, that the *prolēpsis* of god forms in our minds in the same way as all the others: by repeated perception, acquired familiarity and consequent ability to associate the concept with a particular word.

TRUE AND FALSE BELIEF

There is a danger here, though, and that is to believe that because we *perceive* the gods in this world they must somehow *act* in this world. As Lucretius points out in his account of the origin of religion (*DRN* 5.1161–1240), it is all too easy a step to pass from this perception of majestic divine figures to ascribing to them responsibility for everything we are unable to explain, and from there to giving them complete control over our lives. The situation of pre-Epicurean humanity was one of utter subjugation: "When human life on earth was disgracefully brought down before our eyes, overwhelmed under the heavy hand of religion, which displayed its head from the regions of the sky, looming over mortals with appalling aspect" (Lucretius, *DRN* 1.62–5). Ignorance is what gives religion this power, and it is ignorance that must therefore be dispelled if we are to return to a true understanding of the gods and how we should respond to them. Hence the course on physics and cosmology is a vital part of our education, since that will show us that the gods have none of the roles that have been traditionally ascribed to them: the thunderbolt has nothing to do with Zeus, nor the earthquake with Poseidon, nor sexual love with Aphrodite. All these are explicable in material terms. That whole elaborate cult structure, with its mythologies, its threats and promises, is all a fabrication: sincerely believed by adherents, no doubt, but a fabrication none the less. A paradigm case for Lucretius is the cult of the Great Mother, described at length (*DRN* 2.600–43), which arose simply from the perceived and at that time inexplicable fertility of the earth. We know better: "No matter how well and convincingly these stories are set out and transmitted, they have been beaten back a long way by true reasoning" (*DRN* 2.644–5). The fertility of the earth is due to the fact that it contains within itself particles that can be taken up by all the plants and animals that it nourishes. Nothing comes from nothing; there is no divine agent at work.

Let us now look in more detail at what Epicurus has to say about the gods at *LM* 123–4 and *PD* 1:

> First, believing that god is an indestructible and blessed animal, as outlined in the common understanding (*koinē noēsis*) of god, do not ascribe to him[5] anything foreign to his indestructibility or incongruous with his blessedness. Believe of him everything which is able to preserve that blessedness associated with indestructibility. For gods do exist, since we have clear knowledge (*gnōsis*) of them. But they are not such as <the> many believe them to be. For they do not preserve them as they believe them to be [i.e. their beliefs about them are not consistent with their professed faith in their blessedness and indestructibility]. The man who denies the gods of the many is not impious, but rather he who ascribes to the gods the opinions of the many. For the pronouncements of the many about the gods are not basic grasps (*prolēpseis*) but false suppositions. Hence come the greatest causes of harm from the gods to the bad and the greatest benefits <to the good>. For they [i.e. the good] always welcome those who are like themselves, being congenial to their own virtues and considering that everything not such is foreign. (*LM* 123–4)[6]

5. I use the masculine pronoun here and elsewhere because Epicurus does.
6. Translation based on Epicurus (1994: 28–9). For a discussion of the textual difficulties of this passage, see Penwill (2000: 23–5).

> What is blessed and indestructible has no troubles itself, nor does it give trouble to another; and so it is not affected by anger or gratitude; for all such things are a part of weakness. (*Scholiast*: "Elsewhere he says that the gods are contemplated by reason, and that some exist as numerically distinct, others in sameness of form, due to the continuous influx of similar complete images to the same place; and that they are anthropomorphic.") (*PD* 1 with scholiast)[7]

The first part of the *Letter to Menoeceus* passage, expanded in *Principal Doctrines*, deals with the logical consequences of predicating 'blessed and indestructible' of anything. The essential nature of blessedness and indestructibility is indicated in *Principal Doctrines*: "not to have troubles itself nor to cause troubles to another, so that it is not affected by anger or gratitude" (*PD* 1). For the mind of god to be perturbed or changed in any way from configuration A to configuration B would be incompatible with both blessedness and indestructibility; to change the configuration would be to change from blessedness to not-blessedness, and to be subject to change implies destructibility. For a god to become angry would entail such a change. Thus gods cannot be induced to be angry with the Trojans and favour the Achaians, as Homer would have it in the *Iliad*, or be angry with the wicked and favourable towards the good. (That any change in god is necessarily a change for the worse is also argued by Plato [*Republic* 381b–c] and Aristotle [*Metaphysics* Λ.8, 1074b.25–7].) Hence traditional religious belief and practice are illogical, in that they are inconsistent with the *koinē noēsis* or common understanding of the nature of god.

PIETY AND ITS BENEFITS

The latter part of the *Letter to Menoeceus* passage deals with the nature of piety. This, of course, carries significant cultural baggage in Athens; a charge of impiety had been levelled against Anaxagoras in the fifth century, against Socrates at the beginning of the fourth and against Aristotle in 323, while Epicurus was himself briefly in Athens (DL 5.5–6). The specific charge against Socrates was that he "does not recognize the existence of the gods recognized by the state, but rather new and different ones" (Plato, *Apology* 24b). Clearly the same charge could be brought against Epicurus, but rather than try to avoid it he meets it head-on: it is the many who are guilty of impiety, whereas the truly pious person is the one who holds correct beliefs about the gods. Not only do the gods not intervene in our lives (that would be incompatible with their blessedness and indestructibility) but they do not even know we exist, because while the *moenia mundi* allow passage of

7. Translation based on Epicurus (1994: 32).

their images to us, they block images of us reaching them as effectively as a brick wall. The only entities they are aware of are each other. They converse with each other and derive indescribable pleasure from their relationship (Rist 1972: 153, citing Philodemus, *On the Gods*). The idea that god is a being totally absorbed in self-contemplation goes back to Aristotle (*Metaphysics* Λ.8, 1074b.33–5); Epicurus adapts it to suit a plurality. Lucretius describes the gods' existence thus, cleverly adapting a passage of Homer (*Odyssey* 6.42–6):

> The majesty of the gods appears and their peaceful abodes which winds do not shake nor clouds spatter with rain nor snow hardened into sharp frost savage in its white fall, but always the cloudless aether covers them and smiles upon them with its light spread abroad. Moreover nature supplies everything, and nothing at any time mars their peace of mind. (*DRN* 3.18–24; cf. 1.44–49 = 2.646–51)

These are the beliefs that the truly pious will have about the gods; indeed, it is vital that one does so, because as in traditional religion the holding of impious or sacrilegious beliefs has seriously negative consequences. These are adumbrated in the last two sentences of the *Letter to Menoeceus* passage and developed at Lucretius *DRN* 6.68–78. Here 'the bad' are those who hold traditional (= impious) beliefs about the gods and 'the good' are those who hold correct Epicurean (= pious) beliefs. Obviously the gods have no interest in punishing the wicked as they are unaware of them, and in any case they are not subject to anger. But holding false beliefs is nonetheless harmful, not only because it subjects us to fear of divine retribution but also because it prevents us from appreciating the true nature of the divine and so benefiting from our contact with it.

For to understand the true nature of the gods confers far more on the true believer than simply freedom from fear. As Lucretius puts it, the problem for 'the bad' is that: "you will not be able to approach [the gods'] shrines with placid heart, you will not have the strength to receive with tranquil peace of spirit the images which are carried to men's minds from their holy bodies, declaring what the divine shapes are" (*DRN* 6.75–8). In fact, we need to open our minds to these images, to engage in contemplation of them, because they are what can provide us with the model for spiritual health that we so desperately need (cf. Philodemus, *On Piety* [hereafter *Piet.*] 1284 Obbink, where the divine is termed *axiozēlōtotaton*, 'most worthy of emulation'). As Lucretius says in the passage from *De Rerum Natura* quoted above (*DRN* 3), the gods are beyond all perturbation; in their singular existence they are paradigms of perfect *ataraxia*, and in their communal existence paradigms of perfect friendship. They give us an image of what the perfect life can be like, and in fact if it were not for them we would not be aware that there must be a better way to live. (Again, nothing comes from nothing.) It is therefore essential to maintain as close contact with them as we can ("our intellect comprehensively viewing their beautiful dispositions"; Philodemus, *Piet.* 1270–72 Obbink, quoting *On Holiness*), and the best context for doing this is the religious festival. According to Diogenes, Epicurus' piety towards the gods was "beyond description" (DL 10.10), while Philodemus records that Epicurus "loyally observed all the forms of worship and enjoined upon his friends to observe them" and that he "took part in all his country's festivals and sacrifices" (*Piet.* 731–4, 793–7 Obbink). Epicurus himself had this to say:

> Every wise person holds pure and holy beliefs about the divine and has understood that this nature is great and august. And it is particularly at festivals that s/he, progressing to an understanding of it through having its name the whole time on her/his lips, embraces <it> with conviction more vehemently.
>
> (*On the Gods*, cited at Philodemus, *Piet.* 757–72 Obbink)

Again, this is not done to avoid charges of impiety, as Epicurus' detractors suggested (Posidonius cited at Cicero, *On the Nature of the Gods* 1.123; Plutarch, *That Epicurus Makes a Pleasant Life Impossible* 1102B–C); rather it is to place ourselves in a milieu in which we can be most receptive to those images constantly pouring into our souls and so conforming our souls as far as possible to them. This, in fact, is the good "welcom[ing] those who are like themselves".

We need finally to make sense of the scholiast (*PD* 1) and the distinction drawn between gods who exist as 'numerically distinct' (*kat' arithmon*) and those who exist 'in sameness of form' (*kata homoeideian*). Dirk Obbink believes that the scholiast is mistaken, claiming that "no god should exist *kat' arithmon*, since all *kat' arithmon* compounds are perishable" (Philodemus 1996: 303), but the evidence cited for this proposition comes from a heavily reconstructed part of Philodemus' *On Piety* (96–104), so I think we have to take the scholiast at face value. We do not possess the context in which the remark attributed to Epicurus was made, and so we do not know whether the distinction is between two types of god or between two aspects of divine existence. The scholiast's language would suggest the former, in which case we may perhaps accept the view put forward by Long and Sedley that those who exist as numerically distinct are "individual Epicurean sages [who have] become 'gods' by taking on the divine role of perpetual ethical models for future generations" (1987: 148). But I am more inclined to the latter view. According to the principle of *isonomia*, for every instance of a *kosmos* there must be an instance of a god; since reason tells us that there are an infinite number of *kosmoi* in the universe, it follows that there must also be an infinite number of gods. But the images we receive do not altogether support this; in spite of the fact that traditional religion is polytheistic, the *prolēpsis* generated in us is more of 'god' than 'gods' or 'pantheon'. Given that the gods are identical in their perfect blessedness and indestructibility (cf. *On Holiness* fr. 3) it may be that the images we receive do not permit us to distinguish them individually, even though we 'know' that there are a plurality of them. Thus we can conceive of them existing both as 'numerically distinct' and 'in sameness of form'. It is in their 'numerically distinct' aspect that they provide paradigms of friendship and in their 'sameness of form' that they provide paradigms of *ataraxia*. Taken together, they give us the model of the life to which we aspire. As Epicurus says at the conclusion of his *Letter to Menoeceus*, the godlike life is within our grasp:

> Practise these and the related precepts day and night, by yourself and with a like-minded companion, and you will never be perturbed (*diatarakhthēsēi*) either when awake or in sleep, and you will live as a god among men. For whoever lives among immortal goods is in no way like a mortal creature. (*LM* 135, after Epicurus 1994: 31)

FURTHER READING

DeWitt, N. 1967. *Epicurus and His Philosophy* (esp. 249–88). Cleveland, OH: Meridian.

Farrington, B. 1967. *The Faith of Epicurus*. London: Weidenfeld & Nicolson.

Festugière, A. 1955. *Epicurus and His Gods*, C. Chilton (trans.). New York: Russell & Russell.

Long, A. A. & D. N. Sedley 1987. *The Hellenistic Philosophers*, vol. 1 (esp. 139–49). Cambridge: Cambridge University Press.

Mansfeld, J. 1993. "Aspects of Epicurean Theology". *Mnemosyne* **46**: 172–210.

Mansfeld, J. 1999. "Theology". In *The Cambridge History of Hellenistic Philosophy*, K. Algra, J. Barnes, J. Mansfeld & M. Schofield (eds), 452–78. Cambridge: Cambridge University Press.

Penwill, J. 2000. "A Material God for a Material Universe: Towards an Epicurean Theology". *Iris (Journal of the Classical Association of Victoria)* **13**: 18–35.

Philodemus 1996. *Philodemus: On Piety, Part 1*, D. Obbink (trans.). Oxford: Clarendon Press.

Purinton, J. 2001. "Epicurus on the Nature of the Gods". *Oxford Studies in Ancient Philosophy* **21**: 181–231.

Rist, J. 1972. *Epicurus: An Introduction* (esp. 140–63). Cambridge: Cambridge University Press.

On COSMOLOGY see also Chs 8, 14, 17; Vol. 2, Chs 4, 10, 16. On PIETY see also Chs 4, 5, 12.

7

THE STOICS

Tad Brennan

The Stoic School was started in the final decade of the fourth century before the Christian era, by a certain Zeno: not the earlier Eleatic paradox-monger, but a native of the Cypriot city of Citium, and thus usually distinguished as 'Zeno of Citium'. His date of birth is unknown – probably around the 330s BCE – but his death can be dated with fair confidence to 262 BCE, when the school that he had founded came under the leadership of his student and successor, Cleanthes of Assos. Cleanthes was succeeded thirty years later by the greatest of the Stoic line, Chrysippus of Soli.

Although none of these three were Athenians by birth, they all studied and worked in Athens, and were deeply influenced by the schools of Athens that preceded them: Plato's Academy, first and foremost, but Aristotle's Lyceum as well, and even, in an adversarial way, the roughly contemporary and rival school of Epicurus. They also absorbed the writings of Xenophon, who had been a student of Socrates alongside Plato and wrote his own Socratic dialogues, although he left no school behind. Many facets of Stoic theory show the influence of the Socratic legacy – their theology as much as their ethics – and the Socrates that they imitated was just as often Xenophon's as Plato's.

Stoicism had intelligent and interesting proponents to its name for the next four hundred years; the school made an easy passage to Rome when Rome eclipsed Greece in the second century BCE, and it even found adherents among the early Christians.[1] The Roman Stoics provide us with the bulk of our written evidence for the school; the writings of Seneca (4 BCE–65 CE), Epictetus (55–135 CE) and Marcus Aurelius (121–180 CE) survive largely intact, whereas the more voluminous writings of Zeno, Cleanthes and Chrysippus survive only in brief and scattered fragments.[2] Nevertheless, this article will focus on the views that can be

1. The Church Father Tertullian (160–225 CE) is the most famous case.
2. It is slightly misleading to refer to the 'writings of Epictetus'; he wrote nothing himself, and the works that bear his name are manifestly transcriptions of his conversations, taken down by Arrian, the historian who studied with him. The fragments of Zeno, Cleanthes

attributed with some confidence to the Early Stoa (as the period of the first three scholarchs is known).

SOME RELEVANT GENERAL DOCTRINES

Before we look in particular at their philosophy of religion, it will be useful to know a few general tenets of Stoic doctrine to which we shall have reason to refer.

The Stoics were materialists, who argued that only bodies exist. There are no Platonic Forms, no immaterial souls or gods: everything that is, is corporeal. They did accept the existence of both souls and gods, as we shall see, but they constructed them both from matter.

The universe in which we find ourselves contains only one organized cosmic system, with our spherical earth at the centre of a spherical heaven. Earth, sky and celestial bodies are also entirely corporeal, and in fact there is no vacuum or void inside the spherical cosmos; it is a continuum of matter from one side to the other. But there is void space outside our finitely bounded cosmos: indeed, an infinite extent of it in every direction.

The Stoics embraced a form of empiricism according to which we acquire beliefs by assenting to impressions; true beliefs by assenting to true impressions, false ones by assenting to false impressions. Some special impressions guarantee the truth of their contents; if we restrict our assent to impressions of this sort, we can avoid error and unjustified belief, and hope to attain a state in which all of our beliefs are consistent, true and have the status of knowledge. But it is extremely hard to train ourselves to assent only to this special subset of impressions, the so-called 'kataleptic' or cognitive ones, and in fact no one that the Stoics knew about had managed the trick. The rewards of success would be great: a perfectly rational mental state, free of falsehood, inconsistency or any possibility of being deceived.

In fact, the rewards would be even greater than that. For on the Stoic account of ethics, all vicious actions are the result of our assenting to false or unjustified beliefs about what is really valuable in the world: believing, for instance, that money is a good thing, when in fact it is merely indifferent. So if someone had the kind of epistemic perfection described above, they would also be ethically perfect as well, and perform only perfectly virtuous actions.[3] And from this life of perfect virtue, they would reap genuine happiness. Such is the figure of the Stoic Sage, a

and Chrysippus are collected in the invaluable four-volume *Stoicorum Veterum Fragmenta* (hereafter *SVF*), edited by Hans von Arnim and Maximilianus Adler (1924).

3. They would never have false beliefs, and so never do any vicious actions. And since – for reasons too complicated to detail here – the Stoics held that every human action is either vicious or virtuous, and that every virtuous action is just as virtuous as any other virtuous action, it would follow that every action they did was maximally virtuous.

kind of epistemo-ethical ideal, not impossible of realization, but "rarer than the phoenix" (Alexander of Aphrodisias, *On Fate* §28 [= Arnim 1903–5 (hereafter *SVF*): 3.658]).[4] Accordingly, the Stoics also thought that happiness, virtue and knowledge were equally rare: they claimed that everyone they knew about, and they themselves, were miserable, vicious and had no knowledge at all. Here we can see on display the Socratic view that virtue is both sufficient and necessary for happiness, as well as the idea that vice is always the result of ignorance.

ZEUS, THE ACTIVE PRINCIPLE

When the Stoics analyse any material object, or any volume of stuff, they divide it into two principles: an active principle and a passive principle.[5] The passive principle is also called 'unqualified substance', while the active principle is called 'God' (Diogenes Laertius, *Lives of the Eminent Philosophers* [hereafter DL] 7.134). Both of these principles are said to be bodies; neither is found anywhere in the cosmos without the other. All of the qualities that things have – the hardness of iron, or the taste of salt – are said to be imparted to them by the active principle. But it is apparently just as accurate to say that a thing's qualities are currents of *pneuma* – a kind of heated air, or blend of fire and air – or to say that God is a kind of *pneuma* pervading things (Plutarch, *On the Contradictions of the Stoics* 1053F–1054B [= *SVF* 2.449]). The active principle, then, is God, as a fiery breath, pervading every portion of the cosmos, and giving each thing the qualities that it has.

Not only is this true of stuffs like iron or salt, but it is also true of organic unities such as a tree or an animal. In these cases, however, the portion of *pneuma* at work is given special names to indicate its job in unifying and animating the whole structure. 'Soul' or *psuchē* is the word properly reserved for the portion of *pneuma* that is the animating principle of non-rational animals. Plants are animated by *pneuma* in a less active and cooler form called a 'nature' (*phusis*); this is also the animating principle of embryos, human or otherwise, in the womb. Rational animals (i.e. human beings aged fourteen and over) are animated by an extremely hot and active portion of *pneuma* called 'rational soul', sometimes referred to as the 'command centre' (*hēgēmonikon*) of the soul.[6]

---

4. All translations are my own unless otherwise indicated.
5. The best discussion of this and related topics is in Frede (2005). Frede also demonstrates how much the Stoic picture is indebted to the theology of Plato's *Timaeus*, following the lead of Sedley (2002).
6. It is an interesting question, not yet answered to my knowledge, whether the embryo's 'nature' survives after birth alongside of the animal's 'soul', or is subsumed and replaced by it at birth (and likewise whether the 'irrational soul' of the child survives alongside of the 'rational soul' of an adult human being after puberty or is subsumed and replaced). The adult human may thus have three animating principles at work – a nature and an irrational soul as well as a rational soul – or only one.

This portion of *pneuma* in every body is not only the source of the body's properties, but is also the active cause for any events that the body may produce or undergo. When an axe splits some wood, the *pneuma* in the woodcutter's reason or command centre causes *pneuma* to extend through the arms swinging the axe, and the *pneuma* in the axe-head makes the iron hard enough to cleave the wood, whose own susceptibility to splitting is also a reflection of the kind of *pneuma* that it has.

The entire sequence of events in the cosmos involves *pneuma* in different appearances and aspects, which once again is simply God in his role as the active principle, and may also be called Fate. Fate simply is the total network of interrelated active causes (Aëtius, *Opinions* 1.28.4 [= *SVF* 2.917]). There is thus a very direct sense in which we may say that everything that happens is caused by Zeus, and happens in accordance with fate.

At the same time, there are other living things that have a special relation to god; they are unusually pure, intelligent and virtuous. These are also called 'gods', and given the names of the ordinary Greek pantheon. These gods are themselves mixtures of the passive principle, matter, and the active principle that is God in the sense of Zeus. We shall look more closely at these gods later in this chapter.

CONFLAGRATION AND ETERNAL RECURRENCE

According to the Stoic doctrine of eternal recurrence, the cosmic period that we inhabit is bound to come to an end at some distant but determinate date. All human life and all earthly things, the earth itself and the heavens around it, will be consumed in a cosmic conflagration or '*ekpurosis*', during which the sun will swallow up everything else and transform it into a homogeneous fiery mass.[7] During this fiery period, the cosmos will contain nothing but the god Zeus in his most active manifestation. At some later time Zeus will cool down, and a new cosmos will precipitate out of his vapours, formed in accordance with his perfectly rational thoughts about how a cosmic sequence should occur. Since he will have no reason to arrive at different conclusions when he next turns his thoughts to the subject, the next phase of the cosmos will be organized and governed in exactly the same way that this one was, with exactly the same kinds of inhabitants doing exactly the same kinds of things in exactly the same sequence. And, indeed, the events of this current cycle are a perfect copy of the events of the previous cycle, and every previous cycle has cycles previous to it. Here we must distinguish between the unique universe, whose history is infinite in both directions, and the

7. The need for greater room entailed by this expansion and rarefaction is one of the reasons behind the Stoic view that the universe is infinite in spatial extent (although evidently not a sufficient argument for that conclusion).

infinite sequence of cosmic periods, each of whose histories is finite in both directions, and bounded by conflagrations before and after.[8]

FATE

The Stoics were determinists: they believed that every action that occurs has been determined to occur from all eternity.[9] They have several arguments for this view. One line of argument starts from thoughts about the causal coherence of events, pointing up the general principle that no motion is uncaused or unconnected to other causes, and concludes that every event happens as the result of causes that were sufficient to its happening (Alexander of Aphrodisias, *On Fate* 185 [= *SVF* 2.982], 191–2 [= *SVF* 2.945]). There is an independent argument from the principle of bivalence, which argues that if all events were not already caused and fated to happen, then there would be propositions that are neither true nor false (Cicero, *On Fate* §21). Then there is a third line of argument for fate from the nature of divination: "the predictions of the soothsayers could not be true he [Chrysippus] says, if all things were not contained by fate" (Eusebius, *Preparation for the Gospel* 4.3.1 [= *SVF* 2.939]). The Stoics argued that the gods provide us with signs that make it possible for us to predict the future. Reliable and accurate divination does still require mastery of the science of divination, and this knowledge – like all other kinds of knowledge – is possessed only by Sages. Still, it is a consequence of the gods' love and providential concern for human beings that they provide us with both signs of things to come and a method for interpreting those signs (whether we acquire it or not) (Cicero, *On Divination* 1.82). Our failures to profit from divination merely reflect our imperfect mastery of the science (*ibid.*, 1.118).

The Stoics were not in the least troubled by the consequence that divination made the future fixed. As compatibilists, they felt they could defend an adequate notion of responsibility within that determined course of events.

HUMAN AFTERLIFE

There are tantalizing bits of evidence for Stoic doctrine about the fate of human beings after death. The Stoics thought that human beings had souls, of course; in agreement with nearly all Greek philosophers, they thought that every living thing

8. It seems very likely that the Stoics were influenced here in some way or other by two previous cosmic cycles: the cosmic cycle of the Presocratic Empedocles, and the cycle of Plato's *Politicus* (269–74).
9. On this topic see the invaluable Bobzien (1998). I express some disagreements in Brennan (2001).

was animated by a soul, and the only interesting questions involved the soul's nature and properties. They also thought, in common with the Epicureans but distinct from the Platonists and Aristotelians, that the soul is material rather than immaterial. This in itself does not pose any bar to immortality, since we have seen that the gods too are material.

And, in fact, there are several passages where the human soul is said to be a sort of fragment or detached bit of god: presumably, the portion of divine *pneuma* we encountered before.[10] The question remains, what happens to this bit after the individual's death? The Stoics seem to have denied the Platonic idea that souls are reincarnated in a succession of new bodies (Origen, *Against Celsus* 1.1.66 [= *SVF* 2.819]). The most explicit accounts suggest that each soul is capable of survival after death, but that the length and coherence of its survival will depend on the individual's virtue (DL 7.157 [= *SVF* 2.811]). The souls of Sages, being maximally coherent, strong and robust, will float to a region around the moon, where they will endure until the next conflagration, which is as long as most traditional gods will last, too, and thus does some rough justice to the idea that the 'immortality' of the soul should give it a 'divine' life like that of the gods (Tertullian, *On the Soul* §§54–5 [= *SVF* 2.814]; Sextus Empiricus, *Against the Professors* 4.71 [= *SVF* 2.812]). The souls of non-Sages (e.g. yours, mine and Zeno's) will disintegrate more quickly. In addition to being an intrinsically odd doctrine, this is also an odd repudiation of Plato's argument in the *Republic* (608e–610e) that souls must be perfectly immortal, since their greatest evil, vice, does not make them any weaker. On the Stoic view, apparently, it does. It is a curious fact that surviving Stoic discussions of ethics make no reference to post-mortem fate. It may be that the souls of the virtuous fare better after death, but in no surviving text is it even hinted that this difference would give us any reason to pursue virtue or avoid vice; the desirability of virtue is always advocated in this-worldly terms.

ATTITUDES TOWARDS POPULAR RELIGION

As partisans of virtue, enemies of Epicurean hedonism and staunch apologists for the rationality of God's government, the Stoics were frequently treated by later sources as natural allies and defenders of traditional religion. But the case is rather more complicated; their philosophical commitments led them to oppose and reject much of traditional religion, or to support it in name only. Thus a Stoic would have no objection to praying and sacrificing to Zeus, Hera and Aphrodite,

10. An '*apospasma theou*', as we learn at DL 7.143 and Epictetus 1.14.6, 1.17.27, 2.8.11. The word '*apospasma*' is sometimes translated as 'offshoot', but etymologically it means a thing that has been pulled or torn off something else, the way a small lump of clay or bread dough might be pinched from a larger mass.

as well as the rest of the traditional pantheon. But in the Stoic view, only Zeus of those three is truly immortal. Hera and Aphrodite are real, and really gods, but they are mortal gods, who will last only until the next conflagration.

This two-level treatment of divinity – a species of henotheism – is fairly common in Greek philosophical theology, and not entirely unknown in popular religion. Even in Homer, Zeus was the pre-eminent god, the father of gods and men. Plato's *Timaeus* features the same doctrine in philosophical dress when it introduces 'created gods' who come after the first, singular Demiurge.[11] But his created gods are still immortal once created; the Stoic insistence that the gods other than Zeus have only a finite future number of years to live will still have seemed strange.

Somewhat oddly, we have evidence of two kinds of treatment of the gods other than Zeus, and it is not entirely clear whether these reflect two categories of gods, two distinct Stoic approaches to theology or simply a problem in the evidence. The following passage shows one approach:

> They call him 'Dia' because everything happens 'through' (*dia*) him, and 'Zēna' in as much as he is the cause of 'being alive' (*zēn*), and 'Athēna' because his command-center pervades the 'aither', 'Hēra' because it pervades the 'air', and 'Hephaistos' because it stretches through the designing fire, 'Poseidon' because it pervades the moist, and 'Demeter' because it pervades the earth. They bestowed the other appellations in the same way, attending to a kind of fittingness. (DL 7.147)[12]

Here it seems that the names of a variety of traditional gods are being applied to one thing, introduced as "him", and most accurately called 'Zeus'. We can see why the gods referred to by this proliferation of names for Zeus can be considered mortal (i.e. lasting no longer than one cosmic cycle), and yet in some sense be the same thing as the absolutely immortal Zeus, if we recall a relevant piece of Stoic metaphysics. The fourth of the four Stoic genera of being is the so-called 'relatively disposed', for example as master is to slave or teacher to student (Simplicius, *Commentary on Aristotle's Categories* fr. 16 [= *SVF* 2.369]). The Stoics agree that such items can go out of existence through 'Cambridge

11. There is a notable divergence at least at the level of names, in that the Stoics clearly think that 'Zeus' is the proper name for the eternal, imperishable and uncreated god, whereas Plato does not use that name for his Demiurge, and indeed lists Zeus as one of the created gods at *Timaeus* 41a. The Stoics are, in this regard at least, more traditional and more Homeric than Plato. They are, however, willing to refer to Zeus as a Demiurge (DL 7.137.11).

12. The names 'Dia' and 'Zēna' are declensional or dialectical variants of the name 'Zeus'. A few of the names exhibit some sort of attempt at etymological connection between the name and the element represented (Hera, Athena, Demeter).

change', that is, the destruction of their defining relata. So if Hera, for example, is simply Zeus relatively disposed in some way to the air, then Hera is destroyed by the destruction of the air at the end of the cosmic cycle, without Zeus' being destroyed.

However, there is another approach to the existence of gods other than Zeus visible in the following passage and elsewhere:

> Those who introduce the conflagration and rebirth of the cosmos [i.e. the Stoics] agree that the stars are gods, though they do not blush to destroy them in their theory.
>
> (Philo, *On the Imperishability of the World* 13 B)

> Once the divinity of the cosmos has been seen, then we must attribute this same divinity to the stars, which arise from the most pure and mobile portion of ether, without any admixture, and are wholly hot and luminous. Thus they too may with perfect propriety be called living things, and be said to feel and think.
>
> (Cicero, *On the Nature of the Gods* 2.15.39)

> The stars in the heavens are living things, rational and virtuous.
>
> (Origen, *Against Celsus* V 10 [= SVF 2.685])

Unlike 'Hera' and 'Athena', these star-gods do not seem to be mere appellations of Zeus, nor are they distinguished from one another by being correlated with the basic elemental stuffs (air, fire, earth, etc.).

> The Stoics declare that god is intelligent, a designing fire that proceeds methodically to the generation of the cosmos, containing all of the seminal principles, according to which everything happens by fate. And god is spirit that pervades the whole cosmos, changing its appellations according to variations in the matter that it pervades. The cosmos is also a god, as are the stars and the earth; and the highest of all is a mind in the ether. (Aëtius, *Opinions* 1.7.33 [= *SVF* 2.1027])[13]

In this last fragment we can see, side by side, two kinds of polytheism. There is the nominalist polytheism we saw first, according to which 'Hera', 'Athena' and so on are different 'appellations' of Zeus, bestowed on him according to the differing material medium in which these relational or aspectual entities are discerned. But the claim that the stars and earth are gods does not seem to reflect the same metaphysical analysis (any two stars seem to be different gods, but they do not

13. It looks as though the first sentence depicts Zeus during an intercosmic conflagration, while the next two sentences depict Zeus in a fully differentiated cosmos.

differ in the kind of matter of which they are composed). These gods seem to be differentiated from Zeus by more than a mere relation. It is true that in some sense these astral gods are still constituted by a portion of Zeus pervading a portion of (fiery, ethereal) matter. But the same is true of our own case; every human being is composed of a portion of Zeus, *qua* active principle, pervading a portion of matter. The astral deities seem to enjoy at least as much distinctness from each other and from Zeus as we do, which, in turn, seems to be a greater degree of distinctness than is enjoyed by the nominalist gods. It is not clear to me whether what we are seeing here is evidence for three kinds of gods – Zeus, the matter-relative appellations of Zeus and the independent astral gods – or whether instead we are seeing two independent attempts to accommodate popular divinities, espoused by different members or periods of the school.

This is one of the reasons why it is not fruitful, I think, to attempt to categorize the Stoics as monotheistic or polytheistic, pantheistic or 'panentheistic'.[14] There is some sense in which their basic account of material stuffs makes them pantheists: everything that is, which means every body, contains a portion of the active principle that is God. But that label obscures the fact that when we are looking at their gods rather than their causes, we find that Saturn and Mars, the star-divinities, are gods in a way that this tabletop is not. Although Zeus pervades all things continuously, he is not, as it were, evenly distributed through the world; he is distributed in lumps, some of which lumps possess, as separate entities, many of the properties traditionally assigned to gods.

PROOFS OF THE GODS' EXISTENCE

The Stoics offered a variety of proofs of the existence of the gods, some of them inherited from earlier philosophers, some of them novel.

In Xenophon's account of Socrates we can already find arguments that the beneficial arrangement of the cosmos and of our human frame gives evidence of an intelligent divine craftsman (*Memorabilia* 1.4). Arguments of this sort play a large role in Stoic theology:

> Suppose someone were to bring to Scythia or to Britain the armillary sphere recently built by our friend Posidonius, which revolution by revolution brings about in the sun, the moon, and the five planets effects identical to those brought about day by day and night by night in the heavens. Who in those foreign lands would doubt that that sphere was a product of reason? And yet these people hesitate as to whether

14. The question whether the Stoics were pantheists or 'panentheists' is well discussed in Baltzly (2003).

> the world, from which all things come into being, is itself the product of some kind of accident or necessity or of a divine mind's reasoning. And they rate Archimedes' achievement in imitating the revolutions of the heavenly sphere higher than nature's in creating them – and that when the original is a vastly more brilliant creation than the copy.
>
> (Cicero, *On the Nature of the Gods* 2.88, trans. in Long & Sedley 1987: 54L)

The Stoics also employed the argument from universal agreement, or *consensus omnium*: "Therefore the main point is agreed among all men of all races. For all have it inborn and virtually engraved in their minds that there are gods. Opinions vary as to what they are like, but that they exist no one denies" (*ibid.* 2.12, trans. in Long & Sedley 1987: 54C). There were also two forms of the argument that our own rationality and superiority over other animals points to the existence of something even more rational and better, which is God:

> Cleanthes put the argument as follows: "If one nature is better than another nature, then some nature is best. If one soul is better than another soul, then some soul is best. And if one animal is better than another animal, then some animal is best. For such things will not go to infinity: nature cannot continue expanding to infinity, nor soul nor animal. But one animal is better than another: a horse than a tortoise, say, and a bull than a horse and a lion than a bull. And what surpasses and dominates practically all the terrestrial animals in both bodily and psychic constitution is the human being. So it would be the greatest and best animal. And yet it is quite impossible that the human being should be the greatest animal; for, to begin with, it spends its whole life in a state of vice. [There follows a list of other imperfections]. So the human being is clearly not a perfect animal; it is imperfect and indeed far distant from perfection. The perfect animal, the best one, would be greater than the human being, and replete with all the virtues and immune to all vice. And a thing like that is no different from god. Therefore, god exists."
>
> (Sextus Empiricus, *Against the Professors* 9.88–91)

Zeno also argued as follows: "Nothing lacking sensation can have a sentient part. But the world has sentient parts. Therefore the world does not lack sensation." He then proceeds to a tighter argument: "Nothing without a share of mind and reason can give birth to one who is animate and rational. But the world gives birth to those who are animate and rational. Therefore the world is animate and rational" (Cicero, *On the Nature of the Gods* 2.22, trans. in Long & Sedley 1987: 54G).

I close by considering a Stoic argument that has intrigued recent scholars, but still, I think, has a further feature of interest that has not been noticed. It emerges from the following exchange:[15]

> Zeno also propounded an argument like this:
>
> (1) One would reasonably honour the gods.
> (2) But one would not reasonably honour things that do not exist.
> (3) Therefore, the gods exist.
>
> But some constructed a parody of this argument as follows:
>
> (1′) One would reasonably honour the wise.
> (2) But one would not reasonably honour things that do not exist.
> (3′) Therefore, the wise exist.
>
> This conclusion is unacceptable to the Stoics, since according to them no wise person has as yet been discovered. So Diogenes of Babylon responded to the parody by claiming that Zeno's second premise had the following force:
>
> (2*) But one would not reasonably honour things that are not of such a nature as to exist.
>
> For when this premise is used, then it becomes clear that the gods are of such a nature as to exist. And once that is granted, it is clear that they actually do exist. For if they ever were, even once, then they are now. (Just as, if atoms ever were, then they are now; for such bodies are indestructible and ungenerated according to their conception.)
>
> So the argument proceeds to a valid conclusion.
>
> But so far as the wise go, it is not true of them that since they are of such a nature as to exist, therefore they actually do exist.
>
> (Sextus Empiricus, *Against the Professors* 9.133–6)

Zeno wanted to prove that the gods exist. His nameless opponent[16] showed that his argument would prove too much; if it could be used to demonstrate the existence of the gods, then it could equally well demonstrate the existence of Stoic Sages, none of whom, they argued, were in existence in that era.

Diogenes' response is of interest not so much for the way he rephrases the second premise – requiring that suitable honorees be at least capable of existence, even if currently non-existent – as for the next stretch of argumentation that he assumes, but does not care to regiment. What is striking about the next few moves

15. This argument received its best published treatment from Brunschwig (1994).
16. Very possibly Alexinus the dialectician, who is quoted crafting similar attacks on Stoic theological arguments at Sextus Empiricus, *Against the Professors* 9.108–10.

is that they are a very direct tense-logical analogue of the modal S5 argument for the existence of God that has been a topic of interest in the last few decades.

The S5 argument – in hasty and informal summary – requires us to grant only that it is possible for God to exist, and that God is, by definition, the sort of thing that exists necessarily, if at all. Perhaps there is no god; perhaps the atheist is right; but even the atheist should concede that it is part of our common conception of God – as the creator of all else, for instance – that if God exists at all, then God's existence is necessary, and necessary as part of the very definition of the concept.

Now we avail ourselves of some model-theoretic machinery to note that 'it is possible for God to exist' entails that there is some possible world at which God does exist. We then step from our world – the actual world – out to the possible world at which God exists: world *G*, let us call it. We then consider that the same definition of God must apply at world *G* as at the actual world (since the definition lays out the necessary conditions for something's being God). One of the parts of the definition says that if God exists at all, then God exists necessarily; but then from the fact that God exists in world *G*, it follows that God exists necessarily in world *G*. And from this it follows that God exists in every possible world that is connected to or accessible from world *G*, since this is what it means to say that something is necessary in world *G*. But our own actual world, the one we started from, is surely connected to world *G*. So God's necessary existence in world *G* entails his actual existence in our own world. Thus we have used the possibility-claim to travel from our own world out to an arbitrary God-world, and then used the definitional necessity of God's existence to step from the God-world back to our own world. Arriving back at the actual, we find that our mere concession of possibility has come to entail God's actuality.

This is not the right place to address the success of the S5 proof itself. But I do want to point out that Diogenes' modification of Zeno's proof has exactly the same form as it. It requires us to grant only that gods are of such a nature as to exist, and that gods are essentially eternal entities. This is the point of the comparison to atoms. No Stoic would concede that there actually are Epicurean atoms, but they must grant that it is part of the conception of them – part of the very concept that they deny is instantiated – that if they exist, they exist eternally.

Now from the premise that gods are of such a nature as to exist, Diogenes infers that they have existed or will exist at least once, at some time or another (by the principle of plenitude). He then asks us to step from our current moment in time, out to this other, arbitrary time-instant, which we may call instant *I*. At instant *I*, whether it is in the distant past or future, it is true that some gods exist. But it is also true at instant *I* that gods are, by definition, eternally existent things; that is just part of the definition of gods, which definition itself holds good at all instants. Since we now know that instant *I* contains actually existing eternal gods, we also know that those gods exist at every other time-instant that is temporally connected to instant *I*. But the present moment is one of those connected instants. So gods exist at the present moment. 'For if they ever were, even once, then they are now.' We have used the 'even once' to travel from our own moment in time out to an arbitrary God-instant, and then used the definitional eternity to step from the God-instant back to our own time. Arriving back at the present, we find that our mere concession that gods exist 'even once' has come to entail that they exist at this very moment.

The conditions on world-to-world accessibility that make the S5 argument work are exactly the conditions on time-to-time accessibility that make Diogenes' argument work; he must be assuming a tense-logic that would validate the temporal analogues of the characteristic S5 axioms.

FURTHER READING

Algra, K., J. Barnes, J. Mansfeld & M. Schofield (eds) 1999. *The Cambridge History of Hellenistic Philosophy*. Cambridge: Cambridge University Press.

Brennan, T. 2005. *The Stoic Life*. Oxford: Oxford University Press.

Inwood, B. 2003. *The Cambridge Companion to the Stoics*. Cambridge: Cambridge University Press.

Long, A. 1985. "The Stoics on World-Conflagration and Everlasting Recurrence". *Southern Journal of Philosophy* suppl. **23**: 13–37.

Long, A. A. & D. N. Sedley (eds) 1987. *The Hellenistic Philosophers*. Cambridge: Cambridge University Press.

Schofield, M. 1983. "The Syllogisms of Zeno of Citium". *Phronesis* **28**: 31–58.

On DIVINATION see also Chs 3, 7, 8. On EMPIRICISM see also Ch. 7; Vol. 4, Ch. 8; Vol. 5, Ch. 17. On HENOTHEISM see also Ch. 4. On *PNEUMA* see also Chs 9, 10. On POLYTHEISM see also Vol. 4, Ch. 6. On VICE/VIRTUE see also Chs 2, 11, 14, 15; Vol. 3, Chs 20, 21.

8

CICERO

Margaret Graver

The philosophical works of Cicero (106–43 BCE) give evidence of a lively interest in what we now call the philosophy of religion, or philosophical theology. That broad realm of study addresses questions of the same kind as are commonly associated with religious thought, in particular the following:

- the nature of the divine; whether any divine beings exist;
- whether the universe is divinely created; whether events are in any sense controlled or directed by the divine;
- whether future events are already fully determined by divine will; whether human beings have any means of discerning and/or influencing god's intentions;
- the nature of the human soul; its prenatal or post-mortem existence; whether there are divinely appointed rewards or punishments; whether human nature is inherently pleasing to the divine;
- the source of religious stirring in individuals and of religious teachings and practices in human cultures.

All of these are addressed by Cicero, most extensively in his treatises *On the Nature of the Gods*, *On Divination* and *On Fate*, but also in the *Tusculan Disputations* and the earlier works *On the Republic* and *On the Laws*. In these writings he makes it his task not only to seek the truth of these difficult matters, but also to record as many as possible of the conflicting theological positions held by earlier philosophers and by his contemporaries in Rome. He is thus a key figure in the transmission of ancient Mediterranean thought.

In addition, Cicero works out a strategy for the systematic examination of theological subjects from the standpoint of reason. In his works, especially the later works, he assumes that it is possible to enquire into the foundations of religious belief whether or not one is antecedently committed to the truth of such beliefs. This, of course, is the primary point of difference between the philosophy of religion and religious thought itself: whereas the latter may accept non-rational justifications for belief (revelation, authority, ancestral custom) and has some degree of tolerance for mystery and internal contradiction, philosophical theology admits only properly rational grounds and insists on tight standards of internal consistency and coherence. This basic distinction is already recognized and articulated by Cicero himself, and subsequent versions of it within the Western tradition have been much influenced by his treatises. In his work the emphasis falls not on theological doctrines themselves but on the challenging and testing of religious claims by sceptical argumentation. Only rarely does he admit to inclining toward a positive doctrine, and while he claims to hold some personal religious beliefs, he denies that these are what is at issue in his theological writings. His is a carefully crafted plausibilism, borrowed from Greek philosophers of the last period of the sceptical Academy. He will not present any position as simply true, for all are faced with forcible objections that remain unanswered; nonetheless he holds that a good sceptic will sometimes accept a position as plausible if it is better grounded than any alternative.

The modified sceptical stance is conditioned as much by the political and intellectual culture in which Cicero worked as by his personal inclinations. Rome's statesmen and civic leaders were expected to maintain, at least publicly, a respectful adherence to the religious practices of earlier centuries, practices considered to have been instrumental in producing and preserving the Roman state. Priesthoods were state offices: Cicero, like many others of his rank, was charged with the public performance of such sacerdotal functions as large-animal sacrifice, augury (divination from bird-signs), and haruspicy (divination from entrails). At the same time, the behaviour of public figures was also subject to the scrutiny of a sophisticated and frequently cynical elite. Among members of Cicero's own class, there was no general expectation that an educated person would give unqualified endorsement to the traditions of polytheism. More fashionable, as well as more satisfying to the intellect, were the major Hellenistic philosophies, of which the most important were Epicureanism and Stoicism, each offering its own theological system. Yet even here a professed adherence to any one set of beliefs could be turned to political advantage by one's opponents: Epicureans could be branded as pleasure-seekers and intellectually thin; Stoics as rigidly committed to impossible ideals. In order to support his role as a public intellectual, Cicero therefore finds it advantageous to display a thorough knowledge of the doctrines of multiple Hellenistic thinkers, while maintaining a critical distance from all of them.[1]

1. On Cicero's intellectual climate, see further Rawson (1985); Beard (1986); Griffin (1989, 1995); on possible political implications, see Momigliano (1984).

THE CELESTIAL MACHINERY OF *ON THE REPUBLIC*

A certain reserve in the handling of religious topics can be traced even in the treatise *On the Republic*, although in this relatively early work (composed in the late 50s BCE) the explicitly sceptical stance is not yet in evidence.[2] Inspired in part by Platonic devices – the Myth of Er in book 10 of Plato's *Republic* and the Myth of Judgement in *Phaedo* 66b–67d – Cicero arranges his treatise in such a way as to surround his extended discussion of systems of government with intimations of the divine. Thus the dramatic theodicy of the Dream of Scipio passage in book 6 is anticipated already in the opening sequence in the imperfectly preserved book 1. As the extant portion of the text begins, the participants in the dialogue are discussing a peculiar celestial phenomenon (the 'doubled sun' or parhelion) and proceed to descriptions of an orrery, or working model of the celestial orbits. These discussions are suggestive of the precise regularity of the cosmos and, by implication, of the truth of divination, for the doubled sun is easily interpreted as a portent of the impending death of the principal speaker, Scipio.

Religious elements are present, too, in Scipio's theory of government, which praises monarchic rule on grounds that there is a single ruler in the heavens. Yet the same passage also introduces questions about the foundation of such beliefs, and Cicero is careful never to let his argument rely on them exclusively.

> Perhaps it was for the sake of expediency that public leaders instituted the custom of believing that there is a single king in heaven, who "by his nod," as Homer says, turns all Olympus, and who is counted both king and father of all. Still it is a very authoritative view, and extensively, indeed universally, attested, that all nations agree – through the pronouncements of their leaders, to be sure – that there is nothing better than a king, since they hold that all the gods are ruled by the power of one. But if we have learned to regard these as make-believe, the delusions of the ignorant, then let us heed those who are, as it were, shared teachers of the educated. (*On the Republic* 1.56)[3]

This is hardly an unequivocal endorsement of religious tradition. Its strongest point is the agreement of all nations, but even that does not rule out legitimate doubt. Scipio therefore proceeds to bolster his argument by reasoning of quite a different kind: first by an appeal to teleological strains in Greek philosophy and then, following a gap in the transmitted text, by an analogy with psychic harmony in the individual. It is noteworthy, too, that when a later passage mentions the

2. MacKendrick (1989) is a standard reference for the dating of the treatises. The differences between the works of the 50s and those of the mid-40s do not amount to a change of philosophical affiliation; see Görler (1995), responding primarily to Glucker (1988, 1992).
3. All translations are my own.

supposed divine parentage and eventual apotheosis of Romulus, founder of the Roman state, the speaker is careful to mark these as matters of legend, indicative of Romulus' personal and political success rather than of the truth of the reports (*On the Republic* 2.4, 2.17–20).

The most daring segment of the treatise as concerns its theological content is the vaunted Dream of Scipio in book 6. To be sure, material couched as dream-narrative can hardly be counted as assertion. Still, there can be no doubt that the dream's dramatic exposition and lofty manner of expression are meant to leave a lasting impression on the reader. Scipio is taken up into an unspecified heavenly realm where he converses with his deceased father and adoptive grandfather, like himself statesmen and military leaders. From this vantage point he is able to view the empyrean sphere, called "the highest god" (*On the Republic* 6.17), together with the lesser spheres that bear the sun, moon and five visible planets, and to hear the celestial harmonies produced by the sound of their rotation. Far below he sees our own diminutive planet, the centre of the universe yet silent and, since situated below the moon's orbit, subject to death and decay. Only the human soul, being a fragment of the fiery substance of the stars, can ever escape the sublunary realm, and that only if it devotes itself to public service. Those who indulge themselves in pleasure, disregarding "the laws of gods and men", instead tumble about the earth for many generations (*On the Republic* 6.29).

Platonic and Stoic ideas here mingle freely. The image of the body as prison-house of course derives from Plato's *Phaedo*, as does the emphasis on rewards and punishments, and the "self-mover" argument for the soul's immortality is imitated word for word from *Phaedrus* 245c–46a. But the mention of divine fire and the divinized celestial spheres recall Stoic thought, and it is hard to escape the impression that Cicero means to commend both those prestigious philosophical predecessors without quite offering allegiance to either.

HUMAN NATURE AND *CONSENSUS OMNIUM* JUSTIFICATION

Also in *On the Republic*, and with even greater emphasis in the largely contemporary *On Laws*, Cicero subscribes to a definitive position on the goodness of human nature. The fact that some people are willing to act in the interests of others, or even to devote their entire lives to public service, is to be explained by certain innate tendencies in all human beings, called the "promptings of nature" in *On the Republic* 1.3 and the "seeds" or "sparks" of virtue in other works (*On the Republic* 1.3, 1.41; *On Laws* 1.33; *On Ends* 5.18 5.43; *Tusculan Disputations* 3.2). The claim has close affinities with Stoic thought, from which Cicero seems to have derived it, although without explicit attribution. There is in the human race no inborn inclination toward vice: we are primed, as it were, to develop toward virtue as we mature. It is therefore not the fault of nature, or of any divine ordinance, that we frequently lapse into injustice and other vices. Responsibility for evil rests always with flawed human institutions and with the individual perpetrators.

The account of this doctrine in *On Laws* 1 gives the seeds of virtue an intellectualist interpretation that again has antecedents in Stoic empiricism. What we have at birth are only "inchoate conceptions" (*On Laws* 1.30, 1.26–7); these are promising in themselves, but require extensive development before they can qualify as moral notions. That they sometimes yield to moral error is explained by the pernicious influences of culture, or by epistemic confusions that interfere with our intellectual development on an individual basis. Yet despite the undeniable fact of corruption, the innate conceptions have sufficient staying power to give rise to the various civic virtues, to religious scruples and ultimately to codes of law (*On the Republic* 1.2; *On Laws* 1.16–19, 1.24–5; *Tusculan Disputations* 1.40–42).[4]

The notion that human nature is initially oriented toward the good is of broad significance in Cicero's thought. Not only does it preserve intuitions concerning the benevolence of the natural order, but it also plays a role in his philosophical method, as the theoretical basis for arguments based on the *consensus omnium*, the shared opinion of all nations and peoples. If a particular belief is held all over the world, independently of transmission, then we have grounds for assuming that it arises from some innate inclination of the human mind. Thus if it is upheld that every innate inclination of the human mind is towards the good, such universal beliefs have at least a *prima facie* claim to acceptance by philosophers. The argument can fail if the belief in question is not in fact universal, or if the concepts involved are subtle enough that most of humankind would be likely to get them wrong. Still, the untutored opinion of many peoples is always to be taken into consideration, and may provide the best available support for some theological claims.

PERSONAL IMMORTALITY

Cicero's most extensive discussion of the capacities of the human soul is to be found in the first book of the *Tusculan Disputations*, written in 45 BCE. In this work, as in others of the mid-40s, Cicero adopts a formally sceptical stance in the manner of his Academic teacher Philo of Larissa: certain knowledge is unattainable, and the task of the philosopher is merely to discover what view appears under scrutiny to be the most plausible (*probabile*) or most nearly resembling the truth (*verisimile*). Argumentation is put forward by a single embedded speaker who, although unnamed, is said explicitly to represent the author himself. The objective is to combat the fear of death, by which is meant not superstitious terrors occasioned by traditional tales of an afterlife in Hades (for "who is so witless as

4. For the Stoic background see Scott (1995: 157–220); Jackson-McCabe (2004); Inwood (2005: 271–301); see also Graver (2007: 149–71).

to believe that?" [*Tusculan Disputations* 1.11]), but more existential worries about not-being or the death of the self. Against these Cicero, like Socrates in Plato's *Apology*, asserts that even if it could be shown that the soul dies with the body, there is no evil in such a death, since no subject remains to incur the evil. If, on the other hand, the soul survives death, it survives to blessedness.

That it does survive has been the view of all peoples, prompted by "nature"; that is, by human nature (1.29). A universal tendency to believe in an afterlife is evidenced in burial customs and in the concern people show during life for future generations and their own posthumous reputations. The instinctive conception is, however, quite limited: it enables us to recognize the soul's existence and capacity for movement, but does not extend to any subtle understanding of its capacities or of the kind of immortality it has. Thus Cicero particularly admires the acumen with which Plato has constructed a proof of immortality based on those very intuitions: again, the self-mover argument from the *Phaedrus*. And in the main he is content "to err along with Plato" (1.39); that is, to opine that the soul is immortal but not to assert immortality as fact.

He is even less inclined toward dogmatic pronouncement when it comes to the further question of the soul's nature and composition. Here he is willing to entertain a range of possibilities: that the soul is a number (although he finds this obscure) or that it is composed of Aristotle's 'fifth essence' or that it is 'fiery breath' as the Stoics say. Only two views are definitively rejected on the basis of inherent absurdity, both positions that render post-mortem survival impossible; these are the atomist position of Democritus and Epicurus and the harmony theory of Dicaearchus and Aristoxenus. On any of the others it may be that soul survives the death of the body and travels upward to the heavenly regions, to dwell in contemplation. Thus Cicero "finds no reason why Plato's view should not be true" (1.49). Accordingly he endorses the Platonic view, but does so in the manner of the Academic sceptic.

THE EXISTENCE AND NATURE OF DIVINITY

For sustained philosophical investigation of the existence and nature of divinity we turn to the treatise *On the Nature of the Gods*, also written in 45 BCE. Unlike the *Tusculan Disputations*, but like the treatise *On Divination* and others of this period, *On the Nature of the Gods* follows a paired-speech format: first Gaius Velleius presents the arguments for Epicurean theology and is answered by Aurelius Cotta, then Lucilius Balbus does the same for the Stoics and Cotta again responds. Throughout it is Cotta who exemplifies the destructive endeavour of the Academic sceptic, working like a defence lawyer to dismantle the positive proofs that others have advanced. The author's personal point of view is represented only by a silent *persona*, the youthful Marcus Cicero, who in the end forms a judgement of what he has heard.

The Epicurean speaker Velleius is represented as overconfident: a brash dogmatist who launches readily into polemic. His position is one with which Cicero has little sympathy: that the gods are "quasi-corporeal" and of human form, and that they neither made the world nor take any active interest in it. Nonetheless his speech holds some methodological interest, for he frequently rests his assertions on an appeal to universal preconceptions, a strategy strikingly similar to that which Cicero himself sometimes employs (see Schofield 1980; Jackson-McCabe 2004). His speech therefore serves not only to demonstrate the utility of *consensus omnium* arguments in criticizing certain philosophical views, but also to expose the limitations of such arguments.

Thus in criticizing the theological positions of the Presocratic philosophers Velleius regularly insists that no view is viable that does not accord with our intuitions that a divine being must be sentient, eternal, of beautiful shape, indestructible and happy. The view of Thales, that god is water, fails because it does not make god sentient; that of Empedocles, that the four elements are divine, fails because it does not make god eternal, and so on. Criticizing Plato's incorporealist view, Velleius complains that the position is simply incomprehensible. "For", he says, "an incorporeal being would necessarily lack sensation, foresight, and pleasure, all of which we include in the concept of divinity" (*On the Nature of the Gods* 1.30). Similarly, in assessing Stoic views of god as ether (i.e. the upper air) or as the regularity in nature, his objection is that such views do not accord with what we think god is: a living being who meets us in prayer (1.36–8).

Cotta's critique of the Epicurean position goes directly to this issue of the sufficiency of the appeal to preconceptions. The argument, says Cotta, carries little weight in itself (it is *levis*; 1.62); his principal objection to it, however, is that it is not in fact true that all people believe in the gods' existence. Many races are so barbarous as to have no religion, and some philosophers have denied the existence of gods also, as do perpetrators of sacrilege implicitly by their actions. Nor can universal preconceptions support the claim that gods have the human form, since some nations picture gods in animal form. And even if all people did favour an anthropomorphic conception, alternative explanations are available for this, in the influence of culture and in the preference of each species for its own form. In this at least Cotta's scepticism mirrors Cicero's own: the anthropomorphic stories are "entirely fictitious, hardly worth the old wives' lamp-light" (*ibid.*). And he speaks for Cicero also in his contempt for Epicurus' efforts to explain the gods' physical nature and activities in terms of the movement of atoms. As an argument against determinism Epicurus' posited "atomic swerve" is outlandish, not even philosophically respectable; similarly, the supposition that divinities possess "quasi-bodies" fails to supply a satisfactory explanation for their continued existence. A theological system cannot be maintained if not grounded in cogent argumentation; that of Epicurus is "quite incomprehensible" (1.76).

Meanwhile Cotta makes no effort to refute a claim that is of central importance to Epicurus: that the gods are not to be feared precisely because they exercise no causal influence on our world or any other. Already in the preface to the entire treatise Cicero identifies this detachment claim as the principal target of his work, for if it is allowed to stand, all religious observance is meaningless and the very basis of human society and all just behaviour gravely threatened (1.2–4). But Cotta, who questions the gods' very existence, cannot argue against it: only Lucilius Balbus, the Stoic spokesman of book 2, can offer any substantive response. Balbus' position is accordingly taken very seriously and is developed at great length, with all the rhetorical and stylistic elaboration Cicero's exceptional talents can supply. Not only is he allowed to build a coherent argument for the existence and providential concern of the Stoic deity – in essence, an argument from intelligent design – but he is allowed to illustrate that argument with large numbers of examples from the orderly arrangement of the universe, the characteristics of plants and animals, the workings of the human body and, finally, the achievements of human reason. In so far as the reader finds these examples persuasive, Velleius has been answered and Cicero's stated purpose achieved.

This optimistic view of the matter is then tested against the arguments that Cotta advances, respectfully but firmly, on behalf of the sceptical Academy. His attack is related in content to that of Velleius in book 1, but goes far beyond it in argumentative power.[5] Portions of it are attributed to Carneades, the brilliant Academic scholarch of the preceding century. Whether derived from Academic sources or devised by Cicero himself, the arguments are clearly ones that Cicero regards as having considerable philosophical merit. They may not be unanswerable, but they are ones to which answers must be found if religious belief is to have adequate foundation.

Cotta first seeks to show that no satisfactory demonstration has been given of the existence of god. The *consensus omnium* argument he again rejects as weak: the Stoics otherwise place little reliance on the judgement of the many, and they cannot both appeal to popular notions and seek to revise those notions by replacing the state gods with heavenly bodies or forces of nature. A favourite Stoic argument, that the universe must be sentient because it is the best of all things, rests on equivocation, and as for their supposed proof derived from the regular movements of the stars, there are many things, from tides to malarial fevers, that occur with impressive regularity and yet cannot be regarded as divine. Finally, Chrysippus is not entitled to infer from the beauty of the universe that it must have been built by divine beings. This would indeed be a reasonable inference if one were to concede that the universe was built in the way that a house is built. But Cotta does not concede this. He suggests instead that it might have been "formed by nature" (*On the Nature of the Gods* 3.26). He means, presumably (for his promised explanation has been lost in transmission), that the operation of various universal principles, such as gravitational forces or natural selection, could

5. For the 'unholy alliance' between Epicureans and Sceptics, see Long (1990: 281).

provide a suitable causal history for the regularities we observe in nature without recourse to divine agency.

Cotta argues further that the very notion of god is incoherent. The Stoic view requires that the god should be a living being, but a living being is of necessity changeable, with a capacity for sensation and for pleasure and pain, and these capacities entail susceptibility to destruction. Hence god cannot be both living and eternal. Another argument derives from god's virtue: to possess any virtue is necessarily to be able to choose between goods and evils, so that if god cannot partake of evils, he cannot be virtuous either. Yet the Stoics wish to say that god is just.

The sceptic's most devastating arguments, however, are those directed against the doctrine that Stoicism shares with traditional religion: that some benevolent deity is actively engaged in promoting human welfare. Although the relevant portion of book 3 survives only in fragments, it is reported by Lactantius that Cicero here formulated what is sometimes known as the 'problem of pain': if god is unable to rid us of the evils we suffer, he is not all-powerful; if he is able and still does not, he is not concerned for our welfare. Extant portions of the text argue, further, that the gift of reason cannot be considered an instance of divine benevolence. If the gods did give us our reason, they also gave us malice and wickedness, for vice is dependent on the cognitive abilities characteristic of human beings. Finally Cotta reasons that the many observed instances of good conduct going unrewarded, and of wickedness unpunished, demonstrate either god's inability or his unwillingness to execute justice in human affairs. It is with reluctance that Cotta makes this argument, since it threatens to undermine the public's motivation for good behaviour. But the fact is that the observed lack of connection between a person's character and his or her fortunes tends strongly to refute the Stoics' claims in favour of divine providence.

Given the tenor of Cotta's arguments, it is hardly surprising that the Epicurean Velleius, who has already expressed enthusiasm for his case against providentialism, declares in the end that the Academic's arguments appear to him "truer" than those of the Stoic Balbus. More remarkable, perhaps, is that Cicero at the same time represents himself as having been more nearly convinced by the Stoic position than by the refutation: it is "more inclined toward a semblance of truth" than that of Cotta.[6] To understand why Cicero sides against his own Academy, it is essential to remember what was noted above: that the stated aim of the treatise includes establishing that the gods are indeed concerned with human affairs. In declaring the Stoic view to be more persuasive than its refutation, Cicero indicates that providentialism remains more satisfactory than the alternative. He can say this without abandoning his usual philosophical stance, for Carneadean plausibilism permits him to accept what appears to be plausible or like truth

6. This disputed passage has been well treated by Taran (1987) and DeFilippo (2000).

(*verisimile*). Moreover, this qualified judgement in favour of Balbus is to his advantage as a politician and public figure. By it he is able to associate himself with the civic-minded religiosity of the Stoics while also acknowledging the doubts that an educated Roman might have concerning specific Stoic doctrines. He can claim to have accomplished the self-appointed task of combating impiety and its attendant malefactions, without appearing in the invidious light of the dogmatist.

For although the content of Cicero's position is at the end of the day that of the Stoic Balbus, his stance in regard to that content remains that of the Academic Cotta. Of great importance for his public profession is the repeated insistence of Cotta that he does in fact believe in the gods and in their providential concern for the Roman people. He believes as a priest, on the authority of his forebears, and he experiences that belief as a deep inner conviction; it "cannot be shaken out of my mind" (*On the Nature of the Gods* 3.7). But belief on that basis is quite different from the conclusions expected from philosophy: "You have heard, Balbus, what Cotta believes as a priest; now give me to understand what you believe. For I ought to believe our ancestors even if no reason is supplied for belief; from you, though, I should get some rational basis for religion, since you are a philosopher" (3.6). This is not the fideism of later ages. Cotta regards it as possible that the intellectual basis he demands for his belief might at some time be supplied, if not by Balbus then by some other philosopher, and that fully rational conviction seems to him preferable to what he now has.[7] That investigation is left for Cicero's readers to pursue on their own; in the meantime the acceptance of ancestral authority remains the fallback position.

DIVINATION AND FATE

More than once in *On the Nature of the Gods* Cicero alludes, through his characters, to an additional department of the philosophy of religion that, although closely related to the subject matter of that work, requires separate treatment. This is divination, or the reading of future events or divine intentions from signs and portents in the present, an important element in both Greek and Roman religious practice. This was to be the topic of Cicero's next composition, the two-book *On Divination*, circulated after the death of Caesar in 44 BCE.

The dramatic date of the work is just at the time of writing, and the speakers are the author himself and the author's younger brother Quintus. The latter has read the recently circulated *On the Nature of the Gods* and is in agreement with its

7. Unlike DeFilippo (2000), I am not inclined to assimilate Cotta's position to that of the more radical Pyrrhonian sceptics. This is consistent with their being considerable overlap between his arguments and those used by Sextus Empiricus in *Against the Professors* 9.138–81 (Long 1990).

conclusion favouring the Stoics, but seeks to offer a further defence of the Stoic position on divination. The role of sceptical questioner is now taken by Cicero himself, in a speech remarkable for its intensity and for the sheer number of its counter-proofs. The mildly favourable remarks on Stoic divination in *On Laws* 2.32–3 appear now to have been forgotten; the dreams and portents Cicero himself had related in his poems on Marius and on his own consulship are dismissed as poetic licence, although Quintus is permitted to quote liberally from them (Schofield 1986: 63; and see Beard 1986). Whatever his earlier position may have been, Cicero now has no hesitation in representing himself as an amused, even contemptuous, unbeliever in every form of divination practised in Rome.

In the course of the work Cicero argues not only against any pseudo-scientific theory of divination based on the notion of cosmic sympathy, but also against the principal argument advanced by Quintus on behalf of the Stoics: that the gods' benevolent concern for humankind guarantees that they have the will to communicate their intentions in a way we can understand, and their omnipotence guarantees that they have the ability (cf. Denyer 1985). Concerning the first, he does not dispute the possibility that all events in nature may be interconnected, but denies that there can be such a connection as would enable a soothsayer to predict the future of an army from the feeding behaviour of a chicken. Where the connections are obvious, as between the phases of the moon and the tides, there is nothing remarkable in the prediction; other supposed predictions are by chance or are mere fictions. Concerning the argument from the gods' benevolence – a point he seems to have conceded in the earlier work, and, as Schofield (1986) notes, the key to the Stoic position – he questions whether it is to our advantage to know the future: would Caesar have been happier in life if he had known that he was to die by assassination?

Cicero's most telling arguments, however, are those that he derives from Carneades, having to do with divine foreknowledge. In order for the gods to deliver signs of future events, they themselves must have knowledge of those events, and this requires that the relevant future-tense propositions must already be true in the present. This amounts to saying that the occurrence of the predicted events must be immutably fixed by fate. But if they are so fated, then we cannot take any action to avoid them, and divination is of no practical use. Conversely, if our actions do change the course of events, then the predictions turn out to have been untrue, so that no divination has occurred after all.

In order to give full scope to the well-developed Hellenistic discussions concerning modal logic, rich in implications for human responsibility, Cicero also composed a further theological treatise, *On Fate*.[8] The short segment of that work that survives makes clear, at least, the extent of his interest in the topic and

8. Text and commentary in Cicero (1991). The issues are discussed in a major work by Bobzien (1998).

something of the arguments he employed. He resists the fatalism of Chrysippus and other Stoics, claiming that if one reasons from the supposed fact of divination that fate is in control of events, then there is no role for will or for self-improvement, and our actions are not in our own power to control. But neither does he grant that Epicurus makes any headway with his appeal to sheer indeterminacy (the atomic 'swerve'). Instead, he draws a distinction between various kinds of causes. While all propositions, including those about the future, must be either true or false, the truth of them can be known only for those which result from 'natural' causes, that is, from those which operate "by their own force", as 'Scipio will die' is necessitated by his being human. Otherwise the truth-value is unknown even to Apollo, the chief oracular deity.

How exactly this constitutes a solution remains unclear, however, and in any case it is likely that Cicero advanced no definitive solution himself. Like Carneades, to whom he credits much of his argumentation, he may be seeking only to dismantle the dogmatists' claims. In this light it is noteworthy that he asks:

> If there were no term "fate," no entity of fate, no power of fate, and if perchance all or most events came about by mere accident, would things come out any differently than they do now? What does one achieve, then, by pushing for fate, since everything can be explained without reference to fate, in terms of nature or chance? (*On Fate* 1.6)

As Cotta in *On the Nature of the Gods* offered an explanation in terms of 'nature' as a viable alternative to explanations that appeal to divine purposes, so Cicero himself here offers 'nature' and 'chance' as alternative explanatory strategies capable of accounting for the phenomena we observe. He is not thereby committed to either strategy, but he may perhaps force a rejection of determinism and its unsavoury consequences.[9]

FURTHER READING

Cicero 1991. On Fate. In *Cicero, "On Fate", and Boethius, "The Consolation of Philosophy"*, R. Sharples (ed.). Warminster: Aris & Phillips.

Cicero 1997. *The Nature of the Gods*, P. Walsh (ed.). Oxford: Clarendon Press.

MacKendrick, P. 1989. *The Philosophical Books of Cicero*. London: Duckworth.

Schofield, M. 1980. "Preconception, Argument, and God". In *Doubt and Dogmatism: Studies in Hellenistic Epistemology*, M. Schofield, M. Burnyeat & J. Barnes (eds), 283–308. Oxford: Clarendon Press.

9. I wish to thank the participants in a symposium on Cicero's Practical Philosophy held at Notre Dame University in October 2006 for improving my understanding of several issues relevant to this chapter.

Schofield, M. 1986. "Cicero For and Against Divination". *Journal of Roman Studies* **76**: 47–65.
Taran, L. 1987. "Cicero's Attitude Towards Stoicism and Skepticism in the *De Natura Deorum*". In *Florilegium Columbianum: Essays in Honor of Paul Oskar Kristeller*, K.-L. Selig & R. Somerville (eds), 1–22. New York: Italica Press.

On COSMOLOGY see also Chs 6, 14, 17; Vol. 2, Chs 4, 10, 16. On DIVINATION see also Chs 3, 7. On DIVINITY see also Chs 18, 19, 20; Vol. 2, Chs 6, 8. On IMMORTALITY see also Vol. 2, Ch. 5; Vol. 4, Chs 2, 6, 16. On INTELLIGENT DESIGN see also Ch. 4; Vol. 3, Ch. 23; Vol. 4, Chs 11, 12.

9

PHILO OF ALEXANDRIA

David T. Runia

In the history of Western philosophy of religion the thought of Philo of Alexandria (*c.*15 BCE–50 CE) represents something new. Hitherto all the leading philosophers had been Greeks, or, even if they had a non-Greek ethnic background (as may have been the case for Zeno of Citium in Cyrus, the founder of the Stoa), they had identified themselves primarily with the Hellenic tradition. In the case of Philo, however, the situation was different. Philo lived in Alexandria, the greatest centre of Greek civilization in the Eastern Mediterranean, and he was certainly a great admirer of the achievements of Greek culture, particularly in the area of Greek philosophy. But if you had asked him who he was, he would have said, 'I am a Jew', or 'I am a disciple of Moses'. In the case of Philo we encounter for the first time a thinker whose primary loyalty is not to Hellenic religion but to a different religious tradition.[1] What he commenced in his own particular way was to have a long and rich history.

Philo was born in about 15 BCE into a prominent and very wealthy Jewish family in Alexandria. Soon after Alexander the Great had founded the city in 331 BCE, large numbers of Jews emigrated from Palestine and settled in the city. By the time of Philo they represented as much as thirty per cent of the city's population and formed their own community, sandwiched in between the citizen body of Greeks and the native population of Egyptians. It was an uncomfortable situation. Philo himself, because of his wealthy background, would have been an Alexandrian citizen, but this was not the case for most of his compatriots. The Jewish community was naturally influenced by the dominant Hellenic culture of their city. But they did not become completely assimilated. The main vehicle for retaining their independence was an uncompromising devotion to their ancestral

1. Obviously Cicero, discussed in the previous chapter, was also not Greek and had his loyalties to Roman religion, but he stood much closer to the tradition of Hellenic religion than Philo.

religion. About two hundred years before Philo's birth the Torah was translated into Greek. Later, the remaining books of the Hebrew Bible were also translated and the entire collection became known as the 'Septuagint'.[2] So, even though the Jewish community (including Philo) no longer had a knowledge of the Hebrew language, they were still able to study their Scriptures in Greek.

From his writings it is plain that Philo had an excellent Greek education in both the liberal arts and philosophy. It has been suggested that, like other wealthy people in his day, he may have had house tutors in philosophy. Certainly his writings bear witness to an astonishing breadth of knowledge in Greek philosophy, from the Presocratics to the schools that were current in his own time. His own thought shows most affinity to the revival of Platonism that was taking place at his time. Yet it would be a mistake to regard him as a Platonist. As we shall see, he put his philosophical knowledge to a different purpose.

There is only one incident in Philo's life about which we have historical information. In two of his works, *Against Flaccus* and *The Embassy to Gaius*, he recounts some extremely unpleasant incidents that befell the Alexandrian Jewish community in the years 38–40 CE. Under the Roman Governor Flaccus, violent anti-Jewish riots took place. In response, the Jewish community decided to send a delegation to the Emperor Gaius Caligula in Rome, and Philo was appointed as its leader. After lengthy delays they obtained the desired interview, which went rather badly, but at least did not cost them their lives. These events are often connected by scholars with a passage at the beginning of book III of *On the Special Laws*, where he complains about how his involvement in political affairs distracts him from more serious pursuits, and he looks back wistfully to the time when he could fully devote himself to the life of philosophy.

From this incident it is quite clear that, for all his love of Greek culture and Greek philosophy, Philo's first loyalty was to the Jewish people and their ancestral customs. He wished to defend his people in the political arena, but also, because he was a thinker and writer, in the exchange of ideas. Philo was convinced that Jews ought not be ashamed of their religion and culture when it was compared with the achievements of Hellenism. Quite to the contrary, they should be proud of their Laws as written down in the Books of Moses. This is his ancestral tradition and he aims to defend it with all the philosophical knowledge that he has at his disposal.

PHILO'S WRITINGS AND METHOD

Philo was a prolific writer. Nearly fifty of his treatises have survived. A few of these are purely philosophical works on subjects such as the indestructibility of

2. Named after the seventy translators who, according to the legend, received divine assistance in their task and all produced an identical translation.

the cosmos, the existence of divine Providence and on whether animals can be said to possess reason. As we have seen, there are also some writings that defend Judaism against its enemies. But by far the majority of his works are commentaries on the Pentateuch, the five Books of Moses. Philo explains the various historical incidents and legal prescriptions that these books contain. But his chief interest is in uncovering the deeper spiritual and 'philosophical' meaning of Scripture. He argues that Moses represents the pinnacle of philosophical achievement. It might seem a tall order to make this claim persuasive. To be sure, the Pentateuch does contain some passages that can be used for philosophical ends. One thinks particularly of the creation account with which it begins, the experiences of Moses on Mount Horeb and Mount Sinai, and the exhortations that Moses addressed to the assembled people in Deuteronomy. Philo exploits these passages to the full, but they are clearly insufficient to demonstrate Moses' philosophical prowess. He needs a stronger weapon, and finds it in the method of allegorical interpretation.

Philosophical allegory was invented by the Greeks and had a long history before Philo adopted it. Its origins lie in the classical period, when tensions arose on account of the attacks that some intellectuals made on authoritative writings by Homer, Hesiod and the Orphic poets.[3] Xenophanes had ridiculed their presentation of the divine. Plato had banned the poets Homer and Hesiod from his ideal state. Philosophers such as the Stoics regarded this move as both unfair and untactful in the light of the great prestige that these poets enjoyed in Greek society. If Homer and Hesiod were read in another way, it would emerge that philosophical truths were present in their poetry. The meaning hidden behind the words had to be decoded. Homer allegorized (literally 'said something in a different way') in that he said one thing, but meant to say another. This is exactly what Moses did, according to Philo. When he tells the story of the Patriarch Abraham, this has a basis in historical truth. Philo would not wish to deny that such a person lived long ago and was the father of the Jewish race. But if Moses' words are examined carefully and interpreted on a deeper level, it will emerge that he is really telling the story of the human soul on the path to perfection and felicity.

Philo is a master of the allegorical method, which undertakes to decode the original text in terms of a deeper philosophical and spiritual truth. He has a whole array of techniques at his disposal: close reading of the text (and particularly of its peculiarities, which are many); etymology of Hebrew names; comparison and contrast with other biblical texts; reference to philosophical doctrines; and so on. In his lengthy *Allegorical Commentary* he is able to use long chains of allegorical exegesis, which make heavy demands on the reader, but certainly succeed in converting scriptural narrative into a highly unusual kind of philosophical discourse. If we were to challenge Philo and say that what he was doing was more

3. It used to be claimed that the Stoa invented allegory, but in recent scholarship there is general agreement that its roots are older, as can be seen in the Derveni papyrus.

like *eisēgēsis* ('leading [ideas] in') than *exēgēsis* ('leading [ideas] out') of the biblical text, he would answer that for him the text is primary, and that there is always a 'starting-point' (*aphormē*) for his interpretation in the text itself. The way he reads the text does not rhyme with modern critical interpretations, but it certainly has its own method (see § 'The doctrine of creation', below).

EPISTEMOLOGY

Given the nature of his writings, therefore, it will not come as a surprise that Philo does not present us with a theory of knowledge in which he gives a systematic account of the criterion of truth and the status of human thought. There is at least one epistemological question, however, that he cannot possibly avoid. If philosophy consists in the exegesis of Mosaic Scripture, what is the origin and status of that original text? How did Moses come to gain insight into the nature of reality to such a degree that it should be the starting-point of our quest for truth?

At the beginning of his commentary on the creation account in Genesis 1, Philo states that Moses not only had attained the pinnacle of philosophical achievement (presumably through natural ability and the instruction he had received at the court of Pharaoh), but had also been instructed in the most essential of nature's doctrines through divine oracles (*On the Creation of the Cosmos* 8). Moses is a prophet exalted beyond other men. When Philo discusses Moses' special prophetic powers he distinguishes between various types of prophecy, of which two are most important. In one kind of prophecy, which enables the prophet to predict the future, the prophet is empowered to 'stand outside' himself and through divine possession become an instrument of the divine voice speaking through him. This may be called *ecstatic* prophecy because the process occurs 'outside' the prophet's own intellect. In the second type the prophet is also inspired by God, but remains in full possession of his rational abilities, which allows his mind to contemplate the nature of reality in its fullness. "The true priest", Philo writes of the wise person:

> is at the same time a prophet, who through virtue rather than birth has advanced to the service of the truly Existent, and to a prophet nothing is unknown, since he has within him a noetic sun and shadowless beams of light, which give him the clear apprehension of things invisible to sense but perceptible to the mind.
>
> (*On the Special Laws* 4.192)

Here we may speak of *noetic* prophecy, because the prophet's intellect (*nous*) is fully involved (see further Winston 1989).

The Platonism of Philo's Mosaic epistemology is evident in this quote (the noetic sun immediately reminds us of the image in Plato's *Republic*), even if the term 'apprehension' (*katalēpsis*) has a Stoic background. Philo is aided here by the fact that in the biblical account Moses is described as being shown the model (*paradeigma*) of the tabernacle and its contents on the mountain (Exodus 25:9, cf. 40). The word *paradeigma* is a technical Platonic term for an intelligible idea that functions as model for a sense-perceptible thing. By extension Philo can use it to support a Platonic epistemology of intelligible ideas contemplated by an exceptionally gifted human mind such as that possessed by Moses through divine grace. The human mind is able to do this because it is created in the image of God. Prerequisite for this activity, however, is human excellence (*aretē*) made possible through the elimination of the affections (*pathē*). As in Plato and Platonism generally, there is an intimate connection between epistemology, anthropology and ethics (see below §§ 'The nature of humanity', 'Ethics').

It is thus in deference to the altitude of the Mosaic achievement that Philo explicitly says of himself that "I am not a teacher but an interpreter" (*On Animals* 8). The interpreter comments assiduously on the text of his master, but is convinced that his efforts will never exhaust its limitless riches. For this reason Philo is very generous in recording the views of other exegetes, and sometimes himself gives multiple expositions of the same material (which are quite impossible to systematize into a coherent account). It also leads to unexpected sceptical remarks, in which he casts doubt on the human capacity to reach the truth (at *On Drunkenness* 166–202 he even cites the ten tropes of Aenesidemus in full). But it goes without saying that Philo is not a true sceptic. There is truth and it is attainable to the extent possible by the wise man, of whom Moses is the paradigm, but not necessarily by his disciple, who is content to play the role of interpreter of the written text.

THEOLOGY

Philo's thought is resolutely theocentric, more so than any other thinker covered so far in this first volume. Here his commitment to Judaism comes strongly to the fore. In its history, Israel had experienced the nearness of the divine presence. The first commandments of the Decalogue canonize the unique position of Jahweh, or the Lord God, as the Septuagint translates. All of Israel's religious observance is focused on this single God. Philo sees it as his task to conceptualize this experience in terms that are drawn largely from the philosophical tradition.

As we saw in the quote on the true priest and prophet cited in the previous section, for Philo God is above all true Being. This sounds very Platonic, but Philo would certainly claim that it is, above all, Mosaic. Did God himself not reveal to Moses (Exodus 3:14) that "I am Being (*ego eimi ho ōn*)"? It is typical of Philo that he speaks of God as Being both in the masculine (*ho ōn*) and in the neuter (*to on*). The former corresponds more to Israel's personal experience of the divine, the latter to the philosophical concept of God as we find in Plato. Philo wishes to combine both.

Who is this God, and what can human beings come to know about him? Crucial to Philo's thought is the distinction between God's *existence* and his *essence*. Through observation and experience of the natural world and particularly of their own intellectual powers, human beings can without any difficulty conclude that God exists and that he is creator of the universe (see *On the Special Laws* 1.32–5; *On the Life of Abraham* 72–80). But gaining knowledge of God's essence is quite another matter. Not even the great Moses, although he made many requests, was granted this privilege (see *On the Posterity of Cain* 168–9). God is unknowable in his essence. This means that he is also unnameable, indescribable and unutterable, that is, there is no name or description that can give accurate expression to his nature.

Philo thus has a negative and a positive theology, rather similar to what one finds in the second-century handbook of the Platonist Alcinous. It has been argued by some scholars (Wolfson 1947, and recently Radice 1991) that Philo was the inventor of negative theology. The difficulty here is that we cannot prove that he had any direct influence on Greek philosophy outside the Jewish–Christian tradition. But certainly this doctrine of the utter transcendence of the divine nature is a first pillar of his thought, which determines the remainder of his theology.

If God is unnameable, then what about the names he is given in the Bible? Philo's answer is that they refer to God's powers (*dynameis*). The two chief titles of God in the Septuagint, *theos* and *kyrios*, refer to God's creative power (*theos* is related to the root *tithēmi*, 'I set in place') and ruling power (*kyrios* means 'lord') respectively. It is by means of his powers that the transcendent God is related to what is not God, that is, created reality. The reader will perceive that this formulation is awkward, since the term 'God' should refer to the powers. It would be more accurate to say that transcendent Being in his/its unknowable essence relates to what comes after him/it. But Philo has another way of approaching this problem that has become much more famous in the history of philosophical theology. In addition to speaking of God's powers, he also speaks of God's Logos.

Philo's Logos doctrine is difficult, and certainly not always consistent, but in short we may follow David Winston (1985) and say that the Logos represents 'the face' of God (or of Being) as it is turned to created reality. As we shall see in the following section, that does not mean that the Logos is necessarily only immanent as the aspect of the divine at work in the world (compare the Stoic immanent Logos or the Platonist World Soul). The Logos also has a transcendent role, and can be identified with the noetic realm, that is, God's thought (compare the *nous* in Platonism). The chief difficulty posed by Philo's doctrine of the Logos is the following. Sometimes Philo speaks of the Logos as if it were simply an *aspect* of the divine nature; namely, that aspect which is accessible to human thought precisely because it is related to that which follows it. At other times, however, the Logos is treated as an *hypostasis*, that is, a self-subsistent theological entity that is at least to some degree independent of God himself (the issue is complicated even further when Philo talks of angels as *logoi*). In the latter case we might suspect that the doctrine of God's Oneness, as prescribed by Jewish monotheism, is endangered, but this does not seem to be a matter of concern for Philo. The main influence of

Philo's Logos doctrine was felt not in the Greek philosophical tradition (although there are some similarities in Plotinus), but in the later Christian tradition.

THE DOCTRINE OF CREATION

A second pillar of Philo's thought is the doctrine of creation. Philo is wholly convinced that visible, material reality has been created by God, and has nothing but scorn for the minority opinion in the ancient world that the cosmos was the result of chance or random spontaneous developments (the view of the atomists and Epicurus). Furthermore, because God has created the universe, he will also take care of it through the action of divine providence (the role of the Logos). Philo agrees with Plato against the Stoics that, although the universe had a beginning, it will not be subject to total destruction. This, he argues, was already Moses' view, as shown by Genesis 8:22 (see *On the Indestructibility of the Cosmos* 1–19).

In his commentary on the Mosaic creation account in Genesis 1–3, *On the Creation of the Cosmos According to Moses*, Philo has the opportunity to present his interpretation of the doctrine of creation in greater detail. The cosmos is created in six days. This does not mean that God needed a length of time in which to complete his work. In fact everything came into being simultaneously, because time commenced with the cosmos itself. Rather, Moses used the device of a narrative account of creation in six days in order to reveal the ordered structure of the universe (Philo most probably is adapting here a theme from contemporary commentaries on Plato's cosmological dialogue, the *Timaeus*, which also has a narrative structure; see Runia 1986). Of particular interest is Philo's interpretation of the first verses of Moses' account. He notes that the Greek text does not speak of the 'first day', but rather of 'day one' (a Hebraism). Moreover, the earth in Genesis 1:2 is called 'invisible and unconstructed'. Philo interprets these features as an indication that Moses is not speaking of the creation of the visible cosmos on this day at all, but rather of the creation of the noetic cosmos, which the creator used as a model for the creation (*genesis*) of his product. In this way the Platonic world of ideas is located in the opening words of the Bible. It might seem strange that one can speak of the creation of eternal and unchangeable entities such as ideas. Creation must here be understood in an non-material and ontological sense, on an analogy with Plato's presentation of the ideas as deriving their being from the Good in book 7 of the *Republic*. God as Being is wholly transcendent. Philo even goes so far as to say that God is superior to the ideas of goodness and beauty (*On the Creation of the Cosmos* 8). He thus deliberately adjusts Plato's theory of the Idea of the Good in a theocentric direction.

The question may be asked how we should conceive of God as creator if he is wholly transcendent. As we might expect, creative activity belongs to the domain of God's Powers or God's Logos. If one would want to have the doctrine of creation in a nutshell, Philo writes, "one might say that the noetic cosmos (of day one) is none other than the Logos of God while he is engaged in his creative task" (24). We note that Philo does not dissociate God from the creative task and attribute it solely to his Logos. This would surely endanger Philo's conviction that God is unique. But all is not as clear as we might like. We would like to press Philo further on this issue. Should we conclude that God's creative activity does not exhaust the fullness of his Being (a Jewish approach)? Or is it better to argue that in his essence (which is unknowable for us) God transcends all relation to the created realm so that one can hardly call him a creator (a Platonist view)? Some tensions between Philo's Judaism and his Platonism seem to come into view here.

Another area in which Philo is less clear than we would like is his views on the role of matter. In sound Platonist fashion, matter is regarded as the source of disorder and evil, although not as the direct source of the worst kind of evil, which is the moral evil of the wicked soul. But where does matter come from? Is it created by God, or is it a principle independent of him? Philo does not tell us in his commentary on the creation account, and elsewhere he appears to vacillate. It is safest to say, in my view, that he was still too much the prisoner of the Parmenidean assumption that nothing can come out of nothing, and so was unable to face up to the full consequences of a doctrine of creation *ex nihilo*. This was a development that did not take place until Christian theology faced the challenge of the Gnostic movement more than a century later.

In spite of these problems, the main direction of Philo's doctrine of creation is clear. All of created reality is dependent for its existence on God the creator. It is impious and wrong-headed to ascribe divinity and eternity to the created universe. The doctrine of creation is a philosophical consequence of the first commandment, which insists on the absolute sovereignty of God (see *On the Special Laws* 1.13–20).

THE NATURE OF HUMANITY

The climax of the Mosaic creation account is the creation of the human being, who is formed on the sixth day. Using an influential phrase, Philo describes him as a 'border-dweller', living on the border of the mortal and the immortal, sharing in mortality on account of his body, but immortal in respect of his mind (*On the Creation of the Cosmos* 135). Philo sets great store by Moses' statement that the human being is created "according to the image of God" (Genesis 1:26–7). The term 'image' (*eikōn*) is a technical philosophical term, indicating a resemblance such as between a model and a copy. Philo interprets the text as indicating a double relation: the human being is created as image not directly of God, but of his Logos, who in turn is an image of God himself (but surely in a somewhat different sense). In what way can the human being be said to resemble God and his Logos? It is certainly not in terms of his body or lower soul with its passions. Humanity resembles God through its rational soul or mind (*nous*), which is also its immortal part. This interpretation of 'man according to the image' is a third pillar of Philo's thought. Without it he would not be in a position to credit such an exalted status to Moses, as the philosopher *par excellence*. Moses is able to contemplate the realm of incorporeal ideas because of the 'image-nature' of his mind, by which he is related to the divine Logos who embraces those ideas.

Arguably it is in this doctrine that we observe the strongest influence of Greek philosophy on Philo's thought. In the Greek Bible (Septuagint) a conviction of human immortality is only to be found in some very late books, but Philo is convinced of its truth. In Greek philosophical thought ever since Socrates, reason had been the hallmark of the philosopher and the sage. Philo gladly takes this over, but gives it a strongly theocentric direction. If humanity's goal is to 'become like unto God' (the Platonic formulation of the *telos*), then this can take place on account of the human being's 'image-nature', that is, through the powers of its intellect. It is in gaining knowledge of God that the human being becomes like God. This was the nature of Moses' quest, even if in the nature of things the ultimate goal of knowledge of God's essence could not be reached. It could not be reached because assimilation would have to become identity, which is impossible on account of the gap between creator and creature (an instructive contrast can be drawn with Plotinus here).

There are other strands in Philo's views on the nature of the human being that we cannot discuss in detail. For example, he has to make room for the Stoicizing concept of divine spirit (*pneuma*) on account of the important text Genesis 2:7, in which God is said to 'inbreathe' the human being with his spirit (a fascinating passage on this is found in *The Worse Attacks the Better* 79–90). The soul is sometimes regarded as consisting of eight parts (Stoic), sometimes as tripartite (Platonic). Philo also uses the concept of a blood-soul, suggested by Leviticus 17:11. The most important division, however, is that between irrational and rational, mortal and immortal. For this dualism Philo is above all indebted to Plato and the Platonist tradition. In his view, however, its origin is to be located in the Mosaic text.

ETHICS

It might be thought that our presentation of Philo's thought so far is rather theoretical. This can be justified in the context of the history of philosophy, which is our primary focus. But there is a danger that we stray too far from the content of much of Philo's writing. As we noted above, Philo is a master of the allegorical method. What allegory discovers, especially in the biblical narratives, is the journey of the soul and the struggle between virtue and wickedness. Here the biblical narrative is brought home to the reader. Not every soul can reach the heights of Moses' achievement, but every reader has to live his or her life, and can be encouraged to embark on the philosophic quest, aided – as Philo thinks – by the close relation between this quest and the observance of the Jewish religious customs.

In the formulation of his ethical ideals Philo takes over much from the Stoa (with some mixture of Platonist ideas). The journey of the soul involves various stages. It begins with the struggle against the passions. The learner has to recognize that these passions are brought about by a yielding to the inducements of the senses and of bodily sensuality. As the learner advances, he develops the exercise of reason and embarks on the path of the virtues. He recognizes that, although the body has to be cared for, he must be careful not to let it distract him from his higher goals. The goal towards which he strives is the life of perfection, the life as lived by the wise person (*sophos*). The wise person is characterized by a freedom from all passion (*apatheia*), not in the sense that he has no emotions whatsoever, but in that he has converted his irrational passions into rational emotional states (*eupatheiai*). He does not succumb to irrational pleasure (*hēdonē*), but rather feels the rational state of joy (*chara*). Philo is even prepared to attribute this state to God, who takes enjoyment in his creation (*Questions and Answers on Genesis* 4.188). The ideal of the wise person is lofty and seldom attained. It is represented above all by the lawgiver Moses. For many, the Patriarchs are more accessible symbols of what humanity can reach, and for Philo they represent three aspects of the quest for perfection: Abraham is the learner; Isaac is the man with natural aptitude for the quest; and Jacob is the practiser who never yields in his struggle to reach the goal. The quest for perfection and the ideal of the wise person is the fourth and final pillar of Philo's thought.

The reader may wish to conclude at this point that, in spite of the biblical names, Philo's ethics is wholly Greek. This conclusion might at first be strengthened if we were to examine his doctrine of the virtues. For example, Philo takes the four rivers of Paradise (Genesis 2:10–14) to symbolize the cardinal virtues, practical wisdom, self-mastery, courage and justice (*Allegories of the Laws* 1.63). But if we look more carefully at his pronouncements on the virtues we shall find that there are other elements that betray the influence of Jewish thought. We briefly mention four examples. First, Philo adopts a more positive attitude towards the ideal of repentance (*metameleia*) than is customary in Greek tradition. Secondly, following a strong biblical tradition, he is prepared to attribute the attitude of mercy or pity (*eleos*) both to God and to the wise person (i.e. it is not incompatible with freedom from passion), whereas in Greek thought this feeling is considered either inappropriate for the philosopher (as in the Stoa), or only to be exercised in well-defined circumstances (as in Aristotle). Thirdly, Philo often states that the greatest of all the virtues is piety (*eusebeia*). The reverence and devotion that ought to characterize one's personal relation to God plays a much more dominant role in Philo's thought than in the writings of Greek philosophers. Philo's ethics are fundamentally religious. Fourthly and most strikingly of all, Philo repeatedly emphasizes humanity's essential 'nothingness' (*oudeneia*) in comparison with God. If the human being is to 'know himself' (the old Delphic ideal), he must realize that he is dust and ashes, truly nothing (see *Who is the Heir?* 29). This runs contrary to the Greek philosopher's sense of his own worth, and anticipates the emphasis on humility that will be a prominent theme in Christian ethics.

CONCLUDING REMARKS

Philo's thought is a splendid illustration of the cultural and ideological power of Hellenism. Philo was utterly loyal to the traditions of his own people, and regarded himself as nothing but an expositor of the Law. It is fascinating to observe, however, how the ideals of Greek philosophy have so strongly impressed themselves on his thinking that he feels constrained to locate many of them at the very heart of Scripture. Philo set out to show both the Jews and the Greeks of Alexandria that true wisdom was to be found in the ancient traditions of the Jewish nation. What he found there is arguably at least as much Greek as it is Jewish. As Peder Borgen (1984: 150–54) has emphasized, Philo set out to conquer Hellenism, but he came close to being conquered himself.

Philo's writings also yield valuable evidence on the direction in which philosophy is moving at this time. It is clear that its chief inspiration is Platonic. This comes to the fore in Philo's epistemology, theology and doctrine of creation. The Hellenistic philosophy of immanence has been left behind and a definite shift to a philosophy of transcendence has taken place. This movement will be continued in the thought of Plutarch and in the movement that we now call 'Middle Platonism'. At the same time many themes from Hellenistic philosophy, and especially from the Stoa, are retained and given new shape.

The future of Philo's thought did not lie in Jewish tradition. Soon the rich tradition of Alexandrian Judaism would be swept away in the tide of political turmoil. Later Judaism was not interested in Philo's version of Judaism and condemned him to silence. It is sad to think that the great medieval Jewish philosopher, Maimonides, who also lived in Egypt, probably never heard of his distant predecessor. Philo's future also did not lie in Greek philosophy, which probably took very little notice of him. It was in the Christian tradition that Philo's thought was continued. Christian theologians and exegetes rescued Philo's writings and made good use of them for their own purposes. It occurred first in Alexandria (Pantaenus, Clement, Origen, Didymus), but later spread well beyond Philo's own city (Eusebius, Gregory of Nyssa, Ambrose). These men were particularly interested in the way Philo interpreted the biblical stories and they were intrigued by his theory of the Logos, which bore some suggestive resemblances to the account of the Logos in the Gospel of John.

More than half a century ago the influential Harvard historian of philosophy Harry Wolfson argued that Philo single-handedly changed the course of philosophy and laid the foundations for religious philosophy in the patristic and medieval periods until it was subverted by Spinoza. This claim in its full extent cannot be sustained. As we have seen in this volume there was religious philosophy before Philo, and his subsequent influence was nowhere near as great as Wolfson postulated. But it is true that Philo is the first philosopher to base his philosophy on the acceptance of an authoritative body of scriptural writings. This method of philosophizing was to have a long future. For this reason, Philo occupies an important place in the history of Western religious thought.

FURTHER READING

Borgen, P. 1997. *Philo of Alexandria: An Exegete for His Time*. Leiden: Brill.

Dillon, J. 1996. *The Middle Platonists: A Study of Platonism 80 BC to AD 220*, 2nd edn (esp. 139–83). London: Duckworth.

Mansfeld, J. 1988. "Philosophy in the Service of Scripture: Philo's Exegetical Strategies". In *The Question of "Eclecticism"*, J. Dillon & A. Long (eds), 70–102. Berkeley, CA: University of California Press.

Runia, D. T. 1993. *Philo in Early Christian Literature: A Survey*. Minneapolis, MN: Augsburg Fortress Press.

Runia, D. T. 2001. *Philo On the Creation of the Cosmos according to Moses* (Philo of Alexandria Commentary Series 1). Leiden: Brill.

On CREATION see also Chs 13, 17; Vol. 3, Ch. 9; Vol. 5, Ch. 5. On JUDAISM see also Ch. 10; Vol. 2, Ch. 8; Vol. 3, Ch. 15; Vol. 5, Chs 8, 15. On LOGOS see also Chs 11, 13; Vol. 2, Ch. 19. On *PNEUMA* see also Chs 7, 9, 10. On SCRIPTURE see also Chs 9, 13, 17; Vol. 2, Ch. 19; Vol. 3, Chs 3, 4, 15; Vol. 4, Ch. 3; Vol. 5, Ch. 12.

10

THE APOSTLE PAUL

Stanley K. Stowers

The thought of the apostle Paul (*c.*2 CE–*c.*64 CE) is perhaps the most important early source for the later development of Christian theology. This is because, although occasional pieces, the letters contain explanations, concepts, arguments, narrative fragments, metaphors, ethical teachings and references to practices important for the formation of coherent doctrines about human nature and its transformation, Christ's work, God's judgement and salvation, the character and futures of Jews and Gentiles and so on. The letters of Paul are the earliest Christian writings and predate the canonical gospels from decades to one-half of a century. Moreover, they were written before the epic-making changes that occurred with the destruction of Jerusalem in 70 CE and of Judaism as it had been known. Paul assumed that Judaism and God's temple would go on and understood himself as working as the missionary chosen to bring the message about Jesus Christ to the non-Jewish peoples. The teachings attributed to Jesus in the gospels do not appear or play any role in his letters. Rather, he develops a form of religion based on the role of Christ as an agent of human transformation and part of God's plans for the consummation of history. Thus interpreters have often said that Paul rather than Jesus was the founder of Christianity.

Scholars agree that the letters are the more trustworthy sources for knowledge of Paul and his teachings. Much later legendary sources such as the Acts of the Apostles and the Acts of Paul frequently contradict what is known from the letters and must be used with extreme caution. The question of which letters in the New Testament attributed to Paul are authentic has long been a matter of dispute among scholars, although there is a strong consensus that some are his and that others cannot be. Broad agreement exists that Romans, 1 and 2 Corinthians, Galatians, Philippians, 1 Thesssalonians and Philemon were written by Paul. Likewise, 1 and 2 Timothy and Titus were written by a Paulinist a generation or more after Paul's death. Opinion tilts against the authenticity of Ephesians, but is divided regarding 2 Thessalonians and Colossians. The seven 'undisputed' letters must be the starting-point for understanding Paul's thought.

The Acts of the Apostles claims that Paul came from the city of Tarsus in Cilicia. This is possible, but the letters only give information to place Paul in and around Damascus in the earliest period of his life that they attest. The claim that he studied in Jerusalem with Gamaliel (Acts 22:3) is almost certainly false. Solid information about his education can be deduced from the literary level and rhetorical characteristics of the undisputed letters. He was a native speaker of Greek and shows no sign of knowing Hebrew or Aramaic beyond a few words and phrases that may have been traditional to the early Christ movement. The letters reflect a knowledge of letter-writing practices far above the common level seen in the numerous letters that have survived from Egypt and elsewhere. They also show an extensive knowledge of the Septuagint, the Greek translation of the Hebrew Bible. His writing displays a level of education that roughly equals and reflects the tradition of the Greek *progymnasmata*, the preliminary rhetorical exercises. At least a level of knowledge about Hellenistic philosophical, and especially moral philosophical, teachings that one might expect from a person of modest education in the interconnected cultures of the Roman Empire also appear in the letters.

In contexts where Paul writes polemically against fellow Jewish competitors, he reveals that he came from a Jewish family of the tribe of Benjamin; that he thought of himself as devoted to the Jewish life in a rigorous way; and that he belonged to the school of the Pharisees. Unfortunately, we do not know enough about the Pharisees, their teachings and practices, in spite of later sources that claim their heritage, to know what this meant for Paul. The claim does help us to locate Paul sociologically and intellectually as probably an intellectual specialist of the retainer class that served and advised the traditional ruling elite. Paul's self-described persecution of the followers of Christ probably reflects this role. The most reliable sources depict the Pharisees as a political-religious interest group in Jerusalem and Judea. What it might mean for a person who was raised and educated outside Judea to be a Pharisee remains unclear.

Christian traditions, especially with the influence of Augustine in the West, have come to depict Paul's turn to Christ as a conversion from Judaism to Christianity, or from law to grace. But Paul's own accounts flatly contradict this interpretation and describe a vision of Christ in the language of a prophet's calling or commissioning in the Hebrew Bible (Galatians 1:1, 11–12, 15–16; 1 Corinthians 9:1, 15:8; Philippians 3:5–6). Specifically, Paul claims that Christ told him that he had been chosen from before birth to be the messenger to the Gentiles, the non-Jewish peoples (e.g. Romans 15:15–18). Thus Paul thinks of himself as a latter-day Jonah (and not an Augustine) who has been chosen to play a decisive role at the climax of history. That he describes this call as a total reorientation of his life-course and ambitions has appeared in the context of later Christian assumptions as a conversion from Judaism and a moral-religious turning.

Scholars believe that Paul wrote his extant letters during a roughly fifteen-year period of establishing what he calls assemblies of Christ in Roman Asia and Greece. Because the letters are occasional writings addressed to varied practical and intellectual issues in situations that scholars can only intuit from the letters, it will be useful to first provide a synthetic account of Paul's thought before discussing some individual letters, influences on his thought and his impact on later thinkers. A key interpretive issue that has emerged in recent scholarship is how and when to generalize or universalize Paul's statements. Since he writes to Gentile assemblies (e.g. Romans 1:5–6, 13; Galatians 2:7, 4:8–9; 1 Corinthians 12:2) and never uses the concept of a generic Christianity, but always speaks of Jews and Gentiles in Christ, does much of what he writes apply only to the situation of Gentiles or, as in traditional Christian interpretation, does he always speak universally about 'the Church', Christianity and humanity?

CENTRAL THEMES OF PAUL'S THOUGHT

The one place where the letters define the gospel that Paul taught is Galatians: "Scripture, foreseeing that God would justify the Gentiles out of faithfulness, preached the gospel beforehand to Abraham, namely, 'All of the Gentiles will be blessed in you'" (3:8). The message that Paul taught addressed a particular and a universal problem at the same time by means of what he understood to be God's plan carried out through Jesus Christ's fidelity or faithfulness to that plan. This larger account may be summarized as follows. The peoples of the world have in the distant past turned away from the one true God and creator of the universe and fallen into the worship of idols. Because of this situation, God chose a faithful individual, Abraham, to be the progenitor of a faithful people who would someday be the means for returning and reconciling the disloyal peoples to him. Paul's claim is that Christ was the chosen agent for this reconciliation and he himself the chosen messenger. But God's plans go far beyond bringing the non-Jewish peoples back to the worship of the creator. In the resurrection, God raised Jesus to a new level of existence by endowing him with his own spirit (Romans 1:4, 8:11). This divine *pneuma* – poorly translated as 'spirit' or 'ghost' – of Christ is shared by believers when they are baptized "into Christ" (Galatians 3:26–9, 4:6; Romans 6–8). Participation in Christ through sharing his *pneuma* does several things in Paul's thought.

Paul interprets the promise of blessing for the Gentiles given to Abraham as the gift of the divine *pneuma* (Galatians 3:14). Because they share Christ's *pneuma*, and they are "in Christ", they have contiguity with Abraham who becomes their father (Galatians 3:29). Thus they become sons of God. Paul associates this new status for Gentiles with their being made righteous before God and their reconciliation to him and sanctification. On the level of moral psychology, the *pneuma* empowers reason to subdue the attempts of emotion and desire to do evil so that individuals can do what God's law requires while also being freed from the condemnation to which Gentiles were formerly subject under the law (Romans 8:1–11; Galatians 5:18). The divine *pneuma* also intermixes or connects with the natural human *pneuma* and facilitates communication with God (1 Corinthians 2:10–11; Romans 8:26–7). In this current age, those who are "in Christ" and share his *pneuma* still have normal fleshly bodies that are fragile, subject to passions and desire, and are mortal. But this will change after Christ returns from heaven where he rules with God. This weak ontological condition was inherited from Adam. There is no idea of a return to a pre-fall state in Paul's letters. Christ became the last Adam in the resurrection by receiving a perfected "heavenly" body consisting of divine *pneuma* (1 Corinthians 15:44–50; Romans 5:12–19). He is thus the pioneer of a new order of existence, sons of God, for all of those who are in him and who have been "conformed to his image" (e.g. Romans 8:29–30). If any person is in Christ, the person is a new creation (2 Corinthians 5:17). Owing to the idea of the extension of Christ's *pneuma*, Paul can speak not only of those who have been baptized as in Christ, but also of Christ being in the one baptized (Romans 8:10; 2 Corinthians 13:3–4; Galatians 2:20). This explains the terminology of participation with Christ such as "to suffer with", "be crucified with", "buried with", "raised with", "glorified with" and "to rule with".

The Western Christian interpretation of Paul since Augustine has often seen the letters as the supreme source for doctrines of total moral–ontological sinfulness or total depravity. This novel understanding and radical change from most of ancient Christianity became the centerpiece of the Protestant Reformation along with doctrines of radical grace. Eastern forms of Christianity maintained continuity with the mainstream of thinkers in the ancient Churches in their interpretations of Paul. This Western understanding runs together three areas of Paul's thinking that need to be kept separate, even if related, and harmonizes them into a theory of fallen human nature. The three are Paul's writings about moral psychology, the origins of sin and the current apocalyptic world situation. Sin began with Adam's disobedience and universal human mortality resulted (Romans 5:12–13; 1 Corinthians 15:21). Just as believers participate in Christ by sharing his *pneuma*, all descendants of Adam participate in him by sharing the 'soulish' form of existence made of inferior earthy matter (1 Corinthians 15:42–9). Human bodies are thus made of an inferior form of flesh (1 Corinthians 15:50; cf. 38–41). Not only are fleshly bodies mortal and subject to decay, but they also host emotions and desires that are prone to acting against the direction of reason or mind (Romans 6:12–14, 7:5–24). Paul's moral psychology is basically Platonic and resembles that of his contemporary fellow Jew, Philo of Alexandria, and later Platonists such as Plutarch and Galen. The core self that naturally wants to do good and to obey the law is reasoning or mind. In a typically later Platonic way, Paul associates the emotions or passions and desire with the body and its flesh. In the person who exhibits complete moral failure, a failure that is typical of Gentiles (Romans 1:18–32, 7:7–25; 1 Thessalonians 4:3–6), reason wants to keep God's law but cannot because it has been conquered and is ruled by emotion and desire.

Paul's statements about the origins of sin and the state of the person who is under the control of emotion and desire should not be blended together and then harmonized with statements about the current sinfulness of Jews and Gentiles and the role of their disobedience in God's plans. This view, however, is controversial and many scholars still take the language of sin in Romans 1–3 and 4–8 to be about an Adamic fall and a uniform human nature, even if they take the statements in 9–11 about Israel's disobedience to be historical claims. In traditional readings, Paul merely uses his discussions of the failings of Jews and Gentiles as examples or proofs for the universal condition of fallenness and the depraved human nature. A newer view reads Paul as describing an apex or limit of sinfulness, an idea found in Jewish apocalyptic literature, so that both Romans 1–4 and 9–11 address the futures of Jews and Gentiles in light of God's judgement and salvation. The topic of sin appears almost exclusively in Romans, although a doctrine of sinful human nature has traditionally been a presupposition for reading the letters in general and paired with corresponding schemes of salvation. One very popular recent variation claims that Paul draws on apocalyptic literature in thinking of sin and even law as demonic powers that keep humans from doing the good. That view, however, has taken two lethal blows in recent scholarship. First, apocalyptic literature provides no parallels to the idea of sin as a power or of evil beings as keeping human beings in bondage against their wills. Secondly, the powerful arguments for construing Paul's moral psychology in Romans 6–8 and elsewhere as basically Platonic permit an alternative explanation for Paul's language and metaphors about sin and the law.

Paul's writings about the law have proved very difficult for interpreters. On the one hand, certain statements in Romans and Galatians seem to be very negative about the law and even seem to associate it with sin. The law provoked sin, made sin worse, led to condemnation, held people captive and is the power of sin (Romans 5:20, 7:5–6, 8–11; 1 Corinthians 15:56). On the other hand, Paul says that the law is *pneumatikos* ('spiritual', or concerns the *pneuma* of God); is holy, just and good; supports God's promises; and was intended to lead to life (Romans 7:7, 12–14). There is wide agreement that by 'the law' Paul means the Books of Moses, the first five books of the Hebrew Bible, and not some idea of a general moral law or moral sense. Interpreters have dealt with these contradictory-sounding statements in many ways. Scholarship in the past thirty years has severely critiqued many of the traditional approaches to this problem. This criticism has been aimed especially at the ideas that Paul's statements oppose an imagined Jewish legalism and perfectionism, posit a distinction between ritual and moral law, and treat the law as a demonic power. The Augustinian–Lutheran tradition has held that for human beings to think that they can do good or keep the law is the essence of evil. To believe that they are totally sinful and can only beg God's mercy in the face of attempting to keep the law is faith. The most important purpose of the law is to drive people to see their sinfulness and to seek God's mercy.

This latter view has been strongly criticized over the past several decades and has led to different interpretations. One solution stresses that Romans and

Galatians, where most of these statements about the law occur, are explicitly addressed to Gentiles and have their non-covenantal relationship to the law in view. The law contains, among other things, teachings about morals and the one true God that are applicable to all peoples, but also condemns and curses those who live in contradiction to those teachings. Paul draws on Greek moral-philosophical ideas about the state of complete moral failure, the condition of one who is the opposite of the sage. Such a person by definition cannot do good, and moral teachings and law are of no help for that person's condition. This condition is precisely the dilemma of idolatrous Gentiles before they are in Christ and share his *pneuma* (Romans 1:18–32, 7:7–25).

Scholars agree that the relationship of Gentiles to the Judean law was a highly controversial matter among followers of Christ and that Paul staked out a position opposed by many. The position had two major components: in the climactic apocalyptic time after Christ's death, no person would be considered right before God by merely doing the law, and Gentile assemblies did not have to keep the law. Some of those who opposed Paul's law-free gospel to the Gentiles thought that Gentiles who had accepted Christ should follow the whole law like Jews and that males should even be circumcised.

If no one in the apocalyptic period after Christ's death and resurrection could be considered righteous before God by doing God's law, how could they be made righteous? The answer to this question depends on how one translates an expression that plays an important role in parts of Romans and Galatians where Paul discusses his gospel to the Gentiles. The past twenty-five years have seen a vigorous debate about *pistis Christou* and related expressions. The Greek genitive case can be taken in two ways and translated either as 'faith in Christ' or as 'the faith(fullness) of Christ'. The implications for understanding Paul's message are enormous. In the former case, emphasized in the West's Augustinian–Lutheran tradition, Paul holds that human salvation from the ontological sinfulness of the Fall depends on the individual's act of faith. Paul's message was that instead of the old, flawed Jewish way of being saved by doing the law, a person would be saved by believing in Christ. God's different historic relationship to Jews and Gentiles makes no difference. Salvation concerns a uniform human plight and a uniform universal solution. On the second understanding of the genitive case, Paul is saying that in the apocalyptic time of crisis and judgement after Christ, the salvation of the Gentiles (and Jews) is based on Christ's faithful life and death on their behalf. Salvation does not hinge on any human doing or believing, but on the benefits of what Christ and, before him, Abraham did. Just as all Jews receive the status and blessings of being Jewish merely by being a descendant of Abraham on the basis of God's promise to the patriarch and Abraham's faithful acceptance of the promise, so Gentiles become descendants of Abraham and children of God by being in Christ. Although he says little about it, since he writes to Gentiles, Paul also expects Jews who are already children of God to accept what God has done through Christ and to receive the *pneuma* of God.

There is broad agreement that Paul's understandings of God and Christ do not fit the standards of orthodoxy established in the controversies and councils of the fourth and fifth centuries and later. Paul is unlikely to have held the idea that God created the world *ex nihilo* ('out of nothing') and probably held normal Jewish views that followed Genesis in having God create the world out of pre-existing matter. There is certainly nothing like the doctrine of the Trinity. Above all, Paul's thought about God is shaped by Jewish scriptural narratives. God is Lord of all the peoples and of the descendents of Abraham, Isaac and Jacob. But he can also speak of God in abstract language used by Stoic and other philosophers (1 Corinthians 8:6).

Whether Paul has an idea of Christ's pre-existence and incarnation is a controversial question. The passages that have traditionally been used to support these two ideas can be explained in other ways that better fit contemporary Jewish thought. If he did have something like these ideas, they are certainly unlike the later orthodox versions. He may have held something like the idea that God's *pneuma* was destined for Jesus Christ and was ordained or prepared beforehand. In Romans 1:3–4, he writes that Christ was of the seed of David in terms of the flesh and was appointed son of God by the power of the holy *pneuma* in his resurrection from death. The letters tell us almost nothing about Jesus. Paul sees his importance entirely in his faithful death, resurrection and heavenly career. The letters describe Christ's post-resurrection work as that of cosmic divine warrior and ruler on behalf of God. He is not God or equal to God, but is second highest in the creation. Every knee will bow to Christ and every tongue will confess him (Philippians 2:10–11). The clearest text is 1 Corinthians 15:24–8. Christ is the first fruit of the resurrection leading to a general resurrection or a resurrection of the righteous.

> Next comes the fulfillment, when he delivers the kingdom to God the Father, when he has destroyed every ruler, and every authority and power. For he must reign until he has placed all his enemies under his feet. The last enemy that will be destroyed is death. For "he [God] has made subject all things under his feet." But when it says, "all things are made subject," it is clear that the one who made things subject is not included in the subjection. And when all things are subjected to him, then even the son himself will be made subject to the one who made all things subject to him so that God may be all in all.
>
> (1 Corinthians 15:24–8)

Much of Paul's writing occupies itself with moral exhortation and the discussion of moral-religious behaviour. One tendency of scholarship since the first half of the twentieth century has been to stress that Paul's ethical thought is shaped above all by the idea that Christ's return was very near so that activities presupposing ongoing life were to be curtailed or modified. While the letters certainly appeal to this eschatology to urge intensity of adherence to Paul's teachings, the view fails to notice that Paul gives positive content to moral teachings and reasons for these that appeal to criteria typical in Jewish and broader Hellenistic thought, especially in practical philosophical literature. Marriage, for instance, is neither a good nor an evil but is to be judged by two factors (1 Corinthians 7:1–20): the way that it affects the ultimate criterion of devotion to Christ (7:7–8, 17–20, 32–5); and its value in aiding the control of sexual desire (7:5–9). The nearness of the end intensifies consideration of these values (7:28–31).

THE LETTERS

A letter has been aptly described as one half of a conversation. This comparison only partly fits Paul's letters, however, because they are highly rhetorical pieces meant to be read before audiences that testify to Paul's intellectual dominance in this 'conversation'. The idea of a conversation does point to the fact that much information important for understanding the letters was implicit between Paul and his audiences and therefore lost to us. In what follows are brief comments on the form, contents and arguments of four of the undisputed letters that represent the early, middle and late phases of his extant letter writing.

The earliest existing letter, 1 Thessalonians, was written about 50 CE to Gentiles that Paul and his associates had recently attracted to Christ. It is packed with well-known rhetorical features from a tradition of Greek moral exhortation. Most of this ethical instruction is familiar in terms of Paul's larger culture, but his claim that Gentiles are inherently controlled by sexual passion would have been odd (4:3–8). One section (4:13–5:11) responds to the dismay of these Thessalonians when some of their number died and, in the view of these believers, had missed out on Christ's return from heaven. Here we get important information about Paul's expectation of Christ's imminent return, his belief that the dead in Christ would be resurrected first, and many details about the apocalyptic context of his thought. A decade or so later in Romans, Paul's expectation of Christ's return seems more distant.

Scholars often date the Corinthian correspondence to the years 52–5. The exchange involved at least one letter from the Corinthians to Paul, oral communication from them and at least three letters from Paul. First Corinthians is a letter of admonition and advice that ostensibly aims to address divisions among the Corinthian believers and give advice on a number of issues. After mentioning factions loyal to different teachers and teachings (1:10), the letter launches into an eloquent discourse about God's wisdom versus human wisdom (1:18–2:16). The two are incommensurable. Paul's wisdom is secret knowledge that comes from God's *pneuma* (2:6–16). The letter takes up a number of issues under the rubric of freedom and self-restraint: incest (5:1–13); lawsuits (6:1–11); prostitution (6:12–20); sexual activity, marriage, passion and related issues (ch. 7); food offered to other gods/idols (ch. 8); Paul's own example of self-restraint for the gospel (ch. 9);

porneia and idolatry (10:1–11:1); women and head coverings (11:1–16); divisions and the Lord's Meal (11:17–34); and the orderly use of certain pneumatic powers and meetings (chs 12–14). Many of these relate to Paul's concept of *porneia*, which literally means prostitution, but in his usage means disloyalty towards God by sexual activity that he connects with his claim that Gentiles worship false gods. Chapter 15 contains very important information about Paul's physical and cosmological views as it discusses the nature of the resurrection body.

Galatians and Romans are the letters that have extended discussions of God's *pneuma* and faith/faithfulness. This is because they both explicitly address the questions of the justification and salvation of the Gentiles. Only a few remarks about Galatians are possible here. It is a letter of strong rebuke and of advice focusing on the argument that Gentiles in Christ should not adopt the law as a Jew would. They are saved and justified entirely by the faithful life, death and resurrection of Jesus Christ that has brought them God's *pneuma*. That *pneuma* makes them sons of God and heirs of Abraham (3:6–4:7). In this way and not through adopting the law they are united with Jews and all who share in God's *pneuma* (3:19–29). On the negative side, these formerly pagan addressees (4:10–11) of the letter were already under the regime of God's law that justly condemned them and made them subject to punishment for their moral-religious rebellion (3:10–14, 19–22). The law was never meant to bring the Gentiles back to God, but rather it is the faithfulness of Christ that is to redeem the Gentiles. Adopting the law means regressing from the freedom of the *pneuma* to their former state of enslavement to the flesh (cf. 4:8–5:26).

Written in or near 58, Romans has been by far the most important letter for Christian theology and for Paul's philosophy of religion. In the Western reading since Augustine, the letter first proves that all human beings are inheritors of the Adamic fall and then argues that God has now offered salvation no longer through the law, but on the basis of the believer's faith. Chapters 5–8 then work out the moral implications of this regime of grace and Chapters 9–11 is an appendix about Jewish unbelief. Scholarship of the past forty years has found this interpretation deeply flawed. In a more plausible reading, the letter addresses Gentiles and their salvation, but relates their salvation to the law and the salvation of God's people, the Jews. God's apocalyptic anger is justly aimed at all, including those peoples who were not directly given the law, because the true nature of the one transcendent creator-God was clear to human perception in the nature of the creation (1:18–20). But human beings somehow rejected this knowledge and adopted the worship of various forms of 'idol worship' such as the anthropomorphic forms of the Greeks and Romans and the animal forms of the Egyptians (1:21–3). It is unclear whether Paul knows that, for example, Greeks and Romans distinguished the human-made representations from the deities, or whether he simply chooses to misrepresent their religions. God punished these non-Jewish peoples by allowing their mental processes to become irrational so that they came to be dominated by their appetites and emotions (1:21–32). Chapters 2–4 take the form of discussions between Paul and an imaginary Gentile (2:1–16) and a Jewish teacher (2:17–4:25), with techniques taught in the standard rhetorical education and important in the style of moral instruction known as the 'diatribe'. In the discussion with both, Paul argues from God's justice and impartiality that both Jews and Gentiles are liable to God's judgement based on the standards of the law. The Jewish teacher cannot hope to make Gentiles right with God through the ameliorative effects of the law. In the current historical moment Gentiles are sinners because of their idolatry and deep immorality (1:18–2:16), but the Jewish people are equally sinful before God because they have failed in their mission to the Gentiles (2:17–3:20). Chapters 9–11 will reveal that this Jewish rejection of Christ is part of God's plan to allow an opportunity for the Gentiles to turn to him (esp. 11:7–32). "When the full number" of Gentiles have turned, then the Jews will repent and "all Israel will be saved" (11:25–26). Gentile believers should not arrogantly presume that God will favour them and not keep his promises to Israel, the Jews.

Paul's complex argument against Gentiles finding salvation in the law or in any way except through Christ and his *pneuma* continues in Chapters 5–8 with a focus on the law and gentile moral psychology. The law condemned human sinfulness, but did not affect the Adamic punishment by death (5:12–14). Christ brought an answer to both apart from the law (5:15–21). Specifically, those who are baptized into Christ die to sin which means freedom from domination by the passion and desire to which Gentiles were sentenced for idolatry (6:1–7:6). Those "in Christ" can now serve God instead of sin. Chapter 7 uses a Platonic moral psychology to argue that this state of extreme immorality exemplified by the Gentiles (1:24–32) makes the attempt to keep the law both impossible and even an enticement to further sin. In this condition, reason that naturally desires to do the good and to keep God's law has been made captive and has been killed by passion and desire. The law is not to blame, but it cannot help. Only Christ and the divine *pneuma* that raised him from the dead can make the morally dead live again (8:1–11). Paul describes this renewal as Christ's *pneuma* engendering a mode of thinking that is radically different from the thinking that belonged to the desires and passions of the flesh. The result is a new order of beings, children of God formed in Christ's image and living in a renewed cosmos (8:1–11).

INTELLECTUAL INFLUENCES ON PAUL

That Paul's thought is Jewish finds unanimity among interpreters, but for more than one hundred years Pauline scholarship has been steadily building the case that he is also the heir to Greek thought in certain areas. Unfortunately there has been a tendency to posit a unique Jewish essence always beneath what is treated as a superficial Greek 'mode of expression'. This Christian and Jewish ideology of uniqueness does not survive critical historical scrutiny. Not only were the quite varied Jewish traditions always partly constituted by continuing streams of 'outside' influences (e.g. 'Canaanite', Babylonian, Persian, Greek), but Jews were no different than others in inhabiting the broader cultural inheritances that they experienced as taken for granted.

At the very centre of Paul's religious thought are narratives about the creation of the world, the origin of various peoples, their sinful revolt, the character of the Israelite God, the history of Israel, and predictions and intimations about the world's future. Even in the rendering of Hebrew Scripture into Greek, translation into Greek conceptions occurred. Moreover, Paul was heir to centuries of Jewish culture, both in and around Judea and in the Eastern Mediterranean, that had sometimes enthusiastically identified Jewish and Greek culture and at other times had assimilated elements with resistance, but was always unaware of the origins of much of its background understanding. Examples of the former that at certain points show strong similarities to Paul's thought are in the writings of Philo of Alexandria and the *Wisdom of Solomon*.

Another tradition exhibited in the letters is that of apocalyptic. Writings in this tradition draw on various cultural codes from the Mediterranean and West Asia, but took a distinctive Jewish form as, for example, in certain writings among the Dead Sea Scrolls and a number of apocalypses. So in Paul's letters one finds appeals to mysteries, visions and revelations, and a strong expectation of a world and a life to come. His ideas of a present evil age and a coming final judgement also find their closest parallels in this literature. The narrative of events from Jesus' death to his return from heaven and activity as God's warrior against the world's evils fits into an apocalyptic framework. Paul understands Jesus' resurrection as the initial instance of the more general resurrection of the dead, and thus as a sign that the climactic events described in apocalyptic literature had begun. These events included an apex of sinfulness and a time of woes.

Scholarship has detailed an extensive list of connections between the letters and more practical, rhetorical and less technical traditions from Hellenistic philosophy. These include the style of the moral-philosophical literature known as the diatribe, various forms of moral exhortation, discussions about how the teacher should find financial support, the endurance of hardships as signs of the philosopher, particular ethical concepts, and practices of mutual moral education. Some of these issues show contacts with Cynic philosophy.

But more substantive influences appear in the areas of moral psychology, the structure of ethical thought, and the conceptions of certain moral qualities, including self-mastery and cosmic–physical notions. These areas have clear connections with Stoic and later Platonic teachings. While one scholar has made a vigorous case that Paul's moral psychology is Stoic, a decisive case has been made that in Romans 7 the apostle displays the divided self of later Platonism. The core self that Paul calls the mind, reason or the inner person should control the emotions and appetites that belong to the body. There are many examples of philosophers and moralists from later Hellenistic and Roman times combining a Platonic divided moral psychology with elements from Stoic ethics.

At the centre of Paul's ethical thought is the Stoic-like idea that there is only one good – commitment to God/Christ – and that other commonly supposed goods are indifferent and relative to the one good. Paul, like his Jewish contemporary Philo, uses the technical Stoic term 'natural moral functions' (*ta kathekonta*; Romans 1:28). Paul's cosmos and human microcosm with a hierarchy of interactive substances is broadly Hellenistic, but the role of divine *pneuma* is quite Stoic-like. All human beings have *pneuma* that is the stuff/power of their mental abilities. The *pneuma* of God is a perfect and more powerful form of *pneuma*. All human beings can share a portion of God's *pneuma*, presumably as with the Stoics, by extension across the cosmos. Human and divine *pneuma* seem able to blend as in the Stoic theory of blending (*krasis*). In Stoic thought, *pneuma* was a body, meaning that it occupied space or had extension. Paul's claim that the resurrection body was to be a 'pneumatic body' makes perfect sense in Stoic theory. There are, of course, many differences. Stoicism combined theism and pantheism. Each cosmic cycle was a creation of and overseen by God or Zeus, but God was also the active principle in the form of *pneuma* in the lower cosmos that gave rational order (form) and powers of activity to the whole world. This general Stoic role of divine *pneuma* does not appear in the letters. Paul does not treat the divine *pneuma* as a kind of independent being, spirit or 'person' as later Christianity often does.

PAUL'S LEGACY

Paul's thought seamlessly combines Jewish traditions with elements of Greek philosophy in developing his ideas about the significance and future role of Jesus Christ and God's *pneuma*. In combining Jewish traditions, especially through interpretation of the Septuagint, and elements from Greek philosophy, his approach became a model for later thinkers in ancient Christianity. Writers such as Valentinus, Clement of Alexandria, Justin Martyr, Irenaeus, Tertullian, Origen, Eusebius and Arius follow Paul in this approach and appealed to his authority. With Augustine in the fifth century, the Western and Eastern traditions of interpreting Paul began to diverge in major ways. In the Eastern tradition, Paul became and remained a teacher of graced ascetic self-mastery and of the goal of divinization (e.g. ontological transformation by God's *pneuma*). At the same time, doctrines of the Trinity, the incarnation and the return to Paradise provided a transforming framework for Paul's thought for both East and West. After Augustine, the West struggled with ideas of divine determination versus free will regarding human nature and the Christian life, and came to focus on sin and its relation to Jesus' death. Passages that featured a core self and the struggle with passions and desire together with those about identification with Christ and Paul's radical self-understanding became the focus of a developing religious interiority that played a significant role in modern ideas of subjectivity.

FURTHER READING

Engberg-Pedersen, T. 2000. *Paul and the Stoics*. Louisville, KY: Westminster John Knox.
Engberg-Pedersen, T. (ed.) 2001. *Paul Beyond the Hellenism/Judaism Divide*. Louisville, KY: Westminster John Knox.
Gager, J. 2000. *Reinventing Paul*. New York: Oxford University Press.
Hodge, C. 2007. *If Sons, Then Heirs: A Study of Kinship and Ethnicity in the Letters of Paul*. New York: Oxford University Press.
Malherbe, A. 1989. *Paul and the Popular Philosophers*. Minneapolis, MN: Augsburg Fortress.
Meeks, W. 1983. *The First Urban Christians: The Social World of the Apostle Paul*. New Haven, CT: Yale University Press.
Meeks, W. & J. Fitzgerald (eds) 2007. *The Writings of Saint Paul*, 2nd edn. New York: W. W. Norton.
Sampley, P. (ed.) 2003. *Paul and the Greco-Roman World* (esp. 524–50). Harrisburg, PA: Trinity Press International.
Sanders, E. 1977. *Paul and Palestinian Judaism*. Philadelphia, PA: Fortress Press.
Stowers, S. 1994. *A Rereading of Romans: Justice, Jews and Gentiles*. New Haven, CT: Yale University Press.
Stowers, S. 2008. "What is Pauline Participation in Christ?". In *Redefining First-Century Jewish and Christian Identities: Essays in Honor of Ed Parish Sanders*, F. Udoh, S. Heschel, M. Chancey & G. Tatum (eds), 352–71. Notre Dame, IN: University of Notre Dame Press.
Stowers, S. forthcoming. "Paul as Hero of Subjectivity". In *Paul and the Philosophers*, H. de Vries & W. Blanton (eds). Chicago, IL: University of Chicago Press.
Wasserman, E. 2008. *The Death of the Soul in Romans 7: Sin, Death, and the Law in Light of Hellenistic Moral Psychology*, Wissenschaftliche Untersuchungen zum Neuen Testament 2(256). Tübingen: Mohr Siebeck.

On CHRISTIANITY see also Chs 14, 17, 18; Vol. 5, Ch. 12. On CHRIST see also Vol. 2, Ch. 3; Vol. 4, Ch. 3. On JUDAISM see also Ch. 9; Vol. 2, Ch. 8; Vol. 3, Ch. 15; Vol. 5, Chs 8, 15. On *PNEUMA* see also Chs 7, 9. On SALVATION see also Ch. 13; Vol. 2, Ch. 3; Vol. 4, Ch. 19. On SIN see also Ch. 13; Vol. 3, Ch. 4.

11

PLUTARCH OF CHAERONEIA

John Dillon

Plutarch of Chaeroneia, Platonist philosopher, biographer and antiquarian, was born to a family of local aristocrats in the small town of Chaeroneia in Boeotia in about 45 CE. He studied philosophy in Athens under Ammonius, a Platonist philosopher from Egypt, who had settled in Athens and had become prominent in Athenian society. He travelled widely around the Mediterranean, visiting Asia Minor and Egypt, and made a number of visits to Rome, beginning in the 90s, where he gave lectures and became acquainted with many prominent Romans, including Q. Sosius Senecio and L. Mestrius Florus (whose name he adopted on becoming a Roman citizen). In later years he retired to Chaeroneia, where he formed a philosophical circle and composed most of his works. He was also closely connected with Delphi, of whose priesthood he was a member. In his old age, he was bestowed by the Emperor Hadrian with the honorary position of Procurator of Achaea. He died about 120 CE.

Plutarch left a vast body of work, much of which has survived (although his more technical philosophical works – of which a list has been preserved – have been lost). His most famous work is the *Parallel Lives*, in which he presents for comparison a series of lives of distinguished Greeks and Romans, but we also have a large collection of *Moral Essays*, including some important dialogues, such as *On Isis and Osiris* (hereafter *De Is.*), *On the E at Delphi* (hereafter *De E*), *On the Oracles at Delphi*, *On Delays in the Divine Punishment*, *On the Daemon of Socrates* (hereafter *De genio*), and *On the Face on the Moon* (hereafter *De facie*). His nine books of *Table Talk* also contain much of interest, as do essays such as *On Moral Virtue* and *On the Creation of the Soul in the Timaeus*.

Plutarch's variety of Platonism grew out of the various developments in Platonism that had occurred over the century or so before his birth, and in particular the developments associated with the names of Antiochus of Ascalon and Eudorus of Alexandria, who, between them, caused the Platonic tradition to embrace many aspects of both Stoicism and Aristotelianism, as well as, in Eudorus' case, significant aspects of the Pythagorean tradition. What may appear to us, therefore, as 'eclecticism' would be taken by Plutarch rather as the assumption into Platonism of certain formulations from these other traditions that did no more than illuminate various essentially Platonic intuitions. In his ethics and his logic, Plutarch inclines to Aristotelianism, while in certain aspects of his physics (notably, in the *logos*-theory that can be discerned in his essay *On Isis and Osiris*) he seems indebted to Stoicism. We shall see at various points also evidence of Pythagorean influence. His early interest in number symbolism (*De E* 387F), as well as his youthful objection to meat-eating, as evidenced by his early double essay *On the Eating of Flesh*, and his sympathy with animals and championing of their rationality, in the essay on *The Cleverness of Animals* and the dialogue *That Irrational Animals Use Reason*, seem to betray a period of more enthusiastic Pythagoreanism before, as he puts it himself in the dialogue *De E* (387F), he learned moderation on "entering the Academy".

In this chapter, some attention will be paid to Plutarch's ethics, but most to his metaphysics. His views on logic, such as they were, are not relevant to our theme.

ETHICS

The telos, or 'end of goods'

For Plutarch, as for all Middle Platonists of whom we have knowledge subsequent to Eudorus, the supreme object of human existence is 'likeness to God' (*homoiosis theói*), not, as for Antiochus (following the Stoics), 'conformity with Nature'. We find this expressed well in a passage of the dialogue *On Delays in the Divine Punishment* (550D), which begins by quoting Plato, *Theaetetus* 176e, and continues by summarizing Plato's encomium of sight in *Timaeus* 47a–c. It is through our eyes, rather than by means of our intellect, that Plutarch says that this likeness is to be achieved. The eyes, however, are obviously only the agents of the intellect in this matter, as we can see by comparing with this passage his remarks at the beginning of *De Is.* (351C–D), where he specifies that God grants us insight and intelligence (*nous kai phronesis*), which is his special characteristic, in order that we may assimilate ourselves to him. This position would doubtless have been developed further in the lost work *What is the End according to Plato?* (Lamprias Catalogue no. 177).

The virtues

On the subject of virtue and happiness, Plutarch inclines on the whole to the more 'broadminded' ethical position of Antiochus of Ascalon, as against the degree of Stoic–Pythagorean asceticism observable in such thinkers as Eudorus and Philo of Alexandria. Significantly, his terminology in this area is Aristotelian rather than Stoic.

In his essay *On Moral Virtue* we find a useful statement of his ethical theory. Probably a relatively early work, it takes the form of an attack on the Stoic, and in particular Chrysippan, position that the soul is unitary, and that there is no such thing as a distinct irrational part. Moral virtue, he specifies at the beginning (440D), in conformity with Aristotelian doctrine (cf. *Nicomachean Ethics* I, 1103a3ff.), is to be distinguished from theoretical virtue, in that it is concerned with emotion (*pathos*) as its matter and reason (*logos*) as its form, whereas theoretical virtue is concerned solely with the rational part of the soul. In what follows (441E–442C), he traces the development of true ethical doctrine from Pythagoras down, first, to Plato, and then to Aristotle, all of whom recognize that the soul is not unitary, but bipartite. This allows Plutarch to adopt Aristotelian ethics unreservedly, in order to combat the Stoics. His doctrine, in fact, is taken from the *Nicomachean Ethics*, particularly book II.5–7, the theory of the mean being expounded at 444C–445A, with much elaboration.

A topic not discussed in this essay is the status of the three levels of good – the psychical, the corporeal and the external – and their relation to the *telos*. Plutarch does, however, as a Platonist with Peripatetic sympathies, favour 'moderation of the passions' (*metriopatheia*) over their extirpation (*apatheia*) (451B–452C). It is interesting to note how, in the process of stating this position (451B–C), he makes use of what we would regard as a piece of Stoic terminology, but which he takes pleasure in using against them – the fourfold distinction of types of combination, cohesion (*hexis*), natural growth (*physis*), irrational soul and rational soul – to argue that an organism that possesses both the lower and higher types, as does the human being, must possess those in between; that is to say, if one possesses cohesion, natural growth and rationality, one must also possess the passionate and irrational soul.

Plutarch does in fact also hold that all three levels of good contribute to the *telos*, or to happiness. We find him in another polemical anti-Stoic treatise (*On Common Notions* 1060cff.) attacking Chrysippus for not admitting bodily and external goods as forming an essential part of happiness, although nature herself commends them to us (cf. also fr. 144 Sandbach, from an admittedly rather rhetorical lost work *In Defense of Beauty*). So he comes across to us as a fairly thoroughgoing Peripateticizer in ethics, although his true views are frequently obscured in his more popular ethical treatises, where the tradition that he is following is predominantly Cynic–Stoic.

PHYSICS

First principles: 'God', Monad and Dyad

Plutarch's view of God – that is, of the active, or 'male', first principle – is very much what one would expect of a Platonist of his era: God is real being, eternal, unchanging, non-composite, uncontaminated by matter (all these attributes derived from the speech of his revered teacher Ammonius at *De E* 392Eff., which may reasonably be taken to express Plutarch's views also). The fact that in this passage the subject of discussion is actually Apollo simply reminds us how, for philosophers like Plutarch, the various traditional gods have become aspects of divinity in general. God also knows all things (*De Is.* 351D) and directs all things (*De Is.* 382B). He thus exercises providence (*pronoia*) over all things, as will be discussed below. He is also presented, for instance at *De facie* 944E, as "the object of striving for all nature", reflecting the influence on Middle Platonists of the Aristotelian doctrine of the Prime Mover (*Metaphysics* Λ.7; *Physics* I.9).

Besides being 'really existent', for Plutarch God also possesses the two other basic Platonic epithets: he is the Good (*On the Disappearance of Oracles* [hereafter *Def. Or.*] 423D), and he is the One (*De E* 393B–C). In this latter guise, he can be accommodated to the Pythagorean–Platonic pair of first principles, the Monad and the Indefinite Dyad (*Def. Or.* 428D). In this important passage, Plutarch portrays the generation of Number from the action of the Monad on the Dyad in a manner reminiscent of the Old Academic Xenocrates, by whom he is much influenced (as we shall see below in connection with the generation of the soul), but a dualistic tone is introduced that seems to be a contribution of Plutarch himself. Admittedly, this pair of principles is produced here in connection with the origin of Number, but they are plainly also to be understood as the principles of all creation. The Indefinite Dyad, or *apeiria*, is presented as "the element underlying all formlessness and disorder", Number, and the cosmos; it is created by the One "slicing off" (429A) greater or smaller sections of this *apeiria*, and thus imposing limit on it; but it is also presented as a constant threat to good order. This second principle manifests itself at every level of Plutarch's universe, as disorderly, irrational Soul, and as matter, but it is plainly something more than either of these.

At *Platonic Questions* (hereafter *Quaest. Plat.*) 3 (1002A), the same process of generation is outlined again, although here with the Dyad presented in a more positive light, and the process is continued from number, through points, lines, surfaces and solids, to bodies and "qualities of bodies that are generated through (physical) impulses": a list designed, presumably, to cover every level of reality. Plutarch is here indebted, ultimately, to the formalization of Plato's thought propounded by Xenocrates.

The Logos and the Forms

The first principles, thus established, must relate to the world through suitable intermediaries. The first of these, although it makes an appearance only rarely in Plutarch's surviving works, is the Logos, which seems to have found a home in at least some strands of post-Antiochian Platonism, as evidenced, a few generations before Plutarch, in the works of the Jewish philosopher Philo of Alexandria. Indeed, its main appearance in Plutarch is in a somewhat mythological mode, in the essay *On Isis and Osiris*. Here, at 373A–B, we find the two aspects of the Logos, the transcendent and the immanent, represented as the 'soul' and the 'body' of Osiris. His soul is 'eternal and indestructible', whereas his body, which equates to the Logos, or sum-total of the Forms, as immanent in the physical world, is (in mythological terms) repeatedly torn asunder by the monstrous Typhon. Typhon, in turn, represents matter, or the Receptacle of the *Timaeus*, in its role as a principle of disorder, and is constantly being reassembled by Isis, representing the World Soul, as an entity that, while being essentially irrational, is nonetheless positively inclined (372F). The reason-principles and Forms emanating from the transcendent Logos are imprinted on the Receptacle like seals on wax (an image taken from *Theaetetus* 191cff.), and from these Isis composes the sensible world, symbolized by Horus.

We see the Forms, then, in *On Isis and Osiris*, in their immanent aspect, as the contents of the immanent Logos. In their transcendent aspect, 'in themselves', Plutarch plainly takes them as the thoughts of God, such as seems by his time to have become the Platonist consensus (cf. Alcinous, *The Handbook of Platonism*, ch. 9). There is a clear instance of this in *On Delays in the Divine Punishment* 550D (cited above, in connection with the *telos*), where God himself is presented as the totality of the Forms, and thus the model (*paradeigma*) for the physical cosmos, indicating that Plutarch has rationalized the myth of the *Timaeus* to that extent at least. At *Quaest. Plat.* 3 (1001E–1002A), we find an interesting extrapolation of Plato's account of the course of higher studies in *Republic* book 6 (525b–531d), where an intellectual progression from the study of harmony, through astronomy and the other mathematical sciences, should lead us by a process of 'abstraction' (*aphairesis*) to the Forms, conceived of as pure monads: something that Plato may imply, but does not specify.

It must be admitted as somewhat troublesome that it is only in *On Isis and Osiris* that we observe the unequivocal appearance of a Logos-figure in Plutarch's philosophical system, but one can only reflect that we are deprived of many of his most serious philosophical works. Certainly, Plutarch shows no sign of wishing to postulate a separate secondary divinity that would serve as a Demiurge, and his World Soul, as we have seen from his characterization of Isis, is not an entity capable of taking demiurgic initiatives. What we do find, on the other hand, rather disturbingly, is some traces of a subordinate divinity rather like a modified form of the Gnostic Demiurge, standing, if not in opposition, then certainly in contrast to the supreme deity, and presiding more immediately over the physical or, more properly, the sublunar world. Such a concept, which seems to owe something to the notion, from wherever derived, that it is actually the sublunar realm in which we dwell that is the realm of Hades, makes its appearance at *De E* 393A–394C, where we find a contrast made between a supreme deity, denominated 'Apollo' (etymologized as 'Not-Many', and therefore One), and 'Plouton', or 'Hades', who is the "god, or rather daemon, that presides over the nature which is involved in dissolution and generation" (394A). This latter entity is not to be regarded as evil so much as simply the immanent and immediate administrator of the world of change and imperfection, freeing the supreme deity from direct involvement in this. It may thus be seen as to some extent taking over the role of the 'Young Gods' of Plato's *Timaeus.*

The irrational Soul and matter, and Plutarch's dualism

Plutarch's dualistic tendencies have manifested themselves in *De Is.* (373A–B), in the description of the Forms being "seized by the element of disorder and confusion which has been driven hither from the upper region". This seems to imply not just the rather impersonal principle of disorder represented by the Receptacle of the *Timaeus*, but a positively disruptive force, which has (if the phrase quoted here can be taken at face value) at some stage itself broken away, or been expelled, from the intelligible realm. We seem thus once again, as in the case of the sublunary deity mentioned in *On the E at Delphi*, to be brought close to a Gnostic thought-world; but in fact Plutarch can claim the authority of Plato in this matter, as indeed he does earlier in the essay (*De Is.* 360E). In *Laws* 896dff., after all, Plato had postulated, in opposition to the beneficent World Soul, another "of the opposite capacity", which is responsible for all irrational motion in the universe (898b) – or, to be specific, in the sublunar world, to which irrational motion is confined. Anything that is soul is also alive and self-moving, so this on the face of it would be a notable extrapolation from the inanimate disorderly principle of the *Timaeus* (which Plutarch, however, would precisely endow also with a disorderly soul, as we learn from his essay *On the Creation of the Soul in the Timaeus*, e.g. 1014B).

The question thus arises as to how far the degree of dualism manifesting itself in Plutarch goes beyond anything attributable to Plato himself (modern scholars, after all, tend to play down even the 'maleficent' soul of *Laws* book 10, in asserting Plato's fundamental monism). It does seem, indeed, as if Plutarch, through whatever intermediary, has been to some extent affected by dualistic influences emanating from Persia. At *De E* 369E, at any rate, he bestows high praise on Zoroastrian theology, referring to it as "the opinion of the wisest men". Just before this, however, he sets out his own view, employing, as was so popular in his time, an appeal to immemorial antiquity. He claims to discern as inherent in Greek thought an understanding that the universe is administered, not just by one supreme divinity, but by "two opposite principles and two antithetic powers, one of which leads by a straight path and to the right, while the other turns us aside and bends backward", and this causes both human life and nature in general to have a mixed character, experiencing both good and evil (369C–D).

This constitutes a definitive statement of Plutarch's dualism, an attitude he shares both with his follower Atticus and with the Neopythagorean Numenius, but that was firmly rejected by Plotinus and all subsequent Neoplatonists. Plutarch held that the 'maleficent soul' – which must be seen as a manifestation of the Indefinite Dyad – has, before God creates the cosmos proper (which thus has a temporal beginning), itself created a dim prefiguration of the cosmos, such as seems to be described in *Timaeus* 52eff., and which in *On Isis and Osiris* is represented by "the elder Horus", a being which is "brought into being crippled, in darkness" (369E). At 373C we find the statement that "before this world became manifest and was brought to completion by the Logos, Matter, being put to shame by Nature, brought forth from itself, imperfect, a first creation". Plutarch here seems to be making creative use of the myth of Hera producing Hephaestus by herself out of spite, in response to Zeus' generation of Athena from his head: Hera here representing the Dyad, as she does in the theology of Xenocrates.

It is this, as it were, anti-cosmos, in Plutarch's view, that is set in order by God in the *Timaeus.* At this point, however, a more positive aspect of this dyadic entity may be observed. Back in 372E, after all, Isis is equated with the Receptacle of the *Timaeus* and with Matter, and even, at the outset of the essay (351E–F), with Wisdom, and indeed seems to take on very much the same character as Sophia in the system of Philo of Alexandria, suggesting a tendency, in the Alexandrian Platonism from which Plutarch emanates, to identify Matter with the World Soul, and connect both of them with the Indefinite Dyad. This amalgam produces an entity that is on the one hand 'fallen' and imperfect, but on the other hand filled with longing for the perfection emanating from the Logos, and thus constituting the instrumental cause of our creation and the vehicle by which we can come to know God.

There is present, then, in Plutarch's thought, alongside the more adversative Dyadic, 'Typhonic' figure, a World Soul that, while essentially irrational, is thoroughly amenable to being brought to order, although never in such a way that its residual irrationality is altogether done away with. In this connection, there is an intriguing passage in *On the Creation of the Soul in the Timaeus* (1026E–1027A), where we find a description of "the nature which presides over the heavens", which may be taken as the Logos, mingling with the (irrational) World Soul, in such a way as to be periodically overcome by it, and "dragged down into a forgetfulness of its proper role", but then reasserting itself before it is too late. This picture borrows much of its imagery from the myth of Plato's *Statesman*, but it is not clear how literally Plutarch intends us to take it; more probably it is a portrayal of a constant tension between rational and irrational forces in the universe.

What emerges, then, as Plutarch's metaphysical scheme, in place of the more traditional Platonist triad of principles, God, Matter and the Forms, is a system where two positive forces confront two (largely) negative ones: God (as the Monad or the Good) and his Logos (constituting the sum-total of the Forms) facing an Indefinite Dyad, as an unregenerately negative principle, and a Soul that, while remaining essentially irrational, is yet susceptible to ordering by the Logos, to produce an ordered, if imperfect, world. As such, Logos and Soul combine, as described in *Timaeus* 35a, on Plutarch's reckoning, to produce both a rational World Soul, which rules over the physical world, and individual rational souls, which reproduce the tensions exhibited on the macrocosmic level, but which can attain to 'likeness to God' by imposing rational order on their passionate, irrational parts, as discussed above in § "Ethics".

Divisions of the universe and hierarchies of being

Plutarch propounds a three-way division of the universe, set out at *De facie* 943F, and based explicitly by him on a remarkable theory of Xenocrates (fr. 56 Heinze), postulating three *pykna* or 'densities' of Matter, which blend respectively with fire, air and water, to form the sun and stars, the moon, and lastly the earth and sublunar regions generally.

Plutarch, however, introduces this theory only incidentally, in the course of specifying the nature of the moon, and it is not quite clear how far he is claiming it for himself. More interesting still, from a philosophical point of view, is a four-level hierarchy of being that appears, like the distinction of types of soul, in the myth of *De genio* (591B), which expands on the Xenocratean tripartite division of the universe by adding a further term on top, the Monad. It seems to deserve quotation, by reason of its oddness and complexity:

> Four principles (*arkhai*) there are of all things: the first is of Life, the second is of Motion, the third of Generation (*genesis*), and the last is of Dissolution. The first is linked to the second by the Monad, at the Invisible, the second to third by Intellect at the Sun, the third to the fourth by Nature at the Moon. A Fate, daughter of Necessity, holds the keys and presides over each link: over the first, Atropos, over the second Clotho, and over the link at the Moon Lachesis. The turning-point of birth is at the Moon. (*De genio* 591B)

Such a passage must be approached with due caution, by reason of its mythological context, but the 'Invisible' may perhaps be taken as the outer rim of heaven, to preserve the analogy, although it is a (perhaps intentionally) obscure term. 'Nature' can be taken as synonymous with Soul, in its irrational aspect. In its firm separation of Intellect and Soul, which are connected with the sun and moon respectively, this scheme is in accord with the dialogue *On the Face on the Moon*. The three Fates also play analogous roles in both myths (cf. *De facie* 945C).

What is new here is the level of 'Life', and the Monad that links it to the level of Motion. The fact that a supreme principle is called 'Monad' does not in fact mean that it is not also to be accounted an intellect; but a distinction is nonetheless being made between it and *nous* proper. This *nous* must be the demiurgic Intellect, combining the Demiurge of the *Timaeus* with the rational aspect of the World Soul. The Monad must therefore be taken as a transcendent, self-contemplating Intellect, analogous, perhaps, to the Paternal Intellect in the scheme of the Neopythagorean Numenius. The introduction of *Zōē*, a life-principle, as apparently superior to the Monad is somewhat unexpected, but it may be that 'Life' (a concept perhaps borrowed from the notable Platonic passage *Sophist* 248e, which was to have such an influence in later Platonism) is to be regarded rather as the salient characteristic of the realm of the Monad than an active principle in its own right. However that may be, we can discern here a sequence 'Monad–Intellect–Soul (Nature)' that anticipates in an interesting way later (Neoplatonic) developments, but also relates to more or less contemporary Neopythagorean speculations.

Another oddity of this scheme, which may indicate that it is not after all to be taken entirely seriously, is the apparent distinguishing of the realms of 'generation' and 'dissolution', which should both be inseparably characteristic of the sublunar realm. Plutarch, however, wants to associate *genesis* more properly with the moon, which is thus endowed with the role of generator, while the earth is assigned that of corruptor. They both, however, cooperate to produce the realm of Nature.

In both myths, as we have seen, Intellect is connected with the sun and Soul with the moon, and a 'double death' is envisaged for the individual, the soul (with intellect) leaving the body and taking up its abode in the region of the moon, and the intellect then leaving the soul behind and rising to the level of the sun. The reverse process also takes place, the sun sowing intellects in the moon, and the moon sowing the now intelligized souls into bodies (*De facie* 945B–C). All this talk of 'sowing' can be referred back to the description of the activities of the Demiurge in the *Timaeus* 41–2, but it is plain that much scholastic elaboration has taken place over the centuries: the Demiurge is now the sun, and the 'young gods' the moon; an essentially 'solar' theology has taken over, which may itself owe much to the speculations of Xenocrates.

Daemonology

The more transcendent the supreme principle becomes, the more it stands in need of other beings to mediate between it and the material world, over which, in Platonism, it exercises providential care (*pronoia*). We have seen above how the Logos serves this function for Plutarch, but, like all later Platonists, he also postulates a daemonic level of being, which figures prominently in his writings.

It is plain that here, as in various other areas of his philosophy, Plutarch is influenced by Xenocrates. In the essay *On the Disappearance of Oracles* (416cff.), we find a doctrine of daemons put into the mouth of Cleombrotus of Sparta that owes much to Xenocrates, who seems to have drawn on the key passage of Plato's *Symposium* (202e), but elaborated on the doctrine of the mediating role of daemons by propounding an analogy with the three kinds of triangle: the gods are to be compared to the equilateral, men to the scalene and daemons to the isosceles. This is because the daemons "possess human emotion and divine power". They are also to be linked in particular with the moon, and are essential to the coherence of the universe, a link between God and men. Both God's providential care and his transcendence must be preserved, and the universe can tolerate no sharp divisions or sudden transitions. The moon, which served in the myth of *On the Face of the Moon* as the place of souls, and indeed as the symbol of the World Soul, is now established as the proper abode of daemons (who are, after all, souls of a kind). In either case, the sphere of the moon is the essential arena of mediation and transition in the economy of Plutarch's universe.

In *On the Disappearance of Oracles*, the chief subject of discussion is the administration by the daemons of oracles, but they are to be credited in fact with all active interventions of the supernatural in human life, which had been credited, in popular belief, to gods. Daemons are subject to passions, and thus can on occasion become degenerate. At *De facie* 944C, we are told that, if daemons misuse their role as mediators as a result of being overcome by one passion or another, they are punished by being condemned to incarnation as human beings. Such a concept, inspired ultimately, we may suppose, by the self-revelations of Empedocles as a fallen daemon (referred to at *De Is.* 361C), may or may not be intended as an explanation for *all* incarnations, but in any case it introduces an interesting dynamic aspect into Plutarch's theory of daemons.

There are, then, 'evil' daemons in Plutarch's system, but not, arguably, *primally* evil ones, as in Zoroastrian or Gnostic systems. Such evil daemons as there are, it would seem, are fallen from a 'good' state, and may again be promoted to that state. In such passages as *De Is.* 360Dff. and *De facie* 945B, such beings as Typhon, and the Giants and Titans, which would generally be regarded as primevally evil beings, are portrayed as fallen souls that are filled with passions and destitute of intellect, but even they, Plutarch declares, "in time the Moon takes back to herself and reduces to order". Admittedly, at *De Is.* 361B, Xenocrates is quoted as an authority for the view that there are "great and strong natures in the atmosphere, ill-conditioned and morose, who rejoice in such (viz., gloomy sacrifices and obscene ceremonies), and after gaining them as their lot, turn to nothing worse". But while Xenocrates may have regarded these beings as having a permanent status in the cosmos, Plutarch can accommodate them into his 'dynamic' system. There will always be such malevolent beings, but they will not always be the same ones.

Apart from such 'evil' beings, there are daemons who are delegated by God to punish us. Plutarch speaks of those "who go about as avengers of arrogant and grievous cases of injustice" (*Def. Or.* 417B), a concept that goes back at least to Hesiod (*Works and Days* 254–5). Such daemons will, of course, be ranked among the good, even if their actions result in unpleasantness for some, and if they exceed their commission in any way they will themselves be punished and demoted. In this connection, Plutarch makes the interesting remark that: "as among men, so also among daemons, there are different degrees of virtue, and in some there is a weak and dim reminder of the passionate and irrational element, a kind of dregs, at is were, while in others this is extensive and hard to stifle" (*Def. Or.* 417B). Here, differences in degree of purification are recognized among the daemons, but nothing that makes any of them totally evil.

Above all, as has been remarked, Plutarch's theory of daemons seems to be dynamic rather than static. He envisages a continual process of promotion and demotion of souls to and from a daemonic state, and even, it would seem from such a passage as *Def. Or.* 415B, the promotion in rare cases of human souls to divine status. This theory is there attributed to certain anonymous authorities (probably Pythagorean), rather than stated directly by Plutarch's spokesman (his brother Lamprias), but there is no reason to suppose that Plutarch does not endorse it:

> Others [viz., Homer and Hesiod] postulate a transmutation for bodies and souls alike; even as water is seen to be generated from earth, air from water, and fire from air, as their substance is borne upward, even so the better souls obtain their transmutation from men into heroes and from heroes into daemons. And from daemons yet a few souls, in the long reach of time, because of supreme excellence, come, after being purified, to share completely in divinity (*theiotēs*). But with some of these souls it comes to pass that they do not maintain control over themselves, but yield to temptation and are again clothed with mortal bodies, and have a dim and darkened life, like mist or vapour.
> (*Def. Or.* 415B)

So even the attaining of divine status on the part of souls cannot be taken as permanent. There is a continuous process of transmutation, as with the four elements. We may note in this connection that heroes have been introduced here as a second intermediate class between gods and human beings. Hesiod is appealed to as an authority for this just above, but the stimulus for the doctrine in Plutarch seems to be a parallel with the system of two means between the extremes of earth and fire in *Timaeus* (although this four-level system is recognized already by Posidonius, who wrote a treatise *On Heroes and Daemons*).

It remains to speak of the personal or guardian daemon, the most notable example of which, for later Platonists, was the daemonic voice by which Socrates claimed to be guided. We have already seen that, in the myth of the dialogue *De genio* 591Dff., we find a description of the *nous* as a daemon. A little further on, however, at 593Dff., the doctrine is propounded that, while the gods themselves take over the guidance of a favoured few, such as Socrates, the remaining human beings are presided over by a class of disembodied souls. These are certainly distinct from any part of the individual's *psyche* or *nous*. The passage suggests that, while every individual has a guardian daemon allotted to him, the daemon can only take an active part in the guidance of an individual when he is already far advanced in the process of escaping from the cycle of rebirth. The implications of this are not quite clear, but somewhat disquieting. Disquieting too is a doctrine adumbrated at *De Tranquillitate Animae* 474B–C, that we possess not one, but two guardian daemons, one good and one evil (Empedocles [31 B 122 DK (= Diels & Kranz 1951–2)] being claimed as an authority for this), either of which one might follow. It is not clear, however, how far Plutarch is personifying the *daimones* that he talks of. He refers to them just below as *pathē,* which suggests that he is thinking of them only as tendencies rather than as spirits, but this in itself points up the ambiguity of the word *daimōn*, which can be understood as 'daemon' or simply 'fate' (Empedocles himself speaks of *moirai*). Comparison with passages such as *Corpus Hermeticum* IX 3, however, or Philo, *Questions on Exodus* I 23, suggests that the concept of an evil genius was circulating in at least the lower reaches of contemporary Platonism, and Plutarch may be picking up on it.

Contact of the immaterial with the material

In connection with the theory of the guardian daemon, and with the topic of modes of divine inspiration in general, Plutarch indulges in some speculation about the mode of contact between the daemonic and the human intellect, and between the intellect or soul and the body. This is a subject that does not seem to have much bothered Plato himself, and perhaps only became acute as a result of the challenge of Stoic materialism. Plutarch addresses the subject at *De genio* 588F–589B. He cannot be said to probe very deeply into the difficulties associated with the concept, but at least he raises them. He compares the soul (borrowing a thought from Plato, *Laws* 645a–b) to a stringed instrument, the strings of which can be played on by the intellect, and which, taut and sensitive as they are, reach down into the body and stimulate "the inert and prostrate mass" of flesh to action. He never here goes beyond this Pythagorean-inspired musical imagery in his attempt to explain the phenomenon, but we may note his use in the passage of a distinctively Stoic term for 'co-ordinated tension' (*synentasis*), which suggests that he is indulging in a creative application of the Stoic doctrine of *tonos*, to elucidate a thoroughly un-Stoic problem.

Once Plutarch has settled to his satisfaction the problem of the interaction between soul and body, the rest is easy. Spirit can communicate with spirit by the lightest touch, "like light producing a reflection" (589B). Daemons do not need language to communicate their thoughts to one another, and they can do the same to the intellects of persons who are suitably attuned to them, even as the air conforms itself to the sounds of articulate language (589C). Such individuals, like Socrates, are truly 'daemonic'. We have here presented to us a theory of divine inspiration, grounded on a 'scientific' basis, through an application of the theory of cosmic sympathy.

A discussion of Plutarch's views on logical questions is not, I think, germane to the present context. From this survey of his ethical and physical doctrines, however, one can observe how intimately, for a man like Plutarch, philosophy is intertwined with what we might regard as 'religion'. For Plutarch, as for any other Platonist philosopher of antiquity, there is really no clear distinction between the two, there being no separate category of accredited 'ministers of religion' to serve as moral authorities in competition with philosophers.

FURTHER READING

Babut, D. 1969. *Plutarque et le Stoicisme*. Paris: Vrin.
Betz, H.-D. (ed.) 1975. *Plutarch's Theological Writings and Early Christian Literature*. Leiden: Brill.
Brenk, F. 1977. *In Mist Apparelled: Religious Themes in Plutarch's Moralia and Lives*. Leiden: Brill.
Dillon, J. 1977. *The Middle Platonists*. London: Duckworth.
Dillon, J. 2002. "Plutarch on God". In *Traditions of Theology: Studies in Hellenistic Theology*, D. Frede & A. Laks (eds), 223–38. Leiden: Brill.
Ferrari, F. 1995. *Dio, idée e materia: La struttura del cosmo in Plutarco di Cheronea*. Naples: D'Auria.
Hamilton, W. 1934. "The Myth in Plutarch's *De Facie* (940F–945D)". *Classical Quarterly* **28**: 24–30.
Mossman, J. (ed.) 1997. *Plutarch and his Intellectual World*. Swansea: Classical Press of Wales.
Russell, D. 1972. *Plutarch*. London: Duckworth.
Vernière, Y. 1977. *Symboles et mythes dans la pensée de Plutarque*. Paris: Vrin.

On ETHICS see also Vol. 2, Chs 4, 8; Vol. 3, Ch. 9; Vol. 4, Chs 13, 19; Vol. 5, Chs 12, 15, 21. On FORMS/IDEAS see also Chs 4, 13; Vol. 2, Ch. 15. On LOGOS see also Chs 9, 13; Vol. 2, Ch. 19. On PLATONISM see also Chs 14, 15, 17; Vol. 5, Ch. 16. On THE ONE see also Chs 3, 14, 16, 19; Vol. 4, Ch. 9; Vol. 5, Ch. 15. On VIRTUE see also Chs 2, 14, 15; Vol. 3, Chs 20, 21.

12

SEXTUS EMPIRICUS

Richard Bett

Virtually nothing is known about the life of Sextus Empiricus. He was a doctor and, as his name implies, a member of the Empiric school of medicine. He probably lived in the second century CE. His importance in the history of philosophy lies in the fact that he is the only ancient Greek sceptic whose complete works survive. Specifically, he belonged to the Pyrrhonist sceptical tradition, taking its inspiration from Pyrrho of Elis (*c.*360–*c.*270 BCE), but organized as a systematic philosophical outlook in the early first century BCE by Aenesidemus of Cnossos. Sextus' surviving works are as follows: (i) *Outlines of Pyrrhonism* (hereafter *PH*, the initials of the title in Greek),[1] which offers a general account of scepticism in the first book and, in the remaining two books, a critical assessment of non-sceptics' views in logic, physics and ethics, the standard areas of philosophy in the Hellenistic period; (ii) a work in six books criticizing the pretensions to theoretical knowledge by experts in various specialized fields such as rhetoric, mathematics and astrology, called *Against the Professors* (*Adversus mathematicos* in Latin, hence the standard abbreviation *M*); (iii) an incomplete work that originally covered the same ground as *PH*, but at much greater length; the surviving parts are *Against the Logicians* in two books, *Against the Physicists* in two books and *Against the Ethicists* in one book.[2] Sextus' own title for this work is *Skeptika Hupomnēmata* (Sceptical treatises). However, owing to a now unaccountable error in the manuscript tradition, these five surviving books were taken to be a continuation of the six-book work on specialized fields; as a result, the logical books are known by the abbreviation *M* 7–8, the physical part by *M* 9–10 and the ethical part by *M* 11. For the subject of religion only *PH* and parts of the incomplete work are relevant.

1. The best translation of this work bears the title *Outlines of Scepticism* (2000), but this is a replacement, not a translation, of the original title.
2. *Against the Physicists* is available in English only in the antiquated and not wholly reliable Bury translation (1936). My more recent translations of *Against the Logicians* and *Against the Ethicists* are available (2005 and 1997, respectively).

Sextus' usual method is to generate suspension of judgement from the conflicting arguments and opinions on any given topic. The arguments and opinions he employs for this purpose typically include those of the people he calls the dogmatists: that is, the believers in positive philosophical doctrines. They also very often include critiques of these, originating either from rival dogmatists or from the sceptics themselves. But even arguments generated by the sceptics are not arguments that the sceptic endorses; rather, they are part of the sceptic's means to a further end. The sceptic's trick, as Sextus presents it – what he calls the sceptic's "ability" (*dunamis*; *PH* 1.8) – consists in setting out these incompatible ideas in such a way that they exhibit the feature of *isostheneia*, 'equal strength'. For two or more positions to be of 'equal strength' is for the person contemplating them to be no more inclined towards any one of them than any other; in other words, it is a psychological notion rather than a logical one. The effect of this lack of inclination, according to Sextus, is that one suspends judgement about the correctness of any of the positions in question. Again, this is not a matter of what one is *rationally required* to do – for that too would involve taking a definite position, albeit at a meta-level, and definite positions are what the sceptics avoid – but simply of what *happens* to one in the situation the sceptic has devised. And suspension of judgement, in turn, is supposed to yield *ataraxia*, "freedom from worry": the same goal that some dogmatists, most notably the Epicureans, claimed to achieve by the discovery of the truth. Scepticism, then, is not a purely intellectual exercise, but has an important practical effect. Indeed, like other philosophies of the time, it can be described as a *way of life*.

This, of course, raises the question how, more specifically, one is supposed to live as a sceptic. The short answer is that one follows the appearances: that is, one acts in light of the way things appear, while taking no stand on how they really are. One of the most perplexing questions about Sextus' treatment of the topic of religion is how this practical stance is supposed to apply in this case; Sextus is clear that it does apply, but it is difficult to make sense of what he says.

Discussions of religious matters, and of God or the gods, appear in Sextus' treatments of both physics and ethics.[3] In the case of physics it appears he was not the first in the Pyrrhonist tradition. According to a summary of the lost work *Pyrrhonist Discourses* by Sextus' predecessor Aenesidemus, gods figured among the topics discussed concerning the cosmos and the nature of things (Photius, *Bibliotheca* (Library) 170a15–17, trans. in Long & Sedley 1987: 72L3); and this is not surprising, since the dogmatists did the same thing, back to the very beginning of Greek philosophy. In any case, Sextus deals with the conception and the existence of God in the physical section of *Outlines of Pyrrhonism* (*PH* 3.2–12) and also, at much greater length, in *Against the Physicists* (*M* 9.13–194). In addition,

3. As often in Greek thought, the question of the *number* of divinities has, from our perspective, surprisingly little importance; and, following Sextus, I shall freely switch between singular and plural formulations.

religious customs and questions of what is pious figure in the ethical section of *Outlines of Pyrrhonism* (*PH* 3.198–234), and in one of the Modes, or standardized forms of sceptical argumentation, that deals with similar issues (*PH* 1.145–62). I begin by discussing these passages in more detail; I then address the question of religion's role in the sceptic's own life.

DETAILS OF THE TEXTS ON RELIGION

The passage in the physical section of *PH* 3 begins (after a prefatory remark to which I shall return) by arguing that there is no clear conception of God. Different dogmatic philosophers have incompatible conceptions of God, and their dispute about this proceeds "undecidably" (*anepikritōs*; 3). And their attempts to convey a clear conception by appealing to standard ideas of God's indestructibility and blessedness do not improve the situation (4–5). But then, in a common argumentative move, Sextus continues by saying that even if God *is* conceivable, we must suspend judgement about the *existence* of the divine, at least, "as far as the dogmatists are concerned" (6; another point to which I shall return).[4] Again, this is because of the 'undecidable dispute' among the dogmatists about what God is really like, a dispute that would not occur if the divine was a matter of plain experience. The only way in which we could move beyond this impasse would be if a proof for the existence of God could be devised, but such a proof is unavailable (7–9): again, a very common motif in Sextus. Finally (9–12), Sextus exploits some well-known difficulties in the notion of divine providence to argue that a firm assertion of the existence of God is necessarily impious, because the God asserted to exist must be either a cause of bad, as well as of good, or lacking in power. The exact purpose of this last argument is not absolutely clear. It might be seen as an argument for a kind of self-refutation on the part of the dogmatists. Alternatively, it might be seen as one side of a pair of opposed arguments about providence, the goal again being suspension of judgement, and the unexpressed other side being a positive conception of God's providence, and of the piety of those who profess it (the Stoics being the most obvious source); this type of approach, too, is common in Sextus, especially when the existence of the unmentioned arguments on the other side is obvious.

The much longer discussion in *Against the Physicists* differs from this in certain ways. But it too begins with a section on the conception of God (*M* 9.14–48) – in this case, on competing explanations of how the conception of God has arisen, all of which are shown to fail – and it then addresses the existence of God (49–194), offering a number of arguments for and against, the inevitable result being suspension of judgement (191). Here, then, the 'undecidable dispute' about this question

4. All translations are my own.

is not merely asserted, but illustrated in some detail. There are some unclarities of structure, but the main outline of the discussion conforms to the pattern sketched in my introduction.

The passages relating to religion in the ethical sections of Sextus' work are rather different. Much of the ethical section of *PH* 3 is devoted to producing suspension of judgement about whether anything is by nature good or bad. This is accomplished partly by abstract arguments concerning what it would take for something to be by nature good or bad. But Sextus also decides to deal:

> more specifically with the suppositions about what is shameful and what is not, what is prohibited [*athesmōn*, i.e. contrary to *thesmos*, which regularly, although not always, refers to divine law] and not such, laws and customs, piety towards the gods, reverence for the departed, and the like. (198)

There follows a large number of examples of inconsistencies, mainly cultural but also involving philosophical positions, in ethical and religious belief and practice (199–234). The same kinds of subject matter, both religious and ethical, are discussed more briefly and less systematically in the last of the Ten Modes in *PH* 1 (145–63); and here again the result is that we must suspend judgement about the nature of things in these areas.

How exactly are the inconsistencies supposed to yield this suspension of judgement? The answer might seem obvious. One suspends judgement because the conflicts concerning what is truly pious, or about what the gods are really like, are undecidable; this is the typical sceptical approach that I have talked about so far. And there is certainly support for this in the passages currently under examination. The tenth Mode speaks constantly of "opposing" (*antitithesthai*) the various different practices and beliefs being considered. This fits with Sextus' initial characterization of scepticism in general as an "oppositional ability" (*dunamis antithetikē*; *PH* 1.8). In the *PH* 3 passage, too, the religious inconsistencies are said to amount to a "dispute" (*diaphōnia*; 218, cf. 233): precisely the term that is regularly used along with *anepikritos*, "undecidable". But both passages also use another word to refer to the inconsistencies: *anōmalia*, "lack of uniformity". This occurs at the conclusion of the tenth Mode (1.163) and numerous times in the *PH* 3 passage. And this suggests another kind of sceptical approach distinct from the one so far observed.

A lack of uniformity is not necessarily the same as a dispute. If one culture does its sacrifices one way and another does them another way, there is no conflict unless one culture claims, or they both claim, that their way of doing them is the way that in the nature of things, or universally, they *should* be done. And a lack of uniformity in beliefs on the same topic is not necessarily the same as a dispute either, provided the two or more sets of beliefs are somehow localized to distinct sets of circumstances. Now, in numerous places in these texts it looks as if Sextus is pressing for precisely this kind of relativization to locations or circumstances. At the end of the tenth Mode he says that because of the "lack of uniformity" in the objects (*pragmatōn*), "we will not be able to say what the existing thing is like in its nature, but how it appears in relation to this way of life or in relation to this law or in relation to this custom, etc." (*PH* 1.163). One could perhaps understand this as just another reference to undecidable dispute: people from different cultures have different views about ethical and religious matters, and there is no way to adjudicate between them. But in that case one would expect Sextus to refer to the lack of uniformity in people's *opinions* about these things, not to lack of uniformity in the *objects*, a phrase repeated in the other passage (3.235). To speak of lack of uniformity in the objects suggests a somewhat different point: that things are not good or bad, pious or impious, across the board, but only in a given set of cultural circumstances.

Evidence of a similar line of thought appears in the *PH* 3 passage, especially in the section concentrating specifically on religious beliefs and practices. We are told that if anything was pious or impious by nature, the practice or belief concerning that thing would be the same everywhere. Most of the differences in question are cultural; for example, things that people in some cultures eat are considered impious to eat in other cultures. But many of the differences concerning sacrifice involve not incompatible practices in different cultures, but differences in what animals get sacrificed to which gods; it is pious to sacrifice goats to Artemis, for instance, but not to Asclepius (221). Yet both types of examples are used indiscriminately as evidence that nothing is *invariably*, or *by nature*, pious or impious.

This is an example of a pattern of thought that occurs periodically in Sextus. There is good reason to believe that it represents the survival of an earlier and distinct variety of Pyrrhonist scepticism: a variety associated with the originator of the later Pyrrhonist tradition, Aenesidemus. The summary referred to earlier of Aenesidemus' book *Pyrrhonist Discourses* (Photius, *Bibliotheca* 169b18–171a4 [almost all reproduced as texts 71C and 72L in Long & Sedley 1987]) makes clear that Aenesidemus avoided assertions issued invariably – or, as the text puts it, "unambiguously" (*anamphibolōs*; 169b40, 170a29 [= 71C5,11]) – and instead favoured assertions that included a relativization to persons, times or circumstances. The summary also makes clear that Aenesidemus took this relativization to be a method for avoiding dogmatism; Aenesidemus criticizes the Academics of his day, who allegedly professed a sceptical philosophy, for making "unambiguous" assertions and thus failing to maintain sceptical caution. Then again, the Ten Modes, as presented by both Diogenes Laertius (9.79–88)[5] and Sextus (*PH* 1.35–163), and elsewhere ascribed by Sextus to Aenesidemus (*M* 7.345), include

5. Diogenes' account of the lives of Pyrrho and Timon (9.61–116) form an important supplement to the evidence on Pyrrhonism supplied by Sextus. The Hicks translation (1925) is complete; a far superior, but excerpted translation appears in Inwood & Gerson (1997: III-22, III-23).

numerous examples of relativity as an apparent means to suspension of judgement; Sextus' tenth Mode is by no means the only instance. And other examples can be found in Sextus, notably in *Against the Ethicists*.[6]

According to this line of thinking, then, sacrificing goats is not pious or impious by nature, because it is not pious or impious in all circumstances but only in some: that is, depending on which god is the recipient. And eating pork is not pious or impious by nature, because it is acceptable to Greeks but thoroughly unacceptable to Jews and Egyptian priests (223). The two types of cases may seem rather different; but, as noted above, Sextus considers both of them alike to be evidence for the failure of these practices to measure up to the standard of invariability. In order for a certain practice to count as by nature pious, apparently, it would have to be considered pious by everyone and its piety would have to be unrestricted with regard to circumstances. It is not surprising that nothing meets this standard.

Before we move on, it should be re-emphasized that the line of thought involving relativity to circumstances is not upheld consistently in the passages dealing with religion in ethical contexts. Alongside it and, arguably, overshadowing it is the other sceptical approach, the standard and official one in Sextus, according to which suspension of judgement is induced by the undecidability of the dispute among opposing positions. This is not the only place where Sextus has not succeeded in fully integrating material from an earlier phase of Pyrrhonism into the version to which he is explicitly committed. But, whatever may be true in other cases, in the particular case of religion the implications of the two versions may be somewhat different. I shall return to this point in closing.

SEXTUS' OWN ATTITUDE TO RELIGION, AND ITS APPARENT INCONSISTENCY

The Pyrrhonist sceptic, then, suspends judgement about the existence and nature of the gods, and does not hold any opinions to the effect that specific religious practices or beliefs are either pious or impious by nature. Where does this leave the sceptic's own attitude towards the ordinary religious practice of his community? Sextus makes clear in several places that he and his Pyrrhonist colleagues do not by any means withdraw from this ordinary practice. It is not unusual for him to claim to be on the side of ordinary attitudes, as against the theoretical abstractions of the dogmatists. The difficulty is to see how to understand this in the case of religion.

As I mentioned earlier, Sextus claims that the sceptic lives by following the appearances. In the opening sections of *PH* he lists four main categories of

6. I have discussed this topic in my translation of *Against the Ethicists* (1997) and in Bett (2000: ch. 4).

appearances that guide one's choices and actions. One of these is "the handing down of laws and customs" (23). And as an example of an activity the sceptic engages in through the prompting of laws and customs, he says "we accept acting piously as good and acting impiously as bad, in terms of ordinary life (*biōtikōs*)" (24). Elsewhere, laws and customs are appealed to as a basis for acting in the face of an ethical crisis (*M* 11.163–6) and as a basis for living more generally (*PH* 1.17, 231, 237); it is clear from the present passage that acceptance, in some form, of everyday religious practice is part of this package. It is also clear that the qualification "in terms of ordinary life" is meant to mark a contrast with the kind of beliefs about the gods that involve dogmatic commitments: or, as Sextus often puts it, the holding of opinions.

Similarly, Sextus prefaces his discussion of God in the physical part of *PH* 3 by saying that "following ordinary life without opinions, we say that there are gods and we revere the gods and we say that they are provident; it is against the rashness of the dogmatists that we say the following" (2). This is picked up later in the passage (6), where we are told that one must suspend judgement about the existence of God "as far as the Dogmatists are concerned"; again, the implication is clearly that there is a level of religious discussion that is unaffected by the arguments in this section. And in *Against the Physicists*, at the start of the section on the existence of God, he says that:

> the sceptic will perhaps be found to be safer than those who philosophize in other ways, since in accordance with his ancestral customs and laws he says that there are gods and does everything that contributes to worship and reverence of them, but makes no rash claims as far as philosophical investigation is concerned. (*M* 9.49)

There are various ways in which one might understand the notion of 'safety' here. But whatever exactly Sextus has in mind, it is clear that he takes the sceptic's suspension of judgement to be somehow compatible with his involvement in the traditional religious practice of his society. In this respect, again, he treats religious customs as no different from any other social customs; in general, the sceptic does what his society prescribes as to be done. The fact that he takes the trouble to emphasize this in discussions of both the existence and nature of God does suggest, however, that he sees a potential for these discussions to be understood as undermining ordinary religion.

Why do they not do so? Or, in other words, what exactly does Sextus mean by claiming that, in a religious context, the sceptic can do and say things "in terms of ordinary life" without violating suspension of judgement? One possible answer[7] is that the sceptic performs the *actions* involved in religious rituals, but does not

7. See Barnes (1997: esp. 84–6); Bailey (2002: 192–3).

hold any of the beliefs that we might think are associated with them; he does these things because he has been raised in a society in which these things are done, but not because he *believes* these are the *right* things to do, or the things the gods want us to do. The things in question include sacrifices, dietary choices and other matters of religious behaviour, but they also include *saying* certain things in appropriate contexts, such as 'the gods are provident'. The sceptic does not, on this interpretation, thereby express any belief, and so there is no conflict between these actions and utterances and the suspension of judgement he declares in his writings. This stance may be regarded as hypocritical or disingenuous, either because it involves him in saying things without believing them, or because it renders dubious his claim to be following ordinary life.

Another interpretation, which arguably puts Sextus in a better light, has recently been suggested by Julia Annas.[8] Annas proposes that we should draw a distinction between theological beliefs, which are the province of philosophers, including the sceptic when debating philosophically, and religious beliefs and practices, which belong to ordinary people, including the sceptic when "following ordinary life". Theological beliefs, then, concern whether or not the gods really exist and what their true nature is, while religious beliefs are beliefs bound up with the everyday business of religion, such as 'it is pious to sacrifice a goat to Artemis but not to Asclepius'. And Annas' suggestion is that sceptical suspension of judgement about theological beliefs is compatible with the holding of religious beliefs; for religious beliefs do not entail theological beliefs; it is only philosophers, not ordinary religious practitioners, who even entertain theological beliefs. Or at least, she suggests, this is true in the context of pagan religion, where there is no overarching doctrine – particularly of a monotheistic kind, which tends by its nature to claim exclusive title to the truth – and where one culture is quite happy to accept that another culture has different gods from its own. In this situation, the question whether the gods recognized in a given culture are *really* the gods that exist in the nature of things is not one that it would occur to ordinary non-philosophical members of that culture to ask. Thus ordinary religious belief and practice can proceed quite happily without any engagement with the kinds of philosophical debates Sextus draws on; and suspension of judgement about the outcome of those debates does not create any difficulty for the sceptic's own involvement with that ordinary belief and practice.

This is an attractive suggestion, which has the merit of taking seriously the important differences between ancient pagan religion and monotheistic religions. And it may be that the religious attitudes of ordinary people in that context were indeed immune to philosophical scrutiny as Annas describes. This interpretation also makes good sense of Sextus' repeated insistence on the fact that his

8. Annas (forthcoming). I have learned a great deal from this paper, despite some significant disagreements.

philosophical discussions are directed against the rashness of the dogmatists. The difficulty, however, is that it does not seem to square with Sextus' own picture of the relation between ordinary religious beliefs and philosophical views about God.

For one thing, the things that Sextus claims the sceptics say in everyday religious contexts seem to include the *same* kinds of things as are subjected to sceptical scrutiny: according to him, the sceptics say *that there are gods* (*PH* 3.2; *M* 9.49) and that they are provident (*PH* 3.2), but these are precisely the propositions that are undermined in the discussions that immediately follow. In addition, although Sextus does emphasize that his philosophical discussions are directed against the dogmatists, this does not prevent him including the views of ordinary people alongside those of dogmatic philosophers in the mix of items to be placed in mutual opposition. At the beginning of the discussion of the existence of God in *Against the Physicists*, he lists as believers in God's existence "most of the dogmatists and the common preconception of ordinary life" (*M* 9.50); these are then contrasted with atheists and with sceptical suspenders of judgement. It is true that the subsequent arguments rehearsed on the positive side of the issue are all dogmatists' arguments. But this is hardly surprising, since *arguments* on this score are precisely the province of philosophers, not ordinary people; this does not negate the fact that suspension of judgement is presented as an alternative to ordinary people's belief in gods just as much as to dogmatists' beliefs in gods.

This point is reinforced at the end of the discussion. Sextus says that the opposing arguments from the dogmatists lead to sceptical suspension of judgement. He then says that to these oppositions can be added "the lack of uniformity about the gods in ordinary life" (*M* 9.191). And although, as noted earlier, the term "lack of uniformity" need not indicate outright conflict, in this case Sextus is quite explicit that this is what is at issue. For he then says that "Different people have different and discordant suppositions about them [i.e. the gods], so that neither are all of them [i.e. the suppositions] trustworthy because of the conflict between them, nor are some of them because of their equal strength" (192). Presumably this conflict is about the nature and perhaps the number of the gods, since he has already said that ordinary people quite generally believe in the existence of gods. But the conflict and "equal strength" among the alternative views nonetheless encourages suspension of judgement about the gods' existence because if no one view of their nature is of greater plausibility than any other, one might well begin to wonder whether there are any gods at all. It is clear, then, that Sextus takes ordinary religious beliefs to be relevant to the sceptical outcome of his whole discussion; while the arguments of the dogmatists are his main focus, he does not take ordinary beliefs to be on a separate level from these, immune to the effects of his sceptical procedure.

The same can be said of the discussion of ethical and religious inconsistencies in *PH* 3. The dispute about the existence and nature of the gods includes numerous named philosophers. But Sextus begins (218) by saying that "most people" (*hoi polloi*) believe that there are gods. And shortly afterwards (219) he makes it explicit that ordinary people's views are included among the conflicting beliefs in this area, saying that "of people in ordinary life, too, some say that there is one god, others that there are many and of different forms", adding a few of the more outlandish examples of the "different forms" gods are supposed by some to take. The same is true of the "oppositions" cited in the tenth Mode in *PH* 1. Among the religious, as opposed to the purely ethical, items here placed in opposition are both "dogmatic suppositions" (145, etc.) and ordinary beliefs about the gods drawn from mythology (*muthikai pisteis*; 145). "Dogmatic suppositions" are opposed to one another (e.g. 151); beliefs from myth are opposed to one another (e.g. 150); and dogmatic suppositions are opposed to beliefs from myth (e.g. 161–2). Here again, then, there is no question of ordinary religious beliefs being treated as distinct from the theological beliefs of philosophers; beliefs from one category can confront beliefs from the other, and all of them are grist for the sceptic's mill.

ATTEMPTS TO MITIGATE SEXTUS' INCONSISTENCY, AND THEIR FAILURE

So we are back where we were before. Sextus claims to be religious just as ordinary people are religious; this includes doing certain things, such as sacrificing the right animals to the right gods, and it includes saying certain things, such as that the gods exist and that they are provident. And yet the existence and providential nature of the gods, among other general features of the gods, are precisely the topics on which his sceptical machinery is used to generate suspension of judgement. Sextus seems to recognize that his sceptical exercises in this area might leave him open to criticism as irreligious; as noted earlier, this is the obvious explanation of the care he takes to emphasize up front that he is religious in the ordinary way, and that his quarrel is with the dogmatists. The trouble is that this does not seem consistent with the fact that ordinary religious beliefs (in general, not just a selected, perhaps non-Greek, set) figure alongside dogmatic theological positions in the material at which the sceptical machinery is directed.

This is not the only case where the beliefs of ordinary people are among the beliefs from which Sextus says the sceptic suspends judgement. Another is the case of beliefs about good and bad, a very important subject for Sextus; this is discussed in the opening section of *PH* 1 (27–30), and in the ethical section of *PH* 3 (235–8) as well as, at much greater length, in *Against the Ethicists* (*M* 11.110–67). Now, in the first of these passages he specifies that it is ordinary people (*idiōtai*; 30) – not just philosophers – who hold that certain things are by nature good or bad. In this case, then, Sextus does not claim to be fully in harmony with ordinary life; while the laws and customs of his native land may shape the sceptic's behaviour, including when he is confronted with appalling ethical dilemmas (*M* 11.163–6), he lacks the additional component of belief that both ordinary people and dogmatic philosophers have. Given the fact that ordinary religious beliefs as well as dogmatic beliefs about the gods serve as material for sceptical scrutiny, one might have expected that the case of religion would be parallel. But in this case Sextus arguably states, and at least strongly implies, that his stance towards religion is no different from that of ordinary people.

To return to a theme introduced earlier, it is hard not to see this as at least somewhat disingenuous. It is by now something of a commonplace that one should not think of ancient pagan religion as centred primarily around beliefs; what is most basic are the rituals themselves, and these did not necessarily – and in some cases, clearly did not in fact – carry with them any particular beliefs about why they were to be performed, or about the character of the gods in whose honour they were being performed. And this might seem to fit rather well with Sextus' description of his own religious attitude as a simple product of law and custom; he engages in certain sacrifices and dietary habits because those are the things he was raised to do – purely as a matter of habit, without any belief that these are the *right* things to do – and so too, one might say, did practitioners of ancient religion in general, if much recent scholarship on the subject is on the right lines. But this does not fit with what Sextus himself says (rightly or wrongly) about ordinary religious practitioners, and it sits uneasily with some of what he says about his own religious practice. On Sextus' picture ordinary people do *not* merely go through rituals as a matter of custom; they also hold beliefs about the gods, and these beliefs are among those on which the sceptic suspends judgement. And Sextus' own religious practice, which he presents as in conformity with ordinary practice, includes saying certain things that are among the very things on which he elsewhere induces suspension of judgement.

None of this is to deny that there may be a level of everyday belief that is immune from sceptical argumentation and that the sceptic may perfectly well adopt. The exact nature of the sceptic's everyday beliefs, if any, is a central and unresolved issue in the interpretation of ancient Greek scepticism. But although Sextus insists that he is in conformity with everyday attitudes when it comes to religion, *this* is not a case where he professes beliefs in an everyday context that can be considered immune from the effects of his scepticism. Rather, it is a case, like that of beliefs about what is really good and bad, where the beliefs of ordinary people – at least, as he himself interprets them – touch on the real nature of things, and are therefore vulnerable to sceptical scrutiny. So despite his claim to be in tune with ordinary life, he cannot consistently hold some of the religious beliefs that, on his own view, ordinary people hold.

CONCLUSION

This is a disappointing and, one might even say, a boring result. Our initial impression turns out to be correct. But it is not, perhaps, quite the end of the story. As we saw, there are traces of a different form of Pyrrhonism in which relativity, rather than undecidability, seems to play a leading role. On this model, the sceptic achieves his desired result by refusing legitimacy to any claims to the effect that something is a certain way *by nature* – where 'by nature' is understood to entail 'invariably and without regard to circumstances' – and by restricting himself to statements in which some form of relativization to circumstances is explicit. In the context of religion, such relativized statements include those concerning the kinds of sacrifices to be made to certain gods (but not other gods), and those concerning the religious practices that qualify as acceptable in a specific society (but not in other societies). Now, if the sceptic permits himself statements of this kind, and if ordinary religious discourse is thought to consist of statements of this kind, then it is easier to see how Sextus could claim that his religious attitudes are in tune with those of ordinary people, and that these attitudes are not liable to be undermined by sceptical argumentation. And in this context, a distinction such as the one Annas draws between religious beliefs and theological beliefs is easier to maintain. On the one hand, philosophers can worry about whether there are gods, and if so what they are like, in the real nature of things; and on the other, ordinary religious practice and discourse can proceed without having to consider such matters. Finally, this picture seems to fit comfortably with the largely practice-centred character of ancient pagan religion, where ordinary religious beliefs, such as 'It is pious to sacrifice goats to Artemis', seem to be ratifications or even descriptions of ordinary practices rather than global statements about the nature of the divine.

The picture is not, of course, immune to question. One might wonder, first, why the fact that a certain practice is not *considered* pious in some culture means that it *is not* by nature pious. Are we to assume that if a practice is not *considered* pious in some culture, then it *is not* pious in that culture (and therefore not invariably, or by nature, pious)? If so, what licenses that assumption? And in any case, what does it mean to say that some practice is pious in one culture but not in another? Might this not lead to a relativism of an arguably incoherent kind? Finally, supposing a philosopher were to interrogate an ordinary religious practitioner and ask 'So do you believe there really are gods or don't you?', can the ordinary person really answer 'That's none of my concern'? Certainly those in antiquity who were accused, rightly or wrongly, of being atheists were taken to be saying something that undermined ordinary religion. But it is hard to see how this could be so unless ordinary religion was understood to be committed to the general claim that gods do exist.

It may be, then, that the version of Pyrrhonism centred around relativity was inherently unstable in the case of religion. But it at least looks as if it might have been a more promising way for Sextus to combine adherence to ordinary religion with sceptical attack on dogmatic beliefs about the gods. Be that as it may, the relativity model, as we have seen, makes only a vestigial appearance in Sextus' treatment of religion. The dominant line of thought here makes quite clear, on the contrary, that ordinary religion *is* committed to the general claim that the gods exist; and Sextus does not even try to evade the consequence, which is that ordinary religion, just like dogmatic theology, is subject to sceptical scrutiny. And if this is accepted, the prospects for reconciling ordinary religion and scepticism about the existence of God seem dim indeed.

FURTHER READING

Burnyeat, M. (ed.) 1983. *The Skeptical Tradition*. Berkeley, CA: University of California Press.
Burnyeat, M. & M. Frede (eds) 1997. *The Original Sceptics: A Controversy*. Indianapolis, IN: Hackett.

On PIETY see also Chs 4, 5, 6. On RITUAL see also Ch. 20; Vol. 4, Chs 9, 20, 21. On SCEPTICISM see also Vol. 3, Ch. 5; Vol. 4, Ch. 11.

13

EARLY CHRISTIAN PHILOSOPHERS: JUSTIN, IRENAEUS, CLEMENT OF ALEXANDRIA, TERTULLIAN

Eric Osborn[1]

The four writers who begin Christian philosophy in the second century are different in their origin and in their philosophical backgrounds. Justin, from Rome, is as much a Stoic as he is a Platonist. Irenaeus, from Lyons, is only a philosopher by fragmentary borrowing and such strong overall argument as caused Erasmus to name him 'Irenaeus Philosophus'. Clement of Alexandria is plainly philosophical and frequently Platonist. Finally, Tertullian of Carthage, who criticized philosophy, is strongly Stoic. As Collingwood (1961) and Skinner (1969) insisted, there are no perennial problems in the history of ideas to which successive solutions are offered, but only problems that vary from thinker to thinker and from time to time.

JUSTIN

Justin was born in Nablus early in the second century, but came to Rome, where he taught as a philosopher. He tells how he moved from one philosophical school to another until he came to Platonism and beyond Plato to Christian faith (*Dialogue with Trypho* 2–8). In another place he insists that he became a Christian because he saw that Christians were "fearless in the face of death and all that men call fearful" (*Second Apology* 12.1). Justin is called an 'apologist' because he defends Christianity against four strong attacks: ridicule from philosophers, persecution

1. Eric Osborn, the principal author of this chapter, died on 11 May 2007 after a lifetime dedicated to scholarship. The editors are very grateful to David T. Runia for not only contributing a chapter on Philo for this volume but also generously agreeing to review and edit the advanced draft for this chapter. The editors also express their gratitude to the Osborn family for granting permission to publish it. We believe that translations throughout are Osborn's. [Editors' note]

by the state, attack from the Jews and strife with heretics. He enlarges the place of argument in Christian discourse.

How can one talk about God? Justin accepts the accusation that Christians are 'atheists' because they reject the many gods of the state. He puts forward a Platonic account of God as ineffable and unbegotten, following the language of Middle Platonists. We cannot name God, but we can speak to him (*First Apology* 9.3, 61.11; *Second Apology* 12.4). As official 'atheists', Christians follow the way of Socrates in rejecting the daemons whom pagans worship as gods.

How is God active in human affairs? The Logos (word, reason) of God is distinct in number from the Father, yet entirely God. The Logos is known by many names in contrast to the unnameable God and offers the link between God and humanity. The whole human race partakes of '*logos*' and those who have lived 'with *logos*' are Christians whether they were Greeks like Socrates and Heraclitus, or barbarians like Abraham, Ananias, Azarias, Misael and Elijah. Those who have lived 'without *logos*' have been evil men and murderers of those who have lived 'with *logos*'. Yet those who continue to live with *logos*, the Christians, are not troubled or fearful (*First Apology* 46.1–4). There are degrees of participation in *logos* and also a difference between the Logos himself and those who participate in *logos*. Plato and the Stoics, the poets of old, all had a part of the seed of *logos*. Their knowledge was incomplete, but whatever they said that contained truth came from the one Logos and the one God. Justin took the Stoic idea of 'spermatic *logos*' and affirmed its universality and its dependence on the Logos himself, who is the Son of God. Those who share in *logos* have limited but real apprehension of the truth of the Son as Logos.

Justin is able to see all biblical and ancient history as a history of the Logos who has spoken in limited, different ways and then finally come in perfection in Christ.

What makes a philosopher? Justin's movement from one philosophical school to another ends with a rejection of loyalty to any particular sect. From the beginning he insists that truth is the only consideration:

> [R]eason directs those who are truly pious and all true philosophers to honour and love only what is true; to decline to follow traditional opinions if these be worthless. Not only does sound reason direct us to refuse the guidance of those who taught anything wrong; but it is incumbent upon the lover of truth, by all means and even if death be threatened, even before his own life, to choose and to say what is right. (*First Apology* 2.1)

Justin describes the Christian as a lover of truth, following Plato's theme in the *Republic* (485–90). His Christian speaker insists, "I do not care whether Plato or Pythagoras ever thought anything like this at all, for this is the truth and that is why you should learn it" (*Dialogue with Trypho* 6.1). Similarly, Justin argues in his *Apology* that "our claim to be accepted is not that we say the same things as these writers, but that we say what is true" (*First Apology* 23.1).

The Bible is important for Justin because the prophets saw the truth that surpassed all other sources. Their vision apprehended the intellectual world (*Dialogue with Trypho* 7.1). So the content of Scripture can be called the 'true philosophy'. It shows how God's law and God's word (*nomos* and *logos*) had been presented in a progressive revelation. The law of Moses is now superseded and the words of the prophets are summed up in the words of Christ. A similar view of history as intellectual development is found in Celsus, a Platonist opponent of Christianity. Some have argued that Celsus wrote his great attack on Christianity (*True Logos*) after reading Justin and that his account of intellectual history is directed against Justin's account of perfection in Christ.

To sum up, Justin took over a Greek philosophical account of God that offered support against his pagan opponents, and gave an account of universal reason or *logos* where Christianity was the final truth towards which both the Old Testament and Greek philosophy moved. Justin died as a martyr in Rome during the prefecture of Junius Rusticus (162–68 CE).

IRENAEUS

Irenaeus came from Asia Minor but lived and wrote in Lyons, where he became bishop after 177. Erasmus called him a philosopher because he made argument central and this thematic contribution to philosophy of religion remains more important than miscellaneous borrowing. First, he gave a clear account of what Christianity was about. The *kerygma* (or proclamation) of the early Church is set out in his short work entitled, "Demonstration of the Apostolic Preaching". In this work, he makes the four points that govern his thinking. What is God like? Everything begins from God, who is universal intellect and love: "he is all thought, all will, all intellect, all light, all seeing, all hearing, the fount of all good things" (*Against Heresies* 1.12.2). "For God excels nature, having in himself the will because he is good, the power because he is powerful and the perfecting because he is rich and perfect" (2.29.2). There can only be one God (1.22.1), without beginning and without end (2.34.2, 3.8.3, 4.38.1). He is perfect, eternal and unchanging. He contains all things but is contained by none. "He is the cause of being to all things" (4.38.3).

Secondly, the one God has, since his creation of the world, acted in history (divine plan or economy). Thirdly, all that he did came to finality and perfection in Christ (recapitulation). Finally, now his salvation is open to all who believe and who wait for the final triumph of his goodness (inauguration and consummation). This fourfold account of the Christian message (God, divine plan, summing up in Christ, participation in salvation) is 'proved' by Irenaeus as the fulfilment of the words of Scripture and set out concisely in his *Demonstration*. However, a fuller account of his ideas comes in his attack on heresies (*Against Heresies*), where he refutes the various views of those who deny his central message. Irenaeus is important both for his statement of the starting-point of Christianity and for the wealth of argument with which he refutes his opponents. From the viewpoint of philosophy he is important because he adopts argument in his response to his opponents. Gnosticism was a complex and variable theosophy. Irenaeus was concerned to show that it lacked rational coherence, insisting that its opinions were *incredibile, fatuum, impossibile, inconstans*, while the teaching of the Church was coherent and credible, *credibile, acceptabile, constans* (2.10.4). For Irenaeus, God is a universal intelligent being, to whom all is known and who shows his reason, love and glory in the world he has made, especially in the words of his prophets and of his Son. As cosmic mind, God is incompatible with anthropomorphism, whether pagan or Gnostic (2.28.5).

God is creator, man is creature. God makes, while man is made. God creates, from nothing, all that is, bringing opposites into order as he creates. Irenaeus uses two images to describe God as creator: sovereign king and wise architect. God's royal will and command produce creation. "He spoke and it was, he commanded and it stood firm" (Psalm 31:9). The plan of creation comes from God as wise architect.

> It is safer and more accurate to confess the truth: the creator who formed the world is the only God and there is none beside him who received from himself the model and figure of things which have been made … From himself God found the model and form of created things. (*Against Heresies* 2.16.3)

One unique first cause is known because the human mind grows weary of infinite regress and in the end recognizes God as sole creator. Irenaeus is the first to give reasons for *creatio ex nihilo*. If God depended on unformed matter that he had not himself created, he could not be the sovereign God. After Irenaeus, the concept of 'creation from nothing' is firmly established in Christian thought.

Irenaeus anticipates recurring themes with his account of the divine plan in history. Hegel later found a dialectic in God's dealings with humanity. The return of the world to God happens through the resurrection of Christ: "negation is thereby overcome, and the negation of negation is thus the impulse of the divine nature" (Hegel 1969: 294–5). Irenaeus has a universal view of history and sees the divine plan as the way in which the shepherd brings the lost sheep home on his shoulders. Development is central to Irenaeus. In history, God and man become 'accustomed' to one another, God reveals himself progressively and man moves upwards to God. Adam never leaves the hands of God. "For his hand encloses us in our hidden and secret ways" (*Against Heresies* 4.19.2).

The divine plan reaches its perfection in the coming of Christ who is *Christus Victor*:

> But indeed our lord is the one true master. He, the son of God, is truly good; he, the word of God, became son of man and endured

> suffering for us. For he has fought and conquered: on the one hand as man he fought for the fathers and redeemed their disobedience by his obedience; on the other hand, he has bound the strong man, set free the weak, and has poured out salvation on the work of his hands, destroying sin. For the lord is patient and merciful and loves the human race. (3.18.6)

The 'summing up' or 'recapitulation' of all things is the centre of God's plan for human history. It does four things: it corrects, perfects, inaugurates and consummates a new humanity. In contrast to the Gnostic division of spirit and matter, God and humanity, invisible and visible, Irenaeus provides an account of God and the world where God is active and present in the world he has made.

Irenaeus does not draw on contemporary philosophy except in his insistence on the transcendence of God and the unity of the cosmos. Yet by his rejection of the dualist theosophies of the Gnostics, his influence on argued Christian thought became immense. Augustine developed a similar view of cosmic history, which remained influential in Western thought.

CLEMENT OF ALEXANDRIA

Clement is the first early Christian thinker to make exuberant use of philosophical sources. Born probably in Athens, he came to Alexandria in the last quarter of the second century. He travelled around the Mediterranean world, studying under different teachers, and he made most of Greek philosophy useful for the purposes of Christian thinking. While influenced more by Plato and Middle Platonism, he uses other forms of philosophy and takes whatever is useful to explain the puzzles that Christianity has brought.

He saw three main problems facing a Christian philosophy of religion. First of all, the central message of Christianity had to do with a divine movement in history that was declared in Scripture and fulfilled in Jesus Christ. How could one move from this narrative of divine action to philosophical answers about God, humanity, right and wrong? Irenaeus had shown that the Christian message was tied to time and movement. How were Christians to bridge the gap from narrative and oracle to metaphysics? Clement answered this first question with what he called 'the true dialectic'. Everything is ordered by "the goodness of the only one true, almighty God, from age to age saving by the Son" (*Miscellanies* 7.2.12). The divine plan moves to fulfilment in Christ and to a new age that offers salvation. The law was given by Moses, but grace and truth came by Jesus Christ. For Clement as for Justin, the divine plan included the gift of philosophy for the Greeks to prepare them for Christ; it brought human beings from sunset to sunrise and now they must respond to God's fullness. Clement finds in Scripture the 'true dialectic'. He takes Plato's concept of dialectic as rational, aesthetic and moral order, and applies it to the biblical narrative. Scripture points to a universal providence (*Miscellanies* 1.6.2, 1.24.160.5, 2.6.29). The 'true dialectic' as found in Scripture is a source of instruction and education, a prophetic source of knowledge and an answer to questions concerning goodness and truth. Dialectic begins as a rational discussion of Scripture, turning its puzzles into coherent argument. As it finds its way through the detail of Scripture it moves towards universal ideas and finally to God. "The mind is the place of the ideas, and God is mind ... When the soul, ascending beyond the sphere of becoming, becomes aware of itself and has converse with the ideas ... it becomes a kind of angel and will be with Christ" (*Miscellanies* 4.25.155.2–4). By the analysis of Scripture, the 'true dialectic' brings a science of divine and heavenly things from which guidance in human affairs is to be derived (*Miscellanies* 1.28.177.1). Clement applies Plato's dialectic to the content of Scripture because the intellectual world is within the mind of God. In the Platonic tradition, the *kosmos noētos* could refer to the patterns of Forms, to the way in which the Forms fit together or simply to a higher world beyond the senses. In Justin and Irenaeus, Scripture had already been identified as the mind and will of God, ordered by the one divine plan. Clement adds to the takeover of the world of Forms by the divine plan a takeover of Platonic method (Osborn 2005: 68). Clement's fusion of Scripture and metaphysics, of prophecy and Plato, opens the way to biblical theology (Mondésert 1944: 237–52). Clement follows Paul in identifying Christ crucified as the one part of Scripture to be taken literally. All else was to be interpreted figuratively as leading to the finality of the incarnate and crucified Lord.

Clement's second main problem, which he also solved by means of philosophy, was the question of how an uncompromising monotheist could believe in both Father and Son as God. This was the claim of the Fourth Gospel: no one came to the Father but by the Son and no one came to the Son but by the Father. There was no Father without Son and no Son without Father. The Word was the revelation of the unknown Father; he was also within the Father and yet related reciprocally to the Father. God (the Father) was beyond God (the Son); God (the Son) was within God (the Father); God (the Son) was beside God (the Father). Clement's solution of this puzzle depended on Platonism and Pythagoreanism. Unity could be simple unity (one and nothing but one) and complex unity (one and many). Moderatus of Gades (*c.*60 CE) states most clearly the difference between the two principles of unity. A modern interpreter traced this move to Plato's *Parmenides*:

> Think of a principle which so completely transcends all plurality that it refuses every predicate, even that of existence; which is neither in motion nor at rest, neither in time nor in space; of which we can say nothing, not even that it is identical with itself or different from other things: and *side by side with this*, a second principle of unity, containing the seeds of all the contraries – a principle which, if we once grant it existence, proceeds to pluralize itself indefinitely in a universe of

> existent unities. If for the moment we leave fragments out of account and consider only the extant works of Greek philosophers before the age of Plotinus, there is one passage, and so far as I know one passage only, where these thoughts receive connected expression – namely, the first and second 'hypotheses' in the second part of Plato's *Parmenides*.
> (Dodds 1928: 132)

The development in Alcinous (second century CE) points clearly to a divine mind that knows itself and whose thinking is a 'thinking of thinking': "But since the first mind is the noblest of things, the object of its thought must also be noblest, and nothing is nobler than it is itself; so therefore, it would have eternally to contemplate itself and its own thoughts, and this activity it has is Idea" (Alcinous, *Didaskalikos* 10.3). Clement is able to use this account of God to describe the Christian account of the unknown God and of his Mind or Logos, the unity and reciprocity of Father and Son.

From this account of God as Father and Son as simple and complex unity, Clement explains the reciprocity of the one God, Father and Son, in the Fourth Gospel. "Reciprocity in mutual knowledge, glory, love, witness and work, points to the unique oneness of father and son" (Osborn 2005: 135). Clement develops divine reciprocity into three 'mysteries of love'. Everything depends on Father and Son as the first ellipse of love; then follows the divine love of God for humankind and finally the love of neighbour for neighbour. He uses the remarkable image of a set of scales to explain the balance between Jesus and the Father (*Teacher* 1.8.71.3). The Father shares the goodness of the Son and the Son shares the goodness of the Father. The highest rung of the ladder of being is not a rung but a beam-balance (Osborn 2005: 140).

The third and final problem to which Clement applies philosophy is the relation between faith and knowledge. For the Greeks, faith was a miserable substitute for knowledge; for the Christian, it was where everything began and ended. Faith was a simple thing that, like the mustard seed, grew magnificently. Faith is the power of God, the perception of what eye has not seen, the searching of divine mystery and the hope that is always pointing ahead. Clement takes several arguments from philosophers to indicate the necessity for faith. First, faith as the 'substance of things hoped for' finds support in the Epicurean demand for preconceptions. For the Epicureans, there was no way into knowledge except by preconception, *prolēpsis*. The Stoics came next to support faith with their account of 'anticipatory choice'. Knowledge was a comprehension that argument could not overthrow. Both Platonists and Stoics insist that this choice or assent is in our power (*Miscellanies* 2.12.54 [= Arnim & Adler 1924: 2.992]). Again, the place of mental perception is acknowledged by philosophers from Heraclitus to Plato and beyond. Plato claimed that it was impossible to learn the truth about God except from God or God's offspring. We have the divine oracles that tell us of God (*Miscellanies* 6.15.123). Faith is the acceptance of unprovable first principles and these depend, according to both Aristotle and Plato, on no higher axiom. Clement also speaks of faith as judgement (*krima*), a Stoic alternative to the notion of assent (Osborn 2005: 194).

From a basis of faith, Clement is able to build his way of argument and dialectic. He reproduces a logic notebook that discusses logical terms and provides a background to his argument elsewhere (*ibid.*: 206).

Beyond all the unceasing dialectic, there lies the final vision of God as the source of truth and goodness. Goodness must be participation in divine goodness and is a recovering of the likeness to God that human beings had forfeited through sin. Knowledge is linked to reciprocity with God, living in continual prayer and dependence on God's guidance. A careful study of Clement's account of the complete Christian shows his dependence on the ideal of the Greek sage. The concept of the life that contemplates eternal truths and that is devoted to instruction and virtue can be most clearly linked to Platonic thought (Wyrwa 1983).

Clement puts forward an account of Christianity that derives much of its argument and shape from the philosophy that he uses. His three great problems – the divine plan, which becomes the true dialectic; the reciprocity of Father and Son, which becomes the unity of the transcendent one with the one-many; and faith as anticipation, assent and perception – enabled him to begin from the New Testament and to proceed along paths that the philosophers had taken. Each of the questions that challenged Christian belief provided enrichment as it opened up the world of Greek philosophy to Christian use.

TERTULLIAN

Tertullian, the fourth of our second-century pioneers, confirms what we have found in his predecessors. He shares a first allegiance to the Christian kerygma of one God, divine plan, summing up and participation. Again, he shows the remarkable originality that has already been noticed in his predecessors. None is derivative from another. Certainly, there are traces of Justin in Clement but they are only traces. The extraordinary thing is that the first Christian philosophers were remarkably different.

Tertullian begins the tradition of Western Christian thought: "In western Christianity, everything seems to commence with Tertullian: the technical language of Christians, theology, interpretation of scripture and other manifestations" (Moreschini 1990: 55). He is "astonishingly original and personal" (Daniélou 1977: 341). He wrote his own kind of Latin and set out arguments. He had a vivid sense of the power of words and lived in perpetual controversy. His final vocabulary centres on the mystery of salvation: "What in the end is for you the total disgrace of my God, is the mystery of mankind's salvation" (*Against Marcion* 2.27). He begins as a Stoic with an undefined consciousness of God and fills that consciousness with Christian content.

He is an elusive writer who has been widely misunderstood. He is best known from two notorious passages: "What has Athens to do with Jerusalem?" (*On the Prescription of Heretics* 7.9), and "It is credible because inept … certain because impossible" (*On the Flesh of Christ* 5.4). The first passage is a puzzle because in Tertullian Athens has a lot to do with Jerusalem; he is constantly drawing on a classical heritage. In the second claim, there is paradox because credibility and ineptness, certainty and impossibility, are opposites. The puzzle of Athens and Jerusalem is solved very simply by the preposition 'after'. The perfection of Christ is the climax of a history that includes Greek philosophy. All is summed up in Christ and there is no sense in going back to Greek preparation in order to elaborate Christianity.

> Let them beware who put forward a Stoic, Platonic dialectical form of Christianity. For there is no need of curiosity *after* Christ, no need of inquiry after the gospel. When we have believed we have no desire to add to our faith. For this is our primary faith, that there is nothing further which we ought to believe.
>
> (*On the Prescription of Heretics* 7.11–13)

Similarly, the paradox of Tertullian (that the ineptitude of Christ crucified makes him credible) is clearly understood when his argument is analysed. We may restate his argument concisely:

> God is wholly other, and differs from man and from all else. If he is joined to man in a way which is not shameful, inept and impossible, then either God is no longer God or man is no longer man. If God is joined to man in a way which is shameful, inept and impossible, then God is truly God and man is truly man. (Osborn 1997: 62)

Recapitulation is the joining of the end to the beginning, the joining of man to God. For Tertullian, "just as alpha rolls on to omega and then omega rolls back to alpha, so he might show in himself the way from the beginning to the end and the way from the end to the beginning" (*On Marrying Only Once* 5.2). God became man either in a way that is apt and therefore untrue, or in a way that is inept and therefore true.

Tertullian's world is Stoic and Heraclitean, governed by the strife of opposites, of light with darkness and good with evil:

> That same reason which constructed the universe out of diversity, so that all things from their antithetical substances agree in a unity – empty and solid, animate and inanimate, comprehensible and incomprehensible, light and darkness, even life and death – has also so disposed the whole course of existence according to a distinct plan, so that the first

> part of it which we inhabit, reckoned from the creation, flows on to its end in the age of time; and the following part, to which we look, extends into boundless eternity. (*Apology* 48.11; Osborn 1997: 69)

The soul is naturally Christian and comes to recognize God in the world. God is known only to himself, yet may be found by all who do not "refuse to recognize him, of whom they cannot be ignorant" (*Apology* 17.3). Despite all the burdens and barriers that surround it, the awakening soul names God: "Good God! Great God! … O testimony of the soul which is naturally Christian!" (*Apology* 17.6).

Tertullian's longest work was directed against Marcion, who posed the major threat to Christian belief. Marcion, in his *Antitheses*, argued that the God of the Old Testament could not be the God of the Gospels. The supreme, merciful bringer of salvation cannot be the ruthless judge of the Old Testament nor the creator of the cruelties of the world. God's goodness cannot be consistent with the justice of the ancient law. Tertullian argues: "I shall by means of these antitheses recognize in Christ my own jealous God. He did in the beginning, by his own right, by a hostility which was rational and therefore good, provide beforehand for the maturity and fuller ripeness of the things which were his" (*Against Marcion* 2.29.4). Tertullian explains the rationality of divine goodness, why the same God creates and redeems, and why a good God must be just. Tertullian is generally (but not always) convincing, as when describing God's declaration 'let us make man' in the following way:

> It was goodness who spoke, it was goodness who formed man out of clay into that noble substance of flesh, a substance built out of one material to possess many attributes. It was goodness who breathed soul into him – soul not dead but living. Goodness gave him dominion over all things, to enjoy, to govern and even to give them names. Still more, it was goodness who gave man additional delights, so that although in possession of the whole world, he had his dwelling in the healthier parts of it: so early was he transferred to paradise as he has been transferred out of the world into the church. The same goodness sought out a help for him, so that no good thing might be lacking: "it is not good", God said, "that man should be alone".
>
> (*Against Marcion* 2.4.4ff; Osborn 1997: 99)

There are antitheses in the biblical account of God, but they must be held within God and not divided between two Gods.

Tertullian's ingenuity shows up in two other problems: Trinity and christology. His account of the Trinity becomes influential for later Christianity. Father and Son are one God, separated not by intrinsic character but by their disposition alone. 'Father and Son' points to a disposition or relation that exists without internal variety. The category 'sweet and bitter' points to a relative difference in the intrinsic character of things, but Father and Son do not differ in intrinsic character but only in relation. "If then, despite being unaffected in themselves they change because of something else's disposition relative to them, it is clear that relatively disposed things have their existence in their disposition alone and not through any differentiation." This account of the fourth Stoic category (Simplicius, *On Aristotle's Categories* 165.32–166.29, trans. in Long & Sedley 1987: 29C) was taken up by Tertullian and applied to the Father and the Son (*Against Praxeas* 10; cf. Osborn 1997: 127).

Equally remarkable is Tertullian's use of Stoic logic to explain the 'two natures' in Christ. Stoics distinguished between three sorts of mixtures: one in which different things were simply juxtaposed, another in which things disappeared into a new substance and a third where two things were blended together totally without losing their initial qualities. Jesus became God and man, not in a new kind of mixture, but by the total blending of Godhead and humanity. In Stoic terms, "blended substances ... preserve their own natures in the mixture" (Long & Sedley 1987: 48D). Tertullian writes, "We see a twofold state, not confused but joined in one person, God and man, Jesus" (*Against Praxeas* 27).

Tertullian's love of strife and the conflict of opposites gives him a much less contemplative approach to prayer than that found in Clement. Prayer is natural, for cattle bend their knees when they rise from rest and look to heaven with a bellow or a roar (*On Prayer* 29.4). Prayer is the way in which Christians join in the conflict between good and evil and the Lord's Prayer declares the present conflict, which will end in God's kingdom.

Sin is important, for man's likeness to God was lost by Adam's sin and restored by grace (*On Baptism* 5.7). Stoicism gives a physical nature to the corruption of sin, which is passed on from parent to child so that the whole race is infected (*On the Testimony of the Soul* 3.2). Yet sin remains culpable and human freedom is central to the relation between sinner and God. Tertullian signs himself, "Tertullian the sinner" (*On Baptism* 20.5).

Tertullian's humour comes out at many points and he regards laughter as a duty in the face of philosophical stupidity. Most interesting is his rejection of Hermogenes in contrast to his rejection of the Valentinians. Both of these opponents were dualist in their account of God and their conclusions held common ground. Yet there is a remarkable difference. Against Hermogenes, who provides arguments, Tertullian gives reasonable, careful and even tedious arguments. Against the Valentinians, who simply tell the story of a Gnostic myth and who offer no arguments, Tertullian presents ridicule. When confronted by theosophy or myth, Tertullian sees ridicule as a Christian duty. The stories of the Valentinians have no basis in logic and no coherence. Against such fables, "derision is a duty" (*risus officium est*) (*Against the Valentinians* 6.2f.).

For the rest, Tertullian has many striking things to say. His account of the resurrection of the flesh is powerfully argued: "the flesh (*caro*) is the hinge (*cardo*) of salvation" (*On the Resurrection of the Flesh* 8.2). Just as a storm-damaged ship that has limped into harbour can be renewed and refitted, so the human flesh will be transformed at the resurrection (*On the Resurrection of the Flesh* 59–63).

***

To sum up our first four Christian philosophers, we may note their originality and imagination. Each is different and tackles different but related problems.

FURTHER READING

Barnes, T. 1985. *Tertullian: A Historical and Literary Study*. Oxford: Oxford University Press.

Behr, J. 2000. *Asceticism and Anthropology in Irenaeus and Clement of Alexandria*. Oxford: Oxford University Press.

Chadwick, H. 1966. *Early Christian Thought and the Classical Tradition*. Oxford: Oxford University Press.

Fredouille, J. 1972. *Tertullien et la conversion de la culture antique*. Paris: Études Augustiniennes.

Lilla, S. 1971. *Clement of Alexandria: A Study in Christian Platonism and Gnosticism*. Oxford: Oxford University Press.

Osborn, E. 1957. *The Philosophy of Clement of Alexandria*. Cambridge: Cambridge University Press.

Osborn, E. 1973. *Justin Martyr*. Tübingen: J. C. B. Mohr/Paul Siebeck.

Osborn, E. 1981. *The Beginning of Christian Philosophy*. Cambridge: Cambridge University Press.

Osborn, E. 2001. *Irenaeus of Lyons*. Cambridge: Cambridge University Press.

Rankin, D. 1995. *Tertullian and the Church*. Cambridge: Cambridge University Press.

Runia, D. T. 1993. *Philo in Early Christian Literature: A Survey*. Minneapolis, MN: Augsburg Fortress Press.

On CREATION see also Chs 9, 17; Vol. 3, Ch. 9; Vol. 5, Ch. 5. On DIALECTIC see also Ch. 15. On FAITH see also Vol. 2, Chs 6, 12, 16, 18; Vol. 3, Ch. 8; Vol. 4, Chs 8, 10, 13; Vol. 5, Chs 7, 18. On FORMS/IDEAS see also Ch. 4, 11; Vol. 2, Ch. 15. On LOGOS see also Chs 9, 11; Vol. 2, Ch. 19. On PRAYER see also Ch. 18; Vol. 3, Ch. 5; Vol. 5, Ch. 21. On SALVATION see also Ch. 10; Vol. 2, Ch. 3; Vol. 4, Ch. 19. On SCRIPTURE see also Chs 9, 17; Vol. 2, Ch. 19; Vol. 3, Chs 3, 4, 15; Vol. 4, Ch. 3; Vol. 5, Ch. 12. On SIN see also Ch. 10; Vol. 3, Ch. 4. On TRUTH see also Vol. 2, Ch. 17; Vol. 3, Chs 3, 8, 13; Vol. 4, Chs 8, 18; Vol. 5, Ch. 4.

14

ORIGEN

Jeffrey Hause

It would seem that Origen (*c.*186–*c.*255) was born into most unpropitious circumstances. His family belonged to the Christian minority, which educated pagans reviled and the Roman Empire outlawed as an unpatriotic religious novelty. In the persecutions of Septimius Severus, his father, Leonides, was beheaded and the family's property confiscated. The seventeen-year-old Origen, as eldest son, was charged with supporting the family of ten, which he did by teaching literature to private students and, later, the elements of Christianity to catechumens, neither job prestigious. What mattered most to Origen, however, was to become ever more Christ-like and to illuminate, for himself and others, the mysteries hidden in the Scriptures. His various biographers, although not impartial, still paint a reliable picture of Origen's remarkable virtue, while many of his views, adopted by Athanasius, Augustine, and the Cappadocians, marked the mainstream of both Eastern and Western Christianity. From his perspective, his circumstances were propitious indeed.

He was born in cosmopolitan Alexandria, in his day one of the world's centres of learning, where Origen had access to a wide array of texts and brilliant instructors. The patronage of wealthy Christians enabled him to study with Ammonius Saccas, the Platonist philosopher who would later instruct Plotinus, as well as other teachers, such as an unnamed Jewish convert to Christianity who introduced Origen to rabbinic traditions of scriptural interpretation. He eventually founded his own school of advanced studies. Justin Martyr and Clement of Alexandria had already worked to integrate Greek philosophy into Christianity, as Philo had into Judaism, and Origen drew on their pioneering work in his account of Christianity as the true philosophy that all philosophies strove to be, but failed. As his published works circulated, his fame grew, and his work took him to cities throughout the Roman Empire, including Antioch, where he was summoned to a debate by the Emperor Alexander Severus' mother, Julia Mammaea. Origen left Alexandria in 233 and eventually settled in Caesarea, where he was ordained a priest. In addition to preaching, he continued to run his own school of advanced studies and write. His years in Caesarea were exceptionally productive until he was arrested and tortured in the persecutions of the Emperor Decius. Weakened by the torture, he died shortly afterwards, probably in 255 when he was 69.

One of antiquity's most prodigious writers, Origen wrote detailed commentaries on nearly every book of the Bible. In his view, the literal sense of Scripture veils its more important spiritual sense, which expresses that portion of divine wisdom God has so far revealed to human beings. However, to see beyond the veil, to grasp the Bible's deepest truths, an exegete needs scholarly aptitude and divine help in the form of moral virtue and inspiration. Devoting himself to study and trusting God to help him, Origen makes spiritual exegesis his life's work and sees it as his duty to help others to grasp the divine wisdom in so far as they can. Origen's most extraordinary exegetical work is his *Commentary on John*, containing his fullest account of the Son's titles, central both to the spiritual interpretation of the Bible and to our return to God. Through this work Origen also sought to reclaim John's Gospel and its spiritual interpretation from prevalent Gnostic misreadings. He also composed homilies on the Bible, treatises on religious themes and two more overtly philosophical works: the late *Against Celsus*, which defends Christianity against the Hellenistic philosopher Celsus' attacks, and the relatively early *On First Principles*. This latter work is sometimes taken as Origen's only original contribution to philosophy as opposed to biblical studies, but that is a mistake. *On First Principles* is no less biblically based than Origen's other works, which Origen would in turn defend as deeply philosophical not despite but because of their scriptural bases. In engaging Greek philosophy, Origen's confidence in orthodox Christianity allows him to read the philosophers charitably, explaining their errors with equanimity, but also pointing out whatever affinities of goal and similarities of doctrine he finds. He feels no need to make concessions to Greek philosophy, but in developing his own worldview he helps himself to the treasures of pagan learning, just as the Hebrews had been allowed to plunder the Egyptians' treasures in Exodus 12:36. His writings express his own life's commitments: placing himself in the discipline of the Word, he strives to know himself and grow ever more virtuous so as to know and love God and his creation ever better, and he seeks to help others along the same path.

ORIGEN AND PHILOSOPHY

Given his scholarly focus on the Bible, Origen often expresses his distrust of the philosophers. In his judgement, their schools have fragmented the discipline and their theories contain "vain deceit" (*Against Celsus* Prol. 5, quoting Colossians 2:8). We might, then, have expected Origen to abandon philosophy entirely, adopting instead a mythological or mystical approach to religion. While Origen does make room for mysticism, he rejects the mythological approach to understanding God and the world that characterizes his distant predecessors Homer and Hesiod, siding with the long tradition of Greek philosophy that the world is a cosmos:

an ordered system that is rationally comprehensible. Moreover, Origen's philosophical learning is prodigious, and he steeped his students in works by pagan philosophers from all schools, except those he deemed atheistic. He employs the concepts and methods of philosophy to resolve conflicts and solve problems; to expand our knowledge of God, the cosmos, and in particular rational creatures; and to discover virtue's demands, help us to find our way to our ultimate goal and help us transform our lives. These are the common tasks of Greek philosophy, and they characterize most philosophy to the present day.

Origen's attitude toward Greek philosophy is complex. He clearly finds it invaluable for exegesis: philosophical concepts can illuminate the Scriptures, while philosophical techniques give the exegete the tools necessary to discover a coherent reading of the entire Bible. What is more, philosophy is crucial for apologetic work. Origen's *Against Celsus* turns philosophy itself against Celsus' philosophical attacks on Christianity. Origen also recognizes that philosophical reflection has uncovered many truths about God and creation, such as that God is eternal, immutable and absolutely simple. Most astoundingly, Origen writes, some Platonists have discovered independently of the Scriptures that "all things were created by the Word or Reason of God", a central doctrine of Christianity (*On First Principles* 1.3.1). It is no wonder Paul himself finds Greek philosophy impressive; yet Paul also sees it as "vain deceit", and Origen echoes this judgement. Origen lacks Anselm of Canterbury's conviction that we can discover by reason the central truths of Christianity, including the doctrines that God is a Trinity and created the world out of nothing. He is nonetheless not as wary as Tertullian, who regards philosophy as the mother of heresy. In Origen's view, the most important subjects tackled by the philosophers – God, the origin of the cosmos, the nature of the soul – are simply too difficult for unaided reason to master, and so Greek philosophy, whatever its triumphs, is doomed to error. Unmoored from revelation, the philosophers cannot detect their mistakes, but set up rival systems of thought that serve only to insulate them from correction and to fragment their discipline. As a result, on Origen's view, no Greek philosopher has an accurate grasp of God and his creation (*Homily on Genesis* 14.3).

The remedy is not to reject philosophy, but to transform it. Origen's work not only makes use of philosophy, but is *itself* philosophy, the true and sacred philosophy that can succeed where Greek philosophy fails because sacred philosophy is anchored in Scripture (*Commentary on the Song of Songs* prol. 3.20). The bulk of Origen's work, even his commentaries and homilies on Scripture, help the reader to develop a philosophical account of Christianity. We can best see this aspect of Origen's project in *On First Principles*. There, Origen explains that the starting-points of his investigations consist of the propositions in the Rule of Faith, that is, those truths taught clearly and plainly in Scripture, the doctrine handed down by the Apostles, and what is universally accepted by the Church. Using this rule as a defence against misinterpretation, we can gather more truths from the Scriptures, and in the effort of reconciling, integrating and developing them, we will eventually discern, at least dimly, the ultimate explanatory principles. We begin with "Jesus Christ, and him crucified", but eventually we discover how the same Christ is the formal, final and efficient cause of the cosmos, and from this glimpse of Christ, who is the Father's image, we grasp what we can of the Father, the ultimate principle of all.

For Origen, what defines philosophy is in part its subject matter and its characteristic methods for resolving problems. However, Origen, like most ancient thinkers, also takes philosophy to be a discipline in the fullest sense: a way to structure one's life. We can glean this not just from Origen's own writings, but most vividly from the testimony of one of Origen's students who lived and studied with him at Caesarea. This student, then known as Theodore, is often thought to be the youthful St Gregory the Wonderworker before he assumed his Christian name at baptism. On leaving Origen's school, Theodore delivered an *Address of Thanksgiving*, detailing his teacher's curriculum and pedagogical strategies. He describes Origen's philosophical instruction as a sort of intellectual, moral and spiritual formation. In addition to teaching the various doctrines of the Greeks and how to evaluate them critically, Origen sought to train his students to live righteously. It was not mere doctrines about the soul's impulses that they learned to master; they learned to master those impulses themselves. Most importantly, Origen trained his students to strive to know themselves, which Theodore describes as philosophy's highest achievement. Theodore also notes that Origen's own life and character served as a model for his students. Origen explains in his own works his reasons for linking intellectual, moral and spiritual formation. All philosophers strive for ever greater enlightenment about God and his creation. However, in his view, unless they reflect on their lives, come to know themselves, purge themselves of their base desires, and never cease to transform themselves through moral and spiritual discipline, they will fail to gain the wisdom they seek. The Son is Wisdom itself, and the more like the Son one becomes, the more enlightened one will be.

THE TRINITY

Origen accepts the view common to Middle Platonism and to most Christian thought that God (the Father) lies beyond human comprehension or measure. Even in our future life, when we return to the Father and shed the gross material bodies that now dull our minds, the Father will still lie beyond our grasp. Some later Christian thinkers explain God's incomprehensibility by appealing to his infinity, but Origen cannot avail himself of this explanation. Because he accepts the commonly held Greek view that what is infinite is unknowable even to God, if he held that God is infinite, he would also have to admit that God cannot comprehend himself (*On First Principles* 2.9.1). Hence, Origen explains the fact that we cannot grasp the Father, despite his finitude, by stressing the gulf between our weak intellects and the Father's surpassing, if limited, greatness.

This same gulf explains why our language is inadequate for describing the Father. However, even if language cannot convey exactly what the Father is, it can still convey what he is not: the Father is uncreated, immaterial, incorporeal, immutable and absolutely simple, that is, incomposite. Of these attributes, the one Origen stresses is incorporeality. Because the Bible speaks of God's face and hands and of his walking in the Garden of Eden, Christians who failed to read the Bible spiritually took these passages to imply that the Father had a body. Moreover, the pagan philosopher Celsus interpreted the biblical claim that human beings are created in God's image to imply that God has a body. If they are right, Origen argues, the Father would be a composite of soul and body. That view is incompatible with the apostolic teaching that the Father is the first principle of all else, for the Father's soul and body, as the elements that constitute him, would be prior principles (*On First Principles* 1.1.5–6; *Against Celsus* 6.63).

Origen also employs a strategy that would later be called 'the way of eminence' (*via eminentiae*) to remedy the inadequacies of our ordinary predicates for describing the Father. If there were some whose weak eyes could stand to see only the flicker of a lamp, we could teach them about the sun only by expressing that the sun's light is unspeakably greater and more glorious than the candle's flame. Likewise, we express God's positive attributes, such as his goodness, most accurately when we say that they are unspeakably greater than what we are able to perceive from his creatures, which nevertheless give us some indication of what their first principle is like (*On First Principles* 1.1.5–6).

The Father eternally generates the Son, a divine hypostasis numerically distinct from the Father. While the Father has his existence and divinity from himself, the Son is begotten of the Father and participates in the Father's divinity. That is why the Gospel of John speaks of the Father as *the* God (*ho theos*), while it describes the Son as God (*theos*) (*Commentary on John* 2.17). Origen's sketch of the relationship between the Father and the Son is motivated by his desire to find an account of the Trinity that is consistent with monotheism. If Father and Son are numerically distinct hypostases, each with a divine nature, then there are two Gods. Hence, some monotheists concluded that Father and Son must be one and the same hypostasis, but we speak of the Son in order to capture certain aspects of the Father, such as his role as saviour. Other monotheists, unwilling to maintain that the Son is merely an aspect of the Father, concluded that the Son is indeed numerically distinct from the Father, but not divine. Finding these views heterodox, Origen resolves the problem by retaining the view that Father and Son are numerically distinct divine hypostases, but avoids falling into polytheism because these two hypostases are strictly speaking one God, for the Son participates in the Father's divinity (*Commentary on John* 2.16–17). The Father and Son are also one in yet another sense. Although each divine hypostasis has its own will, the Son conforms his will to the Father's: in their content, the two wills are indistinguishable. While some creatures also conform their wills to the Father's in so far as they understand it, no creature has a complete grasp of his will: some fail to see all that he wills, or fail to see it distinctly. Only the Son fully comprehends the Father's will and conforms his will to it, and therefore only the Son is the Father's image (*Commentary on John* 13.228–32).

In his *Commentary on John*, after noting that the Father is absolutely one and simple, Origen adds that the Son, in contrast, becomes the many things that creatures need for their salvation (*Commentary on John* 1.119). These many things, which Origen calls his "aspects", excellences" or "titles", play a central role in Origen's thought. The project of spiritual interpretation is to deepen our understanding of them, since they reveal to us who the Son is, and our only knowledge of the Father is through his image, the Son (Wolinski 1995). Moreover, they reveal the route of return to the Father, since many of them are the names of the virtues we must acquire and the names of the Son in so far as he helps us at various stages on the road of return.

Origen divides the Son's titles into two groups: those that belong to the Son in so far as he is the mediator between the Father and the fallen world (such as 'Shepherd', 'Redemption' and 'King'), and those that belong to him in so far as he is the Son (such as 'Wisdom', 'Truth', 'Power', 'Justice' and 'Logos', that is, 'Word' or 'Reason'), titles that would belong to him even if there had been no creatures in need of salvation. When Origen says that the Son "becomes" these things, he does not mean that the Son undergoes changes by acquiring certain properties. Like the Father, the Son is immutable. However, we will bear a different relation to him depending on the state of our own spiritual progress. For those who are meek but who lack control over their non-rational desires, the Son is Shepherd. The Son rules as King over those who have more rational control over themselves. Those very advanced, whose wills already conform to the Son's, need only a deeper vision of the Son, and for them he is Logos, and finally Wisdom. In none of these cases is there a distinction in the Son himself except in so far as some of these titles are grounded in the activity of Jesus Christ, the Son incarnate. We conceive of the Son differently, and bestow various titles on him, in so far as we receive different sorts of help from him in the various stages of our return.

When Origen speaks of the Son's "acquisition" of those titles belonging to him as Son, once again he does not mean that the Son gains various properties one by one, but rather that certain titles are logically dependent on others and in that sense are 'later' than others. Origen asserts that the Son's most ancient title is 'Wisdom' on the basis of Proverbs 8:22–30, which reports that Wisdom is the beginning. On the other hand, John reports that the Logos was in the beginning (1:1), and that Life came to be in the Logos (1:3–4). Among these titles, 'Life' is posterior to 'Logos', which is in turn posterior to 'Wisdom'. What Origen seems to mean is that the explanation of the Son's later titles requires mention of the earlier ones.[1] Hence, Origen

1. Many scholastic philosophers, especially the Scotists, speak of prior and posterior metaphysical (as opposed to temporal) moments, which they called 'instants of nature'. See Normore (2003: 134), to which I am indebted for my formulation of Origen's views.

says that as Wisdom, the Son comprehends all things. As Logos, he communicates what he comprehends to rational creatures. Because we cannot explain this role as Logos without appealing to his role as Wisdom, the title 'Logos' is later than the title 'Wisdom'. Origen offers this account of the relative priority and posteriority of the Son's titles in so far as they belong to him as mediator between the Father and rational creatures. However, even if we restrict ourselves to those titles in so far as they belong to the Son as Son, we can still see why 'Wisdom' is a more ancient title. The Son is Wisdom because he contains in himself an intelligible cosmos, that is, the exemplars of all things that God creates or could create. As Logos, the Son is the expression of the Father's mind, just as human beings' words are the expressions of their minds. Origen could say, then, that it is precisely because he contains the intelligible cosmos that the Son expresses the Father's mind and is the Father's image. In that case, we must appeal to the Son's being Wisdom in order to explain why he is Logos, and so 'Wisdom' once again would turn out to be prior to 'Logos' among the Son's titles.

Origen admits that even without Scripture, philosophers have come to know truths about the Father and the Son. In fact, Platonists, like Christians, argue for a divine Triad; in Plotinus' well-developed system, they are the One, Intellect and World Soul. However, while the first two hypostases correspond to some extent with the Father and the Son, the third does not correspond at all with the Holy Spirit. Origen contends that without Scripture, no philosopher has had any inkling of the Holy Spirit's existence (*On First Principles* 1.3.1). Just as the Son derives his existence and divinity from the Father, the Holy Spirit derives his from the Father and Son, and from the Son he derives his wisdom, rationality, justice and other perfections identified by the Son's titles. There was in antiquity, as there is now, controversy about how to understand the Son and Holy Spirit's subordination to the Father. Origen clearly teaches that they depend on the Father as their origin and are in that respect subordinate (e.g. *Commentary on John* 2.19–20, 72, 86). The controversy focuses on several passages in which Origen seems to suggest that the Father's knowledge of himself surpasses the Son's and, by implication, the Holy Spirit's, including two in the *Commentary on John* (1.187, 32.350) and one in *On First Principles* (4.4.8), which Rufinus omits from his Latin translation, presumably to preserve Origen and the so-called 'Origenists' of the fourth and fifth centuries from accusations of heresy. (I say 'so-called', since even the Origenists' opponents, in particular Jerome, are also Origen's intellectual heirs.) However, Origen's thoughts in these passages remain undeveloped, and in none of them does he clearly assert that the Father's knowledge surpasses the Son's or Holy Spirit's (Crouzel 1989: chs 9–10). On the other hand, he does plainly state that the Apostles "conveyed that the Holy Spirit is united in honour and dignity with the Father and the Son" (*On First Principles* preface 4). No controversy surrounds Origen's teaching on the Holy Spirit's central role in our lives. The Son is revealed through Scripture, but in order to gain access to that revelation we need the Holy Spirit to sanctify and transform us, for unless we read with spiritual eyes we cannot grasp the Scripture's spiritual sense.

THE COSMOS

In addition to the eternal Trinity, we must also admit an eternal creation, since maintaining that there was a time before God created the world would saddle us with the absurd consequence that God would once have been idle, and surely God cannot be a do-nothing. Moreover, when God eventually did create, he would have changed, and changed for the better at that, since only then would he have been a sovereign. Because God is immutable, he must always have been a sovereign, and so must always have had a world to rule (*On First Principles* 1.2.10, 1.4.3). Origen does not spell out all the premises of this argument, and it remains unclear why he thinks becoming a sovereign would constitute a change in God. He might base this conclusion on the assumption that acquiring any relation constitutes a change in a subject, an assumption that most philosophers would reject. After all, if I should unknowingly inherit a large company and thereby become an employer, it is hard to see how *I* have changed. On the other hand, he might more plausibly take God's change to consist in his new act of governing the world over which he is sovereign.

God's eternal creation is not the material world we inhabit, but an intelligible cosmos that serves as the archetype, the blueprint, of his later creation. The world we see around us, the world containing many instances of human being, of donkey, of triangle, is a reflection of that intelligible world containing the Ideas, perfect exemplars of these kinds. Origen's own version of this Platonic cosmology evidently owes much to Philo, himself deeply influenced by Middle Platonists (Sorabji 1983: 250–53). In *De opificio mundi* (On the world's creation) 4.15–6.25, Philo argues that God creates an intelligible cosmos in the Logos, who is God's agent of creation. As a result, the Logos is the Idea of Ideas, a claim Origen echoes at *Against Celsus* 6.64. When Origen speaks of the Ideas in this cosmos as 'parts' of the Son, he means only to distance himself from the more ancient Platonic view that they exist independently, not to assert that the ideas are themselves constitutive of the Son. However, if it is the eternal creation of the intelligible cosmos that is supposed to save God from charges of idleness, progress and mutability, it might seem that Origen simply pushes the problem back one stage rather than resolving it. Does God not change by creating and ruling over the rational creatures that come into existence at a certain point in time? Origen does not explicitly address this concern, but he has a ready reply. God does not change by becoming sovereign of a new cosmos, since this material world is simply an extension of God's 'original' cosmos. Nor does his will change; from eternity, God willed that rational creatures and the material world appear at an appointed time.[2] God remains industrious and immutable.

2. In *On Prayer* 5–6, Origen applies this solution to similar concerns about God's changing his will after hearing petitionary prayer. See Sorabji (1983: 240–41).

When God expands his cosmos beyond the Ideas, he first creates a finite number of intelligences who enjoy the blissful contemplation of the Son. Most future Christian philosophers, at least through the Middle Ages, agree with Origen that God's motive for creating them is his own goodness. However, these later thinkers typically add that the myriad kinds and ranks we find among creatures, including the ranks of rational creatures, from the highest seraphim to the lowest human beings, manifest in their order and variety, the only way creatures can, the Creator's infinite but absolutely simple goodness. Origen disagrees: there is in God's goodness no basis for diversity (*On First Principles* 2.9.6). It is this assumption that leads him to one of his most distinctive views: that God originally created all the intelligences equal in rank and kind. Otherwise, God would have acted unjustly, favouring some creatures over others for no reason (*On First Principles* 3.5.4–5). In the world we inhabit, of course, there are striking inequalities: some creatures are angels, others demons, and still others human beings; among the human beings, not all are born into circumstances equally conducive to moral and spiritual progress. To avoid impugning God's goodness, Origen constructs an account of creation in which God assigns each creature its metaphysical and social place out of justice and benevolence.

Origen postulates that most of the intelligences grew cloyed with their contemplation of the Son. Losing their passion, they turned from him. As their punishment, God created this material world, casting the offending creatures into various ranks and circumstances in keeping with the gravity of their offence; to express this truth, Origen explains, the authors of Scripture describe the material world's creation as a "casting down" (*katabole*).[3] The greatest offenders became demons, the lesser offenders angels or celestial souls, and those in between became human beings. However, this punishment is not merely an expression of divine retributive justice. As Origen insists against the Gnostics, the God of creation is merciful and benevolent as well as just, and desiring that his creatures return to him, fashions this world to purge them of their vice and instruct them in virtue and wisdom.

THE RETURN TO GOD

When rational creatures fell, they were disfigured. Although, as rational and capable of restoration, they are still in God's image, they have lost their perfection and are no longer in God's likeness. The path of return to God is the path of transfiguration. It comes to an end when we ourselves become gods by sharing in the Son's divinity. We progress along this path by acquiring and exercising virtue.

3. Matthew 25:34, John 17:24, Ephesians 1:4; see *On First Principles* 3.5.4; *Commentary on John* 19.149.

The outline of Origen's account of virtue is similar to Plotinus'. The Father, like the One, transcends virtue, but is virtue's ultimate source. Plotinus' Intellect contains the archetypes of virtue, and Origen's Son is the archetype of virtue: many of his titles name virtues, such as Wisdom, Logos and Justice. Both Plotinus and Origen hold that virtues themselves lie in souls. Perfect virtues are found in the soul of Christ, the rational creature who is identical with the Son and whose example we are to follow. The souls of those who are still walking the path, however, contain not perfect, but purgative virtue. We acquire them in stages, one by one, and with effort. When we have acquired them all in their perfection, our souls will have perfect virtues, as Christ's does, and once again we shall be in the likeness of God.

To regain that likeness, we must be vigilant in following the injunction 'Know thyself', prominent in Greek thought but in Origen's view anticipated by Solomon in the Song of Songs. In his commentary on that biblical work, Origen distinguishes two sorts of self-knowledge (*Commentary on the Song of Songs* 2.5). Each of us is enjoined to acquire the first sort, the knowledge of our character and actions. To make progress in virtue, we need an accurate grasp of our defects and faults; and if we already have virtues, we need to know how to perfect them. This self-knowledge is, in short, the prudence we need to return to godhood, a knowledge so important that God providentially arranges for us to face temptations so that the secrets of our hearts will be revealed; without temptation, we would never know our virtues and vices. As his student Theodore reports, Origen trained his students to acquire this sort of self-knowledge as part of their programme of moral formation (*Address of Thanksgiving* 11–12). The second sort of self-knowledge God enjoins only on those souls endowed with "many graces of perception and understanding". This is metaphysical knowledge of the soul, including knowledge of its nature (is it corporeal or incorporeal, simple or compound, different from or the same as the angels?), its origin (is it eternal or created, and if created, is it created with the body or does it pre-exist the body?), and its future (is it incarnated only once or multiple times?). A large portion of *On First Principles* is devoted to answering these questions, which Origen also treats in his commentaries on the Bible, as the need arises. Those gifted souls who fail to carry out these investigations misuse their knowledge, indulging in the 'wisdom' of this world rather than undertaking these holy studies. While the first sort of self-knowledge leads us along the path of virtue to our perfect flourishing and happiness, the second sort seems itself to be a flourishing and happiness, for it forms a part of whatever share of wisdom we can have in this life.[4]

4. The necessity of metaphysical self-knowledge for happiness has its roots in ancient philosophy and figures prominently in Boethius' *Consolation of Philosophy*. In antiquity, Socrates makes moral self-knowledge (or self-reflection, at any rate) a condition of a life worth living, and in the Middle Ages Abelard would highlight the importance of self-knowledge for proper repentance and meritorious living in his *Know Thyself* (or *Ethics*).

Once equipped with self-knowledge, we return to God, the Holy of Holies, by climbing the Temple steps, one by one, in both this earthly life and the next; the effort is ours, but the steps are the Son in his various aspects (*Commentary on John* 19.38–9). At an early stage of our spiritual journey, he comes to us as our Shepherd to guide the sheep of our irrational parts. As we progress, we find in him our King to rule over us as subjects. With each step we climb, for most of the journey, we progress concomitantly in virtue, faith and knowledge. When we purge ourselves of vice and wayward desires, devoting ourselves to the task of understanding God through his word, the Holy Spirit graces us so that we progress morally and spiritually and our grasp of God and his creation grows fuller and deeper. At each stage, we acquire a new virtue or strengthen an old one, and we acquire new knowledge or see what we already knew in a better light (*Homily 27 on Numbers*). As we near the Holy of Holies, we reach the stage of the Son as Logos. At this stage, we will not need the purgative training we receive now, but receive the Son's tutelage. At the final stage we meet Christ as Wisdom, who will perfect the wisdom we have been nursing through so many prior stages. Only then will we be perfected, in the likeness of God, for "we speak wisdom among the perfect" (1 Corinthians 2:6), and we will be ready to be re-admitted to our original intimacy with the Son.

When, after long discipline in this life and beyond, all rational creatures have been restored to this intimacy, their journey will come to an end like its beginning, and God will be "all in all" (1 Corinthians 15:28). This teaching drew condemnations from Origen's critics, who were particularly appalled at the idea that even the Devil would be saved. When these criticisms threatened to undo his position in the church at Caesarea, he wrote a *Letter to Friends in Alexandria* explaining that he had never asserted the Devil's salvation. In fact, in his debate with the Gnostic Candidus, an early and explicit treatment of this issue, he asserts only that the demons retain the power to return to God, not that they would in fact return. Likewise, creatures restored to intimacy with God retain free will and might again fall, but Origen never teaches that they will. Origen never loses sight of human freedom and moral responsibility, but he also attests to God's provident and patient benevolence, which sends us into this long and bitter exile to teach us to cleave to him eternally in our homeland.

FURTHER READING

Crouzel, H. 1989. *Origen*, A. Worrall (trans.). Edinburgh: T&T Clark.

Eusebius of Caesarea 1989. *The History of the Church: From Christ to Constantine*, G. Williamson (trans.), A. Louth (rev.). New York: Penguin.

McGuckin, J. 2004. *The Westminister Handbook to Origen*. Louisville, KY: Westminster John Knox.

Torjesen, K. 1986. *Hermeneutical Procedure and Theological Method in Origen's Exegesis*. Berlin: De Gruyter.

Trigg, J. 1983. *Origen: The Bible and Philosophy in the Third-Century Church*. Atlanta, GA: John Knox.

On ANGELS/DEMONS see also Chs 16, 20. On CHRISTIANITY see also Chs 10, 17, 18; Vol. 5, Ch. 12. On COSMOLOGY see also Chs 6, 8, 17; Vol. 2, Chs 4, 10, 16. On PLATONISM see also Chs 11, 15, 17; Vol. 5, Ch. 16. On REVELATION see also Vol. 2, Ch. 11; Vol. 3, Chs 7, 11, 16; Vol. 4, Chs 5, 11; Vol. 5, Chs 8, 23. On THE ONE see also Chs 3, 11, 16, 19; Vol. 4, Ch. 9; Vol. 5, Ch. 15. On THE TRINITY see also Chs 17, 20; Vol. 2, Chs 2, 8, 15; Vol. 3, Chs 3, 9, 17; Vol. 4, Ch. 4; Vol. 5, Chs 12, 23. On VIRTUE see also Chs 2, 11, 15; Vol. 3, Chs 20, 21.

15

PLOTINUS

Lloyd P. Gerson

In this chapter, I shall discuss the philosophy of religion of Plotinus (*c.*204–70) under three headings: general metaphysical principles; personal psychological aspects; and critique of alternative approaches. All of these need to be understood against the background of Plotinus' unswerving Platonism. Plotinus did not aspire to originality; certainly not to the founding of a new philosophy, something that only in the eighteenth century came to be pejoratively referred to as 'Neoplatonism'. Nevertheless, in the 600 or so years between Plato and Plotinus, an enormous amount of work appeared reflecting on the revelations of the 'divine' founder of the Academy. As Plotinus' biographer and student Porphyry tells us (*Life of Plotinus* 14.10–25), an impressive amount of this material served as the starting-point for Plotinus' philosophical seminars. In his defence of Plato against both older and newer opponents, and in his efforts to assess the various interpretations of Plato's thought that had over time accrued, Plotinus did develop arguments and insights that we, if not he, would no doubt regard as original. I shall not here offer an opinion on the question of whether 'Platonism' is what Plato taught or whether it is what Plotinus (and his predecessors and disciples) created. In the matter of the philosophy of religion, this is an especially good question, as we are about to see.

GENERAL METAPHYSICAL PRINCIPLES

The focus of Plotinus' philosophy of religion is a proof of the existence of an absolutely simple first causal principle of all that exists in the universe. The provenance of this principle is clear enough: it goes back at least to Plato's Idea of the Good, most famously introduced in his *Republic* (509b6–10). It is this Idea that provides being (*einai*) and essence (*ousia*) and knowability to the eternal and immutable Forms. The Idea of the Good is itself "beyond *ousia*" and is superior to that which possesses it "in prestige and power". And yet, as many have noted, this evidently does not mean that the Good is altogether beyond being in any sense. It is, we are told, "the brightest part of being" (518c9); "the most blessed part of being" (526e3–4); and "the best among beings" (532c5–6). The entire Platonic tradition, including Plotinus, concurs in accepting Aristotle's testimony that Plato indeed believed in an Idea of the Good and that he identified it with 'the One' (*Metaphysics* N.4, 1091b13–14; cf. A.9, 990b17–22; *Eudemian Ethics* 1218a24–8).

In *Ennead* 5.4.1, Plotinus argues for two conclusions: (i) every composite must be accounted for by that which is incomposite or absolutely simple; and (ii) there can be only one absolutely simple being. We can better understand the reasoning for (i) if we concentrate first on the reasoning for (ii). Assume that there were more than one absolutely simple being. Then, there would have to be something that each one of them had that made it at least numerically different from the other, say, for example, a unique position. But that which made it different would have to be really (not merely conceptually) distinct from that which made it to be the one thing it is. That which had the position would be really distinct from the position itself just as something that has a size has to be distinct from that size. But then something that had a position and so was distinct from it would not be absolutely simple. So, that which is absolutely simple must be absolutely unique. Only the first principle of all is unqualifiedly self-identical; the self-identity had by anything else is, therefore, necessarily qualified. This argument suggests the meaning of 'composite' that Plotinus has in mind when he argues for (i). A composite is anything that is distinct from any property it has. What we might call a 'minimally composite individual' is one with one and only one property from which it is itself distinct. Accordingly, the self-identity of that which is composite can only be qualified self-identity.

So, now the question is: why should any composite need the unique, absolutely first principle of all to account for it? Plotinus' concise answer is: "All beings (*onta*) are beings by the One" (i.e. the first principle of all) (6.9.1.1). Here, the word 'being' refers to that which partakes of whatever property it has. Why is it that the One explains this? Plotinus answers that if anything is deprived of the 'oneness' that is said of it, then it is not that 'one' (6.9.1.4). Here, 'one' or 'oneness' refers to the qualified self-identity of whatever has being, the composite (6.9.1.27). Thus, a being is one being having whatever properties it has owing to the first principle of all. The 'oneness' belongs not to the *ousia* alone nor to the subject that has it, but to the composite.

The One is needed to explain any composite being because no composite being is self-explicable. The One explains as an efficient cause of the being of any composite whatsoever (cf. 5.3.15.12–13, 28; 5.3.17.10–14; 6.4.10; 6.7.23.22–4). Composites are necessarily what we may call 'heteroexplicable'. Heteroexplicability follows from the fact that the *ousia* in which something partakes could not uniquely constitute the being's identity. If it could, then that being would be unqualifiedly identical with its *ousia*, a possibility that has already been excluded by the argument for the uniqueness of that which is absolutely self-identical. Something gets to be what it is by partaking of some *ousia*, which means, minimally, that the *ousia* is what that thing is. The One is, however, as Plato said, "above *ousia*". It cannot itself, therefore, be the *ousia* that explains the being of anything with *ousia*. Instead, the One is "virtually all things" (*dunamis tōn pantōn*) (5.4.1.23–6; cf. 5.4.2.38, 6.7.32.31, 6.9.5.36, etc.) roughly in the way that 'white' light is virtually all the colours of the spectrum. As such, it is absolutely self-explicable or 'self-caused' (6.8.14.41).[1]

The proof for the existence of the One is equivalent to Plotinus' central proof for the existence of God. Although the One is said by Plotinus to be "above all predicates" owing to its absolute simplicity (3.8.10.29–35), there are fundamentally two ways in which the One can be spoken of. First, since the One is virtually all that is, it is "in a way" (*hoion*) all that is intelligible. Secondly, the One can be spoken of negatively; we can say what it is not. Thus, we speak about it "from what comes after it" and in negation of that (5.3.14.1–8; cf. 6.9.3.59–64). The One is self-sufficient (1.8.2.4–5), perfect (5.6.2.13), omnipresent (3.8.9.25), meaning that there is nowhere it is not nor anywhere where it is particularly (3.9.4.3–9). The One is goodness itself, and is specifically identified with Plato's Idea of the Good (1.3.1.3, 5.9.2.23–7, 6.5.1.18–20). But apparently unlike the Idea of the Good, the One has a life, specifically a cognitive life (6.8.16.12–29, 5.4.2.12–22). It also possesses will (*boulēsis*), although this does not entail that it engages in deliberation (6.8.13.1–8). Owing to the One's will and goodness, it is eternally providential or, more precisely, it is the source of the providence that resides in Intellect (2.9.15.12, 6.7.39.26–7). It has a kind of intellection (*katanoēsis*) and self-consciousness (*sunaisthēsis*) of itself (5.4.2.16–19). Most remarkably, the One is "love itself and love of itself" (6.8.15.1). All of the 'positive' attributes must be prefaced by the qualified 'in a way'.

The first (atemporal) 'product' of the One is Intellect (*nous*). Intellect is the principle of essence or 'whatness' or intelligibility or substantiality *and* the principle of the activity of intellection. Following Aristotle's argument in *Metaphysics* and *De anima* (*On the Soul*), Plotinus affirms the cognitive identity of intellect and intelligibles.[2] This principle is equivalent to Aristotle's Prime unmoved mover, interpreted as eternally cognitively identical with all that is intelligible and with Plato's Demiurge, similarly cognitively identical with the paradigms of intelligibility.[3] The principle of Intellect is subordinate to the One owing to its complexity,

1. One may usefully contrast here Thomistic metaphysics wherein the first principle of all, God, is virtually *and* eminently, that is, paradigmatically, all things. For Plotinus, to be something of a specific or particular nature eminently entails the possession of some *ousia*, and therefore, some complexity. God's eminence, for Aquinas does not entail this complexity.
2. See Aristotle, *Metaphysics* Λ.7, 1072a31; Λ.8, 1073a30; Λ.9, 1074a33–4, b34; and the references in note 10.
3. See *Timaeus* 29e1–3 with 30c2–d1.

that is, the complexity implied by there being a distinction between an Intellect and intelligibles, and among intelligibles as well. By contrast, the One is absolutely simple.

The third hypostasis, ontologically subordinate to both the One and Intellect, is Soul, the principle of embodied desire of all types. Every living thing has desire in two senses: all desire the Good, but all desire it by desiring something that answers to their embodied needs. The first sort of desire might be termed 'vertical' and the second 'horizontal'. For living things without an intellect, the only way that these things achieve their good is through the attainment of what their embodied selves desire. For living things with intellects, there is a constant lived ambiguity between the search for the satisfaction of embodied psychic desires and the satisfaction of the desire of intellect, a desire that is satisfied only in the contemplation of what the One is virtually, that is, all that is intelligible. The recognition that one's good is purely intellectual is supposed to follow on the recognition that one is truly identical with an intellect, not with an embodied soul. Plotinus here is quite clearly relying on Plato's distinction between the immortal and mortal parts of the soul, which he takes to be equivalent to Aristotle's distinction between soul and intellect.[4]

The three fundamental hypostases are the starting-points for addressing the wide array of perennial philosophical problems that constitute the history of philosophy for Plotinus. We begin to explain psychic phenomena with an understanding of Soul; the intelligible structure of things with Intellect; and the being of everything with the absolutely simple One. Plotinus' philosophy of religion has as its starting-point a hierarchical metaphysics with the One at the 'top' and with matter at the 'bottom', where 'matter' indicates utter formlessness or unintelligibility. Union with the One in some sense is identical with the attainment of the Good for anything; separation from the One in the direction of matter is just the path to evil.

PERSONAL PSYCHOLOGICAL ASPECTS

Porphyry famously reports that Plotinus proclaimed that "the end or goal [of human life] was to be united (*henōthēnai*) with the god who is over all things; while I was with him, he himself attained this goal four times, not in potency but in unspeakable actuality" (*Life of Plotinus* 23.15–18). There is an obvious puzzle in this account. If the One is absolutely simple, it is entirely unclear what 'being united' with the first principle is supposed to mean. The claim that this occurred on at least four occasions hardly serves to clarify the matter. If the union does

4. See *Timaeus* 41c–d, 61c, 65a, 69c–d, 72d–e, 89d–90d; cf. *Republic* 611b–612a; Aristotle, *De anima* 2.2.413b26.

not add to or alter the One in any way, how does the actuality of it differ from the potency? In other words, if the One is virtually all things, it seems to follow that the inverse of this 'relation' does already indicate a kind of actual union. What more could Plotinus have attained?

Famously, in the last words of the *Enneads* (in Porphyry's edition), Plotinus characterizes the contemplative life as "the flight of the alone to the alone" (6.9.11.50–51). The achievement of this flight is the life of gods and of godlike and blessed men. This achievement is neither personal obliteration nor absorption into the One. But it is also something more than the wisdom that consists in contemplating all that is intelligible. Wisdom is a *means* to union with the Good (6.9.11.48). I shall return to the details of this last stage at the end of this section. For the moment, though, we can summarize Plotinus' view of religion as consisting of whatever practices bring us closer to union with the One. The enemy of religion is whatever impedes our union or drives us in the opposite direction.

Plotinus is sufficiently attuned to the Stoic ideal to insist that the impediments to our union with the One are largely self-imposed. As Plotinus put it rhetorically at the beginning of one of his most accessible treatises:

> What can it be, then, that has made souls forget the god who is their father and be ignorant both of themselves and him even though they are parts of the intelligible world and are completely derived from it? The starting point for their evil is audacity, that is, generation or primary difference, or wanting to belong to themselves.
>
> (5.1; cf. 4.4.3.1–3, 4.8.5.28, 6.9.8.31–2)

The 'god' referred to here is probably Intellect, not the One; return to the 'father' is, however, a necessary stage in the ascent to union with that which is 'above' Intellect. The phrase 'wanting to belong to themselves' indicates the trajectory of every embodied soul. The desires of an embodied human soul are all for concrete apparent goods, that is, for things we believe will satisfy us. But our desire for these is only provisional; we desire them *if* they are what they appear to be, namely, really good. Only the first principle of all, however, is unqualifiedly good. The state of ordinary embodied souls is a continuous wanting of the apparent goods of individual human beings. These apparent goods, however, can at best add up to a simulacrum of unity or integrity.[5] The narrative of any ordinary human life has as its constant underlying theme a denial of one's true identity. The 'forgetting' of the father is reflected in every action springing from an embodied desire. Each human being is the composite of body and soul in so far as he acts on desires originating in the composite; he is his true self when he acts on or identifies with his reason

5. Cf. Plato, *Republic* 443e1 on the ideal for a human being as "becoming one out of many"; also, 554d9–10; *Phaedo* 83a7.

(1.1.9.15–18). While one is occupied with the embodied self, one typically forgets one's real or true self (4.4.18.11–16).

Accordingly, while Plotinus recommends the practice of civic and purificatory virtue as a stage in the dissociation of the self from embodied life, he rejects the possibility of such virtue as a substitute for religion (1.2.3–5). For although virtue "intellectualizes the soul" (6.8.5.35; cf. 6.7.35.4–6) and in a way makes us "godlike" (1.2.1.1–6), the practice of virtue is itself a kind of self-subordination to the sensible world. As Plotinus tendentiously puts it, if circumstances compel us to act virtuously, how are we then in control of ourselves (6.8.5.13–37)? 'Being in control of oneself' suggests the self-identification that comes from self-recognition. Following Plato, those practices that lead us to 'assimilate to the divine' are the essence of religion.[6] But the divine transcends virtue. So the practice of such virtues is purely instrumental.

And yet, someone who practices the virtues begins to separate himself from ownership of the appetites and emotions that he discovers in himself. The mechanism of separation is concrete and specific. To do something because one regards it as the virtuous thing to do is to make a second-order judgement on one's first-order desire. If, for example, I think it virtuous to stand fast in the face of an attack even though I would earnestly prefer to flee, I thereby discover in the subject making this judgement an intellect. And this, as we already know, is the *real* me. If, however, one takes the use of intellect in practical action as ideal, then one is still removed from the divine, that is, from the divine to which one ought to desire to be assimilated. The practice of virtue as ordinarily conceived can actually be an impediment to self-identity if its instrumentality is not recognized.

So, the question for Plotinus becomes: "what art is there, what method or practice, which will take us up there where we must go?" (1.3.1.1–2). The answer is that the practice of philosophy itself – in particular, dialectic – is the vehicle of ascent. The description of dialectic that follows relies entirely on Plato's account in the dialogues.[7] Briefly, the religious relevance of dialectic is derived from the nature of the cognition of the intelligible world. When we think about Forms or intelligibles, we 'access' not only the intelligibles but our 'undescended' intellects as well (4.7.13, 4.8.8).[8] Plotinus says that although intellect is not a part of the embodied soul, it is both "ours and not ours". For this reason, "we use it and do not use it" (5.3.3.25–9). Intellect is ours although not a part of the embodied soul because we are neither soul–body composites nor souls, but intellects. That is, we are intellects when we identify ourselves with our intellects. Plotinus is here

6. The central text is Plato, *Theaetetus* 176b. Plotinus refers to this text in many places: see 1.2.4.5–6, 1.4.16.12, 1.6.6.20, 1.8.7.12, 2.9.6.40 and so on.

7. See *Republic* 531c–533a; *Sophist* 253c–d.

8. The reason why Forms or intelligibles could not exist apart from intellect is that if they did, then what intellect would possess would only be representations of the truth, not the truth itself.

drawing out the implication of Aristotle's claim that "the human being is especially intellect".[9] We embodied persons use our own intellects and are identical with them whenever we think. Since intellect is identical with intelligibles, our accessing of what is intelligible is identical with our accessing or use of our own intellects. Since intelligibles are eternally separate from their sensible manifestations, so, too, are our intellects. So, when we engage in dialectic, we are launched on a project of self-discovery.

Even more specifically, and again following Aristotle, Plotinus insists that when we use our intellects we become identified with intellect's intelligible objects (3.8.8.1–10, 5.5.1.52–3).[10] One is able to think oneself when one thinks that which is intelligible; indeed, it is only then that one becomes intelligible to oneself. It is only then that one becomes aware of one's "parentage" (5.1.1.10) and only then that one is in a position "to hear the voices from above" (5.1.12.20–21). It is then that one is poised to attain or experience the "principle and cause and god of Intellect", and to receive it in a way "as something other than it is itself" (5.1.11.10).[11]

Although the One is in us as "other", it is possible to receive it owing to the fact that it is "the same as us" (3.8.9.22–3). That a product of the One should be the 'same' as the One although other than it is precisely the way that Plato explains the mitigated intelligibility of the sensible world in relation to its eternal paradigm. So, for example, the equality of equal sticks or stones is genuine equality, although there is something 'missing' in them.[12] Equality itself is the self-identical nature that is paradigmatically present in Intellect, or, for Plato, the Demiurge, and also present in a diminished way in all its instances. Since the One is virtually all things, everything is in a way the same as the One. The One is the unqualifiedly self-identical 'nature' present in a diminished way in everything else. Sameness, however, is primarily a property of things sharing an identical *ousia* or nature. The One is "above *ousia*". So, the 'sameness' we and everything else have to the One is, as it were, twice removed from that self-identical source. We are the same as intelligible reality, although ontologically diminished in relation to it, and so we are again the same as the wholly transcendent first principle, which is virtually all that is intelligible. That is why it must be received as other than it is in itself. But that it can be received at all is owing to this sameness.

---

9. See Aristotle, *Nicomachean Ethics* IX.8, 1168b35–9a2; X.7, 1178a2–7; cf. *Timaeus* 90c on the immortal part of the soul, the intellect.
10. See Aristotle, *De anima* 3.4.429b9, 430a2; 3.5.430a20; 3.7.431a1; 3.8.431b22–3.
11. The point of this difficult line is probably that the reception of the One inevitably requires that one receive it as other than it is, since it is itself no one thing nor is it limited by *ousia* in any way. To receive it as other than it is means to receive some image or representation of it. The One itself is, however, virtually every one of these images or representations.
12. See *Phaedo* 74a6. Cf. *Republic* 479c6–d1, where sensibles are said to be "between being and not being". And at *Parmenides* 132d3 Socrates concedes that sensibles are "the same as" (*homoiomata*) their paradigms.

Here we return to the problem of what 'union' with the One is supposed to be beyond one's self-identification as intellect. As Plotinus says, if we wish to see it, we have to be "not altogether intellect" (3.8.9.32; cf. 6.9.11.45–8). We have to attain a super-intellectual mode of cognition of the self-identical source. We do this, presumably, by recognizing that all intelligible objects are virtually one. In order to see what this might involve, we can begin by considering the cognitive state of one who, say, grasps the unique scientific law underlying diverse phenomena. Seeing the one-behind-the-many is analogous to the penultimate stage of ascent where one sees *that* there is a virtual unity of all that is intelligible. The ultimate stage is, presumably, a hypernoetic grasp of that unity itself wherein what is unified is left aside. Since all higher cognition is self-cognition, this ultimate stage might be fairly described as 'actual unification with the One' (cf. 6.9.10.9–21, 6.9.11.1ff.).

If the techniques of ascent are limited to the purificatory practice of virtue and dialectic, the motive for ascent is our natural love of the beautiful. Plotinus is perhaps the first of Plato's disciples to see his *Symposium* as a religious or theological treatise. Plotinus aims to bring the Platonic account of *erōs* to the fore as an essential ingredient in 'assimilation to the divine'.

In Socrates' report of Diotima's 'mysteries' of love, he tells us that she claims that the love of the beautiful is really nothing but the desire for the possession of the good.[13] Plotinus has no hesitation in interpreting this to mean that the beautiful is the attractive aspect of the Good or the One (6.7.30.29ff.).[14] 'The beautiful' actually stands for all the Forms (1.6.9.35–6, 6.7.22.5–7). Just as the One is present virtually to all things, so everything regarded as beautiful or attractive is so regarded because it is an image of the One. However, as Plato, followed by Plotinus, notes, although human beings are willing to settle for the apparently beautiful, they will never settle for the apparently good.[15] The ascent to the One consists in the unfolding recognition of images of the really beautiful for what they in fact are.

This ascent is hierarchical. The ordering of the hierarchy is according to proximity to the One. The very act of recognizing that the physical beauty in one individual is not identical with the unqualifiedly good is itself a stage on the ascent. Prior to the ultimate state of the ascent, the birth in beauty that is the work of love always, therefore, produces images of true virtue. It is only with the attainment of the beautiful itself – with the cognition of it – that true virtue is produced.[16] This true virtue is contrasted by Plotinus with the 'popular and political' virtue mentioned in *Phaedo* and with the so-called virtues of the soul

13. See 205a5. Later (206a11–12), she defines love as "desire for the possession of the good forever".
14. Cf. *Philebus* 64e5–65a5, where the Good is said to reveal itself in three aspects: beauty, symmetry and truth.
15. See *Republic* 505d5–9; *Enneads* 5.5.12.19–25.
16. See *Symposium* 212a4–5.

in *Republic*.[17] Remarkably, the achievement of the ascent is described by Plotinus as self-identification with "the best of ourselves" (6.7.30.35–7) and with one's "natural state" (6.9.9.26–7); it is the achievement of "oneself glorified" (*heauton ēglaïsmenon*; 6.9.9.56–7). So, in one way the ascent is a self-discovery; in another, it is a self-transformation from the embodied soul desirous of the apparently beautiful to the disembodied intellect desirous only of the Good itself.

In this way, Plotinus' account of the beautiful – Plotinian aesthetics, as it is often referred to – can be said to be, without irony, an element of his philosophy of religion. In fact, it is a crucial element, since it focuses on the central motivation of embodied life, namely, the fulfilment of desire for *whatever* attracts us. All human desire, for Plotinus, connects us or aims us to the apparently beautiful. The philosopher realizes that the apparently beautiful is not what is really desired after all.

THE CRITIQUE OF RELIGION

The philosophy of religion hitherto described needs a supplementary discussion of Plotinus' criticisms of the religious doctrines of his day. The most famous of these criticisms are found in his treatise "Against the Gnostics" (2.9). In this treatise, Plotinus attacks the doctrines of certain unnamed thinkers.[18] The focus of his attack is evident in the alternate title recorded by Porphyry, "Against those who say that the universe and its maker are evil". As we saw above, Plotinus argues that the central teaching of Platonism is the existence of an absolute simple and unique first principle of all, the One or the Good. On this principle the entire universe depends. Everything of which the Good is the cause must be inferior to it, but nevertheless good, being the effect of a good cause. This includes the multiplicity of visible and invisible gods (cf. 2.9.9.38–40). If, then, anything in the universe is evil, it must be outside the causal scope of the Good. But to claim that anything can be outside the causal scope of the Good is to misrepresent its infinite nature; that is, to assume its limitation in one way or another. Such a position – and

17. See *Enneads* 1.2 on the grades of virtue. Cf. *Phaedo* 82a10–b3; cf. 69b6–7; *Republic* 365c3–4, 500d8, 518d3–519a6, 619c7.
18. Porphyry in ch. 16 of his biography mentions contemporary individuals who in Plotinus' opinion had abandoned Greek wisdom in favour of alien and indefensible innovations. Among these were Zoroastrians and Christians. Some of the primary Gnostic material was recovered in the last century from the Nag Hammadi Library in Egypt. It is worth emphasizing that contemporary scholars have often identified this Gnostic material with heretical Christian doctrines. By contrast, Plotinus seems to use the term 'Gnostic' for any putative source of wisdom that rejects Greek wisdom. Thus, Plotinus does not dismiss out of hand Indian, Persian or Jewish wisdom literature unless he sees it as contradicting the divine revelations of Plato.

whatever religious practices might be thought to flow from it – are, for Plotinus, unqualifiedly irreconcilable with Platonism.

In the light of this fundamental opposition, it is not surprising that Plotinus begins the treatise with a reassertion of the soundness of positing three and only three hypostases: the One, Intellect and Soul. The causal dependence of Soul on Intellect and the Good, and of Intellect on the Good is eternal and necessary. So, the Gnostic doctrine of an evil soul or a product of it creating the universe has no metaphysical support. Specifically, if this soul is a craftsman of this ordered material universe, it must have employed intelligible reality as a model and in that case the images of the model, just in so far as they are images of what is 'goodlike', will themselves be good. But if the putative craftsman 'forgot' intelligible reality, how could it have crafted anything (2.9.3)? For Plotinus, then, there is no basis for the Gnostic complaints about the evil that is the material universe and the necessity of finding some occult practice (or form of knowledge, *gnōsis*) to escape it.

And yet Plotinus himself and the entire Platonic tradition recommend 'escape' from this universe.[19] What is wrong with the Gnostics seeking out alternative means of escape? According to Plotinus, the profound difference between authentic Platonic otherworldliness and its Gnostic counterfeit is this. The ascent from the exterior to the interior and from the lower to the higher – as Porphyry describes Plotinus' religious thinking – cannot proceed if at each stage the hierarchical order is not recognized. To think of the material universe, our bodies, and the desires that both engender as evil amounts to rejecting the connections within the hierarchy. That is, it amounts to denying that the material universe really is an image of intelligible reality; it amounts to a refusal to see an image as good just in so far as it bears some intelligibility. What this does psychologically is to leave the ascent unmotivated. Merely wanting to be rid of the travails of embodiment is too drearily common a thing to constitute a stage on a philosophical ascent. Wanting what is good for oneself is not equivalent to wanting the Good. But one cannot really want the latter without recognizing that there *is* a Good. Given that the Good is virtually all that is intelligible, one does this by recognizing the goodness of all of the intelligible images of Intellect. If one starts with revulsion for this world, then one is going to do what anyone does when overcome with revulsion: flee in the opposite direction. There is, however, no opposite direction, since the One or the Good is everywhere. There is only a chimerical Eden appropriately imagined as home for a false self.

Plotinus notoriously seems to give back to the Gnostics what he seeks to take away when he identifies matter with evil.[20] This doctrine, however, is easily misconstrued. Following Aristotle, Plotinus argues that matter is opposed to form;

19. See especially *Phaedo* 65a–d and *Theaetetus* 176a, passages to which Plotinus frequently refers; cf. 4.8.1.29.

20. See 1.8.7.1–4, 17–23; 1.8.4.50–51. On matter as privation, see 2.4.16.3–8; 1.8.5.6–13, 11.1–7.

that is, it is utterly formless in itself, even though it is always present with matter (2.4.5.3). It is, to put it simply, the inevitable and necessary condition for the products of the One, and Intellect and Soul with the One. There could be no images without matter, and images are the result of the necessary activity of the primary hypostases. The One or the Good is virtually all that is formed and its 'opposite' is the absolutely formless. As opposite of the Good, then, matter is evil, but just as the Good is so-called 'in a sense' (*hoion*) because it is the necessary cause of all that is intelligible and good, matter is evil 'in a sense' because it is the necessary effect of intelligible production.

Against the Gnostics, Plotinus insists that Soul and individual souls are not evil (1.8.4.6–7). Owing to embodiment, however, we are susceptible to evil (1.8.4.44–50). So, matter is only evil for an embodied soul, one weakened by embodiment. Plotinus' subtle position is that a Gnostic make-believe rejection of the material world is to be contrasted with the psychological stance of one who has turned himself in the direction of that which is truly real. Such a person neither confuses the body – which of course has its own form – with matter nor confuses a longing for the Good with a hatred for that which is not even intelligible. Just understanding that matter is absolute formlessness is enough to enable one to recognize that it cannot even be an object of disdain. All the same, the longing for a return to one's authentic self is equivalent to the renunciation of evil.

CONCLUSION

Porphyry in his *Life* records Plotinus' last words before dying as "try to bring back the god in you to the divine in the all" (2.26–7). In ancient Greek generally, there is little difference between the use of the noun 'god' and the adjective 'divine'. Still, it is remarkable that the two termini of endowment and achievement should suggest the personal, on the one hand, and the impersonal, on the other. What need is there, after all, to bring a god back to the divine? In the light of the above discussion, what Plotinus seems to mean is this. First, through the practice of dialectic one discovers oneself to be a god, that is, an immortal intellectual soul. Secondly, through the practice of virtue and the pursuit of the objects of love one begins to divest oneself of the idiosyncratic and ephemeral, or the "wanting to belong to oneself" (5.1.1.5). The achievement of union with the god that Porphyry reported Plotinus as having experienced four times in his life is here presented as 'bringing back' the god in us to its source. There are no shortcuts to the goal, theurgical in nature or otherwise.[21] As quoted above, in the final words of the *Enneads* (in

21. Cf. Porphyry's (10.33–8) story about Plotinus' colleague and companion, the philosopher Amelius, who once invited Plotinus to attend a temple on the occasion of a lunar festival for the gods. Plotinus replied, "they ought to come to me, not I to them". Porphyry says he dared not ask Plotinus the meaning of this exalted remark, but it is not implausible that it

Porphyry's arrangement of the treatises), religion is "the flight of the alone to the alone" (6.9.11.51; cf. 1.6.7.8, 6.7.34.7).

FURTHER READING

Armstrong, A. 1976. "The Apprehension of Divinity in the Self and Cosmos in Plotinus". In *The Significance of Neoplatonism*, R. Harris (ed.), 187–98. Norfolk: International Society for Neoplatonic Studies.

Bussanich, J. 1996. "Plotinus's Metaphysics of the One". In *The Cambridge Companion to Plotinus*, L. Gerson (ed.), 38–65. Cambridge: Cambridge University Press.

Bussanich, J. 1997. "Plotinian Mysticism in Theoretical and Comparative Perspective". *American Catholic Philosophical Quarterly* **61**: 339–65.

Gerson, L. 1994. *Plotinus* (esp. ch. 10). London: Routledge.

Hadot, P. 1993. *Plotinus, or the Simplicity of Vision*, M. Chase (trans.). Chicago, IL: University of Chicago Press. [Published in French as *Plotin ou la simplicité du regard* (Paris: Plon, 1963).]

Kenney, J. 1997. "Mysticism and Contemplation in the *Enneads*". *American Catholic Philosophical Quarterly* **61**: 315–37.

O'Meara, D. 1980. "Gnosticism and the Making of the World in Plotinus". In *The Rediscovery of Gnosticism: Proceedings of the International Conference on Gnosticism 1978, I: The School of Valentinus*, B. Layton (ed.), 365–78. Leiden: Brill.

Rist, J. 1967. *Plotinus: The Road to Reality* (esp. chs 15–17). Cambridge: Cambridge University Press.

Rist, J. 1989. "Back to the Mysticism of Plotinus". *Journal of the History of Philosophy* **27**: 183–97.

Sinnige, T. 1975. "Metaphysical and Personal Religion in Plotinus". In *Kephalion: Studies in Greek Philosophy and its Continuity Offered to Cornelia de Vogel*, J. Mansfeld & L. de Rijk (eds), 147–54. Assen: Van Gorcum.

On AESTHETICS see also Vol. 4, Chs 13, 18. On DIALECTIC see also Ch. 13. On FIRST CAUSE see also Ch. 16; Vol. 2, Ch. 14; Vol. 3, Ch. 6. On HIERARCHY see also Ch. 20; Vol. 2, Ch. 4. On PLATONISM see also Chs 11, 14, 17; Vol. 5, Ch. 16. On VIRTUE see also Chs 2, 11, 14; Vol. 3, Chs 20, 21.

---

indicates Plotinus' lack of interest in ritual practices. This is especially striking in the light of the shared polytheism of Plotinus and his contemporaries. The very meaning of this polytheism seems to evanesce when detached from ritual practice, as later Iamblichus and Proclus so clearly saw.

16

PORPHYRY AND IAMBLICHUS

Mark J. Edwards

Porphyry was born in 232, and commenced his philosophical studies in Athens under the eminent critic Longinus. He spent the years from 263 to 268 with Plotinus in Rome, as we learn from his own report in his *Life of Plotinus*, a preface to his edition of the *Enneads*, which became ours (*Life of Plotinus* 4, 11, 23). On the evidence of an ancient source, Iamblichus is believed to have been his pupil, and on evidence that some might think no evidence at all, his birth has been dated to 245 (Cameron 1968). What is certain is that Iamblichus was the younger, that, like Porphyry, he was a Platonist, and that both men hung a religious superstructure on a scaffolding erected by Plotinus, who in outward show was the least religious thinker of late antiquity. Porphyry was a Greek-speaking Phoenician from the great city of Tyre; the Chalcis that is said to have been the birthplace of Iamblichus is generally supposed to have been the town of that name in Syria. No date for the death of either is recorded, and we know little of their careers save what can be gathered from their writings. Porphyry was perhaps the more conventional, a stenographer to oracles and public cults, where Iamblichus purports to be an expositor of deep mysteries. Yet both, as heirs of Plotinus, were intolerant of irrationality even in the study of things above reason, and both were aware that, in framing a theology for barbarians, they were preserving a Greek tradition of enquiry for the Greeks.

A PREFACE TO PORPHYRY

If Porphyry had a philosophy of religion – if, that is to say, he would not be more properly styled a religious polymath – it must be reconstructed from lost writings, the remains of which we owe to Christian sources. No dates can be attached, without circular reasoning, to his *Philosophy from Oracles*, *On Statues*, *On the Regression of the Soul* or *To Anebo*, as the aim of our principal tradent, Bishop Eusebius of Caesarea, was not to furnish matter for a biography, but to illustrate the wilful gullibility of a Greek thinker who occasionally admitted to knowing better. Modern readers of Eusebius, finding sceptical passages from the letter to Anebo cheek by jowl with the pious credulity of the *Philosophy from Oracles*, have sometimes assumed that the latter represents only the cast-off weeds of Porphyry's schooling before his encounter with Plotinus, while the letter to Anebo testifies to a change of wardrobe in his intellectual prime (Bidez 1913 *passim*). But if that is so, we must posit a second childhood at the end of his career when, in writing the life of his mentor Plotinus, he included a number of miraculous episodes which that austere freethinker would certainly not have recounted in the same style. We must also assume that his idiom did not keep pace with his thoughts, since his *Philosophy from Oracles* and *Regression of the Soul* – the first a specimen of his apprenticeship and the second of his maturity, according to the most celebrated theory of his development – are in fact so alike in diction, tenor and content as to persuade one notable scholar that we have to do with a single work passed down under different titles.[1]

One change in his opinions is attested in his own works. To pass from the school of Longinus to that of Plotinus was to embrace the latter's innovatory doctrine that "the Forms are not external to the Intellect": that is to say, that the Demiurge or creator of the phenomenal realm and the paradigm that he contemplates in creating it are not distinct, as subject and object are in the lower plane, but one and the same. Plotinus would add that, if the intellect and the intelligible manifold are one, it follows that the one is at the same time many, and hence that the intellect cannot supply its own principle of unity. The One that he postulates as the cause of unity therefore lies beyond intellect, beyond determinate being, beyond all that is commonly called divine. It is often affirmed that Porphyry doubles back on his master's teaching and conflates the first principle with intellect; but the argument requires us to identify him as the anonymous referent in authors who are accustomed to use his name, or to accept the disputed attribution to him of an anonymous and undated commentary on the *Parmenides*.[2] It was indeed said of him that he took *nous* or intellect to be the Father of the first triad in the Chaldaean system (fr. 267 Smith);[3] but this is his exegesis of a text that, so far as we know, he did not regard as an infallible, or even a peculiarly authoritative, scripture.

It is certain that he speaks from time to time of the highest principle in more quotidian terms than those customarily employed by either Plotinus or his successors. But it seems that, in certain instances at least, he was accommodating his speech to that of his vulgar interlocutors. He is credited in the *Suda* (a Byzantine lexicon) with some fifteen *logoi* or discourses against the Christians. We have at most a few vestiges of any work under that title, but excerpts survive from

1. See O'Meara (1959), against Bidez (1913).
2. See further Bechtle (2000).
3. On the Chaldaeans see below.

essays under different names that obliquely rebuke the new sect for its failure to see the fruit beneath the rind of custom. The treatise *On Statues* undertook to explain the symbolism of divine images to unlettered men who lacked the art to read them (fr. 1 Bidez [1913: appendix 2]);[4] the false apocalypse of Zoroaster, which he rebutted more than once, is ascribed in *Life of Plotinus* 16 to certain "Gnostics", whom he regards as heretical Christians. Perhaps it was in the hope of suborning the faith of Christians under persecution that he spoke of the One as "god above all" in his memoir of Plotinus (*Life* 23.16), and affixed the title *On the Three Hypostases* to a text (*Enneads* 5.1) in which his master traced the procession of mind and soul from the suprasubstantial source of unity. If more of Porphyry's extant work were strictly exegetic – if there were less that could be discounted as polemical, accommodatory or experimental – we could hope to ascertain whether this apostle of Plotinus upheld his master's teaching on the ineffability of the first principle. As it is, we can study only what remains, with the caveat that what remains is only what was not suppressed in the triumph of his adversaries.

PORPHYRY'S *PHILOSOPHY FROM ORACLES*[5]

Philosophers of the Roman world debated not the existence of divine beings, but their number and variety. Platonists could deduce the true marks of deity from first principles, but hitherto they had owed their knowledge of lesser gods, or demons, to the lore of priests, the long memories of the poets and the discernment of a few enlightened souls. Porphyry's *Philosophy from Oracles* seems to have been the first attempt to lay an incorrigible foundation for beliefs that were otherwise merely intuitive or hereditary. The first extract in Eusebius, which appears to come from the proem to the opening book, declares that none of the oracles collected in the treatise have suffered change or augmentation, but for occasional corrections to the syntax, metrical supplements and pruning of otiose matter (fr. 303.15–22 Smith). Wherever, then, the reader of this collection meets a philosophic doctrine, it is not because the editor has insinuated his own thoughts into the text but because the gods have a natural propensity to speak the truth. The veracity of the oracles will be gauged best by those who, after years of fruitless labour in search of truth, have seen that there is no escape from perplexity except through revelation (303.30–34). This, however, the gods will not vouchsafe to those of dissolute life or sluggardly understanding: they reserve the gift for those

4. Here, and nowhere else to my knowledge, Porphyry opines that God is luminous (fr. 2), and that his properties, which the sculptor is forced to represent symbolically, can be adequately rendered by an Orphic poet's collage of human and bestial attributes (fr. 3).
5. See Porphyry (1993). Most excerpts are drawn from the *Preparation for the Gospel* by Eusebius, a Christian apologist born a generation after Porphyry.

whose one concern in life has been the liberation of the soul.[6] Such is the disparity between mortals and immortals that the most formidable powers can be known only from the verses in which they state their own name and lineage (310–13, 317, 319, 320). From Apollo, the chief expositor of divine mysteries, we learn that gods are of four orders – chthonic or earthly, marine, subterranean and celestial – each demanding the sacrifice of a different kind of victim (314, 315). To the gods of earth one offers four-footed animals – swine to Demeter, for example – which, in keeping with their habitat, must be black (315.29–34). A trench must be dug for offerings to subterranean powers; to those who live above the soil we raise altars (315.35–7). Winged fowl suffice the other gods, and these again must be black for those who dwell in the dusky ocean (315.20). White birds are the portion of the supernal gods, the whole carcase being presented to those of the air, while those of the aether and upper heaven require no more than the extremities (315.21–5). Precepts for the fashioning of images follow. Those of Pan should be goat-legged, cloven footed and two-horned (318); Hecate's waxen effigies should bear a lamp, a whip and a sword and be encircled by the figure of a snake (319, 320). Her colours should be white and red and gold, which reinforce her triple character; this in turn corresponds (308.21–2) to the three divisions of the soul and to the demiurgic and unitive power that Hecate exerts in all three provinces of matter.

Porphyry's second book defines the instruments and the bounds of divine activity. A long oracle divides angels into three classes: those who are always in the presence of the Almighty, those who depart to carry out his errands or convey his decrees, and those who intone perpetual hymns of praise (325.15–23). In addition to these ministers, there are evil daemons, subjects of the Egyptian god Sarapis, who must be exorcised in preparation for the approach of gods (316). It is to them that the ignorant offer bloody and unwholesome sacrifices, and their reward is to be puffed up with crass vapours that give rise to wordless gibbering and bombast (326.26–34). The daemons have their symbol, the three-headed Cerberus, who once again represents the three realms ensouled and ruled by Hecate (327). Apollo tells one suppliant that he cannot reveal himself until the daemons have received their tribute of wine, milk, fruits and entrails (329); asked on another occasion to foretell the sex of an unborn child, he replies that she will be a girl by the edict of the stars (333).

In the third book Apollo warns us still more candidly of impending deceit (341). Verses ascribed to Pythagoras make Hecate submit to the conjurations of a "mortal man", while other lines prescribe expressly that incantations should be accompanied by a "mortal flute" (fr. 347.23, 349.9, from Eusebius, *Preparation for the Gospel* 5.8). A passage eagerly cited by Augustine declares that only ignorant and brutish folk would worship any god below the heavens, and that even the higher deities are subject to one whose law has been enshrined in the Hebrew

6. This claim suggests that this is not an early work, as some scholars have opined.

scriptures (Augustine, *City of God* 7.23 [= fr. 346 Smith]). But for this passage, Porphyry's regulations for animal sacrifice in this treatise would have stood in bald contradiction to his repeated advocacy of bloodless sacrifice in other works.[7] That is some evidence of its authenticity and, if a Christian had interpolated the reference to the Hebrews, he would surely have deleted two other texts that are hostile to followers of Christ, although they spare the man. "Man he was and all that man can be", declares an oracle that is attributed to Hecate (fr. 345 Smith, from Eusebius, *Preparation for the Gospel* 3.7.1–2), although Augustine hints that Porphyry himself had more than a hand in it (Augustine, *City of God* 19.23.107 [= fr. 346 Smith]); the oracle goes on to lament that worshippers of Christ parade their folly by paying to his exalted soul the honours due to a god alone. Another passage, cited only by Augustine, relates that when a pagan asked Apollo how to reclaim his Christian wife, the god replied that one might as well attempt to write on water as to cure those who have succumbed to this disease (*City of God* 19.22.17 [= fr. 343.8–14]).

PORPHYRY AND THEURGY

We have remnants of another book in which Porphyry commended the practice commonly known as theurgy, or divine work, as a purgative to the lower soul, and hence as a means of freeing the higher soul from the contagion of the body. The conventional title *On the Return of the Soul* is attested only in Augustine's *City of God*, and even there was intended only as a description of its contents (*City of God* 10.29).[8] The excerpts in Augustine are compatible with the teaching of the *Philosophy from Oracles*, but coincidences of thought and style are not common enough to justify the thesis that the two works were identical. It is only in the Augustinian excerpts that the Chaldaeans are represented as the true adepts in theurgy, and only here that we find express quotations from the *Chaldaean Oracles*.[9] By their precepts angels are brought down from the fiery space beneath the firmament to assist in the exorcism of the passions; other rites must be observed to persuade our evil genius not to hinder the approach of a better guardian; offerings to the sun and moon, however, are proscribed because

7. See, above all, *On Abstinence*, books 1 and 3, a book undoubtedly written after the death of Plotinus in 270.
8. The fragments, all derived from Augustine, are collected in an appendix to Bidez (1913). O'Meara (1959) contends that the *Return of the Soul* is the same work as the *Philosophy from Oracles*.
9. *Chaldaean Oracles* is a work ascribed to two second-century prophets, in which the divine world is conceived as a series of descending triads, in each of which power or *dunamis* mediates between being and life, although being predominates in the first triad, power in the second and mind in the third. Porphyry seems to have held that the One is the Father of the highest triad.

the destiny of the rational soul is to rise above the spheres and join the Father in incorporeal beatitude (Augustine, *City of God* 10.23). Theurgy differs from magic in aiming only at the good, and in being collaborative rather than coercive: it is not by charms but by the virtue of continence, nurtured inwardly, that ignorance is expelled from the rational soul (10.29).

Yet angels, too, are prone to vice, and in this daemonic character are ready to assist a malignant theurgist. "A good man in Chaldaea", Porphyry writes, "complains that his laboured efforts to purge the soul were baffled when a man skilled in the same arts, touched by envy, checked the powers from granting his petitions though he adjured them in sacred prayers" (Augustine, *City of God* 10.9). Nevertheless, when Porphyry admits that he has not discovered a universal means of purification (10.32), he appears to be speaking only of the lower soul. The purgatives that Greek philosophy offers to the higher soul, on the other hand, are sufficient, and (for all that we know) unique.

THE LETTER TO ANEBO[10]

Porphyry has no quarrel with the Egyptians in most of his writings. Nevertheless in the shortest of his extant works – if the letter to Anebo is an entire work, not an excerpt – he accosts the Egyptian priesthood with a series of paradoxes that, to judge by the growing acerbity and sarcasm of his tone, he considers fatal to their pretensions. The interrogation commences bluntly: how is it, Porphyry wonders, that the priests invoke the gods as their superiors, yet command them as inferiors? Why is spotless purity demanded of the postulant when the gods themselves not only assist us in lechery, but command it? Why does 'theagogy' make use of carcases when its adepts are required to abstain from meat and shun the smoke of sacrifice? How can gods as powerful as the sun and moon be awed into speaking the truth by threats that they know to be fictitious? Are they children, to believe that a man can open the pit of Hades or disperse the limbs of Osiris once again? The Egyptians may profess to have seen their deities ensconced in mud or seated on a lotus, or even changing form to match the constellations of the zodiac; but in that case they have failed to unmask the products of their own fantasy, having no conception of any god who is not a physical element. If all this is said in riddles, can they not divulge the meaning of the riddle? Why are all their mysteries wrapped up in barbarous terms that (we are told) will not bear translation into Greek? We cannot suppose that Egyptian is the language of the gods, or indeed that they use any language heard among mortals. If the higher gods are

10. For text and commentary, see Eusebius, *Preparation for the Gospel* 14.10 and Scott (1936: 28–102).

impassible, then none of our menaces, prayers and immolations can subdue them, while the lower gods will be too weak to do us good or harm.

This, then, is the assault to which the great treatise *On the Mysteries* replied under the pseudonym of an Egyptian priest, Abammon, who is generally assumed to be fictitious. That Iamblichus was the true author would appear to be proved not only by the testimony of Proclus (see Saffrey 1971), but by the dense and convoluted prose of the treatise, by coincidences in detail with his undisputed writings and, above all, by the theology of the eighth book, which concurs with his at the points where he diverged from his predecessors. In the following summary I shall argue that he makes his defence on grounds that would have seemed rational and cogent to fellow-Platonists, and indeed to most Greeks. Where he contradicts a view held by Porphyry, it is not because he is reasoning less Platonically, less systematically or with less concern to vindicate the dignity of reason and the absolute transcendence of the gods.

IAMBLICHUS, *ON THE MYSTERIES*

Theurgy, as Iamblichus defines it, is a human work, but one that owes its efficacy to *sumbola*, which unite divine powers to those of the mortal adept. The Greek word, like its English derivative 'symbol', denotes the use of a cryptic locution or image to convey truths for which common speech provides no glossary, but at the same time it retains its etymological sense of 'contract'. It is the bounty of the gods, not any force that earthbound wisdom can impart to our words and actions, that makes such a contract possible. Beings who can be threatened or cajoled are not gods, but daemons of low rank who share the traits of their seducers. True deity is bodiless and therefore imperturbable; it is not affected even by the operation of that cosmic sympathy which vouchsafes to the soul some knowledge of things to come in the lower realm. When we speak of divine necessity, we mean not that the gods are subject to coercion, but that goodness has an indefeasible tendency to impart itself to lower planes of being. Such benefits are proportioned to the capacities and deserts of the recipient, and the rites that cannot sway a supernal intellect may nonetheless help the worshipper to rid himself of ignorance, vice or passion. Success depends, in short, on a friendship that can be earned but not exacted: if the Greek magus clings to the barbarous formulae with which Egypt and Chaldaea have clothed their mysteries, that is not because reason sleeps, but because the rational man is one who does not presume to correct the gods.

We meet the same proviso against translation in the *Hermetica*, a collection of Greek tracts in which the gods of Egypt blend a cosmopolitan theology into an idiom drawn from Plato and the Stoics. Yet just as in this Hellenistic broth there are some ingredients that are genuinely Egyptian, so in the treatise of Iamblichus *On the Mysteries* – and above all in the theology that his eighth book ascribes to Hermes Trismegistus – there are elements that do not belie his priestly pseudonym.

The cause of all, according to this account, is One, "remaining immovable in the singularity of his own onehood" (*On the Mysteries* 8.2, in Places 1971: 262). From him proceeds the "first god and king", the self-fathering Good, who, as the monad prior to essence, is the transcendent source of intellect and its objects. Hermes, we are told, could not give a full account of these transcendent principles in fewer than a hundred volumes: after them he places another monad, the unitive principle of the intellectual realm, in whom resides the "primordial object of intellection", to be worshipped only in silence (*ibid.*). The intellectual realm takes shape through Kneph, the "self-thinking mind" (*ibid.*), who is the leader of the celestial gods; the visible world, however, is shaped and governed by a demiurgic intellect, who is called Amoun when he brings forth, Ptah or Hephaestus when he perfects his work, and Osiris when he makes this work productive of further goods (8.3, in Places 1971: 265).[11] In another text the elements are assigned to an Ogdoad or group of eight, in which four masculine deities are paired with their feminine counterparts under the regency of the sun, while the generated world itself is subject to the authority of the moon (*ibid.*). Of matter the Egyptians say – in contrast to the Greeks – that it is not a mere passivity but a source of life, abstracted from the principle of essence by the self-fathering god who entrusts it to the Demiurge (*ibid.*, *finis.*).

In his reference to the Ogdoad, Iamblichus may be thinking of the sodality of eight gods, male and female, who are depicted in a famous relief at the city of Hermopolis (Gwyn Griffiths 1996: 260). It is wrong, he maintains, to imagine all such agents as a single genus, divided (as in Plato) by dichotomous characteristics or (as in Aristotle) by constellations of accidental properties that are notionally, if not physically, separable from the universal substance in which they inhere (*On the Mysteries* 1.4). The truth is that the higher gods, the daemons and the heroes – the only species named at this point, although Abammon will later add angels and archangels – differ in essence as in rank, and that it is only when the properties that define each class are ascertained that we know what to hope from any member of it. In the class of gods, we cannot speak, in fact, of individuated members, for deity is pure intellect, identical with its thoughts and grasping all thought in the undivided unity of truth (1.6–7).

The contemplative faculty of a daemon or a hero, on the other hand, is limited and discrete, although this is not, as Porphyry seems to presuppose, the consequence of their being confined to the regions that furnish the elements of their bodies (1.5). Porphyry shows his ignorance by assigning an aerial body to the gods themselves, thus rendering it impossible for them to know, let alone to regulate, whatever is done outside their own sight and hearing (1.8). And he commits another fallacy when he supposes that the daemon or hero owes his identity to his

11. Cf. Porphyry, *On Statues* fr. 10 Bidez. All these gods appear (although not together) in Egyptian triads: Gwyn Griffiths (1996: 100–110).

corporeal envelope, for the principle of individuation at any level of being resides not in the substrate but in the form: that is to say, in the higher entities from which all form proceeds. The more remote a class of beings is from the unity of the ruling principle, the greater will be the difference among its members, but it is not the remoteness itself that differentiates. Even the soul, which dwells in matter, is characterized by immaterial properties (1.10); heroes, daemons and gods are properly incorporeal, and hence imperceptible to our physical senses. Bodies, when they employ them, remain extrinsic, so that if, for example, the gods employ such visible instruments as the sun and stars, they remain superior to the daemons, however tenuously the latter may be clothed (1.17). It is almost a logical consequence that heroes, daemons and gods alike are immune to the passions that afflict their votaries (1.10). It is in fact our own rebellious spirits that we propitiate when we offer prayers to wrathful gods, and the evils that we hope to avert by sacrifice are born of our own false reasoning and desire (1.11). If obscenity and licence are admitted in public rituals, it is not to amuse the gods, but to remind us that these ceremonies are tempered to human understanding – often to the grossest understanding – and can offer us at best a turbid image of the reality beyond sense and imagination (1.12). Impassibility and incorporeality are universal properties in the transcendent realm, which, for all disparities of rank and nature, is as continuous as a field of radiant light.

Why so many gradations of divinity? Because its operations are as manifold as the cosmos that it governs and sustains. Daemons represent the creative and generative powers of deity, heroes represent those which communicate life and shape the conduct of the soul (2.1). Archangels and angels rank between the gods and daemons; archons are of two kinds, the cosmic or sublunary and the material or hylic. The first resembles the gods in its stability while the second is diverse in aspect, turbulent in action. In most of the subsequent catalogues, the heroes (if present at all) precede both categories of archon, and the soul holds the lowest place, although it often seems to be the hylic archons who sit furthest from perfection. The properties of each order are now described, with a scholastic predilection for taxonomy far more redolent of Iamblichean commentary on Plato than of any ancient work from a priestly hand. We have room here only for a few specimens:

- Gods are simple and uniform in aspect; archangels and angels may fall short of their simplicity, but do not adopt such heterogeneous guises as the daemons. Variety is more pronounced in subaltern beings who inhabit matter, while souls present themselves "in every form" (2.3, in Places 1971: 71).
- Gods are immutable, even in semblance; archangels fall short of them in "sameness", but even angels, although inferior, cannot yet be said to change. Daemons "appear at different times in different forms"; heroes resemble demons, while the soul is a weak simulacrum of the hero (2.3, in Places 1971: 72).
- Gods bestride earth and heaven in their epiphanies, while an archangel has only so much light as he has authority. The radiance of an angel is still more

circumscribed, while that of a daemon is prone to fluctuation. Heroic apparitions are smaller in bulk but nobler in bearing. Cosmic archons are capable of great epiphanies, hylic archons only of pretending to greatness; the soul is more mercurial than the hero (2.4, in Places 1971: 75–6).

- Through the approach of a god we receive perfection and deliverance from passion; archangels bring serenity of contemplation, angels rational wisdom, daemons a longing to complete the works required of us in the sphere of generation. From heroes we derive zeal, and from the archons an inclination of the soul to heaven or earth (2.8, in Places 1971: 87).

We have noted above that Iamblichus does not ascribe any power of illumination to a psychic or physical "sympathy" between elements in the cosmos. True divination, he argues, is imparted by the gods, although receptivity may be perfected by an exquisite attenuation of the senses: the prophetess at Delphi yields herself to the "fiery spirit", while her counterpart at Branchidae is overwhelmed by the radiance that proceeds from her sacred wand (1.11). It is not, as Porphyry thinks, because the soul contains scintillae of divinity (1.20) that it serves the gods as a vessel of inspiration, but because it submits to powers that it does not possess by nature. Souls of females or males unmanned by ecstasy are favoured because they offer less resistance to their divine mentors, while the orgies of Sabazius and Bacchus are all the more efficacious because they expel all "human and natural qualities". To propose that it is only through cosmic sympathy that the irrational and inanimate can become portents is to suggest that we acquire knowledge from something lower than the intellect, and thus to overthrow the very premise on which Porphyry attributes vaticination to the soul (3.15–17).

Practitioners of the mysteries are unjustly accused of making the gods accomplices in unjust designs (4.1). It is often the case, Iamblichus explains, that the gods appear to condone injustice because they see that it conduces to a more distant goal, which we too – could we perceive it – would acknowledge to be just (1.5). When an act performed in the name of the gods miscarries, it is not because there is ignorance or error in the divine realm, but because the practitioner lacked the means to make better use of the strength that he acquired by exploiting the sympathy of the elements (1.6). While there are daemons who effect their illicit purposes through just but unlearned ministers (1.7), that is only a further proof that the wisdom by which gods judge good and evil is not immanent to the world or to our own unassisted faculties. The object of theurgy is in fact to make a science of our religion, purging the mind (with divine assistance) of its natural and hence superstitious propensity to imagine that a crime against one's neighbour may be a duty to the gods.

But why – the question is Porphyry's – are priests enjoined to shun contact with the dead, when they habitually avail themselves of the carcases of beasts in their invocations (6.1)? Iamblichus replies that priests are not required to hold aloof from every corpse, but only from those of human beings, since the animal form has never housed a divine soul and is thus not rendered unclean by its departure. It is not through the animal's flesh but through its emancipated soul that we approach the divine, for a soul acquires some kinship with the daemons by the mere fact of having shed its carnal envelope (5.3). A corpse creates no defilement in a daemon, because these super-human beings are not susceptible of corruption (5.2). But now it seems that Iamblichus has bared his flank to the next thrust: how can beings so impassible be intimidated by the threats of mortals? The great ones, he replies, suffer no coercion (6.5): it is not such potentates as the sun and moon but lower agents – senseless, limited, irrational – who permit themselves to be overawed, or perhaps the terrestrial daemons, not because they are compelled but because they are not so indifferent as the higher powers to the threat of sacrilege (6.6). Furthermore, it is possible that the magician gains an ascendancy over lesser gods by becoming one with their overlords, whose symbols he employs (6.6).

DIVINE SYMBOLISM, HUMAN UNDERSTANDING

Iamblichus proceeds to explain these symbols in his seventh book, with the caveat that a symbol fails in its purpose unless we grasp the intellectual truth behind the pictured emblem (7.1). Mud, for example, signifies the corporeal, and (by virtue of this) whatever gives life and nourishment, hence the generative principle, and finally (for those who can ascend so far) the First Cause (7.2). The lotus enthroned on mud betokens mastery of the corporeal, while the image of a piloted ship bears witness to the divine administration of the cosmos (7.2, in Places 1971: 252). The stars are both the symbols and the instruments of divine government, and the sacred guides of Egypt are therefore not ashamed to parcel out the heavens into spatial quarters, the twelve signs of the zodiac, or even thirty-six decans (8.4). It would not be true, however, to say with Porphyry that the Egyptians imagine human life to be subject to the stars, for soul and intellect have their origins outside the natural realm. We have in fact two souls, the higher and more elusive of which is naturally receptive to divine influence. It can indeed afford to despise the lower manifestations of divinity, for it is only the supracosmic gods who are able to assist it in its ascent from the toils of matter (8.6).

The Egyptians can be acquitted of maintaining that our destiny is fixed for us at birth by a personal daemon, or that a soul can procure its happiness by appeasing it with material sacrifices (9.1). The daemon – a product of not one element but of all the elements in due combination – represents the lot that the soul elects for itself before descent into the body. It is therefore not the agent of the soul's release but only its coadjutor in fulfilling the sublunar decrees of fate. When this is achieved the daemon yields to a higher god, whom the astrologers style the *oikodespotēs*, "master of the house" (9.2). The aim of theurgy is the realization or enjoyment of the Good. The soul that aspires to union with this sublime and ineffable source of being must not only attain to the "plenitude of intellect" but submit to divine assistance, and for most this will entail some use of theurgical machinery (10.5).

Iamblichus is perhaps the first Greek philosopher to forbid the representation of the gods in painted or sculpted images (see especially *On the Mysteries* 3.28). He is, in fact, the arch-rationalist among the Platonists: more rational than Porphyry, who believed that in this lower world we are answerable to daemons who are themselves weaker than fate.[12] The true god, in Iamblichus' view, personifies all that is highest in the intellectual faculty, and is thus superior both to the natural sympathies between the powers and elements of the cosmos and to the arts by which the sorcerer transforms these cosmic sympathies into instruments of vanity and greed.

FURTHER READING

Blumenthal, H. & E. Clark (eds) 1993. *The Divine Iamblichus*. London: Bristol Classical Press.

Lewy, H. 1956. *Chaldaean Oracles and Theurgy*. Cairo: Institut Français d'Archéologie Orientale.

Shaw, G. 1995. *Theurgy and the Soul*. University Park, PA: Pennsylvania State University Press.

Smith, A. 1974. *Porphyry's Place in the Neoplatonic Tradition*. The Hague: Nijhoff.

On ANGELS/DEMONS see also Chs 14, 20. On FIRST CAUSE see also Ch. 15; Vol. 2, Ch. 14; Vol. 3, Ch. 6. On SYMBOLS see also Vol. 5, Ch. 11. On THE ONE see also Chs 3, 11, 14, 19; Vol. 4, Ch. 9; Vol. 5, Ch. 15. On THEURGY see also Ch. 20.

12. In addition to the literature cited above, see *To Marcella* 275.5–25 Nauck on the necessity of appeasing the natal daemon, who seems in this case to personify the sexual instinct.

17

THE CAPPADOCIANS: BASIL OF CAESAREA, GREGORY OF NAZIANZUS, GREGORY OF NYSSA

Anthony Meredith

Prior to the advent of the Cappadocian Fathers – Basil of Caesarea (*c.*330–79), his friend Gregory of Nazianzus (329–89), and Basil's brother Gregory of Nyssa (*c.*335–*c.*395) – Cappadocia, to the north-east of modern Turkey, seems to have been something of a cultural backwater. Hence comes the epigram, 'It is as hard to teach turtles to fly as to teach Cappadocians to write good Greek'. The three Fathers came from very respectable and prosperous families, and at any rate two of them received a good classical education in the university of Athens for about five years. An elaborate account of their life is provided by Gregory of Nazianzus' *Oration* 43, a panegyric of his friend and younger contemporary, Basil.

Unfortunately what we should most like to know, the nature of their philosophical background, is much more difficult to arrive at. The education at Athens was largely rhetorical and we know little or nothing about the sort of philosophy they would have encountered. A general acquaintance with some sort of Platonism must be assumed. But that apart, we are reduced to conjecture. The great period of revived Neoplatonism was to occur during the fifth century, with Proclus and Macrobius being worthy of note, the former because of the influence he exercised on Pseudo-Dionysius. Although the fifth century saw an increased interest in Platonism, this came too late to affect the Cappadocian approach.

It is true that Eunapius (346–414), in his *Lives of the Philosophers and Sophists* (hereafter *Lives*), does mention some disciples of Iamblichus, among whom were Maximus and Chrysanthius, who, although much admired by the Emperor Julian, were theurgists or miracle workers, rather than philosophers in the strict sense. Aedesius, himself a Cappadocian and also the preceptor of the Emperor Julian, was indeed a philosopher but we know next to nothing about what he taught from the account in Eunapius (*Lives* 461, in Philostratus 1921: 376). Aedesius died *c.*355 and no writings of his survive.

Before an account of the nature and influence of philosophy on the teaching of the Cappadocians is offered it is important to note that the actual word 'philosophy' in their writings refers less to their systematic use of Plato, Aristotle and the

Stoics than to a particular way of life, above all, a moral and ascetic one. Basil regularly applies the word 'philosophy' to the monastic life, as does his brother Gregory of Nyssa in his *Life of Macrina* (section 1) and in the prologue to his treatise *On Virginity*. (The whole subject has been thoroughly treated by Malingrey 1961.)

The basic assumption underlying what follows is that the three Cappadocian Fathers, and above all Gregory of Nyssa, ought to be treated seriously as philosophers. However, it must be admitted at the outset that this is not a self-evident proposition. It not only seems to contradict certain explicit statements of all three Cappadocians, but has also been vigorously contested by several scholars, particularly by Christopher Stead (1976). It cannot be denied that the two Gregories, in particular, were renowned preachers. Gregory of Nyssa, despite his apparent lack of formal rhetorical education, was much valued by the emperor, Theodosius I, and two funeral orations for the emperor's wife, Flaccilla, and daughter, Pulcheria, survive. This indicates that there is in Gregory of Nyssa, as in many ancient writers, a tension between rhetoric and philosophy.

The question of the influence exercised by Platonism in its various forms on the thought of the Cappadocian Fathers, above all Gregory of Nyssa, has been variously answered at least as far back as Cherniss' seminal article, "The Platonism of Gregory of Nyssa" (see Cherniss 1934). For Cherniss, Gregory was little more than a Hellenized wolf in the clothing of a Christian sheep. In other words, although Gregory continues to use the language of Christian tradition, the meaning he attaches to this language is Hellenic rather than Christian. Doerrie (1983), however, preferred to use the language of *Umdeutung*, or transformation, with which to define the approach of Gregory. On this view, Gregory did indeed take over the language and some of the ideas of philosophy, notably those to be found in Plato's *Phaedo, Theaetetus* and *Timaeus*, but (on this hypothesis) Gregory did not do so uncritically, instead giving these philosophical concepts and ideas a meaning distinct from that found in the Platonist tradition. Stead (1976), by contrast, radically questions Doerrie's whole approach, and does not treat Gregory as a philosopher at all, but rather as a rhetorician without a coherent point of view. There is some truth in this, as Gregory does not provide us with a clearly articulated standpoint on the subject of the person of Christ or the relation of freedom and salvation.

Of the Cappadocians' philosophical education, as has already been mentioned, we know very little. Their own at times disconcertingly hostile attitude to secular philosophy, coupled with their failure to mention any contemporary pagan philosopher, may lead to the false conclusion that they were uninfluenced by what they either ignored or affected to despise. So, for example, Basil on several occasions in his letters – with echoes of 1 Corinthians 2:6, where the wisdom of this age is contrasted with the wisdom of Christ – criticizes the value of human learning (e.g. *Letters* 223:2, 258:2; nor are these the only examples we could cite). Even so, Basil is not entirely consistent at least in his attitude to classical culture in general, if the correspondence between him and Libanius in his *Letters* 335–59 is genuine (part of it is certainly so). We also need to remember that Tertullian, in the beginning of the third century, despite his apparent total rejection of philosophy as a poisonous root (*Apology* 46:18), was happy elsewhere to speak of the Stoic philosopher Seneca as "our Seneca".

Again, Basil's friend Gregory of Nazianzus, in a well-known passage in *Oration* 23.12, writes that it was fishermen rather than students of Aristotle who spread the Gospel. Even Gregory of Nyssa, arguably the most philosophically literate of all three Cappadocians, is happy to attribute the errors of Eunomius to the influence of Aristotle, which he does in *Against Eunomius* 1.46 and elsewhere. The last two examples more than suggest that Aristotle was regarded by some Christians as at least a suspicious ally in their attempts to articulate their faith. Yet, in *Against Eunomius* 2.404 and 405, Gregory of Nyssa accuses Eunomius of being overly influenced by the *Cratylus* of Plato in his treatment of the nature of language as natural rather than conventional.

It should in fairness be stated that a similar wall of indifference or hostility existed on the pagan side also. For example, two fifth-century pagan philosophers, Macrobius and Proclus, provide no indication at all of their awareness of the existence of Christianity. The same is true also of Sallustios and Iamblichus. By contrast, Porphyry provided learned ammunition for the persecution of Diocletian in 305 in the shape of a fifteen-volume *Against the Christians.*

An exceedingly useful summary of the various possible approaches to the problem of the differing degrees of influence exercised on the Cappadocian Fathers, notably Gregory of Nyssa, by non-Christian philosophy is provided by Jaroslav Pelikan in his 1992–93 Gifford lectures, *Christianity and Classical Culture* (1995: ch. 1). Pelikan alerts the reader to the ambiguous character of the Cappadocians' approach to classical culture, for although they were happy to use the philosophical tradition, as we have seen they affect on occasion to despise it.

The central aim in what follows is to explore the extent to which, in all three Cappadocian Fathers, it is possible to detect evidence of the influence of philosophical ideas in their different writings. I shall distinguish three differing ways in which such influence may be discerned:

(i) An actual acknowledged citation from a non-Christian writer, of the type of reference we find, for example, in Augustine's *City of God*: "As Porphyry says in his work entitled *The Letter to Anebo*" (10.11).

(ii) A verifiable citation from a classical author, but one that goes unacknowledged. Some such usages will occur in passages from the Cappadocians, later to be discussed.

(iii) An unacknowledged and general dependence on a classical (especially philosophical) author, but without any clear verbal echoes. So, for example, Gregory of Nyssa's treatise *On Virginity* portrays the upward progress of the created soul in an idiom unmistakably influenced by the *Symposium* of Plato, but shorn of any precise citation of any length.

(I) AN ACKNOWLEDGED CITATION FROM A NON-CHRISTIAN WRITER

It can be asserted at the outset that in none of the Cappadocian Fathers does there occur any example of category (i). This is quite remarkable: although both Basil and Gregory Nazianzus had an elaborate education at Athens from 350 to 356, nowhere in the writings of either do we find any mention of their pagan preceptors or contemporaries. This may be owing to the fact that their education in Athens was rhetorical rather than philosophical in content.

Why the Cappadocians were so reserved and why instead Augustine was so much more forthright is a question that deserves exploration. It may have been because of the pronounced hostility to Christianity portrayed by the celebrated School Law of Julian in June 362, which effectively excluded Christians from occupying teaching posts in universities. Even though Julian was dead within a year of this 'cruel' edict, it may well have challenged men of the intellectual calibre of the Cappadocians to be cautious in advancing too explicit a connection between Christianity and philosophy. Their reticence is all the more remarkable when it is set beside the *Preparation for the Gospel* by Eusebius of Caesarea, composed some time after the peace of Constantine in 312/313. There we find Eusebius quoting considerable and acknowledged extracts from Plotinus' *Enneads* 5.1 and 4.7 (at *Preparation for the Gospel* 11.17 and 15.10 respectively).

The only possible exception to this general approach occurs in Gregory of Nazianzus' *Third Theological Oration*, in the course of which Gregory offers an account of the derivation of the dyad and triad from the monad, from which all begins. But Gregory insists that this is *not* to be compared to the overflow of goodness, as from a *krater*, as "one of the Greek philosophers has dared to claim". The passage alluded to is, according to Arthur James Mason, Plato's *Timaeus* 41d (see Gregory of Nazianzus 1899: 76 n.2), but according to Hermann Josef Sieben it refers to Plotinus' *Ennead* 5.2.1 (see Gregory of Nazianzus 1996: 176 n.16).

(II) A VERIFIABLE CITATION FROM A CLASSICAL AUTHOR

When it comes to actual verbatim quotations, or ones that are nearly so, we have two good examples in Gregory of Nyssa. One, discovered by David Balás (1966: 168), is a passage from Plutarch's treatise *On Isis and Osiris* 25, which is cited, but without any reference to Plutarch, in Gregory's *Against Eunomius* 3.10.41. Gregory accuses the author, whom he terms "the wise theologian", of introducing the names of Egyptian gods into Christianity. Interestingly, this passage does not appear to occur in Eusebius' *Preparation for the Gospel.*

The only other passage where it may be possible to detect verbal dependence without any apparent acknowledgement is in the opening words of Gregory's treatise, *De Instituto Christiano* (in *Gregorii Nysseni opera* VIII.1.40.1), which may echo the opening words of Plotinus' *Enneads* 4.8.1. Even here direct dependence of

Gregory on Plotinus is denied by Staats (1984), although asserted by Mühlenberg (1966: 82).

(III) AN UNACKNOWLEDGED AND GENERAL DEPENDENCE ON A CLASSICAL AUTHOR

Despite the relative paucity of extended, identifiable passages of philosophical provenance in all three Cappadocians, the attempt to articulate a certain basic Christian understanding within a largely Platonist framework is evident in them all. However, before the particular usage of Platonism is addressed it is important to remember not only that our knowledge of the Cappadocian philosophical education is slight, but also that it is unclear to what extent they depended on an actual knowledge of the Platonic corpus and how much they were indebted to now lost florilegia, the existence of which is vouched for by Henry Chadwick (1969).

This latter issue is raised because of the relative frequency with which certain phrases recur. Two instances illustrate the point and the difficulty. The ideal of perfection as "becoming as much like god as possible" is taken verbatim from Plato's *Theaetetus* 176b. Again, the thought that, "It is hard to know and impossible to reveal to all the divine nature" is a quotation from Plato's *Timaeus* 28c and is described by Chadwick in his note to Origen's *Against Celsus* 7.42 as "perhaps the most hackneyed quotation from Plato in Hellenistic writers" (Origen 1953: 429). The Cappadocians make use of Platonic ideas, particularly in their spiritual writings: Basil in his *Rules*, and Gregory of Nyssa in his treatises *On Virginity* and *On the Soul and Resurrection*.

All three Cappadocian Fathers, but especially Basil, were well aware of the challenge presented to the Gospel, especially after Julian's edict of June 362, by the use of Hellenistic letters. In order to face the issues raised for the Christian community by the surrounding culture, Basil and Gregory of Nazianzus put together a collection of texts from Origen, called the *Philocalia*, with the aim of drawing from Origen's writings (mainly his *De principiis*) a defence of freedom and of an allegorical understanding of Scripture.

Basil himself at a slightly later date composed a treatise, probably for the benefit of his nephews, entitled *To Young Men On How They May Be Helped By Greek Literature* (Letter 22). Basil here makes much use of the idea of *chresis* (use). The expression occurs on several occasions and the underlying thought is that when reading Homer the notion of moral usefulness should be to the fore. Nigel Wilson describes Basil's thesis (as found in 2.37–39 of Letter 22) as follows: "the utility of all types of author, whether poets, orators or other prose writers are to be exploited, if they can lead to benefit for the character" (see Basil of Caesarea 1975: 10). This more positive approach to classical literature should make us cautious in taking too seriously the negative attitude previously mentioned in several of Basil's letters. Both the *Philocalia* and the *Letter* indicate the importance the Cappadocians attached in making an alliance between Christianity and culture. It should be remarked, however, that Basil's approval of Homer and others is a moral, not a metaphysical, approval. In other words, although Basil admits that there is a close harmony between the moral outlook of pagans and Christians, he is not persuaded of the truth of pagan legends and philosophy.

But how in practice does this affect the other writings of Basil? Two examples of his method shed some light on this. In the preface to his *Longer Rules*, section 3 (*Patrologia Graeca* [hereafter PG] 31, 896b), and in section 1 of Rule 2 (PG 31, 909b–c), we find Basil in his description of the upward mobility of the created spirit using language that is clearly indebted to the *Symposium* of Plato. In the *Symposium*, Diotima, usually assumed to be the mouthpiece of Socrates himself, outlines the upward movement of the human spirit in terms of the search for absolute beauty, "the divine, the original, the supreme, the self-consistent, the monoeidic beautiful itself" (211e). In Rule 2, Basil writes: "By nature we desire beautiful things, though we differ as to what is supremely beautiful ... Now what is more marvellous than the divine beauty?".

Very similar language occurs in Gregory of Nyssa's treatise *On Virginity*, above all in chapter XI, especially in section 5, where the ascent of the created spirit to absolute beauty moves upward in precisely the same way as it does in Plato's *Symposium* 210aff. Clearly, in the moral and spiritual sphere Basil and Gregory seem to have experienced little difficulty in using language and ideas of Platonic provenance. But what of other areas?

Both Basil and his brother, Gregory of Nyssa, composed commentaries on the opening chapter of Genesis, entitled *Hexaemeron*, the six days of creation. Basil's work took the form of nine homilies delivered in Caesarea probably in the Lent of 375. Gregory of Nyssa's work is a treatise, which contains frequent references to his teacher, Basil, and was probably composed after his brother's death in January 379. Gregory's audience was very different from Basil's and was probably much less various than his brother's whom, as stated by Gregory himself, were many in number and not all of them academic (*in Hex.* PG 44, 65a). By contrast, Gregory of Nazianzus, who was later accorded the title of 'The Theologian', left no series of sermons on similar subjects, although he is the author of forty-five extant sermons.

The genre of Basil's work may account for the fact that there is some evidence in the sermons of Hellenic influence. The main source used is the *Timaeus* of Plato. This is hardly surprising in as much as Plato's dialogue, like Genesis, is concerned with the fashioning of the physical universe. In Basil's first homily (section 2), the primary motive for the creation of the universe is stated to be the goodness of God, without any trace of envy, a conception clearly borrowed from *Timaeus* 28b–30a and familiar already from Athanasius' treatise *On the Incarnation* 3.3. It is perhaps worth remarking that the popularity of Plato's *Timaeus* was not restricted to Christian authors. The index to Plotinus' *Enneads* (see Plotinus 1964–

82) reveals the interesting fact that that dialogue was more popular with Plotinus than were its near rivals, the *Phaedrus* and the *Republic*.

Despite his willingness to use the *Timaeus*, Basil makes it abundantly clear, especially at the beginning of his ninth homily, that the Bible is not a treatise on cosmology. It is not intended to answer the questions posed by physicists and philosophers alike as to whether the world is a sphere or a cylinder or a disc. Basil shows considerable awareness of the views held by secular philosophers and physicists. But, as Stanislas Giet points out in his introduction to the Sources Chrétiennes edition of Basil's nine homilies *On the Hexaemeron*, one of the difficulties in trying to evaluate the extent of Cappadocian dependency on philosophy is that "the realm of philosophy is too imprecise to allow of any neat comparison" (see Basil of Caesarea 1950: 46).

According to Gregory of Nazianzus' *Panegyric on Basil* (*Oration* 43.23), the education that he and Basil received at Athens was not narrowly rhetorical but also embraced astronomy, logic and geometry. Even so, Basil's attitude to the classical culture he had received is decidely ambiguous. On the one hand, he treats it with some reserve, if not outright contempt, when he calls it a foolish waste of time in Letter 223/2 and elsewhere. On the other hand, there exists a collection of letters between Basil and the leading pagan sophist of the day, Libanius (*Letters* 335–59). All may not be genuine, but they are enough to show that Basil possessed a divided mind on the subject of the value of pagan literature.

By contrast, Gregory of Nyssa, despite his apparently total dependence on his brother for education (Basil is invariably for him "the teacher", as at PG 44, 64b, 65b), is far more willing to treat Genesis 1 as a coherent account of the divine foundation of the universe, in which all is linked together by the idea of what he terms *akolouthia* or connection (as at PG 44, 76b, 85b, 117b). In fact, it is precisely in his search for the sequence of the narrative of Genesis 1 that Gregory consciously distinguishes his position from that of his brother (PG 44, 68b–d). As Gregory points out, Basil's work was a series of sermons designed for a popular audience, which could not be expected to grasp philosophical niceties (PG 44, 65a). Another word Gregory uses to articulate the stages of creation is *taxis* (order) or *heirmos* (close connection), as at PG 44, 76b and 77c, the prevailing assumption being that the power and will of God are inseparable and that God works in an orderly way.

It is a favourite device of Gregory to do this. For example, in his eight *Homilies on the Beatitudes* he is forever trying to relate the eight beatitudes to the ordered steps of a ladder leading up to God. A similar search for this sort of coherence dominates his *Catechetical Oration*, where more than twenty instances of the key word, *akolouthia*, occur. In his work on the six days of creation, Gregory is always on the search for the ordered sequence. The frequency with which Gregory employs the word *akolouthia* can be gauged from the fact that the *Lexicon Gregorianum* devotes no fewer than fifteen columns to the word itself, in addition to thirteen columns to its correlatives (Daniélou 1970: ch. 2).

Gregory is endeavouring to discover an ordered structure. In other words, he is searching for an overall design and to that end he is on the search for the meaning of the words and so to arrive at what he calls their particular *skopos* or direction. In order to further his search for coherence, Gregory appeals in chapter 5 of the *Catechetical Oration* to what he terms 'common ideas': that is, ideas or notions that are common to all rational enquiry, whether philosophical or Christian. With their help he endeavours to establish both the rational and the revealed basis of the doctrine of the Trinity. Saint Paul had attempted something very similar at Romans 2:15, where he appeals to a law written in human hearts. Origen, likewise, in his work *Against Celsus* 1.9, appeals to the universal ideas shared by all human beings. Basil, also, in his *Treatise on the Holy Spirit* (9.22) makes use of the expression "common or universal ideas", but he is appealing there less to some general, philosophical background than to the unwritten or oral tradition of the Fathers.

This fact illustrates well one of the differences between Basil and Gregory. The latter uses the expression 'common ideas' very frequently, especially in *Against Eunomius* (e.g. at 1.186, 2.11), and this despite the fact that one of his complaints against his adversary is his dependence on Aristotle. Gregory even composed a treatise on the Trinity for the benefit of the Greeks with the title *From Common Ideas*, in the course of which he attempts to establish the rational character of the Trinity. In a not dissimilar fashion, the central purpose of Gregory's *Catechetical Oration* was to enable catechists to deal with the articulate objections of those being prepared for baptism. (The expression 'common ideas' does not occur in Gregory Nazianzus' *Five Theological Orations*, this possibly suggesting that he is primarily concerned with helping the faith of those to whom he was preaching.)

One of the primary consequences of the importance Gregory of Nyssa assigns to common ideas in the *Catechetical Oration* is his endeavour to establish the fact that the doctrine of the Incarnation, which lies at the heart of the divine economy, does not conflict with the idea of what it is fitting to predicate of God, that is, with *theoprepeia*. This does not include, perhaps rather surprisingly, the notions of either incomprehensibility or infinity; nor does it include the notions with which Gregory articulates the nature of God and the soul's approach to him in the *Life of Moses* and *Homilies on the Song of Songs*. Rather, Gregory is establishing from the outset of his *Catechetical Oration* (*Gregorii Nysseni opera* III.IV.8 3,4) four basic ideas – the goodness, justice, wisdom and power of God – which are also to be found in Origen's *Against Celsus* 3.70. Gregory's debt to Origen is everywhere evident.

The remainder of Gregory's treatise is devoted to showing in a quite unusual way how the salvation of the world was realized by God without him acting in a tyrannical or unjust way to the devil, who had his rights. Gregory, in common with other Christian writers, was anxious to exonerate God from the injustice of stealing from the devil his lawful prey, which the devil had won by human folly and his own cunning. Chapter 20, above all, is devoted to establishing precisely this point. It begins with the words, "Everyone agrees that we must believe not only in the power of God, but also in his justice, goodness and wisdom." It looks very much as though Gregory is determined to do what Plato had done in book 2 of the *Republic* and establish the nature of God by reflection on those characteristics that help define human excellence. In other words, our perception of what it means to be a good person determines our perception of the nature of God.

In order to substantiate this theory of the justice of God in dealing with the rights of Satan, Gregory employs the celebrated image of the fish hook in chapter 22 and following. The devil swallows the bait of the humanity of Jesus and in the process is overcome by the hidden divinity of Christ. The deceiver is deceived. God is not unjust.

Although Origen's homily *On Matthew* (16.8) seems to have been the source of what Gustaf Aulen (1970) has called "the ransom theory of atonement", this theory found no favour at all with Gregory Nazianzus in his *Oration* 45.22. The point is that Gregory of Nyssa seems to have elaborated his theory in order to establish the justice of God in dealing with fallen humanity. This fact reinforces a point already made; namely, that Gregory of Nyssa, in his eagerness to interpret the message of the Gospel in ways acceptable to our ideas of justice, removes the mystery of redemption in so doing. But it should also be remembered that his motive is the desire to render the Gospel message acceptable and palatable to pagan converts. Such an approach is far less evident in the other two Cappadocians, who write 'from faith to faith'.

Little has so far been said about the attitude adopted by Gregory Nazianzus towards philosophy. As was noted previously, it is to him that we owe in his third *Theological Oration* (section 2) any direct reference to Greek philosophy. There Gregory refers to the metaphor of an overflowing cistern with which to explore and explain the organic relationship between Father and Son. The Father is treated as some sort of overflowing vessel from which the Second Person springs. A similar illustration does indeed occur in Plotinus' *Enneads* 5.2.1. However, despite his acquaintance with the passage in question, Gregory is not happy about employing it, because it seems to make the generation of the Son too organic and necessary. "Let us", he writes, "never look on this generation as involuntary, like some natural overflow, hard to be retained, and by no means befitting our conception of the deity" (*Theological Oration* 3.2). The upshot is that, despite Gregory's awareness of this Plotinian image, he mentions it only to reject it.

Gregory Nazianzus' *Oration* 21, a sort of funeral oration in honour of Athanasius who had died in 373, is very instructive on Gregory's general attitude towards classical culture. On the one hand, he is clearly aware of the terminology of Neoplatonism. In section 13, for example, he uses the language of 'triad', as he had done in his *Third Theological Oration* (section 2) as well as in *Oration* 23.8. The question is how much this tells us about his commitment to philosophical ways of thinking: probably very little. Later on in *Oration* 21 (section 12), Gregory launches an attack on the destructive effect of philosophy in the last third of the fourth century. Gregory reinforces his point by likening the heretics of his own day to the philosophers encountered by St Paul on the hill of the Areopagus at Acts 17:21.

In general, therefore, Gregory is much more reserved about the value of philosophy than the two brothers. Like Gregory of Nyssa, Gregory of Nazianzus had indeed censured Eunomius for reducing religion to philosophy and, above all, to the atheistic philosophy of Epicurus and to the philosophy of Aristotle with its denial of providence (*First Theological Oration*, section 10). Gregory of Nazianzus, however, is more consistent in this respect than are Basil and Gregory of Nyssa.

In his fifth *Oration*, for instance, Gregory Nazianzus is clearly aware of the existence of various analogies to illustrate the unity and trinity of God. But he also perceives (in section 32) that employing the analogy of the sun and its rays to illustrate the relation of Father and Son is problematic. He is anxious to avoid the suggestion that only the Father has an independent personality. Gregory therefore writes, "Neither the ray nor the light is another sun, but they are only effulgences from the sun and qualities of its essence". It may be that Gregory Nazianzus' reserve towards philosophy accounts for his subsequent reputation as 'The Theologian'.

CONCLUSION

What has emerged from the above is that any discussion of the philosophy of the Cappadocians is primarily concerned with Gregory of Nyssa. This is in many ways surprising. We know next to nothing about his philosophical training or indeed of any other form of education he may have had. He was also cautious about spreading his views. Even so, the use to which he put the *Symposium* in his treatise *On Virginity*, and his use of the *Phaedo* and *Phaedrus* in his treatise *On the Soul and Resurrection*, together with his search to find structure and order in creation and revelation and to relate the mystery of the Trinity and the Incarnation to the realms of common ideas and God-fittingness, mark him out as a thinker of some originality and importance. A negative consequence of this approach is that it can easily be interpreted as an abandonment of the divine mystery. To insist on the importance of justice, order and goodness alongside power may have the effect of reducing the wonder of faith. But this is a risk that any serious attempt to grapple with the divine mystery is bound to undergo.

What underpins Gregory's whole approach is the conviction that there is an ultimate harmony between Hellenism and Christianity, between faith and reason. In this, as in other respects, he is a disciple of Origen, under whom Gregory the Wonderworker, the apostle of Cappadocia, had studied. And the same Gregory had also instructed Gregory of Nyssa's and Basil's grandmother, the elder Macrina, in the faith, as Basil tells us in Letter 204.

The two other Cappadocians have less to offer on this front. They were more concerned with establishing peace and order within the Church and with defending and expounding Christian teaching for the benefit of those who already believe. Basil indeed had dealings with outside culture. His *Philocalia*, however, does not seem to have affected his attitude to, or use of, philosophy. The same is also true of Gregory of Nazianzus, who despite editing the *Philocalia* along with Basil and displaying great verbal familiarity with the philosophical language of his day, does not hesitate to attribute all adverse criticism of St Athanasius to philosophical perversity (*Oration* 21.12).

All three Cappadocians owe a considerable debt to Platonism. This can be summed up in the emphasis we can detect in each of them on the reality and importance of the spiritual world within and outside us, and in their insistence that God is real, good and beautiful, language that recalls Plato's *Timaeus*, *Republic* and *Symposium*. Alongside these obvious points of contact there exist two points of divergence: (i) both Basil and Gregory of Nyssa (the latter in *Against Eunomius* 1.271–4) emphasize the radical distinction, even within the spiritual realm, between creature and creator, something not readily found in the Platonic tradition; and (ii) the Platonic insistence on the importance of the soul needed to be modified by the Christian conviction that the body was also made by God and made for salvation, and that Christ had a body in addition to his soul (Gregory of Nyssa, for instance, insists on the bodily resurrection of Christ and on our bodily resurrection in *To Theophilus*, and also on the importance of the sacraments of baptism and the eucharist in *Catechetical Oration*, chs 32–7).

FURTHER READING

Basil of Caesarea 1950. *Ascetical Works*, M. Wagner (trans.). Washington, DC: Catholic University of America Press.

Gregory of Nyssa 1967. *Ascetical Works*, V. Callaban (trans.). Washington, DC: Catholic University of America Press.

Gregory of Nyssa 2007. *Gregory of Nyssa: The Letters*, A. Silvas (trans.). Leiden: Brill.

McGuckin, J. 2001. *St Gregory of Nazianzus: An Intellectual Biography*. Crestwood: St. Vladimir's Seminary Press.

Meredith, A. 1995. *The Cappadocians*. London: Geoffrey Chapman.

Meredith, A. 1999. *Gregory of Nyssa*. London: Routledge.

On CHRISTIANITY see also Chs 10, 14, 18; Vol. 5, Ch. 12. On COSMOLOGY see also Chs 6, 8, 14; Vol. 2, Chs 4, 10, 16. On CREATION see also Chs 9, 13; Vol. 3, Ch. 9; Vol. 5, Ch. 5. On PLATONISM see also Chs 11, 14, 15; Vol. 5, Ch. 16. On SCRIPTURE see also Chs 9, 13; Vol. 2, Ch. 19; Vol. 3, Chs 3, 4, 15; Vol. 4, Ch. 3; Vol. 5, Ch. 12. On THE TRINITY see also Ch. 14, 20; Vol. 2, Chs 2, 8, 15; Vol. 3, Chs 3, 9, 17; Vol. 4, Ch. 4; Vol. 5, Chs 12, 23.

18

AUGUSTINE

Gareth B. Matthews

Augustine was born in 354 in Thagaste, a provincial town in what is now eastern Algeria. After studying rhetoric in Carthage and sailing to Italy for what turned out to be a seven-year stay, he returned to North Africa where he became Bishop of Hippo Regius and stayed until his death in 430. In Carthage he had been attracted to Manicheanism; he was, in fact a Manichean 'auditor' for nine years. But about the time he left Carthage for Rome he had become disillusioned with Manicheanism. While in Italy he came under the influence of Ambrose, Bishop of Milan, who eventually baptized him. The experience of his conversion to Christianity is described in his famous autobiography, *Confessions*, at the end of book 8.

We have more writings from Augustine than from any other ancient author. His extant 100 books and treatises, 500 sermons and 250 letters are eloquent testimony to his magisterial role in the early formation and development of Christian philosophy and theology. He wrote the great *City of God* in 410 in response to critics who suggested that Christianization had led to the fall of Rome. He died twenty years later, shortly before Hippo itself was attacked and partly burned.

Augustine made a number of seminal contributions to the philosophy of religion. They can be organized under six headings: (i) faith and reason; (ii) proof for the existence of God; (iii) the divine attributes; (iv) the problem of evil; (v) the problem of God's foreknowledge and human free will; and (vi) prayer and religious ritual.

FAITH AND REASON

Early in book 2 of the dialogue *On Free Choice of the Will*, Augustine asks his interlocutor, Evodius, whether he is certain that God exists (2.2.5.12). Evodius replies that he accepts God's existence by faith, not by reason. Augustine then asks him what he would say to a fool who had said in his heart, echoing a verse from Psalms 14:1 and 53:1, 'There is no God'.

Evodius responds to this challenge by suggesting that they appeal to the evidence of Scripture. Augustine is not satisfied with that response. Why then, he asks, should we not simply accept the authority of the scriptural writers on other matters, rather than engage in our own philosophical investigation. Evodius answers, "We want to know and understand (*nosse et intellegere*) what we believe" (2.2.5.16).[1]

Augustine compliments Evodius on his having grasped the nature of their project, which is to come to understand what they already affirm by faith. Quoting the 'Old Latin' text of Isaiah 7:9, "Unless you have believed, you shall not understand",[2] as well as the admonition of Jesus, "Seek and you shall find" (John 17:3), he agrees that their purpose is to seek to understand what they believe.[3]

We might well ask whether one might gain faith through developing one's understanding, as well as gain understanding by examining one's faith. Augustine, in one of his sermons (43.3.4), acknowledges what is in any case perfectly obvious: that his hearers cannot believe of what he is saying that it is true unless they first understand his words. But in matters of religious doctrine, Augustine insists, faith must precede understanding. Thus in his *Tractate* 29 on the Gospel of John, he writes, "If you have not understood, I say, 'Believe!'. For understanding is the reward of faith". He goes on: "Therefore do not seek to understand that you may believe, but believe that you may understand" (29.6, my translation).

PROOF OF THE EXISTENCE OF GOD

Augustine was certainly not the first philosopher to conceive an argument for the existence of God, but perhaps he was the first one to conceive a purely *a priori* argument for God's existence. His argument is, one might also say, the forerunner of Anselm's ontological argument. Anselm's argument is so much more interesting than Augustine's that it has almost totally eclipsed its forerunner. Still, it may be useful to outline the Augustinian argument, if for no other reason than to appreciate Anselm's argument all the more.

Early on in book 2 of *On Free Choice of the Will* Evodius makes a move that anticipates Descartes's 'method of doubt'. Unwilling simply to accept Augustine's assurances about evil and free will, Evodius suggests, "Let us take up our investigation as though everything were uncertain" (2.2.5.11).

1. Unless otherwise noted, all quotations from this work are taken from Augustine (1964).
2. *Nisi crederitis, non intelligetis*. Modern translations, based on a better Hebrew text, render this verse as "If you will not believe, surely you will not be established", which fails to make Augustine's point.
3. Anselm, who was strongly influenced by Augustine, initially chose the Augustinian slogan 'faith in search of understanding' for the work he later decided to call *Proslogion*, where he presents his famous ontological argument.

Somewhat later Augustine follows Evodius's suggestion: "Therefore, to start at the beginning with the most obvious, I will ask you first whether you yourself exist. Are you, perhaps, afraid that you are being deceived by my questioning? But if you did not exist, it would be impossible for you to be deceived" (2.3.7.20). With this anticipation of the Cartesian *cogito* we might expect Augustine and Evodius to produce a rational reconstruction of what they know based on the foundation stone of what one expresses by saying 'I exist'. But that does not happen. Instead, Augustine leads Evodius to accept a scale of being with a division among (i) inanimate things, for example a stone; (ii) animate things without understanding, for example a beast; and (iii) those animate beings with understanding, for example Evodius, or Augustine himself. The main point of this division is to make conceptual space for the idea that one kind is superior to another.

At 2.6.13.52, Augustine develops a parallel hierarchy among natures, or souls. Thus the nature or soul of a beast is superior to the nature of a stone and the nature or soul of a human being is superior to both of the others. Augustine then asks Evodius whether, if they found something superior to reason, he would agree that the entity they had found was God. Evodius replies that the entity would have to be something to whom nothing is superior (*quo est nullius superior*; 2.6.14.54). Thus we have this definition of God:

(D) x is God = *df* x is superior to the rational soul (or mind) and nothing is superior to x.

There follows a long discussion aimed at establishing that truth is superior to our minds. With the superiority of truth established, Augustine presents (at 2.14.38.152–15.39.153) the following argument:

(1) Anything that is more excellent than our mind and to which nothing is superior is, or would be, God. [from definition (D) above]

(2) Truth is more excellent than our minds.

Therefore,

(3) Either truth itself is God, or if there is something superior to truth, then it is God.

Therefore,

(4) God exists.

The idea that truth might be God may seem sufficiently implausible to a reader to render this argument unpersuasive. However, the saying of Jesus, "I am the way, the truth, and the life" (John 14:6), just by itself, opens the way for Augustine to think that the supposition that God simply is truth cannot be ruled out.

Another objection to Augustine's proof might be that it fails to prove that there is only one God. But to have established that there is *at least* one God would still be a significant achievement, even if there were additional work to be done to establish that there is *at most* one God.

Although this argument is quite different from, and much less impressive than, Anselm's ontological argument in his *Proslogion*, it is nevertheless a significant attempt to offer an argument for the existence of God. For one thing, it is a purely *a priori* argument, whereas most other arguments have at least one empirical premise. Thus, for example, Thomas Aquinas' argument for God as a first efficient cause uses the empirical premise, "For we find there to be in sensible things an order of efficient causes" (*Summa theologiae* Ia.2.3). One might think that Augustine's premise, "Truth is more excellent than our minds", is an empirical premise. But, in fact, it seems to be supported only by the *a priori* thought that the mind is judged by truth, and a judge is superior to what is judged.

Augustine's definition of 'God' – "that which is superior to our mind and nothing is superior to it" – is a little like Anselm's "something than which nothing greater can be conceived", although it is not as close as Augustine's characterization of God in other passages. Consider, for example, this passage from Augustine's *Confessions*: "I confessed that whatever you are, you are incorruptible. Nor could there have been or be any soul capable of conceiving that which is better than you" (7.4.6, in Augustine 1992: 114).

DIVINE ATTRIBUTES

Augustine has many philosophically interesting things to say about the divine attributes, both individually and as a group. Here he offers a general characterization of God:

> Let us think of God, if we are able, and insofar as we are able, in the following way: as good without quality, as great without quantity, as the Creator who lacks nothing, who rules but from no position, and who contains all things without an external form, as being whole everywhere without limitation of space, as eternal without time, as making mutable things without any change in Himself, as a Being without passion. (*On the Trinity* 5.1.2)[4]

As the above quotation suggests, Augustine is particularly good at bringing out how paradoxical each of the divine attributes is. Consider, for example,

4. All quotations from *On the Trinity* are taken from Augustine (1963). With slight emendations, the latter part of this work is published as *On the Trinity* (Augustine 2002).

God's wisdom. God, according to Augustine, is maximally wise. But that means, Augustine thinks, that God, by his wisdom, knows all things past and future, not as past or future, but as present. Moreover, by that same wisdom God knows individual things, not one at a time, but all together as in a single glance (*On the Trinity* 15.7.13).

Or consider the ineffability of God. The greatness of God is inexpressible, according to Augustine. But, as Augustine also points out (*On Christian Doctrine* 1.6.6), to say that God is indescribable is already to describe God.

Augustine is perhaps the most important source for the doctrine that God is by nature perfectly simple. His doctrine of the 'Divine Simplicity' is part of a carefully worked out account of the metaphysics of God's nature in book 5 of *On the Trinity.*

In chapter 5 of book 5 Augustine tells us that "in God nothing is said to be according to accident, because there is nothing changeable in Him" (5.5.6). However, Augustine adds, not everything that is said of God refers to his substance either:

> For something can be said of Him in regard to relation, as the relation of the Father to the Son, and of the Son to the Father. There is no question here of an accident, because the one is always the Father and the other is always the Son, not indeed in the sense that the Father, from whom the Son is born, never ceases to be the Father because the Son never ceases to be the Son, but in the sense that the Son was always born and never began to be the Son. (5.5.6)

In the next chapter Augustine introduces the doctrine of divine simplicity in this way:

> But God is not great by a greatness that is not that which He Himself is, so that God becomes as it were a sharer in it when He is great. For in that case the greatness would be greater than God, but there cannot be anything greater than God; therefore He is great by that greatness which is identical with Himself. (5.10.11)

In the last book of *On the Trinity* Augustine offers this more general statement of the idea of divine simplicity:

> For one and the same thing is therefore said whether God is called eternal, or immortal, or incorruptible, or unchangeable; and similarly, when He is called living and understanding ... one and the same thing is said. For He has not obtained the wisdom by which He is wise, but He Himself is wisdom. And this life is the same as this strength or this power, and the same as this beauty by which He is called powerful

> and beautiful ... Or again are goodness and justice also different from each other in the nature of God, as they are different in their works, as if they were two different qualities of God, one His goodness and the Other His justice? Certainly not! (15.5.7)

THE PROBLEM OF EVIL

The problem of evil occupied Augustine's theological and philosophical thinking throughout most of his adult life. In fact, it was doubtless the need to make sense of evil in the world that attracted him to Manicheanism during his young adulthood. And the challenge of understanding the place of evil in a God-created universe is an important theme in his writings in all periods of his life. He faced it head-on in his early work, *On Free Choice of the Will*, where his interlocutor, Evodius, starts things off with the following request: "Tell me, I ask you, whether God is not the cause of evil [or the author of evil, *auctor mali*]" (1.1.1.1). Augustine responds by questioning whether Evodius means to ask for the cause of the evil that is done or the evil that is suffered. "Both", replies Evodius.

Augustine then tries to assure Evodius that it cannot be God who causes evil, for God is good and so does not do anything evil; moreover, God is just, and therefore does not allow unjust punishment (1.1.1.1–2). In fact, as Augustine goes on to say, there is really no single cause of evil in the world. Each of us, he maintains, is the cause of our own evil deeds, indeed, the originating cause of our own evil deeds, since each of us has free will as a gift from God. Here is the way Augustine states his own position near the beginning of book 2 of *On Free Choice of the Will*:

> If a human being is something good, and cannot act morally [or with moral rectitude, *recte facere*] unless he wills to do so, then he must have free will [*liberam voluntatem*], without which he cannot act morally. We must not believe that, just because sin is committed through free will, God gave it to us for this reason. It is a sufficient reason for why he had to give free will to us that, without it, a human being could not live a moral life [*recte non potest vivere*]. (2.1.3.5, my translation)

Evodius is not satisfied. He thinks that if free will is a gift from God, God should have made that gift to be like justice. No one, he maintains, can use justice to do wrong and so produce evil. God should have given us free will in the way he has given us justice. That is, God should have given us free will, Evodius thinks, in a way that would allow us to do morally good things but would not allow us to do morally bad things (2.2.4.8).

One might think that the answer to Evodius' puzzle should be obvious. Justice is a virtue. The will is a power. It is incoherent to suppose that God could have given us a virtue as a power. But, for Augustine, a virtue *is* a power. Indeed the

Latin word, *virtus*, is sometimes translated 'virtue' and sometimes as 'power'. In any case, Augustine does not make this move.

So far as I can see, Augustine never offers a direct answer to Evodius' challenge in *On Free Choice of the Will*. That is, Augustine never in that work explains why God could not have given us human beings free will in such a way that we could never have used it to produce evil. Instead, he tries to convince his readers that it is we who are responsible for the use we make of our free will, not God. If we use it to sin, then we are responsible for the sin that results, not God. Free choice of the will, he maintains, is an intermediate good, not, like justice, an unqualified good. When we use our free will to act rightly, then the result is something good. Indeed, it is something that could not have been produced except by a genuinely free action. When we use it to sin, however, the result is certainly something evil, but it is an evil for which we are responsible, not God. Maddeningly, Augustine never directly addresses Evodius' question as to why God could not have given us free will in such a way that we could have used it only to act in a morally upright way.

One could put Augustine's reasoning this way. In his view, God is the creator of free human agents and those human agents use their free wills to create evil. But it does not follow that God creates evil. Augustine, in effect, insists that creation is not a transitive relation. That is, from

(5) God created agents with free choice of the will

and

(6) Human agents through their free choice of the will created moral evil

this does not follow:

(7) God created moral evil.

Evodius can agree that (7) does not follow from (5) and (6). But he still asks why the following could not have been true:

(8) God created human agents and gave them free choice of the will in such a way that it could not be used to create evil.

His idea seems to be that if (8) were true, then so would this be true:

(9) There is no evil.

But, of course, (9) is false.

Augustine might have argued that (8) does not state a real possibility. That is, Augustine might have argued that there is not, nor could there be, any such thing as a free will that could not be used to create evil. More circumspectly, he could have argued, as Alvin Plantinga has argued recently, that it is possible, *for all we know*, that not even an omnipotent being could create free agents who never sin. In Plantinga's jargon, it is logically possible that each free human being God could have created suffers from "transworld depravity" (Plantinga 1974: 49ff.). That is, it is logically possible that each human being with free will God could have created is such that there is no possible world in which that being fails to commit a sin. Augustine, however, does not argue that way, at least not in *On Free Choice of the Will*. Moreover, and even more surprisingly, the Plantinga thesis is contradicted by what Augustine writes late in his life. I shall turn to the late-life response in a moment. But first I want to say something about Augustine's indirect response to Evodius.

In book 3 of *On Free Choice of the Will* Augustine tells us that we should praise God for our creation even if our soul is "wasted by sin". He warns us against saying of sinners "It would be better if they had not existed", as well as against saying "They ought to have been made differently". The last warning is, no doubt, directed at Evodius. "If", Augustine goes on,

> you conceive of something better, you can be sure that God, the Creator of all good, has already made it. Moreover, it is not a true reckoning [*ratio*], but simply an envious weakness, if you wish that the lower should not have been made because you think that something higher should have been created. (3.5.13.45)

Here Augustine appeals to something like the idea of the 'great chain of being'. We human beings are lower than the angels, but higher than the brutes. We have reason and free will. We can act morally, as well as immorally. But we should not complain that we are not made as good angels, who never sin.

Although this response is clearly meant to silence Evodius, it does not answer his question: why could we not have been given free will as we are given justice?

We do find Evodius' question addressed in Augustine's later writings, including his *Enchiridion* (at 105), written perhaps in 423 seven years before his death, and somewhat more extensively in the last book of *City of God*, completed perhaps four years later. Here is a passage from the latter work in which Augustine discusses the perfect freedom the blessed will enjoy in heaven:

> Now the fact that [the blessed in heaven] will be unable to delight in sin does not entail that they will have no free will. In fact, the will will be the freer in that it is freed from a delight in sin and immovably fixed in a delight in not sinning. The first freedom of will, given to man when he was created upright at the beginning, was an ability not to sin (*potuit non peccare*), combined with the possibility of sinning (*potuit et peccare*). But this last freedom will be more potent, for it will bring

> the impossibility of sinning (*peccare non poterit*); yet this also will be the result of God's gift, not of some inherent quality of nature. For to be a partaker of God is not the same thing as to be God; the inability to sin belongs to God's nature, while he who partakes of God's nature receives the impossibility of sinning as a gift from God.
>
> Moreover the stages of the divine gift had to be preserved. Free will was given first, with the ability not to sin; and the last gift was the inability to sin. The first freedom was designed for acquiring merit (*meritum*); the last was concerned with the reception of a reward (*praemium*). But because human nature sinned when it had the power to sin it is set free by a more abundant gift of grace so that it may be brought to that condition of liberty in which it is incapable of sin.
>
> (*City of God* 22.30)[5]

According to the view presented in this passage, it is quite possible, as Evodius had suggested in Augustine's dialogue thirty-five years earlier, for God to give his human creatures free will without their having any possibility of sinning. But, if this is right, we may well want to know why God did not do that, that is, why God did not give Adam and Eve, or their descendents, this perfect freedom of the will to choose freely without any possibility of sinning.

One suggestion might be that, since the first kind of freedom, the kind that brought with it only the ability *not to sin*, "was designed for acquiring merit", none of us would be able to merit eternal salvation if we had the sort of free will that rules out any possibility of sinning. But that cannot be Augustine's view. According to him, nothing we do merits eternal salvation anyway; if we do gain eternal salvation, it will be only through the grace of God. So we must reject this first suggestion as an interpretation of Augustine.

Here is a more promising suggestion. There would have been some goodness and merit missing from creation if Adam and Eve and their descendents had had, from the very start, the perfect freedom that cannot be used for sinning. After all, as Augustine maintains, the blessed in heaven receive the impossibility of sinning by partaking of God's nature. But God is, by nature, eternally unable to sin. In theological jargon, God is by nature eternally and immutably impeccable. The human goodness added in creation arises from the righteousness of those agents with the ability to sin who nevertheless freely choose not to sin. If Adam and Eve had started out partaking in God's perfect freedom, without the possibility of sinning, they would not have added anything to the goodness and merit that was already in existence, namely, God's goodness.

Even if this suggestion is right, however, what I have said so far cannot be the whole story. After all, in the passage I have quoted from *City of God* 22.30,

5. All translations from the *City of God* are taken from Augustine (1984).

Augustine does link the idea of acquiring merit (*meritum*) with the idea of receiving the reward (*praemium*) of eternal happiness. This linkage suggests that the elect actually earn their reward, which cannot be Augustine's real view. But how else can this passage be understood?

We get an indication of a strong possibility in Augustine's *On the Trinity*, where he writes:

> What else could have made [the mind] miserable under the omnipotent and good God, except its own sin and the justice of its own Lord? And what shall make [the mind] happy, except its own merit and the reward of its Lord? But its merit is also a grace from Him whose reward will also be its happiness. For it cannot give itself the justice which it has lost and no longer has, because man received it when he was made, and by sinning has certainly lost it. He receives justice, therefore, and on account of it he may merit to receive happiness.
>
> (*On the Trinity* 14.15.21)

Here we have the characteristic Augustinian line of thought according to which any good we do, we do through the grace of God. So the merit we earn, we earn with the help of the grace of God. Moreover, even though we could not earn that merit unaided by the grace of God, we could, by our own will, refuse it. Here in book 14 of the *City of God*, Augustine makes clear that we have the power of refusal:

> Now man could not even trust in the help of God without God's help; but this did not mean that he did not have it in his power to withdraw from the benefits of divine grace by self-pleasing. For just as it is not in our power to live in this physical frame without the support of food, and yet it is in our power not to live in it at all (which is what happens to suicides), so it was not in man's power, even in paradise, to live a good life without the help of God, yet it was in his power to live an evil life.
>
> (*City of God* 14.27)

So my suggestion is that heavenly bliss, without the power to sin, is the just reward of merit that can be earned through the grace of God, but not without the agreement and consent of the sinner.

Plantinga's thesis about transworld depravity is, of course, part of his 'free will defence', which is a response to what we can call the 'consistency (or logical) problem of evil'. The consistency problem is an issue about whether it can be logically consistent to affirm the conjunction of these claims:

(10) God is all-good.
(11) God is all-powerful.
(12) There is evil.

In fact, the conjunction of (10), (11) and (12) is not, strictly speaking, logically inconsistent. But we would have a logically inconsistent conjunction if we were to add this fourth claim:

(13) No all-good being would allow any evil to exist if she/he/it could prevent it.

Or alternatively, and more simply:

(13*) If there were an all-good and all-powerful being, there would be no evil.

The free will defence offers the goodness of free will as a basis for rejecting (13) and (13*). But that defence will be ineffectual if it were possible for God to create creatures with free will who are nevertheless unable to sin. Plantinga's thesis about transworld depravity has it that, for all we know, even an omnipotent being could not do that.

The passage from the last book of the *City of God* makes clear that Augustine, at least in his later life, would have been unable to mount the standard free will defence as a response to the consistency problem of evil. In particular, his mature view is not that God could not possibly have made free human moral agents who never sin. In fact, according to him, God's gift to the elect in heaven is precisely the kind of freedom of the will that carries with it an inability to sin. His idea, rather, seems to be that, if God had first given human beings free will together with the inability to sin, God would have precluded the possibility of there being any moral good besides his own. For to give human beings free will with the inability to sin would require that they partake in God's own nature, which is, of course, eternally impeccable and yet perfectly free. But by first giving human beings free will with the ability to sin, as well as the ability not to sin, God provided for the possibility that there would be some merit in addition to the goodness of his own impeccable nature.

GOD'S FOREKNOWLEDGE AND HUMAN FREE WILL

It was Augustine who framed, for all later philosophy, the question of how human free will could be compatible with God's complete foreknowledge of all that has happened and will ever happen. He does this in book 3 of his treatise *On Free Choice of the Will.* This problem was not exactly Augustine's own discovery. As he makes clear in *City of God* (book 5, chapter 9), he himself took the problem from Cicero. But it is not Cicero that later philosophers have turned to in discussing this topic, but Augustine.

The guarantor solution

One solution Augustine presents to the problem we may call the *guarantor solution*. "Our will would not be a will", Augustine says,

> unless it were in our power. Therefore, because it is in our power, it is free … Nor can it be a will if it is not in our power. Therefore, God also has foreknowledge of our power. So the power is not taken from me by His foreknowledge, but because of His foreknowledge, the power to will will more certainly be present in me. (3.3.8.33–5)

According to this reasoning, we can understand God's foreknowledge to guarantee our free action. For, necessarily, if God foreknows that we will do something voluntarily in the future, that foreknowledge guarantees that we will do it voluntarily.

The divine-case solution

A second solution to the problem of foreknowledge and free will we may call the *divine-case solution*. Augustine asks Evodius whether God foresees what God himself will do. "Certainly if I say that God has foreknowledge of my deeds," Evodius answers, "I should say with even greater confidence that he has foreknowledge of his own acts, and foresees with complete certainty what He will do" (3.3.6.23). Augustine then points out that the same reasoning from God's foreknowledge that leads us to rule out human free will should lead to the conclusion that God's own future acts will be done, not voluntarily, but by necessity. However, if the divine case is to be rejected, then, it seems, the human case should be rejected as well.

The eternality solution

Evodius points out that nothing ever happens, or comes to pass, within God, since everything within God is eternal (3.3.6.24). Thus there is in God no such thing as his knowing beforehand what he will choose to do, not because he is ignorant of what he will choose but because in him there is no 'beforehand'. If, however, there is no 'beforehand' in God, then, strictly speaking, God does not have *fore*knowledge.

Neither Augustine nor Evodius, however, makes anything of that conclusion in *On Free Choice*. Instead, they go on talking about God's foreknowledge. But Evodius' self-correction, that is, his withdrawal of his own claim that God sees beforehand what God will do, introduces the idea of God's eternal present, which Augustine describes eloquently in the following passage from book 11 of the *City of God*:

> It is not in our fashion that God looks forward to what is future or looks directly at what is present or looks back on what is past, but in some other mode far and away different from our way of thinking. Indeed, He does not go from this to that by a change in thought but he sees altogether, unchangeably, in such a way that those things which come to be temporally – not only future things that are not yet, but also present things that are already and past things that are no longer – he comprehends them all in a firm and eternal present. (11.21)

We can call the idea that there is no problem of foreknowledge and free will since there really is no *fore*knowledge in God the *eternality solution*. One might well wonder, however, how effective this solution would actually be. The idea of foreknowledge is especially troubling for free will, since it seems to 'lock in' all future actions and leave no room for free choice. However, the idea that an omniscient being knows *timelessly* what we will do also seems to 'lock in' our (to us) future actions in a way that is at least as threatening to free will as genuine foreknowledge would be.

The modal-placement solution

A fourth solution to the problem of foreknowledge and free will is what we might call the *modal-placement solution*. From

(14) Necessarily, if God foreknows that Adam will sin, Adam will sin

it does *not* follow that:

(15) If God foreknows Adam will sin, Adam will necessarily sin.

Moreover, from (14), together with

(16) God foreknows that Adam will sin

we may validly infer

(17) Adam will sin

but not

(18) Adam will necessarily sin.

If, then, the claim of necessity, as in (14), governs the *connection* between God's foreknowledge and the occurrence of what God foreknows will happen (what later medieval philosophers, including Aquinas [*Summa theologiae* Ia.14.13.3], call 'necessity *de dicto*'), God's foreknowledge will not preclude the possibility that among the things God foreknows are free actions of human agents. On the other hand, if God is omniscient and all the things God foreknows will happen are themselves necessary events, as in (15) – what is later called 'necessity *de re*' – God's foreknowledge will rule out human free will.

Boethius seems to have been the first to mark this distinction clearly (see his *Consolation of Philosophy* 5.6). But Augustine comes close. He asks Evodius whether, if he foreknew that someone was going to sin, it would be necessary that he sin. Evodius answers that it would be necessary (3.4.9.38). Here Evodius seems to be relying on the assumption that all objects of foreknowledge are necessary events, things that have to happen, as in (15) above.

Augustine's reply, "You do not compel someone to sin whom you foreknow will sin, although without doubt, he will sin" (3.4.9.39), may suggest to a reader a distinction between the necessity of the conditional (*de dicto* necessity), as in (14) above, and the necessity of the consequent (*de re* necessity), as in (15) above. But Augustine does not express himself that way.

PRAYER AND RELIGIOUS RITUAL

Augustine raises philosophical problems about prayer and religious ritual in various passages. One recurrent concern bears a strong resemblance to the Paradox of Inquiry in Plato's dialogue *Meno*. Meno asks how he and Socrates, not already knowing what virtue is, can aim their search for what it is at the right target; and even if they should come upon the nature of virtue, how they can, not already knowing what it is, recognize what they have found to be virtue (*Meno* 80d). Augustine, at the beginning of his *Confessions*, prays to God for help in coming to know and understand him. But he then asks, in perplexity, "Who calls upon you when he doesn't know you? For an ignorant person might call upon someone else instead of the right one" (*Confessions* 1.1.1).

For Augustine this worry about how he can direct his prayer at God for help in coming to know him is not an idle concern. After all, he had himself been a Manichean novitiate or 'hearer' for some nine years. In retrospect he may well have viewed his prayers as having been directed at a false god.

Augustine's response to the targeting problem is not clear. His response to the recognition problem seems to be that when he comes to know God, his "restless soul will find rest in Him". This resolution bears some similarity to the idea of Plato's Socrates that learning what virtue is may be recollecting knowledge that the soul had from its previous life.

Like almost any philosophically inclined believer, Augustine asks why we need to tell God in prayer what God, being omniscient, already knows. This statement of the problem and response to it is typical for Augustine:

> But again it may be asked (whether we are to pray in ideas or in words) what need there is for prayer itself, if God already knows what is necessary for us – unless it be that the very effort involved in prayer calms and purifies our heart, and makes it more capacious for receiving the divine gifts, which are poured into us spiritually. For it is not on account of the urgency of our prayers that God hears us, who is always ready to give us his light, not of a material kind, but that which is intellectual and spiritual. But we are not always ready to receive.
> (*On Our Lord's Sermon on the Mount* 2.3.14; Augustine 1991: 38)

When Augustine asks himself why our bodily gestures can be important in prayer, he faces another philosophical puzzle. It seems to him that prostration and other physical movements can increase the fervour of prayer. But he has a metaphysical principle according to which nothing 'lower' can have any causal effect on anything 'higher'.[6] Thus no bodily movement can affect the mind or soul of the suppliant. In this passage Augustine reveals that he does not know how to resolve the puzzle:

> For when men pray they do with the members of their bodies what befits suppliants – when they bend their knees and stretch out their hands, or even prostrate themselves, and whatever else they do visibly, although their invisible will and the intention of their heart is known to God. Nor does He need these signs for the human mind to be laid bare to Him. But in this way one excites oneself to pray more and to groan more humbly. Although these motions of the body cannot come to be without a motion of the mind preceding them, when they have been made, visibly and externally, that invisible inner motion which caused them is itself strengthened. And in this manner the disposition of the heart which preceded them in order that they might be made, grows stronger because they are made. (*On the Care of the Dead* 5.7)

As is often the case, Augustine leaves the question unanswered. How can bodily motions affect the mind of the suppliant? 'I do not know', Augustine admits.

FURTHER READING

Brown, P. 1967. *Augustine of Hippo*. Berkeley, CA: University of California Press.

Mann, W. (ed.) 2006. *Augustine's Confessions: Critical Essays*. Lanham, MD: Rowman & Littlefield.

6. See, for example, Augustine's *De musica* (On music) 6.5.8 and *De Genesi ad litteram* (The literal interpretation of Genesis) 12.16.33.

Matthews, G. 2005. *Augustine*. Oxford: Blackwell.
Matthews, G. (ed.) 1999. *The Augustinian Tradition*. Berkeley, CA: University of California Press.
Rist, J. 1994. *Augustine: Ancient Thought Baptized*. Cambridge: Cambridge University Press.
Stump, E. & N. Kretzmann (eds) 2001. *The Cambridge Companion to Augustine*. Cambridge: Cambridge University Press.
Wetzel, J. 1992. *Augustine and the Limits of Virtue*. Cambridge: Cambridge University Press.

On CHRISTIANITY see also Chs 10, 14, 17; Vol. 5, Ch. 12. On DIVINITY see also Chs 8, 19, 20; Vol. 2, Chs 6, 8. On EVIL/PROBLEM OF EVIL see also Ch. 19; Vol. 2, Ch. 16; Vol. 3, Chs 13, 18 19; Vol. 4, Ch. 12; Vol. 5, Chs 18, 19, 22, 23. On EXISTENCE OF GOD see also Ch.19; Vol. 2, Chs 5, 6, 13, 14; Vol. 3, Chs 6, 12, 13, 14, 15, 21, 6, Vol. 5, Chs 11, 16. On FREE WILL see also Vol. 2, Chs 2, 7, 9, 19; Vol. 3, Chs 9, 15; Vol. 5, Ch. 22. On PRAYER see also Ch. 13; Vol. 3, Ch. 5; Vol. 5, Ch. 21.

19

PROCLUS

Dirk Baltzly

The question of the contribution of Proclus (411–85) to the history of Western philosophy of religion is complicated by the fact that Proclus would not himself have distinguished philosophy of religion as a distinct sub-branch of philosophy. When we moderns think about this subject, we think about it as the philosophical study of religious phenomena, and in particular the assessment of the truth-claims made explicitly or implicitly by various religions. In this way, philosophy and religion have different goals. The goal of philosophy is truth, and the specific goal of philosophy of religion is an assessment of the truth of various propositions about God or the afterlife. The goal of religion, if we may speak this way, is not merely truth, but salvation and a godly life.

It seems unlikely that Proclus would have recognized either of these divisions: that between philosophy of religion and the broader area of metaphysics or that between philosophy and religion itself.

The first point is one that should by now be familiar. Lloyd Gerson (1990) makes the point that *theologia* in ancient Greek philosophy generally is best thought of as part and parcel of the attempt to give an account of the first principles (*archai*) of things. Hence metaphysics or 'first philosophy' in Aristotle coincides with theology (*Metaphysics* E.1, 1026a24–33). As we shall see, Proclus' theology takes in the systematic study of all intelligible beings – roughly, those things that make up the realm of Intellect or *nous* for Plotinus – in addition to the utterly transcendent One or Good.

With respect to the second point, the aim of philosophy is one with the goal of living: to become like God in as much as this is possible. The Neoplatonists take Plato's *Theaetetus* 176a–b and *Timaeus* 90b–d to indicate that this is the *telos* or objective of living. The life of philosophy is one way in which we accomplish this assimilation to the divine. But the life in which one practises religious mystery rites also plays a role – perhaps an even greater role – in facilitating the soul's return to the divine. These two pathways to the divine, however, find their unification in the exegesis of the texts of Plato. This is because, as Proclus sees matters, Plato's philosophy provides the purest distillation of the wisdom that is common to all earlier philosophical texts, as well as to inspired texts such as the *Chaldean Oracles* or the Orphic writings.[1] Thus the boundaries that moderns see between philosophy, the history of philosophy and religion are not sharply drawn in Proclus.

LIFE AND WRITINGS

We have a biography of Proclus by his successor in the Athenian Neoplatonic school, Marinus.[2] He was very probably born in 411 and died in 485 (cf. Siorvanes 1996). His father was a lawyer and Proclus was intended to follow him into the law. This training, however, was aborted when Proclus had a vision of the goddess Athena, who instructed him to pursue the study of philosophy (*Life of Proclus* [hereafter *VProc.*] 9). At the age of nineteen, he went to Athens to fulfil this divine command.

In Athens, Proclus' talent was quickly recognized by Syrianus, who was then head of the Academy. The date of Syrianus' death is not clear. Proclus became *Diadochos* or 'Platonic successor' either immediately afterwards or perhaps after a brief interlude in which Domninus assumed leadership (cf. Diller 1957: 188; Siorvanes 1996: 6). Proclus was head of the Academy for roughly the next fifty years. As befits the head of the Neoplatonic School, Proclus lived a life of strict asceticism. He abstained entirely from sex, and ate meat only in the context of sacrifice where he deemed it necessary. His habits included ritual bathing in the sea, all night vigils and fasts. He died at seventy-five years of age (*VProc.* 26).

Marinus' biography makes it clear that Proclus was not only a teacher and interpreter of Plato's works, but a practitioner of magic and theurgy as well (*see* this volume, Ch. 16, "Porphyry and Iamblichus"). The latter is a form of ritual magic in which the aim is to become united with the gods.

These things were, strictly speaking, illegal. An imperial decree in 391 notionally prohibited all pagan cults and closed their temples. Proclus nonetheless performed ceremonies in which he invoked the aid of the gods for the healing of the sick by rituals and hymns (*ergois te kai hymnois*; *VProc.* 17). Marinus comments on one of Proclus' acts of healing as follows: "Such was the act he performed, yet in this as in every other case he evaded the notice of the mob, and offered no pretext to those who wished to plot against him" (*VProc.* 29, trans. Edwards). 'The mob' in this context is very likely to be Christians. However, Proclus did not inevitably escape

1. The *Chaldean Oracles* is a collection of hexameter verses composed during the late second century CE. The 'Orphic' writings that Proclus and the other Neoplatonists quote most frequently are from the 'Rhapsodic Theogony', which is mostly a product of the post-Hellenistic period.
2. For the Greek text see Marinus (1966), and for an English translation see Edwards (2000).

their notice, since he took a one-year 'leave of absence' from Athens following an event in which Marinus says he "entered the billowing tempest of affairs at a time when monstrous winds were blowing against the lawful way of life" (*VProc.* 15). Saffrey (1975: 555–7) has speculated that the "tempest of affairs" might have been the closure of the temple of Asclepius and its conversion to a place of Christian worship.

Thus Proclus not only wrote on theology, but was also a deeply religious man. This perhaps explains why Proclus' writings range so widely, including topics that we might hesitate to regard as philosophical. It also helps to explain the deep, albeit rather alien, sense of piety that pervades his work.

Proclus' writings divide into roughly four genres: commentaries, large systematic works, shorter essays, and religious hymns and exegesis of sacred texts. In the first category, we still possess in one form or another Proclus' commentaries on *Alcibiades I*, *Parmenides*, *Timaeus* and a collection of studies on the *Republic* (Proclus 1965, 1966–8, 1970b, 1987, 2007a,b, 2008). A summary of his commentary on the *Cratylus* has been preserved (2005). The other surviving work in commentary form is on book I of Euclid's *Elements* (1970a).

Three of Proclus' systematic treatises survive. The best known is his *Elements of Theology* (1963). The least well known is his systematization of Aristotelian physics (1912, 1958). The third is the massive *Platonic Theology*, which attempts to chart the hierarchy of divinities from the highest to the lowest gods (1968–97).

We also possess three essays: *Ten Problems Concerning Providence* (1977), *On the Subsistence of Evil* (1982), and *On Fate* (1979). The content of his *Eighteen Arguments on the Eternity of the World* can be reconstructed from Philoponus' criticisms (2001a).[3] There are also two astronomical works. The first, *Outline of the Astronomical Hypotheses*, is a critical examination of Ptolemy's astronomy (1909). The other is a paraphrase of some difficult passages in Ptolemy's *Tetrabiblios*.

We possess fragments of a variety of works that demonstrate Proclus' interest in the canon of pagan Neoplatonic religious texts, as well as in theurgic practices. Among these are the fragments of his commentary on the *Chaldean Oracles*.[4] In addition to this, a portion of Proclus' work "On Sacrifice and Magic" survives (1928).[5] Finally, we have a number of hymns to various gods (1957, 2001b).

---

3. Although manuscripts of this work carry the subtitle 'Against the Christians', it seems likely that Proclus' book was not intended as an attack on Christianity. (Proclus maintains a circumspect and perhaps contemptuous silence on that subject.) Rather, *Eighteen Arguments* was written against Platonists such as Plutarch of Chaeronia who took the creation in the *Timaeus* literally.
4. Text and French translation included in Places (1971).
5. The 1928 Bidez edition is in Greek. For a French translation see Festugière & Massignon (1944).

THE SUBJECT MATTER OF THEOLOGY AND HOW WE MAY COME TO KNOW ABOUT IT

On the one hand, the subject matter of theology is god or the gods (*theos*/*theoi*). On the other hand, it could also concern all those things that are divine (*ta theia*). At some points, Proclus appears to separate the noun, 'god', from the adjective, 'divine'. Other times, things that possess the quality of divinity may be gods in virtue of what they do. This requires some explanation.

Like Plotinus, Proclus accepts the existence of the One or the Good: that is, an utterly simple principle of all things, more ontologically basic than Plato's Forms. (I shall discuss Proclus' arguments for the One below.) Like Plotinus and others, Proclus also calls the realm of Forms "Being, Life and Intellect". Hence, the One is said to be *beyond Being* (cf. Plato, *Republic* 509a–b). The One counts as a god for two reasons. It is a god because the One, as final cause, is "that toward which all things aspire" (Proclus, *Elements of Theology* [hereafter *ET*] prop. 13), but also because it is beyond all things, including even Being. As such it is "super-essential" (*hyperousios*; *ET* 115). This is precisely what a god is according to Proclus (*ET* 113).

However, Proclus does not confine the title of 'god' to just the One. The One is certainly super-essential, but Proclus accepts the additional, super-essential *henads* (literally 'units') of his teacher Syrianus.[6] Every henad is a god. They are like the One in being superior to Being – roughly the realm of Forms – but unlike the One in that henads can be *participated in* by other things (*ET* 116).

When a Form or intellect participates in a henad, it is thereby divine. By extension, souls may be divine through participation in a divine intellect that, in turn, participates in a henad. Even bodies may be 'deiiformed' (*theoeides*) through participation in a divine soul. (An example would be the cosmos that is animated by the divine World Soul; *Commentary on Plato's Timaeus* [hereafter *in Tim.*] II 5.26.)

It seems that each such divine participant counts as a god in as much as it exercises *providential care* over the effects that result from it (*ET* 134). Things lower in Proclus' ontology than the henads exercise providence, not through their own natures, but by virtue of their participation in henads (*ET* 120). This is perhaps what distinguishes henads as self-perfective (*autotelēs*) gods (*ET* 114), but divine entities that exercise providence are gods nonetheless.

This means that theology has *many* gods to study: the One, the henads and all the things that are divinized through their participation in the henads. However,

6. There has been scholarly dispute on the origins of the doctrine of the henads. On the one hand, in his edition of *Elements of Theology* (1963), E. R. Dodds suggested an origin among the Neopythagoreans prior to Plotinus (*Enneads* 6.6.9). In their introduction to volume 3 of *Theólogie Platonicienne* (1968–97: ix–xvii, li–lxxxvii), H. D. Saffrey and L. G. Westerink assign the doctrine to Syrianus. Dillon (1972) argues for Iamblichus.

it would be a mistake to contrast this apparently profligate polytheism with the 'mature monotheism' of Proclus' Christian or Jewish contemporaries. As Polymnia Athanassiadi and Michael Frede (1999) argue, the pagan philosophers of late antiquity subordinated the plurality of manifestations of the divine to a single god. It is perhaps better to see the contrast as one between two general religious and philosophical attitudes. Judaeo-Christian theology makes God wholly transcendent and separate from creation, while pagan Neoplatonism makes God transcendent but also allows divinity of various degrees to be immanent in all that depends on the One. Pagan Neoplatonism is thus a form of panentheism (cf. Cooper 2006).

Nor should we see Proclus' divine henads merely as convenient placeholders for the Olympian gods.[7] It is true that Proclus assigns different chains or series descending from a particular henad to different Olympians. However, the different gods are assigned different properties and so play different roles in generating the subsequent working out of the One's emanation to its lowest levels (*ET* 145).[8] So, for instance, the series of entities descending from Hephaestus (who forges things such as chains) has a causal role in binding things together (*in Tim.* II 27.19–31), while the series that descends from Dionysius (who was cut into many pieces) plays a role in multiplying things (*in Tim.* II 197.19–20). This allows Proclus to read Homer as an allegorical way of describing both the theological landscape and the principles that govern the 'generated' (i.e. everlastingly dependent) world of nature (cf. Lamberton 1989).

But gods are not easy to study, and super-essential gods are particularly problematic. Since the One is 'beyond being', strictly speaking, it eludes language. Indeed, it eludes even the unified sort of cognition through which intellect apprehends all the Forms as one (*Commentary on Plato's Parmenides* [hereafter *in Parm.*] 808.17–18). Proclus shares Plotinus' insight that, when it comes to the One, seemingly positive assertions about it are actually a way of talking about ourselves (*in Parm.* 1073.26–30). That is, the attempt to characterize the One in positive language reveals more about our cognitive limitations than it does about the object we seek to describe. However, Proclus adds a new dimension to negative predications of the One. There is a sense in which affirmation is often superior to negation, since in most cases assertions tell us that a subject possesses some property, and do not merely indicate an absence. The sense of not-being that goes with absence is indeed inferior to being. However, just as there is a way of not-being that is superior to being – the sense in which the One transcends Being – so

7. Dodds puts this complaint in his usual, stylish way: "That Homer's Olympians, the most vividly conceived anthropomorphic beings in all literature, should have ended their career on the dusty shelves of this museum of metaphysical abstractions is one of time's strangest ironies" (Proclus 1963: 260).
8. This differentiation in the distinctive features of the divine henads seems to be explained by appeal to two other super-essential principles in Proclus' ontology, Limit and Infinity (*ET* 159).

too there is a form of negation that is superior to affirmation. Indeed, the negative predications of the One indicate that it is the causal source of the properties whose predicates are negated in relation to it (*in Parm.* 1072.19–1077.18). This means that it is not-*F* in a way that transcends and is prior to the distinction between those things that we can think as *F* or not-*F*.

Knowledge of the divine henads is not so problematic. Since they are participated in by those intellects below them within the realm of Being, they are intelligible (*noēton*) in relation to them. This means we can know something of these henads by the way in which their distinctive characteristics are transmitted to lower orders by the intellects that participate in them. On the other hand, considered in relation to the One, they are hidden (*kryphios*), just as It is. By 'hidden' Proclus means super-essential and subject only to negative predications. This relativity of opposed predicates is typical of Proclus' metaphysics. Things at the limit of one hypostasis are *F* in relation to what comes before them, but not-*F* in relation to what comes after them.

The One, the henads and the things divinized by participation thus form the subject matter of theology. Our understanding of it, Proclus tells us, is inextricably intertwined with the interpretation of Plato's dialogues. The entire philosophy of Plato was revealed through the beneficent will of higher beings (*Platonic Theology* [hereafter *Pl. Th.*] I 5.6–8). But Plato's philosophy does not reveal itself to just anyone. Proclus is indebted to previous philosophers to whom the truth of Platonism has been revealed. They are like a chorus of Bacchants, following the leader of mystic initiations: Plato. Proclus sees himself following a chorus that includes Plotinus, Amelius and Porphyry, Theodore of Asine and Iamblichus, and his own teacher, Syrianus.[9] This conception of Plato's philosophy as divinely inspired and interpreted to us through the work of previous Platonists explains the predominance of the commentary form in Proclus' own writing. The sentiment that he is merely a chorus member perhaps explains why we seldom see Proclus taking credit for any philosophical innovation that he may be making.

While Plato's philosophy is thus the royal road to theology, Plato does not reveal the truth about the gods in the same manner in all cases (*Pl. Th.* I 17.18–24). Sometimes Plato communicates this truth in the manner of divine possession (*entheasiastikōs*), for example in the *Phaedrus* (238cff.). In other cases, Plato communicates dialectically, for example in the *Sophist*. Elsewhere, as in the *Timaeus*, he guides us from physical theory to divine matters by means of mathematical teachings (*Pl. Th.* I 19.6–9). But Plato also communicates 'iconically', using images to convey his philosophy. For instance, Proclus thinks that in the *Statesman*, the statesman is an image or *eikōn* of the Demiurge. Proclus contrasts the use of

9. Proclus' relation to these philosophers is actually quite complex. Plotinus and those who come after him disagree among themselves, of course, and Proclus does take sides in these disagreements. On this and other puzzles about this passage in the *Platonic Theology*, see Buckley (2006).

images, which he thinks of as a Pythagorean mode of teaching, with symbols, which he associates with the Orphics.[10] The divinely inspired mode of teaching is also exemplified by the *Chaldean Oracles*, as well as Homer (Proclus, *Commentary on Plato's Republic* [hereafter *in Remp.*] I 102.2). It is Plato, however, who – while sometimes also employing these modes – really has the market cornered on the *scientific exposition* of theological truth (*Pl. Th.* I 20.19–20). The purest distillation of this Platonic theology occurs in the *Parmenides* (*Pl. Th.* I 32.1).

This (incomplete) catalogue of all the ways in which Plato communicates the truth about the gods gives us some idea of the multiplicity of reading strategies that Proclus will take up toward the dialogues. Nothing in one of Plato's dialogues is too trivial to ignore. Every aspect is relevant to the goal (*skopos*) of the dialogue.[11] The fact that Plato sometimes employs the modes of exposition associated with Pythagoras, Orpheus and the divine Homer points to another salient aspect of Proclus' commentaries on Plato's dialogues. Proclus is always anxious to show that, properly interpreted, there is a confluence of wisdom in all these sources of theological insight. Thus, for example, at *in Tim.* II 82.3–20, Proclus provides quotations from the *Chaldean Oracles*, the Orphic poems and Homer to show that they agree with Plato that the entire cosmos has its own power of perception. The study of the gods is thus one and the same not merely with the interpretation of Plato's dialogues, but with the synthesis of Plato's divine wisdom and those other sources that prefigure it in iconic or symbolic ways.

THE ARGUMENT FOR THE EXISTENCE OF THE ONE IN *ELEMENTS OF THEOLOGY*

The foregoing suggests that Proclus' arguments for the existence of god(s) will be somewhat diffuse, since his method of exposition consists in line-by-line interpretation of Plato's dialogues. This expectation is confirmed by an examination of the remains of his Plato commentaries. In view of this, it is perhaps unsurprising that the most carefully studied of Proclus' works is the one that is in many ways least characteristic: the *Elements of Theology*.[12] Will it yield an argument for the existence of the One that we may hold up alongside such proofs of God's existence as Aquinas' Five Ways?

10. On the distinction between symbol and image, see Dillon (1990).
11. This is an approach to reading Plato that Proclus perhaps takes over from Iamblichus. See Tarrant (2000: 92–6).
12. Dodds contrasts *Elements of Theology* with Proclus' other works in these terms: "The vast prolixities of exposition which uncoil their opulence in the bulky and shapeless sentences that fill most of the 1100 pages of the *Timaeus* commentary, and riot unchecked in the jungle of the *Platonic Theology*, are here pruned to a brevity which leaves no room for parenthetic digression or rhetorical ornament" (Proclus 1963: xi).

Proclus begins by claiming that every plurality of things participates in unity (*ET* 1). If this were not so, then each of the parts of the plurality would not be itself one but would instead be bottomless, as it were: an infinity of parts, each of which is subject to infinite decomposition. However, each thing that participates in unity is both one and also not one (*ET* 2). That is to say, it has some character other than being one, for this is presupposed by its being a subject able to participate. So it seems that 'not one' here has the sense of 'other than one': a treatment of negation familiar from Plato's *Sophist* 257bff. It follows that all participants are other than unity itself (*ET* 4). The argument for this proposition provides a foundation for the strong non-identity assumption that Vlastos found implied by the logic of the so-called 'third man' argument of the *Parmenides*. If unity were not distinct from its participants, it would be a participant, since everything is one. But as a participant, it would be both one and not one (by *ET* 2). But unity itself cannot be both one and not one, so it is distinct from the participants. *ET* 5 registers the difference between distinctness and logical priority, and argues that unity must be prior to the participants, rather than being coordinate with them or dependent on them. So it must be a *cause* of all that is one through participation. Since it is the cause of all that is one through participation, it must be superior to everything, since causes are superior to what they produce (*ET* 7). *ET* 11 provides something of a 'first cause' argument that all things are the result of a first cause. There must be such a cause on pain of things existing without a cause, or an infinite regress of causes, or a circle of causes. There must be a *single* cause of all effects since every plurality is logically posterior to the One (*ET* 5).

At *ET* 8, Proclus shifts from discussing the One to discussing the Good, and draws the implication that it has no other character than being good. (Were this not so, given the treatment of otherness as negation, it would be both good and not good: an unacceptable consequence.) *ET* 13 argues for an identification of the One with the Good on the ground that every good tends to unify that thing whose good it is. Everything that is unified is thereby made complete or perfect (*teleios*), and so not lacking. But this is good for the thing so unified. So the One and the Good are the same. *This* is the origin and first cause of all things (*ET* 12).

As can be seen from even this very brief sketch, the line of argument in *ET* falls short of the deductive method in Euclid's *Elements* on which Proclus' *Elements of Theology* is modelled. This is unsurprising, since there is nothing that plays the role of axioms and definitions. If Proclus' presuppositions about, say, negation or participation were explicitly spelled out, they would probably not strike most people as quite as self-evidently true as Euclid's axioms.

Refuting Proclus' arguments in *ET* is a sport with a long history, one that we know goes back at least as far as Nicholas of Methone in twelfth-century Byzantium (Athanasios 1984). If Proclus' arguments have drawn less admiration than those of Aquinas – even though many admirers of Aquinas are just as unconvinced – this is perhaps owing to the fact that Proclus' premises are drawn from a Platonic metaphysical tradition that we find more alien than Aquinas' Aristotelian presuppositions.

EVIL, PROVIDENCE AND DIVINE FOREKNOWLEDGE

If the Good is the cause of all things, what shall we say about evil? As is usually the case, the Neoplatonic account of evil and its causes presupposes Plato's texts as an essential backdrop and attempts to give a solution within these terms.

Proclus has three essays relevant to the problem, but the most philosophically rigorous one is "On the Existence of Evils" (*De malorum subsistentia* [hereafter *De mal.*]).[13] His views in this essay proved very influential, since they were incorporated with only minimal changes into the text of Pseudo-Dionysius' *On the Divine Names* (4, 18–34).

A central task of Proclus' essay is the rejection of what he takes to be Plotinus' position that matter is a principle or source (*archē*) of evil. Plotinus argues that evil is that specific kind of not-being that is opposed to Form, since Form is a source of order and measure. Plotinus characterizes Beauty as the domination of matter by Form (*Enneads* 5.8). Since Plotinus thinks that shortcomings in Beauty are the result of the incomplete mastery of Form over matter, it is unsurprising that he treats matter as the principle of evil. While matter is 'thing-like' enough to be this principle of evil, it is also a kind of not-being. Plotinus argues against Aristotle's analysis of the principles of change in *Physics* I and for the view that matter should actually be *identified with* privation (*Enneads* 2.4.14–16). In treating matter as the cause of evil Plotinus seems to apply the Platonic 'one over many' assumption to the case of evil: just as there exists the Good itself, which is the cause of all good things, so too there must be a cause of evil (*Enneads* 1.8.3.23–5). This assumption is the fundamental difference between Plotinus and Proclus.

Proclus has a number of arguments against Plotinus' assumption that we must identify a principle or origin of evil in the first place. If we do so, we face a dilemma. Either this *archē* of evil really is an *archē*, and not the product of something else, or it is the product of some cause distinct from itself. In the first case, there cannot be two such principles, for if each is *one* principle, then each must be subordinate to some common cause of unity prior to both. If, however, the origin of evil is a product of the One or the Good, then since the cause of any thing is *F* to a greater degree than the product, the Good will have to be evil to a higher degree than the (purported) *archē* of evil (*De mal.* §31). To avoid this dilemma, we should posit not a single cause of evil, but rather many sources. This view purportedly explains why Socrates speaks of causes of evil in the plural in *Republic* 379c (*De mal.* §47).

Proclus also argues that nothing is evil *per se* (§9). Rather, each thing that we call an evil is such in relation to some other particular good (§51). This does not mean that there is no such thing as evil, any more than there is no such thing as

13. Proclus (1977, 1979) belongs to the same established tradition of discussions of providence and freedom as Plotinus, *Enneads* 3.1–3.

a father or a son: each of these are examples of predicates that are relational. Evil, like fatherhood, is a property that supervenes on the intrinsic properties of things. Proclus conveys this idea by calling evil something that has "parasitic existence" (*parypostasis*; §49).

Unlike fatherhood, however, we cannot locate even a single uniform cause among the properties on which it supervenes. This is the effect of denying that it has an *archē*. So it turns out that evil is *uncaused* in a sense (§50.29–31). Within the framework of Aristotle's theory of causes, it lacks a formal and final cause (§49.7–11). It lacks a formal cause since there is no one property that 'causes' relational evil in the way that being male and having offspring causes fatherhood. Since the final cause is 'that for the sake of which' something comes to be, and all things come to be for the sake of some good, relational evil also lacks a final cause. Proclus thinks that evil has only the kind of accidental cause that chance events have. Since nothing in nature brings a chance event about regularly (else it would not be chance), there is no *per se* cause of evil analogous to the way in which the doctor is the *per se* cause of health. This is not to embrace a form of indeterminism. Cause here is not being contrasted with randomness. Rather, we have a *per se* cause when the description of the cause shows why citing it is explanatory. To say that evil has no *per se* cause is to say that there is no uniform, informative explanation of evils. Each one is like an unhappy counterpart of the happy chance by means of which you go to the market to buy wine and meet someone who owes you money (cf. Aristotle, *Physics* II.5). If evil has only a kind of parasitic existence and is not something that has a *per se* cause – a unified explanandum that can be understood by reference to a unitary cause – then the divine is surely not responsible for it.

PHILOSOPHY, THEURGY AND THE SOUL'S RETURN TO THE DIVINE

I noted above that Neoplatonists take Plato's *Theatetus* and *Timaeus* to set out the *telos* or goal of living. Our well-being requires the soul to "become like god in as much as this is possible" (*Theaetetus* 176b1), a specification of the *telos* summed up in the phrase *homoiōsis theōi*, or 'assimilation to god'.

Since this is a form of Platonism, it is unsurprising that the achievement of this goal requires the virtues. However, the exact connection between possessing the virtues and becoming like god is mysterious, since the gods themselves do not seem to possess virtues such as self-control or justice, or at least not in the sense in which we possess them. As Aristotle remarks, the gods do not have to control bad appetites or return money deposited with them (*Nicomachean Ethics* 1178b7–22). The response of the Neoplatonists is to articulate an ordered series of *levels of virtue* in which each level verges more and more toward the kind of intellectual activity in which the gods engage. The basic distinction in Plotinus (*Enneads* 4.2) is between civic virtues, modelled on the account in *Republic* book 4, and purificatory virtues, for which the Platonic source text is *Phaedo* 69a–c. Porphyry (*Sentences* 32) identifies four levels, while Iamblichus goes further to identify six (as quoted by Damascius, *Commentary on Plato's Phaedo* §138–51).[14]

It seems likely that Proclus adopted Iamblichus' account of the virtues. This, however, raises the question of Proclus' attitude to theurgy, for Iamblichus' highest level of virtue is *hieretic* or priestly virtue. The role of sacrificial and magical practice in elevating the soul to god was debated between Iamblichus and Porphyry (*see* this volume, Ch. 16, "Porphyry and Iamblichus"). This debate tended, even in antiquity, to invite a division between those who supposed that the royal road back to god was through philosophy (Plotinus, Porphyry) and those who thought that we returned to god by means of the science of the priestly arts (Iamblichus, Syrianus, Proclus).[15] It must be admitted that, while Proclus gives philosophy some credit for removing the 'accretions of generation' that the soul acquires in its descent into a body, he gives 'the life of ritual' even more (*in Tim.* III 300.13–20). But this remark has a quite specific context. Like the other Neoplatonists, Proclus takes *Timaeus* 41e2 to license the notion of 'psychic vehicles': concentric spherical bodies made of aether that acquire accretions in the soul's descent into the body.[16] The *Chaldean Oracles*, which they seek to integrate into their understanding of Platonism, speak of such "stains of generation" (fr. 196). The Neoplatonists after Iamblichus suppose that these accretions may be removed by theurgic ritual. This form of purification is said by Proclus to be the soul's salvation (*in Tim.* III 297.16–24). My own view is that Proclus somewhat overstates his case here. He should perhaps say that the removal of the accretions that the psychic vehicle acquires in its descent is a necessary but not sufficient condition for assimilation to god. Proclus also thinks that there is a purification effected by philosophy through which the soul is purged of false beliefs (*Commentary on Plato's First Alcibiades* [*in Alc.*] 174.13–14).

Good Platonist that he is, Proclus naturally accepts the *Timaeus*' vision of the circles of the Same and the Different rotating within the individual soul in an imitation of the movements of the fixed stars and the planets along the path of the ecliptic. Successful imitation of the divine requires us to master the disruption to our psychic circles that is introduced by embodiment. This achievement is the soul's assimilation to god. However, when Proclus describes these disruptions,

14. A sense of the rather attenuated connection between these higher levels of virtue and what we might regard as morally noble character traits can be seen by considering Porphyry's description of the paradigmatic virtues: his highest level. At this level, the virtue of self-control is intellect's 'being in relation to itself', while doing justice is simply performing intellect's proper function. Cf. Brisson (2006).

15. Cf. Damascius, *Commentary on Plato's Phaedo* §172. For Iamblichus and theurgy, see Shaw (1995). For the predominance of theurgy over philosophy in Proclus' soteriology, see van den Berg (2003).

16. On these vehicles, see Sorabji (2005: 221–38).

he does so in *cognitive terms*. Implicitly accepting a contradiction is one kind of disruption we may experience and we cure this *by philosophy* (*in Tim.* III 341.4–342.2). Of course, all our philosophical efforts at purifying ourselves may come to no avail if the 'stains of generation' that have become attached to our psychic vehicles continue to throw us psychically off balance, so to speak. But nothing in Proclus suggests that merely removing these stains through ritual practice will be sufficient in itself for making us think straight: or, more accurately, to think circularly as the World Soul does![17] So, while Proclus' soteriology doubtless has some ritual elements, philosophy plays an important role too.

CONCLUSION

The *individual* contribution of Proclus to philosophy of religion (or any other area of philosophy) is hard to gauge because of the convention of the Neoplatonic commentary tradition. Whatever Proclus' individual contributions to the philosophy of the Athenian school, he was clearly its most influential conduit. We have already observed the connection between his work and the work of the philosopher identified as Dionysius the Areopagite. Moreover, Proclus' own works were studied – albeit quietly! – in Byzantium (Perry 2006). In the fullness of time, his works were translated into Arabic (Morewedge 1992; Shayegan 1996). A consequence of this was the composition, probably at some time in the ninth century in Baghdad, of the *Kalam fi mahd al-khair* (Discourse on the pure Good), which was translated into Latin as the *Liber de causis* and attributed to Aristotle. In fact, however, it represents a certain synthesis of propositions from Proclus' *Elements of Theology* with the simpler metaphysics of Plotinus, as well as ideas from Islamic or Christian monotheism. This, together with John Scotus Eriugena's translation of Dionysius, was the main conduit for Proclus' theology to the Latin West (cf. Boss & Seel 1987; Bos & Meijer 1992). The Platonists of the Italian Renaissance read Plato with Proclus at their elbow (Allen 1994). Of the 900 philosopical theses that Giovanni Pico della Mirandola (1463–94) proposed to defend in his *Conclusiones*, Proclus' *Elements of Theology* provides fifty-five. Proclus' direct influence on philosophy of religion and theology begins to peter out in subsequent centuries, although his *Platonic Theology* is cited by Berkeley near the end of *Siris*. Hegel engaged in a serious study of Proclus in the period 1797–1800 and interprets his divine, intelligible triads within the terms of his own metaphysics in his *Lectures on the History of Philosophy*. With the growing movement to read Plato without the filter of Neoplatonism, Proclus fell out of favour (Tigerstedt 1974). In some ways this is understandable. If one is not antecedently committed to a Neoplatonic worldview, little in Proclus will seem convincing to

17. The case is developed at more length in Baltzly (2006).

you. Nonetheless, he bequeathed to Western philosophy of religion: (i) a rigorous thinking through of the central notions of negative theology; (ii) a precise formulation of the metaphysics of emanation; (iii) a solution to the problem of evil that seeks to evade divine responsibility by denying divine causation of evil; and (iv) a geometric form for philosophical argument in the *Elements of Theology* that subsequent philosophers sought to emulate.

FURTHER READING

Brisson, L. 2004. *How Philosphers Saved Myths: Allegorical Interpretation and Classical Mythology*. Chicago, IL: University of Chicago Press.

Rappe, S. 2000. *Reading Neoplatonism: Non-discursive Thinking in the Texts of Plotinus, Proclus and Damascius*. Cambridge: Cambridge University Press.

Sorabji, R. 2005. *The Philosophy of the Commentators, 200–600 AD: A Sourcebook, vol. 2: Physics*. Ithaca, NY: Cornell University Press.

Sorabji, R. 2005. *The Philosophy of the Commentators, 200–600 AD: A Sourcebook, vol. 3: Logic and Metaphysics*. Ithaca, NY: Cornell University Press.

Watts, E. 2006. *City and School in Late Antique Athens and Alexandria*. Berkeley, CA: University of California Press.

On DIVINITY see also Chs 8, 18, 20; Vol. 2, Chs 6, 8. On EVIL/PROBLEM OF EVIL see also Ch. 18; Vol. 2, Ch. 16; Vol. 3, Chs 13, 18, 19; Vol. 4, Chs 12, 18; Vol. 5, Chs 19, 22, 23. On EXISTENCE OF GOD see also Ch. 18; Vol. 2, Chs 5, 6, 13, 14; Vol. 3, Chs 6, 12, 13, 14, 15, 21; Vol. 5, Chs 11, 16. On NEOPLATONISM see also Ch. 20; Vol. 2, Chs 3, 4; Vol. 3, Ch. 9; Vol. 4, Chs 4, 9. On THE ONE see also Chs 3, 11, 14, 16; Vol. 4, Ch. 9; Vol. 5, Ch. 15. On TRIADS see also Ch. 20.

20

PSEUDO-DIONYSIUS

Kevin Corrigan and Michael Harrington

For many centuries the four major works and ten letters that form the *Corpus Dionysiacum*[1] were thought to be by St Denys the Areopagite, a member of the Athenian Areopagus converted by St Paul (Acts 17:34), just as their author represents them to be. Doubts about the authorship were raised as early as 532 by a Synod in Constantinople after a pro-monophysite group had claimed support for their views in the corpus, and later still by Peter Abelard (1121), Lorenzo Valla (1457) and John Grocyn (1501), but they were first widely published by Erasmus in 1504. Hardly anyone doubted a generally Platonic background to the corpus, although some, like Luther, thought it "pernicious": Dionysius "Platonizes more than he Christianizes" (1888: 562). The Neoplatonic character of parts of the corpus was definitively demonstrated in 1895 by Hugo Koch and Josef Stiglmayr (independently): Denys' presentation of evil as a *parhypostasis*, or by-product of reality without genuine existence on its own account, was dependent on Proclus' *De malorum subsistentia*.[2] In fact, the corpus employs language and quotations from Hellenic authors stretching back through Proclus, Iamblichus and Plotinus to Aristotle, Plato and Parmenides. We will probably never know the identity – or gender – of the real author (although many candidates have been proposed[3]), but we can date the public circulation of the corpus approximately to 518–28 since there are references to it in the treatises written by Severus of Antioch in his dispute with Julian of Halicarnassos (which were translated into Syriac in 528 by Paul of Callinicus), since these important works by such a resourceful and mysterious author would hardly have gone uncommented on for long, and since the

1. Hereafter abbreviated as follows: *On the Divine Names* (*DN*), *Mystical Theology* (*MT*), *Ecclesiastical Hierarchy* (*EH*), *Celestial Hierarchy* (*CH*), and *Letters*. For Greek text (page and line numbers) see Dionysius (1990, 1991). For translation, see Dionysius (1987). For the ordering of the works and letters, see Hathaway (1969).
2. See *DN* 713D–736B.
3. See Hathaway (1969: 31–5), for a survey.

corpus reveals a thorough knowledge of Athenian Neoplatonism and of elements of Christian liturgy thought to be current in the late fifth century.[4] So St Denys or Dionysius the Areopagite, the supposedly ancient apostolic authority, became the modern Pseudo-Dionysius, perhaps of Syrian birth, misleadingly – and wrongly – labelled as late as 1997 as a 'ruthless' usurper of late Neoplatonic philosophy.

Pseudo-Dionysius' contribution to the philosophy of religion, however, is more original and subtle than some modern assessments have supposed. Originality is, after all, a modern notion. 'To introduce new things' (*kainotomein*)[5] could be a verb of abuse in late antiquity, not a recommendation. Moreover, to borrow from earlier traditions is not to eliminate creativity; charges of syncretism or hybridism often presuppose a standpoint of doctrinal purity that can be incapable of crossing religious boundaries. Dionysius transforms the whole of pagan Neoplatonism (from Plato and Plotinus to Proclus) into a new Christian form, cutting right across the major issues that framed his or her own time: first, the Council of Chalcedon in 451, by answering definitively the question whether Christ had one nature or two,[6] had only exacerbated the conflict between partisans for either side; and, secondly, Justinian's closing of public schools to non-Christians in 529 effectively put an end to living conversation between Christians and others. Dionysius' pseudonym not only gives him impeccable apostolic credentials. It also permits him: (i) to stand outside the monophysite controversy altogether, since the original Denys had died long before it began, and yet at the same time to incorporate language from both sides of the controversy that nonetheless transcends it;[7] (ii) to provide a bridge between Christianity and Hellenism that actually foregrounds the problem of their encounter since the pseudonym derives from a passage in the Acts of the Apostles where Christianity and Greek philosophy/religion are in conflict, yet in living contact; and (iii) to wrap his own identity within that of a mysterious intermediate figure who represents the instantaneous translation of one tradition (Greek philosophy) through a two-way intermediary (Denys) into another (Judaeo-Christianity/apostle Paul and Timothy). Dionysius hides his own identity just as he insists mysteries must be concealed from those who would not understand them (*CH* 140A–B). This subtle pseudonym therefore marks an

4. See Rorem & Lamoreaux (1998: 9ff.).
5. Cf. *DN* 68C; Dionysius 1990: 143,3–7.
6. "... one and the same Christ, Son, Lord, Only-Begotten, acknowledged to be without confusion ... without separation in two natures, since the difference of the natures is not destroyed because of the union, but, on the contrary, the character of each nature is preserved and comes together in one person and one hypostasis ..." (*Definition*, Council of Chalcedon).
7. For example, on the one (monophysite) side, as God made man, Christ gave us "a new theandric activity" (*Letters* 4, 1072C; 1991: 161,9–10); and, on the other (Chalcedonic) side, see Dionysius' use of 'unconfused' terminology (see *Definition* in note 7) as in Christ being formed out of love for humanity "by a complete and unconfused humanization" (*EH*, 44C; 1991: 93,16–17).

important synchronic moment in the history of the philosophy of religion and of inter-confessionalism.

This intermediary function of the pseudonym also indicates the way the author sees his own task within the corpus and provides an insight into some of the simultaneous transformations at play within it. On one level, Dionysius represents his teaching as a transmission by, first, St Paul and, then, Hierotheus through himself to Timothy. Hierotheus has been thought to be "part of the overall fiction" (Dionysius 1987: 69 n.128), but Dionysius tells us that Hierotheus wrote the *Elements of Theology*, which is the title of one of Proclus' most famous works. Timothy, on the other hand, is identifiable as the recipient of two letters from St Paul and traditionally thought to be the Bishop of Ephesus. Dionysius therefore represents himself as a medium through whom Christian teaching and the Hellenistic wisdom subsidiary to it are transmitted to ordinary Christians like Timothy. On another level, this transmission is to represent how the Trinity or Thearchy (God-beginning), revealed in Scripture and Christ, reaches down in creation and sustenance into all things, without departing from itself, to draw all things back through the various hierarchies of Law (in the Old Testament), the church and sacramental life (in the orders of the *Ecclesiastical Hierarchy*), and the whole of angelic creation (in the *Celestial Hierarchy*) to the 'luminous darkness', beyond discourse or reason, of the Source and present Ground of their existence.

On yet another level, this chain of transmission both embodies and transforms many of the principles of classical Neoplatonism to entirely new purposes. The hypostases (or levels of being) and triads of related terms (such as abiding–procession–conversion/procession–abiding–conversion or again being–life–intellect) are fundamental to Neoplatonism as a means of expressing the ontological derivations and relationality of all beings. All things abide in their cause, flow out of it, and yet return to it.[8] Or – a variation – all things flow out of their cause, become themselves by abiding in their cause, and return to their cause in love and yearning to become more themselves and more than themselves.[9] Or again, within any entity (for example, Intellect as that which includes all intelligible things), there is a triadic internal relationship in which a first moment of unrestricted being is mediated through the outpouring of life into a final moment of fully realized self-thinking intellect and all three are linked together in a dynamic two-way synergy. Here in Dionysius we meet these triads and many more (e.g. in *CH* 208B–D and *EH* 500C–509A, in relation to the sacraments, one of the most famous traditional triads – purification, illumination and perfection). In Dionysius, however, these abstract terms are given concrete reference. They become actual

8. Cf. "Every effect remains in its cause, proceeds from it, and converts to it" (Proclus, *Elements of Theology*, prop. 35). For different triads, see Wallis (1995: 132–3).
9. For this triadic variation in both Dionysius and pagan Neoplatonism, see Schäfer (2006: 55–74). For being–life–thought, see the still classical work by Hadot (1960: 107–41); for Dionysius see *DN* 816Aff.

orders of individual/specific living beings ranging from angels to priests, monks and catechumens. They also become definite characters in a living conversation faithful to the spirit of Plato's dialogues. Just as, according to Proclus, Socrates in Plato's *Parmenides* can approach the unity of Parmenides' thought only through the medium of Zeno's less unified thought (*in Parmenidem* 700, in Proclus 1987), so too Timothy – who had found Hierotheus' work to be over his head because of its "comprehensive and unitary enfoldings" (*tas synoptikas kai heniaias ... synelixeis*) (*DN* 681B) – needs Dionysius to unfold Hierotheus' thought into a more accessible form (681C). Dionysius' choice of the word *synoptikos* is precise. Socrates uses it in his argument to Glaukon in *Republic* book 7 of the comprehensive, all-round vision to which the dialectician finally attains in the "study" of the Good (*Republic* 537C). As Glaukon is to Socrates, so is Socrates to the Good. And as Aristodemus to Socrates, and Socrates to Diotima, so is Diotima a medium for Socrates in relation to the Beautiful in the *Symposium*. In Dionysius, then, as in some of Plato's most influential dialogues, actual characters help to create a linked universe. Mediation separates and explicates, but also lifts up the ordinary through the less ordinary to what is beyond both.

RELIGION: GOD, THEOLOGY, PHILOSOPHY, THEURGY

Dionysius does not have a notion of religion as such. This is to say, religion is a term derived from Latin with no exact Greek equivalent. The approximate terms Dionysius employs (*threskeia*, worship; *theologia*, theology; *hierourgia*, holy work; *leitourgia*, liturgy; *theourgia*, theurgy) involve a 'theology' of lived experience that does not separate philosophy, practice, prayer and community. Equally, Dionysius does not divide life up into its various domains (social, political, philosophical, etc.) and then add 'religion' as another category. The 'religious' pervades all other categories from the beginning. Philosophy is "divine" (*DN* 684B), involving "the received knowledge of divine things", "purity of mind", "accuracy of exposition", analytic discernment and the unpacking of the implicate, compressed order into a rational, discursive examination of individual detail (684C–D).

Dionysius' theology builds on earlier forms but goes beyond them. As in Plotinus, God's unrestricted existence precedes any determinate essence. However, while Plotinus characteristically describes his God as a One that is beyond even Being, Dionysius' One is the Trinity that is at once unrestricted Being and yet beyond any determinate being (*hyper-ousia*) (cf. *MT* 997A–B; 1991: 141,1, 142,4). It is even 'beyond God' in the sense that God is manifested to us in any determinate way (such as 'providence' or 'goodness', for instance).

This permits Dionysius to develop a subtle positive (kataphatic) and negative (apophatic) theology. With Basil the Great and Gregory of Nyssa, he holds that while we know nothing of the "hidden, beyond-essential God", we can by Scripture (the "holy oracles"), through the overflowing generosity of the Trinity, develop a kind of language or grammar of speaking about God. This language would allow us to take account of all the scriptural evidence of God's manifestation throughout history and also to take seriously the major problems confronting language and thought when we deal with such mysteries as the Trinity or Incarnation. Dionysius envisages this generosity as an outpouring of God's creative and sustaining power at all levels of creation, reaching down as a form of discourse or explication (*logos*), corresponding to the order of his various works (some lost or never written) into a multiplicity proportionate to each level of descent and then rising to greater and greater unity where language falters until having "passed up and beyond the ascent it will turn silent completely" (*MT* 1033c). Alongside our affirmations, therefore, Dionysius insists that none of our conceptions (*ennoiai*) are applicable to God, especially negative or privative conceptions (just as Basil and Gregory had argued against Eunomius' position that 'Unbegotten' was the only proper name for God).[10] Our negations of God are not privations:

> What has actually to be said about the cause of everything is this. Since it is the Cause of all beings, we should posit and ascribe to it all the affirmations we make in regard to beings and, more appropriately, we should negate all these affirmations, since it surpasses all things. Now we should not conclude that the negations are simply the opposites of the affirmations, but rather that the cause of all is considerably prior to this, beyond privations, beyond every denial, beyond every assertion.
> (*MT* 1000b; 1991: 143,2–7; trans. from Dionysius 1987)

Negation in this sense is not the absence of a predicate or a substitution of negative for affirmative images, as if one were to substitute 'God is not life' or 'God is a rock' for 'God is life'. Metaphorical utterances can be simultaneously affirmed and negated in so far as they together convey the failure of discourse to grasp what is beyond discourse. So when Dionysius says that dissimilar similarities are more appropriate symbolic names for God than more conventional titles (*CH* 137b–141d), he does not mean that to call God a 'worm' is more literally true than to call God 'good' but rather that the psalmist (Psalm 22:6; cf. *CH* 145a) who uses such language subverts our conventional tendency to think that we know what we mean by traditional epithets and so hides the sacred, yet points to it anew in a subversive way. Affirmation and negation together push our language to its breaking points, to reveal the limitations of all literal and metaphorical discourse in relation to God, who transcends both.[11]

At the same time, reason is not eliminated by theology. Faith grounds philosophical thought. With Gregory of Nyssa, existential faith precedes essential

10. For *agenetos* (unbegotten) against Arianism (and Eunomianism) implicitly, see *DN* 912c–d. For Basil and Gregory generally as well as on *ennoiai*, see Ayres (2004).
11. Compare *Letters* 6, 1077a; 1991: 164,3–8. See also Turner (1995: 19–49).

knowing and yet simultaneously informs it, holding together pagan and Christian yearning in what we might call their 'affective' approaches to mysticism. Hierotheus, Dionysius tells us in *On the Divine Names*, has been enlightened either by his own research or by "more mysterious inspiration" from elsewhere (an intertextual memory of Simmias' conjecture in the *Phaedo* [85c–d] that all knowledge is provisional like a "raft" for sailing the seas of life, "having learned either from oneself or from another" until one finds something better), "not only learning but also experiencing divine things", Dionysius continues (*pathein ta theia*; *DN* 648B – a phrase from Aristotle [fr.15 Rose], St Paul [Hebrews 5:8] and Plato [*Phaedrus*, 238c5–6]; "For he had a sympathy with such matters … and was perfected in a mysterious union with them … independent of any education" (*DN* 648B). Sympathy and affective mysticism, however, do not obliterate human reason, for Dionysius immediately tells us that he wants to present "the blessed visions" of Hierotheus' "most powerful *reasoning* (*dianoia*)". Demonstration and teasing out the implications of an experience or an argument go hand in hand with emotional aptitude, theological passion and ordinary practice. Some scholars have accordingly sought to identify the erotic and emotional strands of such an approach with an anti-intellectualist position. In reaction, others have re-emphasized that Dionysius' affective mysticism occurs entirely within an intellectual tradition.[12] Dionysius' language favours neither option exclusively. This is perhaps not only because mind and ordered feeling go together in the Platonic–Aristotelian tradition,[13] or because mind and heart are roughly coextensive in biblical literature as well as in the Christian ascetic and theological tradition, but also because these categories are anachronisms that cannot be used to characterize the past without distortion.

Iamblichus adopts the word theurgy, 'god-work', together with theology, 'god-word', to describe the inmost reality of contemplative *practice*, on the basis of a hidden sympathy or interconnectedness between material things and the sacred, divine significances resident in them by virtue of divine power itself. He denied that pure human thought or contemplation could bring about union with the divine. What was crucial was the divine gift as well as the performance of certain ritual actions or theurgy, 'god-work', in the belief that one could attain to the divine through divine *philia* in the first place and by means of the incarnation of divine forces themselves in material objects, statues or human beings, as well as by means of the power mirrored everywhere in the universe and in the natural sympathy of all parts, and not just by talking about the gods (*theo-logy*) or by looking at them (*theoria*).

While Iamblichus is clear that all principles of inspiration come from above (*De mysteriis* [hereafter *De myst.*] 3.7–8), human theurgists nonetheless order the

12. For both tendencies, see Turner (1995: 47).
13. This is perhaps why a treatment of pleasure only comes into focus in *Republic* book 9 at the culmination of the arguments of books 1–9 and in the *Nicomachean Ethics* X as a similar culmination of the arguments to that crucial point.

powers of the universe by investing themselves with "the hieratic role of the gods" (*De myst.* 4.2; Iamblichus 2003: 184,9–10).[14] This last is not a Christian prerogative for Dionysius. The orders of the Celestial and Ecclesiastical hierarchies have their own places 'in proportion to their capacity', as the Neoplatonic dictum has it, but theurgy is primarily God's work in nature and history, not our work. Theurgy complements theology: "The theurgies are the consummation of the theologies" (*EC* 432B), that is, the actual works of God in the New Testament perfect the theological foreshadowings of the Old. Speaking about God, therefore, thinking and reasoning one's way through divine manifestations in nature and community, and celebrating sacramental mysteries are all theurgical acts, not appropriations of divine powers, but forms of actually being made like God or divinization (cf. *EH* 376A1–2; 436B) and means of singing or 'hymning' the actual working (*pragmateia*) of God that makes our substance and life as like to the Good as possible (*EH* 436C).

Consequently, prayer is neither coercive power nor manipulation, but the primary form of free address to any free Other:

> [W]e must begin with a prayer before everything we do, but especially when we are to talk of God. We will not pull down to ourselves that power which is both everywhere and yet nowhere, but by divine memories and invocations we may commend ourselves to it and be joined to it. (*DN* 680D)

Iamblichus too – like Origen and other Church Fathers – had held that prayer changes us, not the divine, but in Dionysius there is no question of investing oneself with any divine prerogative.

Dionysius, in fact, brings new tensions to his theology/theurgy. Created beings are related hierarchically or mediately to God, yet while God establishes the hierarchies, God is immediately related to everything created. All viewpoints somehow have to be held together (on hierarchy, see immediately below). Furthermore, in late Neoplatonism, Iamblichus and Proclus had introduced new Christian-sounding theological triads such as faith–good hope–love as well as a divine providential eros for everything emanating from the One.[15] Dionysius goes beyond this to suggest that God's love for creation actually has an *affect* within God by analogy with our own experience of love. In Iamblichus, "the divine is not brought down into the signs of divination" (*De myst.* 3.18) and "the divine is exempt from external bewitchment (*akelēton*) or affection or constraint" (1.14). For Dionysius, by contrast, God's love is so real that it becomes (as it were) "outside of itself", "is

14. In *De myst.* 4.2, it is not entirely clear whether this refers to pneumata that have no reason of their own (2003: 183,1–14) or to theurgy as a whole (*ibid.*: 184,1–9).
15. See Wallis (1995: 154–5).

charmed (*thelgetai*)[16] by goodness, affection and love" and *is* "led down … to dwell in all things" without simultaneously departing from itself (*DN* IV, 13). To suggest not only that we suffer divine things, but also that the Trinity does so in its own hyper-essential way is to go beyond anything in previous thought.

HIERARCHY

Each of Dionysius' two treatises on hierarchy is in some way a pioneer. *On the Heavenly Hierarchy* was not the first Christian work to discuss the nature of angels, but it was the first to provide a complicated, specific and exhaustive account of the ranks within their hierarchy, although it would soon be followed by a competing account by Gregory the Great. The discrepancies between the two would later be noted and resolved by, among others, Thomas Aquinas (*Summa theologiae* I, q. 108) and Dante (*Paradiso* canto 28). Dionysius' second hierarchical treatise, *On the Ecclesiastical Hierarchy*, was not the first treatise to deal with liturgical theology, having predecessors in Ambrose, Cyril of Jerusalem and Theodore of Mopsuestia, as Paul Rorem (1993: 118–21) has noted, but its complete and systematic approach to the Christian rites has no extant model.

On the Heavenly Hierarchy answers many minor questions about the angels, such as: what does the word 'angel' mean (ch. 4)? Why are names for particular ranks like 'angel' (ch. 5) and 'power' (ch. 11) sometimes used to describe the whole heavenly hierarchy? Why are human bishops sometimes called angels (ch. 12)? Why are human beings sometimes said to interact directly with higher ranks of angels, skipping over the lower ranks of the angelic hierarchy (ch. 13)? How many angels are there (ch. 14)? What is the meaning of the various symbols used to describe them (ch. 15)? But, beyond answering these subordinate questions, the treatise may be said to have two purposes as a whole. The first is the more famous purpose of organizing into nine ranks the various terms used apparently of the angels in the Hebrew and Christian scriptures, grouped into three sets of three: seraphim, cherubim and thrones; dominions, powers and authorities; and principalities, archangels and angels (summarized in ch. 6 and explained at length in chs 7–9). The second purpose is to clarify the nature of mediated contact with God, primarily among the angels, but also among human beings.

Mediated contact with God is necessary because not all beings are of a single rank. They differ in rank as an image of the difference in activities exercised by God in them (508c–509a). His activities are three – purification, illumination and perfection – and so their ranks will likewise be ordered in groups of three. The higher ranks of angels hand down the activities of God to the lower ranks in a completely

16. This is perhaps a memory of Agathon's *Eros* "enchanting the mind of all gods and human beings" (*Symposium* 187e4–5).

immaterial manner. The highest rank of human beings – whether they are called theologians, apostles or bishops – also receives these activities in an immaterial manner, "from intellect into intellect" (376C), being worthy, as Dionysius says, of "thoughts that are the equal of those belonging to the angels" (868C). At this point, the nature of the transmission changes. The theologians do not hand down the divine activities intellectually because human beings, or at least the vast majority of them, "cannot extend themselves to intelligible contemplations without mediation (*amesos*), but need an elevation that is their own and natural to them" (140A). The theologians provide this elevation in two ways: by writing the Hebrew and Christian scriptures, and by establishing the liturgical rites of the Church. These texts and rites perform the same divine activities that are present in the minds of the angels, but this time they act "in the diversity and multiplicity of divided symbols" (376B).

One might assume that treatises such as *On the Divine Names* and the *Symbolic Theology* would address the first of these two symbolic forms of mediation: the Hebrew and Christian Scriptures. And, in a limited sense, this is true. The treatises on naming explain the different ways in which scriptural language can and does address the divine, but the context in which these names can be meaningful is liturgical. The Scriptures do not speak "from intellect into intellect", but in the spatial and temporal diversity of the liturgical rite. Their language is diversified by being spoken over the course of time by one person to another across a space. Only in this way can the Scriptures become the "elevation" that is natural to human beings. Both Scriptures and rites as forms of mediation constitute the subject of the second of the two hierarchical treatises, *On the Ecclesiastical Hierarchy*.

Dionysius does not claim to give advice about what should be done in these rites. He presents his text as a description of the already-existing rites of the Christian Church. He selects for special discussion the rites of baptism (ch. 2), the Eucharist (ch. 3), consecration of the chrism (ch. 4), ordination and activity of deacons, priests and bishops (ch. 5), ordination of monks (ch. 6) and burial (ch. 7). Each rite receives an introduction, then a more or less literal description of what bodily actions take place over the course of it, and finally a contemplation of its meaning. This contemplation often has two parts: an exoteric one for the uninitiated, and an esoteric one for initiates.

There has been some question among scholars as to whether Dionysius' selection and discussion of the rites is a work of description or creation. René Roques has suggested that, by omitting those aspects of the rites that do not suit his Neoplatonic conceptual structure, Dionysius is presenting a system that "does not correspond to the living reality of the church" (1954: 199). Roques directs his argument primarily against the triadic structures of *On the Ecclesiastical Hierarchy*, which seem more to be constructed by Dionysius than to be found in the existing Church hierarchy. While his triad of clergy – bishops, priests and deacons – does roughly map onto a division described in other texts of the time, his triad of laity – monks, faithful and the impure – does not seem to correspond to any historical formal division in the Church.

If these triadic structures sometimes feel laid down with a heavy systematic hand, it is also true that the treatise has its decidedly non-systematic side. Dionysius includes the adverb 'reasonably' (*eikotōs*) in the arguments he makes in *On the Ecclesiastical Hierarchy* with a frequency unmatched by any other text of his corpus. The term in its various forms has a long history in the Platonic tradition, beginning with Plato himself, who used it to qualify the reach of the arguments in his *Timaeus* and the *Critias*. In both dialogues, the 'reasonable' (*eikos*) is opposed to the 'precise' (*akribēs*). The speakers in the dialogues, Timaeus and Critias, make arguments that are reasonable but fall short of precision or necessity.

Dionysius uses the term not so much to qualify his arguments, but to qualify the rationality of the rites themselves. It is reasonable that the hierarch be consecrated while holding the Scriptures on his head, because the Scriptures contain everything we can know about God, and the hierarch is set in charge of providing that knowledge (513c). Is it possible to imagine a church where hierarchs were legitimately consecrated without holding the Scriptures on their heads? Yes. Dionysius' justification for this action does not then make the action necessary, but reasonable. The rite conforms to a certain degree of rationality, but it is not governed by reason. In other words, the rite cannot be deduced from a set of rational presuppositions. It must be given within a tradition.

The restriction of human knowledge of God to the context of rites that are rational only in a limited sense, and that are material and so confined to the lower levels of the hierarchy, has made some scholars wonder whether the hierarchical treatises are compatible with his treatises on naming. *On the Divine Names* seems to provide a purely rational means of ascent to God through the simple interpretation of names, while the *Mystical Theology* seems to break with the hierarchic structure altogether in describing a human ascent to God that goes beyond both the senses and the intellect to union with God himself.

It was Jean Vanneste (1959) who answered this question most forcefully for twentieth-century scholarship, dividing the Dionysian corpus into so-called 'theological' and 'theurgical' works, and suggesting that the two categories described mutually exclusive paths to God. The theological works, as the etymology of the name suggests, describe a work of reason (*logos*), ascending through the various forms of name towards a mystical encounter with God (*Theos*). The theurgical works, on the other hand, describe a work of bodily action (*ourgos*), not necessarily a rational action, performed within the institutional structure of the hierarchy so as to gain some contact with God, or benefit from God. The tension between the theological and the theurgical paths is the tension between the rational and the irrational, the immediate and the mediated, the personal and the institutional. This characterization of theurgy as irrational has its roots in the scholarly mood generated by various works of Eric Dodds, who describes the development of liturgical theology in the third century CE as the demise of classical rationality. This strict separation of rational mysticism from irrational liturgy has been criticized by a number of more recent authors, among them Gregory

Shaw (1995) on behalf of Iamblichus and Alexander Golitzin (1994) on behalf of Dionysius.

It must be said that the distinction between *On the Heavenly Hierarchy* and *On the Ecclesiastical Hierarchy* on the one hand, and the remaining major works of Dionysius on the other, is to some extent suggested by Dionysius himself. He treats *On the Divine Names*, the *Mystical Theology* and the apparently unwritten *Theological Representations* and *Symbolic Theology* together, as having a single subject matter: the naming of God (1032D–1033D). The two hierarchical treatises are not included in this organizational scheme, but form their own pairing based on their distinctive subject matter: the ranks of created beings below God.

On the other hand, it is not clear that the works are separated by the mediated or unmediated character of the encounter with God they describe. Each hierarchy, Dionysius says, "sacredly enacts the mysteries of its own illumination in ranks and in hierarchic knowledge, and is likened to its own principle, as much as is permitted" (165B). How the problem of mediacy and immediacy arises depends on how we interpret the 'in', when Dionysius says that the action of illumination and the likening to God occurs "in ranks and in hierarchic knowledge". An immediate contact with God would seem to require that the aspirant depart from his own rank and ascend to the rank of God. Such contact would be ruled out by Dionysius' claim that likening to God occurs 'in' ranks, and not outside them. It may be, however, that we draw this conclusion only if we do not think of 'likeness' as the Neoplatonists did. When we look at likeness in a very generally Neoplatonic manner, we see that where two things already of the same rank become like each other, then the same thing is present immediately in both, and the question of mediation does not arise. The union of a lower rank with a higher rank, on the other hand, has a different character. The lower participates immediately in the higher, but in such a way that its participation constitutes an image of the higher, and so is mediated by its very distance from the higher. Only in such a way is its character as an image safeguarded. Dionysius shows this concern to preserve the character of the image with his constant use of "as much as possible" and "as much as is permitted" when referring to the likening of the lower rank to the higher. If this mediation poses a problem, then it is a problem even for the highest rank of angels, who, although they have nothing above them but God himself, nevertheless participate as images of God rather than as God himself. The lower ranks also participate in God himself (immediate participation), but in order to safeguard their character as lower ranks, this participation comes to them through the higher ranks (mediate participation). Neoplatonists as varied as Plotinus (in *Enneads* 1.2.2) and Proclus (in his *Commentary on Plato's Parmenides* 912), would presumably not see this mediated immediacy as a problem.

In another sense, the problem of mediacy and immediacy in the hierarchical works cannot be so easily resolved, but in this case it is a problem for the Dionysian corpus as a whole. It can be found in the so-called 'theological' treatises just as it can in the two hierarchical works. At the beginning of *On the Divine*

Names, Dionysius stipulates that he will not "say or conceive anything concerning the divinity that is hidden and beyond being, other than what has been said to us in the holy discourses" (588A). God is beyond what our reason can grasp, and so we should not use reason to discover names for him. We must rely on the names given to us within the historical tradition of the Hebrew and Christian Scriptures. And yet the divine names or, as Dionysius also calls them, the intelligible names, have as their proper referent the intelligible structures that underlie all created things: being, truth, unity, goodness, and so on. As intelligible and universal, they are accessible not only through the mediation of a particular scriptural tradition, but also to the unmediated use of human reason. Dionysius acknowledges this in practice, if not while accounting for his method, discussing the intelligible names in the language of Greek philosophy and using divine names more common outside the Hebrew and Christian tradition than within it.

The comparable tension in the hierarchical works can be brought out by juxtaposing Dionysius' explicit concern for bodies only as symbols inside the church, with the universal intelligible structure that he says is contemplated through those bodies, a structure that is equally responsible for the bodies outside the church. In other words, the beauty of the intelligible archetypes, explained by Dionysius as the source of the beautiful symbols in the church, is also responsible for the beauty of the world outside the church. Some scholars have resolved this tension by denying its second pole and concluding that Dionysius finds nothing redemptive in the natural world, "an existence entirely sunk in deception and enslavement to the seeming good of the world, the flesh, and the devil", as Golitzin (1994: 158) describes it. This conclusion may resolve a tension that Dionysius himself does not address, perhaps because the tension is bound up so intimately with Christianity itself: the tension between Christ as a historical figure and Christ as a cosmic figure (the *logos* of the prologue to the Gospel of John), between Christ the establisher of the Church and Christ the establisher of creation.

INFLUENCE

The first commentary on the works of Dionysius appeared within a century of the works themselves. This commentary took the form of short paragraphs, or scholia, on particular words or phrases in the original text. The scholia could be as short as one word intended to clarify a term used by Dionysius, or as long as a brief treatise, sometimes going far beyond the context of the original text. In general, the scholia are concerned with showing how Dionysius fully subscribes to the credal statements adopted by the first four ecumenical councils of the Christian Church, while introducing to him a strain of late antique Neoplatonism that does not seem to match perfectly the thought of either Dionysius or the credal statements of the councils. Medieval manuscripts attribute the scholia sometimes to John of Scythopolis alone, and sometimes also to Maximus the Confessor. Although they may not initially have been written in the margins of a manuscript containing the text of the Dionysius corpus, they soon found their way there, and were transmitted throughout the Middle Ages side by side with the original text.

Each treatise within the corpus exercised its own influence and generated its own set of commentaries throughout the Middle Ages, although in the Latin West the corpus did not begin to exercise a wide influence until Eriugena produced its definitive Latin translation around 860. Perhaps the most influential treatise in both East and West was the *Mystical Theology*, with the limitations it placed on language about God, and its provocative but only briefly described concept of unknowing as the culmination of human interaction with God. Authors influenced by it tended, unlike Dionysius, to enrich the concept of unknowing with language drawn from ordinary human activities. Some, beginning with the Greek scholiast and Eriugena, and continuing most famously with Albert the Great and Thomas Aquinas, described unknowing as a cognitive activity, a kind of knowing. Others, such as Maximus the Confessor, the Victorine school, and, later, Gregory Palamas and Marsilio Ficino, described unknowing as an affect, akin to or identical with the experience of love.

After it was accepted in the early sixteenth century that the Dionysius of Acts 17:34 did not write the works attributed to him, their influence waned, generating a faint and generally indirect interest among the German Idealists, as well as romantics on both sides of the Atlantic. The corpus resurfaced in the twentieth century, when its pseudonymous character became intriguing rather than repelling for philosophers influenced by 'the death of the author' in literary criticism, and when its description of a God beyond being began to resonate with contemporary efforts to get beyond traditional metaphysics.

FURTHER READING

Andia, Y. de 1996. *L'union à Dieu chez Denys l'Aréopagite*. Leiden: Brill.

Andia, Y. de (ed.) 1997. *Denys l'Aréopagite et sa postérité en Orient et en Occident*. Paris: Institut d'Études Augustiniennes.

Ayres, L. 2004. *Nicaea and Its Legacy: An Approach to Fourth-Century Trinitarian Theology*. Oxford: Oxford University Press.

Corrigan, K. 2004. *Reading Plotinus: A Practical Introduction to Neoplatonism*. West Lafayette, IN: Purdue University Press.

Dionysius 1987. *Pseudo-Dionysius: The Complete Works*, C. Luibheid (trans.). New York: Paulist Press.

Gersh, S. 1978. *From Iamblichus to Eriugena: An Investigation of the Prehistory and Evolution of the Pseudo-Dionysian Tradition*. Leiden: Brill.

Hadot, P. 1960. "Être, vie, pensée chez Plotin et avant Plotin". In *Les Sources de Plotin: Dix exposes et discussions*, E. Dodds *et al.* (eds), 107–41. Geneva: Fondation Hardt.

Louth, A. 1989. *Denys the Areopagite*. Wilton, CT: Morehouse-Barlow.

Schäfer, C. 2006. *The Philosophy of Dionysius the Areopagite: An Introduction to the Structure and the Content of the Treatise On the Divine Names*. Leiden: Brill.

Shaw, G. 1999. "Neoplatonic Theurgy and Dionysius the Areopagite". *Journal of Early Christian Studies* 7: 573–99.

On ANGELS/DEMONS see also Chs 14, 16. On DIVINITY see also Chs 8, 18, 19; Vol. 2, Chs 6, 8. On HIERARCHY see also Ch. 15; Vol. 2, Ch. 4. On NEOPLATONISM see also Ch. 19; Vol. 2, Chs 3, 4; Vol. 3, Ch. 9; Vol. 4, Chs 4, 9. On RITUAL see also Ch. 12; Vol. 4, Chs 9, 20, 21. On THEURGY see also Ch. 16. On TRIADS see also Ch. 19. On THE TRINITY see also Chs 14, 17; Vol. 2, Chs 2, 8, 15; Vol. 3, Chs 3, 9, 17; Vol. 4, Ch. 4; Vol. 5, Chs 12, 23.

CHRONOLOGY

776 Traditional date for the first Olympic Games

*c.*750 The *Illiad* and the *Odyssey*, epic poems ascribed to Homer, are composed.

621 Draco develops first written constitution of Athens, with the death penalty the punishment for most offences.

594 Solon revises Draco's constitution and establishes Athenian timocracy, thus making wealth, not birth, the criterion for holding political office.

570 Birth of **Xenophanes**, Greek poet, philosopher and religious critic.
Death of Sappho, one of the great Greek lyric poets, known for her songs of love towards women.
Death of Jeremiah, Old Testament prophet who witnessed the Babylonian destruction of Jerusalem.

563 Birth of Siddhartha Gautama, who is said to have reached enlightenment at the age of thirty-five and thence became known as 'the Buddha'; founder of one of the four largest active religious traditions today (Buddhism).

550 Death of Zoroaster (or Zarathustra), Persian prophet and founder of Zoroastrianism, a religion containing both monotheistic and dualistic elements, which served as the state religion of various Persian empires until the seventh century CE.

546 Death of Thales, first of the Greek natural philosophers and founder of the Milesian School.
Death of Anaximander, also a member of the Milesian School, who speculated on 'the boundless' or 'the unlimited' (*to apeiron*) as the source of all that is.

527 Death of Vardhamana Mahavira, Indian prophet who founded Jain religion.

525 Death of Anaximenes, philosopher who taught that air is the primary constituent of the universe.

521 Death of Lao-tzu, founder of Taoism and considered to be the author of the *Tao Te Ching*.

509 Beginning of Roman Republic.

*c.*507 Death of **Pythagoras**, founder of a religious-philosophical community in southern Italy.

480 Death of **Xenophanes**.

479 Death of Confucius, China's most famous philosopher, whose teachings are preserved in the *Analects*.

475 Death of Heraclitus, the 'obscure' philosopher of becoming and contemporary of Parmenides, the latter of whom founded the Eleatic School, which denied the reality of becoming or change.

469 Birth of **Socrates**, the first of the three giants of ancient Greek philosophy. He wrote no philosophical works but his discussions in public places in Athens were immortalized in the early dialogues of his pupil **Plato**.

460 Birth of Hippocrates, the 'father of medicine'.

438 Death of Pindar, greatest of the Greek choral lyricists.

435 Death of Empedocles, philosopher and poet, known for his view that everything is composed of four material elements (fire, air, earth and water), which are moved by two opposing forces, Love and Strife.

431 Beginning of twenty-seven-year Peloponnesian War between Athens and Sparta.

429 Birth of **Plato**, the second of the three giants of ancient Greek philosophy, perhaps best known for his Socratic dialogues and his theory of Forms.
Death of Pericles, who led Athens to the height of political power and artistic achievement.

428 Death of Anaxagoras, philosopher of nature who was compelled to flee Athens after being charged with impiety for claiming that sun was not a divine being but an incandescent stone.

424 Death of Herodotus, first great historian of the ancient world. He wrote a history of the wars between Greece and Persia.

401 Death of Thucydides, author of *History of the Peloponnesian War.*

399 Death of **Socrates** at the age of seventy, sentenced to die on charges of corrupting the youth and not believing in the Olympian gods.

391 Death of Mo Tzu, Chinese philosopher who propounded, against Confucianism, a doctrine of universal love, which became the basis of the religious movement known as Mohism.

390 Rome sacked by the Gauls.

384 Birth of **Aristotle**, third of the three giants of ancient Greek philosophy. He was a member of **Plato**'s Academy, and went on to establish his own School and to construct a philosophical and scientific system that heavily influenced Christian scholasticism and medieval Islamic philosophy.

370 Death of Democritus, philosopher who developed (together with his teacher, Leucippus) an atomist theory of the world.

347 Death of **Plato**.

341 Birth of **Epicurus**, philosopher who taught that the goal of human life (happiness) cannot be achieved unless the fear of the gods and of death are banished.

334 Birth of **Zeno of Citium**, founder of the Stoic school of philosophy, which taught that happiness lies in living in accordance with nature or the rational order of things.

323 Death of Alexander the Great, pupil of Aristotle and king of Macedonia who overthrew the Persian empire and conquered much of the Near East.

322 Death of **Aristotle**.

Death of Demosthenes, Athenian statesman and famous orator who opposed the imperial ambitions of Philip of Macedon and his son, Alexander the Great.

310 Birth of Aristarchus of Samos, a Greek astronomer who was the first to maintain that the earth has an axial rotation and that it revolves around the sun.

300 Euclid completes his treatise on geometry, the *Elements*.

289 Death of Mencius (Meng-tzu), a Confucian philosopher who was a champion of the common people and an advocate of democracy.

276 Birth of Eratosthenes, a Greek astronomer who was the first person to calculate the circumference of the earth.

271/70 Death of **Epicurus**.

262 Death of **Zeno of Citium**.

240 Death of Callimachus, Greek poet and scholar who produced a comprehensive catalogue of the works contained in the Library of Alexandria.

238 Death of Asoka, Indian emperor who renounced warfare, converted to Buddhism and provided vigorous patronage to Buddhism during his reign.

212 Death of Archimedes, famous mathematician and inventor, known for discovering the buoyancy principle that has come to be called 'Archimedes' principle'.

159 Death of Terence, one of the greatest Roman comic dramatists.

149 Death of Cato the Elder, Roman soldier, orator and statesman who was noted for his conservative and anti-Hellenic policies.

125 Death of Hipparchus, Greek astronomer and mathematician who made important contributions to solar and lunar theory, and is considered to be the first person in the West to compile a star catalogue.

122 Death of Polybius, second only to Thucydides among ancient historians. He wrote a history of the rise of the Roman Empire.

106 Birth of **Cicero**, Roman statestman and scholar who is widely considered one of Rome's greatest orators.

87 Death of Wu Ti, autocratic Chinese emperor who made Confucianism the state religion of China.

71 Death of Spartacus, gladiator-slave who led an unsuccessful revolt against the Romans.

43 Death of **Cicero**.

30 Death of Cleopatra, Queen of Egypt who committed suicide soon after the suicide of her lover, Mark Antony, which led to the Roman conquest of Egypt and brought an end to the Hellenistic era.

27 Roman senate grants Octavian the title of 'Augustus', following the demise of the Roman Republic and the beginning of the Pax Romana, a period of relative peace and prosperity in the Roman world.

20 Birth of **Philo of Alexandria**, Greek-speaking Jewish philosopher known for his method of allegorical interpretation of biblical texts.

19 Death of Virgil, great Roman poet, whose masterpiece is the *Aeneid*.

12 Death of Agrippa, deputy of Augustus (the first Roman emperor) and responsible for many of the emperor's military triumphs.

8 Death of Horace, one of the foremost poets of the reign of Augustus.

4 BCE Birth of Jesus of Nazareth, founder of the Christian religion.

3 CE Birth of **Paul** (originally 'Saul'), who was brought up as a Pharisee, subsequently converted to Christianity and embarked on missionary journeys to the Gentiles.

17 Death of Livy, Roman historian who wrote a comprehensive history of Rome from its foundation until the reign of Augustus in his own time.

*c.*23 Death of Strabo, Greek geographer and historian whose *Geography* records the history of the people and places of the world known to the Greeks and Romans of his time.

30 Death by crucifixion of Jesus of Nazareth.

49 Claudius (Roman emperor, 41–54) expels Jews from Rome.

50 Death of **Philo of Alexandria**.

64 Great fire of Rome, blamed by Emperor Nero on the Christians who are therefore persecuted and severely punished.

65 Death of Seneca, philosopher and statesman who tutored the future Roman emperor, Nero.

66–73 First Jewish–Roman War: Jews of Judaea province rebel against the Romans, but rebellion ends with the fall of Jerusalem and the destruction of the Temple in 70 and the capture of Masada in 73.

69 Death of **Paul**.

79 Death of Pliny the Elder, Roman author of an encyclopaedic *Natural History*, who died in the eruption of Mt Vesuvius that destroyed Pompeii.

100 Death of Josephus, a Jewish historian who wrote *The Antiquities of the Jews*, an account of Jewish history from its early beginnings to the revolt against Rome in 66.

115–117 Second Jewish–Roman War, the Kitos War: Jews of Palestine and the Diaspora rebel but again fight unsuccessfully against Rome.

*c.*120 Death of **Plutarch**, Greek biographer who wrote the *Parallel Lives*, a collection of biographies of Greek and Roman heroes in pairs.
Death of Tacitus, Roman senator and historian.

130 Birth of **Irenaeus**, Bishop of Lyons and author of *Adversus Omnes Haereses*, an attack on Gnosticism.

132–5 Third Jewish–Roman War, Bar Kokhba's Revolt: Jewish rebellion against Roman rule in Judaea was crushed in 135 and Jews were forbidden to enter Jerusalem.

150 Birth of **Clement of Alexandria**, an Athens-born pagan who converted to Christianity and became head of the Catechetical School in Alexandria.

155 Birth of **Tertullian**, who grew up as a pagan in Carthage, North Africa, converted to Christianity, and eventually joined the Montanist sect (an apocalyptic group that taught that the Heavenly Jerusalem would soon descend on earth).

165 Death of **Justin Martyr**, Christian apologist who was trained in philosophy, converted to Christianity (in about 130), and was executed in Rome.

*c.*170 Death of Ptolemy, Egyptian astronomer, geographer and mathematician of Greek descent, best known for his geocentric model of the universe.

*c.*185 Birth of **Origen**, biblical exegete and theologian who taught in Alexandria and Caesarea and became one of the most influential figures in the early church.

189 Victor I becomes the first Latin-speaking pope.

190 Death of Athenagoras, Christian apologist who was the first to elaborate a philosophical defence of the doctrine of the Trinity.

c.200 The first written record of the Jewish oral law, the *Mishna*, is compiled by Judah ha-Nasi.

202 Death of **Irenaeus,** bishop of Lyon who fought against Gnosticism.

c.204 Birth of **Plotinus**, Neoplatonist philosopher who established his own school in Rome and authored the posthumously published and highly influential *Enneads.*

212 Death of **Clement of Alexandria**.

c.216 Death of Galen, Greek physician often considered to be the most important contributor to medical theory and practice in antiquity following Hippocrates.

230 Death of **Tertullian**.

232 Birth of **Porphyry**, a student of **Plotinus**. He wrote a *Life of Plotinus* and edited his teacher's works, as well as writing many treatises of his own, including *Against the Christians.*

245 Birth of **Iamblichus**, Neoplatonist philosopher who taught in Syria.

c.255 Death of **Origen**.

258 Persecution of Christian clergy and civil servants by Emperor Valerian.

270 Death of **Plotinus**.

276 Execution of Mani, Iranian founder of Manichaeism, a dualistic religious system that posits a cosmic conflict between the primordial powers of light (good) and darkness (evil).

c.285 Death of Diophantus of Alexandria, mathematician who introduced symbolism into algebra.

303 Roman emperor Diocletian launches last major persecution of Christians.

305 Death of **Porphyry**.

312 Constantine the Great defeats Maxentius at the battle of the Milvian Bridge, becomes sole ruler of the West, and adopts Christianity as his favoured religion.

313 Edict of Milan extends freedom of worship to Christians.

324 Constantine becomes sole ruler of the whole Roman Empire.

325 Death of **Iamblichus**.
The Council of Nicaea, the first 'ecumenical council', is summoned primarily to deal with the Arian controversy (whether the Son is a finite, created being or is of the same substance as the Father).

329 Birth of **Gregory of Nazianzus**, one of the 'Cappadocian Fathers', best known for his *Five Theological Orations.*

330 Birth of **Basil the Great**, brother of **Gregory of Nyssa**, who was appointed Bishop of Caesaria in Cappadocia in 370.

c.335 Birth of **Gregory of Nyssa**, Cappadocian Father, who was widely regarded as the leading theologian of the later fourth century.
Death of Bhasa, pioneer of Sanskrit classical drama.

336 Death of Arius, priest in Alexandria, who was condemned by the Council of Nicaea (in 325) for teaching that the Son of God was not eternal but created by the Father.

339 Death of Eusebius, Bishop of Caesarea, best remembered for his *Ecclesiastical History*, this being our principal source of the first three centuries of the Church.

354 Birth of **Augustine**, initially a follower of Manichaeism, who converted to Christianity in 387, becoming Bishop of Hippo and one of the leading theologians in the history of Christian thought (chief writings include *Confessions* and *City of God*).

355 Birth of Pelagius, British theologian, who taught in Rome, and was accused by **Augustine** of the heresy that human beings can achieve salvation largely through their own efforts, apart from divine grace.

362 Roman emperor Julian 'the Apostate' restores paganism.

373 Death of Athanasius, Bishop of Alexandria, author of *De Incarnatione* and implacable opponent of the Arian heresy.

379 Death of **Basil the Great**.

381 Council of Constantinople, regarded as the 'second ecumenical council', convened to unite the Eastern Church at the end of the lengthy Arian controversy.

c.382 Death of Wulfila, Gothic bishop and missionary, inventor of the Gothic alphabet, and first translator of the Bible into a Germanic language.

389 Death of **Gregory of Nazianzus**.

c.395 Death of **Gregory of Nyssa**.

397 Death of Ambrose, Bishop of Milan, famous as a powerful preacher and for his confrontations with Emperor Theodosius I.

350–400 Compilation of the *Talmud of Jerusalem*.

411 Birth of **Proclus**, Neoplatonic philosopher and opponent of Christianity, who provided, in his *Elements of Theology*, a systematic exposition of Neoplatonic metaphysics in the form of 211 propositions.

415 Death of Hypatia, notable Alexandrian mathematician and philosopher, and prominent pagan, who was murdered by a mob of Christians.

420 Death of Jerome, best known for his translation of the Bible into Latin (the Vulgate).
Death of Kalidasa, Indian poet widely regarded as the outstanding writer of classical Sanskrit.

430 Death of **Augustine**.

431 Council of Ephesus, the 'third ecumenical council', condemned the doctrine, associated with Nestorius, that Christ is divided into two persons, one human and the other divine.

c.450 Death of Sushruta, Indian physician who made seminal contributions to science of surgery.

451 Council of Chalcedon, the 'fourth ecumenical council', rejected monophysite doctrine that Christ had only one nature.
Death of Nestorius, patriarch of Constantinople who was deposed from his see owing to his teachings.

455 Rome plundered by the Vandals.

461 Death of Pope Leo I, known for his emphasis on the primacy of the see of Rome, his campaign against heresy and his success in persuading Attila the Hun not to invade Rome.

c.450 St Patrick's mission to Ireland.

476 Traditional date of the fall of the Roman Empire.

*c.*476 Birth of **Boethius**, Roman theologian who wrote *The Consolation of Philosophy* while in prison awaiting execution (*see* Vol. 2, Ch. 2).

*c.*480 Birth of Benedict of Nursia, Italian monk who established the Benedictine order.

485 Death of **Proclus**.

BIBLIOGRAPHY

Adam, J. [1908] 1965. *The Religious Teachers of Greece: Gifford Lectures on Natural Religion Delivered at Aberdeen University*. Edinburgh: T&T Clark.

Adomėnas, M. 1999. "Heraclitus on Religion". *Phronesis* **44**: 87–113.

Alcinous 1993. *Didaskalikos*. In *Alcinous: The Handbook of Platonism*, J. Dillon (trans. & comm.). Oxford: Clarendon Press.

Allen, M. 1994. *Plato's Third Eye: Studies in Marsilio Ficino's Metaphysics and its Sources*. Aldershot: Variorum.

Allport, G. 1960. *The Individual and his Religion: A Psychological Interpretation*. New York: Macmillan.

Annas, J. 1981. *An Introduction to Plato's Republic*. Oxford: Oxford University Press.

Annas, J. 1982. "Plato's Myths of Judgment". *Phronesis* **27**: 119–43.

Annas, J. forthcoming. "Ancient Scepticism and Ancient Religion".

Aristotle 1984. *The Complete Works of Aristotle: The Revised Oxford Translation*, 2 vols, J. Barnes (ed.). Princeton, NJ: Princeton University Press.

Armstrong, A. 1966–88. *Plotinus*, 7 vols, Loeb Classical Library. Cambridge, MA: Harvard University Press.

Armstrong, A. 1992. "Dualism: Platonic, Gnostic, and Christian". In *Neoplatonism and Gnosticism*, R. Wallis (ed.), 33–54. Albany, NY: SUNY Press.

Arnim, H. von 1903–5. *Stoicorum Veterum Fragmenta*, 3 vols [*SVF*]. Stuttgart: Teubner.

Arnim, H. von & M. Adler (eds) 1924. *Stoicorum Veterum Fragmenta*, 4 vols [*SVF*]. Leipzig: Teubner.

Arrighetti, G. 1973. *Epicuro: Opere*. Turin: Einaudi.

Athanasios, A. (ed.) 1984. *Nicholas of Methone: Refutation of Proclus' Elements of Theology*. Leiden: Brill.

Athanassiadi, P. & M. Frede (eds) 1999. *Pagan Monotheism in Late Antiquity*. Oxford: Oxford University Press.

Atticus 1977. *Fragments*, É. des Places (ed. & trans.). Paris: Les Belles Lettres.

Augustine 1963. *The Trinity*, S. McKenna, (trans.). Washington, DC: Catholic University of America.

Augustine 1964. *On Free Choice of the Will*, A. Benjamin & L. Hackstaff (trans.). Indianapolis, IN: Bobbs-Merrill.

Augustine 1984. *Concerning the City of God against the Pagans*, H. Bettenson (trans.). Harmondsworth: Penguin.

Augustine 1991. *Our Lord's Sermon on the Mount*. In *Nicene and Post-Nicene Fathers*, First Series, vol. 6, P. Schaff (ed.), 1–63. Edinburgh: T&T Clark.

Augustine 1992. *Confessions*, H. Chadwick (trans.). Oxford: Oxford University Press.

Augustine 1993. *On Care to be Had for the Dead*. In *Nicene and Post-Nicene Fathers*, First Series, vol. 3, P. Schaff (ed.), 539–51. Edinburgh: T&T Clark.

Augustine 2002. *On the Trinity: Books 8–15*, G. Matthews (ed.). Cambridge: Cambridge University Press.

Aulen, G. 1970. Christus Victor: *An Historical Study of the Three Main Types of the Idea of the Atonement*, A. Hebert (trans.). London: SPCK.

Ayres, L. 2004. *Nicaea and Its Legacy: An Approach to Fourth-Century Trinitarian Theology*. Oxford: Oxford University Press.

Bailey, A. 2002. *Sextus Empiricus and Pyrrhonean Scepticism*. Oxford: Oxford University Press.

Balás, D. 1966. *Metousia Theou: Man's Participation in God's Perfections According to Saint Gregory of Nyssa*. Rome: Herder.

Baltzly, D. 2003. "Stoic Pantheism". *Sophia* **42**: 3–33.

Baltzly, D. 2006. "Pathways to Purification: The Cathartic Virtues in the Neoplatonic Commentary Tradition". See Tarrant & Baltzly (eds) (2006), 169–84.

Barnes, J. 1997. "The Beliefs of a Pyrrhonist". In *The Original Sceptics: A Controversy*, M. Burnyeat & M. Frede (eds), 58–91. Indianapolis, IN: Hackett.

Basil of Caesarea 1950. *Homélies sur l'Hexaéméron*, Sources Chrétiennes, vol. 26, S. Giet (trans.). Paris: Editions du Cerf.

Basil of Caesarea 1975. *Saint Basil on the Value of Greek Literature*, N. Wilson (ed.). London: Duckworth.

Beard, M. 1986. "Cicero and Divination: The Formation of a Latin Discourse". *Journal of Roman Studies* **76**: 33–46.

Bechtle, G. 2000. *The Anonymous Commentary on Plato's Parmenides*. Berne: Haupt.

Beckman, J. 1979. *The Religious Dimension of Socrates' Thought*. Waterloo: Wilfrid Laurier University Press.

Benson, H. 2000. *Socratic Wisdom*. Oxford: Oxford University Press.

Berg, R. van den 2003. "'Becoming Like God' according to Proclus' Interpretations of the *Timaeus*, the Eleusinian Mysteries, and the Chaldaean Oracles". In *Ancient Approaches to Plato's Timaeus*, R. Sharples & A. Sheppard (eds), *Bulletin of the Institute of Classical Studies*, supp. vol. 76, 189–202. London: Institute of Classical Studies.

Berti, E. 2000. "Metaphysics Lambda 6". In *Aristotle's "Metaphysics" Lambda*, M. Frede & D. Charles (eds), 181–206. Oxford: Oxford University Press.

Betegh, G. 2004. *The Derveni Papyrus: Cosmology, Theology and Interpretation*. Cambridge: Cambridge University Press.

Bett, R. 2000. *Pyrrho, His Antecedents and His Legacy*. Oxford: Oxford University Press.

Bidez, J. 1913. *Vie de Porphyre*. Ghent: Van Goethen.

Bobzien, S. 1998. *Determinism and Freedom in Stoic Philosophy*. Oxford: Oxford University Press.

Borgen, P. 1984. "Philo of Alexandria: A Critical and Synthetical Survey of Research since World War II". In *Hellenistisches Judentum in römischer Zeit: Philon und Josephus*, W. Haase (ed.), Aufstieg und Niedergang der römischen Welt II 21.1, 98–154. Berlin: De Gruyter.

Bos, E. & P. Meijer (eds) 1992. *On Proclus and His Influence in Medieval Philosophy*. Leiden: Brill.

Boss, G. & G. Seel (eds) 1987. *Proclus et son influence: Actes du colloque de Neuchäatel, juin 1985*. Zurich: GMB Editions du Grand Midi.

Boyancé, P. 1966a. "L'Apollon solaire". In his *Mélanges d'archéologie, d'épigraphie et d'histoire offerts à Jérôme Carcopino*, 149–70. Paris: Hachette.

Boyancé, P. 1966b. "L'Influence pythagoricienne sur Platon". In *Filosofia e scienze in Magna*

Grecia: Atti del quinto Convegno di Studi silla Magna Grecia, Taranto, 10–14 ottobre 1965, 73–113. Naples: L'arte tipografica.

Boyancé, P. 1972. *Le Culte des Muses chez les philosophes grecs: Études d'histoire et de psychologie religieuses*. Paris: E. de Boccard.

Bremmer, J. 1995. "Religious Secrets and Secrecy in Classical Greece". In *Secrecy and Concealment: Studies in the History of Mediterranean and Near Eastern Religions*, H. Kippenberg & G. Stroumsa (eds), 61–78. Leiden: Brill.

Brenk, F. 1986. "In the Light of the Moon: Demonology in the Early Imperial Period". *Aufstieg und Niedergang der romischen Welt II* **16**(3): 2068–2145.

Brenk, F. 1998. "Genuine Greek Demons, 'In Mist Apparelled'? Hesiod and Plutarch". In *Relighting the Souls: Studies in Plutarch, in Greek Literature, Religion, and Philosophy, and in the New Testament Background*, F. Brenk (ed.), 170–81. Stuttgart: Franz Steiner.

Brennan, T. 2001. "Fate and Freewill in Stoicism". *Oxford Studies in Ancient Philosophy* **21**: 259–86.

Brickhouse, T. & N. Smith 1983. "The Origin of Socrates' Mission". *Journal of the History of Ideas* **44**: 657–66.

Brickhouse, T. & N. Smith 1994. *Plato's Socrates*. Oxford: Oxford University Press.

Brisson, L. 1987. "Usages et fonctions du secret dans le pythagorisme ancien". In *Le Secret*, P. Dujardin (ed.), 87–101. Lyon: University of Lyon Press.

Brisson, L. 2006. "The Doctrine of the Degrees of Virtue in the Neoplatonists: An Analysis of Porphyry's Sentences 32, Its Antecedents, and Its Heritage". See Tarrant & Baltzly (eds) (2006), 89–106.

Brunschwig, J. 1994. *Papers in Hellenistic Philosophy*, J. Lloyd (trans.). Cambridge: Cambridge University Press.

Buckley, T. 2006. "A Historical Cycle of Hermeneutics in Proclus' Platonic Theology". See Tarrant & Baltzly (eds) (2006), 125–34.

Burkert, W. 1964. "Review of Detienne, *De la pensée religieuse à la pensée philosophique*". *Gnomon* **36**: 563–7.

Burkert, W. 1972. *Lore and Science in Ancient Pythagoreanism*, E. Minar (trans.). Cambridge, MA: Harvard University Press.

Burkert, W. 1985. *Greek Religion*, J. Raffan (trans.). Cambridge, MA: Harvard University Press.

Burnyeat, M. 2008. *Aristotle's Divine Intellect*. Milwaukee, WI: Marquette University Press.

Bussanich, J. 2006. "Socrates and Religious Experience". In *A Companion to Socrates*, S. Ahbel-Rappe & R. Kamtekar (eds), 200–213. Oxford: Blackwell.

Cameron, A. 1968. "The Date of Iamblichus' Birth". *Hermes* **96**: 374–6.

Chadwick, H. 1969. "Florilegium". In *Reallexikon für Antike und Christentum*, vol. 7, 1131–60. Stuttgart: Anton Hiersemann.

Cherniss, H. 1934. "The Platonism of Gregory of Nyssa". In *University of California Publications in Classical Philology, vol. 11: 1930–33*, J. T. Allen, H. C. Nutting & H. R. W. Smith (eds), 1–92. Berkeley, CA: University of California Press.

Cherniss, H. 1971. "The Sources of Evil According to Plato". In *Plato*, vol. 2, G. Vlastos (ed.), 244–58. Garden City, NY: Anchor Books.

Cicero 1991. *On Fate*. In *Cicero, "On Fate", and Boethius, "The Consolation of Philosophy"*, R. Sharples (ed.). Warminster: Aris & Phillips.

Cicero 2003. *De Natura Deorum, Liber I*, A. Dyck (ed.). Cambridge: Cambridge University Press.

Clay, J. 2003. *Hesiod's Cosmos*. Cambridge: Cambridge University Press.

Cohen, S. M. 1971. "Socrates on the Definition of Piety: Euthyphro 10A–11B". *Journal of the History of Philosophy* **9**(1): 1–13. Reprinted in *The Philosophy of Socrates*, G. Vlastos (ed.), 158–76 (Garden City, NY: Anchor Books, 1971).

Cohen, S. M., P. Curd & C. D. C. Reeve (eds) 2005. *Readings in Ancient Greek Philosophy: From Thales to Aristotle*. Indianapolis, IN: Hackett.

Collingwood, R. 1961. *The Idea of History*. Oxford: Oxford University Press.

Cooper, J. 2006. *Panentheism, The Other God of the Philosophers: From Plato to the Present*. Grand Rapids, MI: Baker Academic.

Crouzel, H. 1989. *Origen*, A. Worrall (trans.). Edinburgh: T&T Clark.

Daniélou, J. 1970. *L'être et le temps chez Grégoire de Nysse*. Leiden: Brill.

Daniélou, J. 1977. *The Origins of Latin Christianity*. London: Darton, Longman & Todd.

DeFilippo, J. 2000. "Cicero vs. Cotta in De Natura Deorum". *Ancient Philosophy* **20**: 169–87.

Denyer, N. 1985. "The Case against Divination: An Examination of Cicero's *De Divinatione*". *Proceedings of the Cambridge Philological Society* **31**: 1–10.

Detienne, M. 1963. *La Notion de daïmôn dans le pythagorisme ancien: de la pensée religieuse à la pensée philosophique*. Paris: Les Belles Lettres.

Diels, H. 1965. *Doxographi Graeci*, 4th edn. Berlin: Walter de Gruyter et Socios.

Diels, H. & W. Kranz 1951–2. *Die Fragmente der Vorsokratiker*, 6th edn [DK]. Berlin: Weidmann.

Diller, H. 1957. "Proklos". In *Real-Encylopadie der Klassischen Altertumswissenschaft*, A. Wissowa & W. Kroll (eds), 186–274. Stuttgart: Alfred Druckenmüller.

Dillon, J. 1972. "Iamblichus and the Origin of the Doctrine of Henads". *Phronesis* **17**: 102–6.

Dillon, J. 1990. "Image, Symbol and Analogy: Three Basic Concepts in Neoplatonic Allegorical Exegesis". In *The Golden Chain: Studies in the Development of Platonism and Christianity*, J. Dillon (ed.), 247–58. Aldershot: Variorum.

Dillon, J. 2003. *The Heirs of Plato: A Study of the Old Academy (347–274* BC*)*. Oxford: Clarendon Press.

Diogenes Laertius 1925. *Lives of the Eminent Philosophers*, 2 vols, R. Hicks (ed.) (Loeb Classical Library). Cambridge, MA: Harvard University Press.

Diogenes Laertius 1972. *Lives of Eminent Philosophers*, R. Hicks (trans.). London: Heinemann.

Dionysius 1987. *Pseudo-Dionysius: The Complete Works*, C. Luibheid (trans.). Mahwah, NJ: Paulist Press.

Dionysius 1990. *Corpus Dionysiacum I* (Greek text of *De divinis nominibus*), B. Suchla (ed.). Berlin: De Gruyter.

Dionysius 1991. *Corpus Dionysiacum II* (Greek text of *De coelesti hierarchia, De ecclesiastica hierarchia, De mystica theologia, Epistulae*), G. Heil & A. Ritter (eds). Berlin: De Gruyter.

Dodds, E. 1928. "The Parmenides of Plato and the Origin of the Neoplatonic 'One'". *Classical Quarterly* **22**: 129–42.

Doerrie, H. 1983. "Gregor III (Gregor von Nyssa)". *Reallexicon für Antike und Christentum* **12**: 863–95.

Drozdek, A. 2007. *Greek Philosophers as Theologians: The Divine Arche*. Aldershot: Ashgate.

Edmonds, R. 2004. *Myths of the Underworld Journey: Plato, Aristophanes, and the "Orphic" Gold Tablets*. Cambridge: Cambridge University Press.

Edwards, M. 1991. "Xenophanes Christianus?" *Greek, Roman, and Byzantine Studies* **32**: 219–28.

Edwards, M. 2000. *Neoplatonic Saints: The Lives of Plotinus and Proclus by their Students*. Liverpool: Liverpool University Press.

Eisen, M. 1974. "Xenophanes' Proposed Reform of Greek Religion". *Hermes* **102**: 142–50.

Epicurus 1994. *The Epicurus Reader: Selected Writings and Testimonia*, B. Inwood & L. Gerson (eds & trans.). Indianapolis, IN: Hackett.

Festugière, A. & L. Massignon 1944. *La Révélation d'Hermès Trismègiste*. Paris: Librairie Lecoffre J. Gabalda.

Finamore, J. 2006. "Apuleius on the Platonic Gods". See Tarrant & Baltzly (eds) (2006), 33–48.

Fontenrose, J. 1978. *The Delphic Oracle: Its Responses and Operations, with a Catalogue of Responses*. Berkeley, CA: University of California Press.

Fränkel, H. 1974. "Xenophanes' Empiricism and His Critique of Knowledge (B34)", M. Cosgrove (trans.). In *The Pre-Socratics*, A. Mourelatos (ed.), 118–31. Garden City, NY: Anchor Press.

Frede, D. & A. Laks (eds) 2002. *Traditions of Theology: Studies in Hellenistic Theology*. Leiden: Brill.

Frede, M. 2000. "Introduction". In *Aristotle's "Metaphysics" Lambda*, M. Frede & D. Charles (eds), 1–52. Oxford: Oxford University Press.

Frede, M. 2005. "La Théologie stoïcienne". In *Les Stoïciens*, G. Romeyer-Dherbey & J.-B. Gourinat (eds), 213–32. Paris: Vrin.

Frede, M. & D. Charles (eds) 2000. *Aristotle's "Metaphysics" Lambda*. Oxford: Oxford University Press.

Gerson, L. 1990. *God and Greek Philosophy: Studies in the Early History of Natural Theology*. London: Routledge.

Gerson, L. (ed.) 1999. *Aristotle: Critical Assessments*, vol. 1. London: Routledge.

Glucker, J. 1988, "Cicero's Philosophical Affiliations". In *The Question of "Eclecticism": Studies in Later Greek Philosophy*, J. Dillon & A. Long (eds), 34–69. Berkeley, CA: University of California Press.

Glucker, J. 1992. "Cicero's Philosophical Affiliations Again". *Liverpool Classical Monthly* **17**: 134–8.

Golitzin, A. 1994. *Et introibo ad altare Dei*. Thessaloníki: Patriarchikon Idruma Paterikon Meleton.

Gombocz, W. 1997. *Die Philosophie der ausgehenden Antike und des frühen mittelalters, vol. IV, Geschichte der Philosophie*, W. Röd (ed.). Munich: C. H. Beck.

Görler, W. 1995. "Silencing the Troublemaker: De Legibus 1.39 and the Continuity of Cicero's Scepticism". In *Cicero the Philosopher: Twelve Papers*, J. Powell (ed.), 85–113. Oxford: Clarendon Press.

Gould, J. 1985. "On Making Sense of Greek Religion". In *Greek Religion and Society*, P. Easterling & J. Muir (eds), 1–33. Cambridge: Cambridge University Press.

Graver, M. 2007. *Stoicism and Emotion*. Chicago, IL: University of Chicago Press.

Graziosi, B. 2002. *Inventing Homer: The Early Reception of Epic*. Cambridge: Cambridge University Press.

Gregory of Nazianzus 1899. *The Five Theological Orations of Gregory of Nazianzus*, A. J. Mason (ed.). Cambridge: Cambridge University Press.

Gregory of Nazianzus 1996. *Orationes theologicae*, H. J. Sieben (trans.). Freiburg: Herder.

Gregory of Nyssa 1952–. *Gregorii Nysseni opera*, W. Jaeger (ed.). Leiden: Brill.

Griffin, M. 1989. "Philosophy, Politics, and Politicians at Rome". In *Philosophia Togata: Essays on Philosophy and Roman Society*, M. Griffin & J. Barnes (eds), 1–37. Oxford: Oxford University Press.

Griffin, M. 1995. "Philosophical Badinage in Cicero's Letters to his Friends". In *Cicero the Philosopher: Twelve Papers*, J. Powell (ed.), 325–46. Oxford: Clarendon Press.

Guthrie, W. K. C. 1962. *A History of Greek Philosophy: Vol. 1, The Earlier Presocratics and the Pythagoreans*. Cambridge: Cambridge University Press.

Guthrie, W. K. C. 1971. *Socrates*. Cambridge: Cambridge University Press.

Gwyn Griffiths, J. 1996. *Triads and Trinity*. Cardiff: University of Wales Press.

Hackforth, R. 1952. *Plato's Phaedrus*. Cambridge: Cambridge University Press.

Hadot, P. 1960. "Être, vie, pensée chez Plotin et avant Plotin". In *Les Sources de Plotin: Dix exposes et discussions*, E. Dodds *et al.* (eds), 107–41. Geneva: Fondation Hardt.

Hadot, P. 1995. *Philosophy as a Way of Life: Spiritual Exercises from Socrates to Foucault*, M. Chase (trans.). Oxford: Blackwell.

Hadot, P. 2002. *What Is Ancient Philosophy?*, M. Chase (trans.). Cambridge, MA: Harvard University Press.

Harrison, T. 2008. *Greek Religion: Belief and Experience*. London: Duckworth.

Hathaway, R. 1969. *Hierarchy and the Definition of Order in the Letters of Pseudo-Dionysius*. The Hague: Nijhoff.

Hegel, G. 1969. *Vorlesungen über die Philosophie der Religion*. Frankfurt: Suhrkamp.

Huffman, C. 1993. *Philolaus of Croton: Pythagorean and Presocratic: A Commentary on the Fragments and Testimonia with Interpretive Essays*. Cambridge: Cambridge University Press.

Huffman, C. 1999. "The Pythagorean Tradition". In *The Cambridge Companion to Early Greek Philosophy*, A. Long (ed.), 66–87. Cambridge: Cambridge University Press.

Huffman, C. 2005. *Archytas of Tarentum: Pythagorean, Philosopher and Mathematician King*. Cambridge: Cambridge University Press.

Hunter, R. 2004. *Plato's Symposium*. Oxford: Oxford University Press.

Hussey, E. 2006. "The Beginnings of Science and Philosophy in Archaic Greece". In *A Companion to Ancient Philosophy*, M. Gill & P. Pellegrin (eds), 3–19. Oxford: Blackwell.

Iamblichus 1991. *On the Pythagorean Way of Life*, J. Dillon & J. Hershbell (trans.). Atlanta, GA: Scholars Press.

Iamblichus 2003. *On the Mysteries*, E. Clarke, J. Dillon & J. Hershbell (trans.). Atlanta, GA: Society for Biblical Studies.

Inwood, B. 2003. *The Cambridge Companion to the Stoics*. Cambridge: Cambridge University Press.

Inwood, B. 2005. *Reading Seneca: Stoic Philosophy at Rome*. Oxford: Clarendon Press.

Inwood, B. & L. Gerson (trans.) 1997. *Hellenistic Philosophy: Introductory Readings*, 2nd edn. Indianapolis, IN: Hackett.

Jackson, B. 1971. "The Prayers of Socrates". *Phronesis* **16**: 14–37.

Jackson-McCabe, M. 2004. "The Stoic Theory of Implanted Preconceptions". *Phronesis* **49**: 323–47.

Johnson, R. 1999. "Does Plato's 'Myth of Er' Contribute to the Argument of the *Republic*?" *Philosophy and Rhetoric* **32**: 1–13.

Kahn, C. 2001. *Pythagoras and the Pythagoreans: A Brief History*. Indianapolis, IN: Hackett.

Kidd, I. 1995. "Some Philosophical Demons". *Bulletin of the Institute of Classical Studies* **40**: 217–22.

Kingsley, P. 1995. *Ancient Philosophy, Mystery, and Magic: Empedocles and Pythagorean Tradition*. Oxford: Clarendon Press.

Kingsley, P. 1999. *In the Dark Places of Wisdom*. London: Duckworth.

Kirk, G., J. Raven & M. Schofield 1983. *The Presocratic Philosophers: A Critical History with a Selection of Texts*, 2nd edn. Cambridge: Cambridge University Press.

Koch, H. 1895. "Proklus als Quelle des Dionysius Areopagita in der Lehre vom Bösen". *Philologus* **54**: 438–54.

Koch, H. 1932. *Pronoia und Paideusis: Studies über Origenes und sein Verhältnis zum Platonismus*. Berlin: de Gruyter.

Koninck, T. de 1994. "Aristotle on God as Thought Thinking Itself". *Review of Metaphysics* **47**: 471–515.

Kouloumentas, S. 2009. "The Early Pythagoreans on Cosmic Justice". In his *The Conception of Cosmic Justice in Early Greek Philosophy*, 146–66, unpublished PhD dissertation, Cambridge University.

Lamberton, R. 1986. *Homer the Theologian: Neoplatonist Allegorical Reading and the Growth of the Epic Tradition*. Berkeley, CA: University of California Press.

Lamberton, R. 1989. *Homer the Theologian: Neoplatonist Allegorical Reading and the Growth of the Epic Tradition*. Berkeley, CA: University of California Press.

Long, A. 1990. "Scepticism about Gods in Hellenistic Philosophy". In *Cabinet of the Muses: Essays on Classical and Comparative Literature in Honor of Thomas G. Rosenmeyer*, M. Griffith & D. Mastronarde (eds), 279–91. Atlanta, GA: Scholars Press.

Long, A. A. & D. N. Sedley 1987. *The Hellenistic Philosophers*, 2 vols. Cambridge: Cambridge University Press.

Luther, M. 1888. *D. Martin Luthers Werke: Kritische Gesamtausgabe*, vol. 6. Weimar: Hermann Böhlau.

MacKendrick, P. 1989. *The Philosophical Books of Cicero.* London: Duckworth.

Macris, C. 2003. "Pythagore, un maître de sagesse charismatique de la fin de l'époque archaïque". In *Carisma profetico: fattore di innovazione religiosa*, G. Filoramo (ed.), 243–89. Brescia: Morcelliana.

Macris, C. 2009. "Charismatic Authority, Spiritual Guidance, and Way of Life in the Pythagorean Tradition". In *Philosophy as a Way of Life: Ancients and Moderns*, M. Chase & M. McGhee (eds). London: Blackwell.

Malingrey, A.-M. 1961. *Philosophia: Étude d'un groupe de mots dans la littérature grecque, des Présocratiques au IVe siècle après J.C.* Paris: Klincksieck.

Mansfeld, J. 1988. "Compatible Alternatives: Middle Platonist Theology and the Xenophanes Reception". In *The Knowledge of God in the Graeco-Roman World*, R. van den Broek, T. Baarda & J. Mansfeld (eds), 92–117. Leiden: Brill.

Marinus 1966. *Vita Procli.* J. Boissonade (ed.). Amsterdam: Adolf M. Hakkert.

McKirahan, R. forthcoming. "Aristotle on the Pythagoreans: His Sources and His Accounts of Pythagorean Principles". In *Polarity and Tension of Being: Pythagoras and Heraclitus*, A. Pierris (ed.), Proceedings of the Symposium Philosophiae Antiquae Quintum, 16–28 July 2005, Pythagoreion (Samos) and Ephesus. Patras: Institute for Philosophical Research.

McPherran, M. 1996. *The Religion of Socrates.* University Park, PA: Pennsylvania State University Press.

McPherran, M. 2000. "Does Piety Pay? Socrates and Plato on Prayer and Sacrifice". In *Reason and Religion in Socratic Philosophy*, N. Smith & P. Woodruff (eds), 89–114. Oxford: Oxford University Press.

Meinwald, C. 2002. "Plato's Pythagoreanism". *Ancient Philosophy* **22**: 87–101.

Momigliano, A. 1984. "The Theological Efforts of the Roman Upper Classes in the First Century BC". *Classical Philology* **79**: 199–211.

Mondésert, C. 1944. *Clément d'Alexandrie: Introduction à l'étude de sa pensée religieuse à partir de l'Ecriture.* Aubier: Paris.

Moreschini, C. 1990 "Aspetti della doctrina del martirio in Tertulliano". *Compostellanum* **35**: 55–70.

Morewedge, P. (ed.) 1992. *Neoplatonism and Islamic Thought.* Albany, NY: SUNY Press.

Morgan, M. 1990. *Platonic Piety.* New Haven, CT: Yale University Press.

Morrow, G. 1966. "Plato's Gods". In *Insight and Vision: Essays in Honor of Radoslav Andrea Tsanoff*, K. Kolenda (ed.), 121–34. San Antonio, TX: Principia Press of Trinity University.

Most, G. 2003. "Philosophy and Religion". In *The Cambridge Companion to Greek and Roman Philosophy*, D. Sedley (ed.), 300–322. Cambridge: Cambridge University Press.

Mourelatos, A. (ed.) 1974. *The Pre-Socratics.* Garden City, NY: Anchor Press.

Mühlenberg, E. 1966. *Die Unendlichkeit Gottes bei Gregor von Nyssa: Gregors Kritik am Gottesbegrift der klassischen Metaphysik.* Göttinger: Vandenhoeck & Ruprecht.

Nightingale, A. 2004. *Spectacles of Truth in Classical Greek Philosophy: Theoria in its Cultural Context.* Cambridge: Cambridge University Press.

Normore, C. 2003. "Duns Scotus's Modal Theory". In *The Cambridge Companion to Duns Scotus*, T. Williams (ed.), 129–60. Cambridge: Cambridge University Press.

Numenius 1973. *Fragments*, É. des Places (ed. & trans.). Paris: Les Belles Lettres.

Obbink, D. 1992. "'What All Men Believe – Must Be True': Common Conceptions and *Consensio Omnium* in Aristotle and Hellenistic Philosophy". *Oxford Studies in Ancient Philosophy* **10**: 193–231.

O'Meara, J. 1959. *Porphyry's Philosophy from Oracles in Augustine.* Paris: Études Augustiniennes.

O'Meara, D. 1989. *Pythagoras Revived: Mathematics and Philosophy in Late Antiquity.* Oxford: Clarendon Press.

Origen 1953. *Contra Celsum*, H. Chadwick (trans.). Cambridge: Cambridge University Press.

Origen 1956. *The Song of Songs: Commentary and Homilies*, R. Lawson (trans.). New York: Newman Press.

Origen 1965. *Contra Celsum*, H. Chadwick (trans.). Cambridge: Cambridge University Press.

Origen 1966. *On First Principles*, G. Butterworth (trans.). New York: Harper Torchbooks.

Origen 1982. *Homilies on Genesis and Exodus*, R. Heine (trans.). Washington, DC: Catholic University of America Press.

Origen 1989. *Commentary on the Gospel According to John, Books 1–10*, R. Heine (trans.). Washington, DC: Catholic University of America Press.

Origen 1993. *Commentary on the Gospel according to John, Books 11–32*, R. Heine (trans.). Washington, DC: Catholic University of America Press.

Osborn, E. 1997. *Tertullian: First Theologian of the West*. Cambridge: Cambridge University Press.

Osborn, E. 2005. *Clement of Alexandria*. Cambridge: Cambridge University Press.

Pelikan, J. V. 1995. *Christianity and Classical Culture: The Metamorphosis of Natural Theology in the Christian Encounter with Hellenism*. New Haven, CT: Yale University Press.

Penwill, J. 2000. "A Material God for a Material Universe: Towards an Epicurean Theology". *Iris (Journal of the Classical Association of Victoria)* **13**: 18–35.

Périllié, J. (ed.) 2008. *Platon et les Pythagoriciens: Hiérarchie des savoirs et des pratiques: musique - science - politique*. Brussels: Ousia.

Perry, K. 2006. "Reading Proclus Diadochus in Byzantium". See Tarrant & Baltzly (eds) (2006), 223–35.

Petit, A. 1997. "Le silence pythagoricien". In *Dire l'évidence: Philosophie et rhétorique antiques*, C. Lévy & L. Pernot (eds), 287–96. Paris: L'Harmattan.

Philodemus 1996. *Philodemus on Piety, Part 1*, D. Obbink (trans.). Oxford: Oxford University Press.

Philostratus 1921. *Lives of the Sophists* (with Eunapius, *Lives of the Philosophers and Sophists*), W. C. Wright (trans.). Cambridge, MA: Harvard University Press.

Places, É. des (ed. & trans.) 1971. *Oracles chaldaïques: Avec un choix de commentaires anciens*. Paris: Les Belles Lettres.

Plantinga, A. 1974. *God, Freedom, and Evil*. New York: Harper & Row.

Plato 1925. *Lysis, Symposium, Gorgias*, W. Lamb (trans.). Cambridge, MA: Harvard University Press.

Plato 1997. *Complete Works*, J. Cooper (ed.). Indianapolis, IN: Hackett.

Plato 2000. *Timaeus*, D. J. Zeyl (trans.). Indianapolis, IN: Hackett.

Plotinus 1964–82. *Plotini opera*, 3 vols, P. Henry & H.-R. Schwyzer (eds). Oxford: Clarendon Press.

Porphyry 1886. *Opuscula*, A. Nauck (ed.). Leipzig: Teubner.

Porphyry 1913. *On the Return of the Soul* and *On Statues*, appendices to J. Bidez *Vie de Porphyre*. Ghent: Van Goethen.

Porphyry 1965. *The Life of Pythagoras*. In *Heroes and Gods: Spiritual Biographies in Antiquity*, M. Hadas & M. Smith (eds), 105–28. London: Routledge & Kegan Paul.

Porphyry 1991. *Life of Plotinus*, P. Kalligas (ed.). Athens: Centre for the Publication of Greek Authors.

Porphyry 1993. *Fragmenta* (including *On Statues, Philosophy from Oracles*), A. Smith (ed.). Leipzig: Teubner.

Porphyry 2001. *Πορφυρίου. Πυθαγόρου βίος* [original Greek text], C. Macris (trans. in modern Greek, & notes). Athens: Katarti.

Proclus 1909. *Procli Diadochi hypotyposis astronomicarum positionum: Una cum scholiis antiquis e libris manuscriptis edidit Germanica interpretatione et commentariis instruxit*, C. Manitius (ed.). Leipzig: Teubner.

Proclus 1912. *Institutio physica*, A. Ritzenfeld (ed.). Leipzig: Teubner.

Proclus 1928. *Proclus: De Sacrificio et magia* (Catalogue des manuscrits alchimiques grecs), J. Bidez (ed.). Brussels: Lamertin.

Proclus 1957. *Hymni*, E. Vogt (ed.). Wiesbaden: Harrassowitz.

Proclus 1958. *Die mittelalterliche Ubersetzung der Stoicheiosis physike des Proclus: Procli Diadochi Lycii Elementatio physica*, H. Boese (ed.). Berlin: Academie.

Proclus 1963. *Elements of Theology*, E. Dodds (ed. & trans.). Oxford: Clarendon Press.

Proclus 1965. *Alcibiades I: A Translation and Commentary*, W. O'Neill (trans.). The Hague: Martinus Nijhoff.

Proclus 1966–68. *Commentaire sur le Timée*, A. Festugière (trans.). Paris: CNRS.

Proclus 1968–97 *Théologie platonicienne*, H.-D. Saffrey & L. G. Westerink (eds & trans.). Paris: Les Belles Lettres.

Proclus 1970a. *Commentary on the First book of Euclid's Elements*, G. Morrow (trans.). Princeton, NJ: Princeton University Press.

Proclus 1970b. *Commentaire sur la République*, A. Festugière (trans.). Paris: Vrin.

Proclus 1977. *Trois études sur la providence I: Dix problèmes concernant la providence*, D. Isaac (ed. & trans.). Paris: Les Belles Lettres.

Proclus 1979. *Trois études sur la providence II: Providence, Fatalité, Liberté*, D. Isaac (ed. & trans.). Paris: Les Belles Lettres.

Proclus 1982. *Trois études sur la providence III: De l' existence du mal*, D. Isaac (ed. & trans.). Paris: Les Belles Lettres.

Proclus 1987. *Commentary on Plato's Parmenides*, G. Morrow & J. Dillon (trans.). Princeton, NJ: Princeton University Press.

Proclus 2001a. *On the Eternity of the World*, H. Lang & A. Macro (eds & trans.). Berkeley, CA: University of California Press.

Proclus 2001b. *Hymns: Essays, Translations, Commentary*, R. van den Berg (ed.). Leiden: Brill.

Proclus 2005. *On Plato's Cratylus: Ancient Commentators on Aristotle*, B. Duvick (trans.). London: Duckworth.

Proclus 2007a. *Commentary on Plato's Timaeus, Vol. 1*, H. Tarrant (ed. & trans.). Cambridge: Cambridge University Press.

Proclus 2007b. *Commentary on Plato's Timaeus, Vol. 3, Part 1*, D. Baltzly (ed. & trans.). Cambridge: Cambridge University Press.

Proclus 2008. *Commentary on Plato's Timaeus, Vol. 2, Book II: The Demiurge and the Model*, D. T. Runia & M. Share (trans.). Cambridge: Cambridge University Press.

Radice, R. 1991. "Observations on the Theory of the Ideas as the Thoughts of God in Philo of Alexandria". *The Studia Philonica Annual* 3: 126–34.

Rawson, E. 1985. *Intellectual Life in the Late Roman Republic*. Baltimore, MD: Johns Hopkins University Press.

Riedweg, C. 1997. "'Pythagoras hinterliess keine einzige Schrift' – ein Irrtum? Anmerkungen zu einer alten Streitfrage". *Museum Helveticum* 54: 65–92.

Riedweg, C. 2005. *Pythagoras: His Life, Teaching, and Influence*, S. Rendall (trans., in collaboration with C. Riedweg & A. Schatzmann). Ithaca, NY: Cornell University Press.

Rist, J. 1972. *Epicurus: An Introduction*. Cambridge: Cambridge University Press.

Robinson, R. 1953. *Plato's Earlier Dialectic*, 2nd edn. Oxford: Clarendon Press.

Romeyer-Dherbey, G. & J.-B. Gourinat (eds) 2005. *Les Stoïciens*. Paris: Vrin.

Roochnik, D. 2004. *Retrieving the Ancients: An Introduction to Ancient Philosophy*. Oxford: Blackwell.

Roques, R. 1954. *L'univers Dionysien: Structure hierarchique du monde selon le Pseudo-Denys*. Paris: Aubier.

Rorem, P. 1993 *Pseudo-Dionysius: A Commentary on the Texts and an Introduction to their Influence*. Oxford: Oxford University Press.

Rorem, P. & J. Lamoreaux 1998. *John of Scythopolis and the Dionysian Corpus*. Oxford: Clarendon Press.

Rowe, C. 1983. "Archaic Thought in Hesiod". *Journal of Hellenic Studies* **103**: 124–35.

Runia, D. T. 1986. *Philo of Alexandria and the "Timaeus" of Plato*. Brill: Leiden.

Russell, B. 1946. *History of Western Philosophy*. London: Allen & Unwin.

Saffrey, H.-D. 1971. "Abamon, pseudonyme de Jamblique". In *Philomathes: Studies in the Humanities in Honour of Philip Merlan*, R. Palmer & R. Hammeton-Kelly (eds), 227–39. The Hague: Nijhoff.

Saffrey, H. D. 1975. "Allusions antichretiennes chez Proclus: Le diadoque Platonicien. *Revue des Sciences Philosophiques et Philogiques* **59**: 553–62.

Schäfer, C. 2006. *The Philosophy of Dionysius the Areopagite: An Introduction to the Structure and the Content of the Treatise On the Divine Names*. Leiden: Brill.

Schefer, C. 1996. *Platon und Apollon: Von Logos zurück zum Mythos*, International Platon Studies, 7. Berlin: Academic Verlag.

Schofield, M. 1980. "Preconception, Argument, and God". In *Doubt and Dogmatism: Studies in Hellenistic Epistemology*, M. Schofield, M. Burnyeat & J. Barnes (eds), 283–308. Oxford: Clarendon Press.

Schofield, M. 1986. "Cicero For and Against Divination". *Journal of Roman Studies* **76**: 47–65.

Scott, D. 1995. *Recollection and Experience: Plato's Theory of Learning and Its Successors*. Cambridge: Cambridge University Press.

Scott, G. (ed.) 2002. *Does Socrates Have a Method? Rethinking the Elenchus in Plato's Dialogues and Beyond*. University Park, PA: Pennsylvania State University Press.

Scott, W. 1936. *Hermetica IV*. Oxford: Clarendon Press.

Seaford, R. 2005. "Mystic Light in Aeschylus' *Bassarai*". *Classical Quarterly* **55**: 602–6.

Sedley, D. 1997. "'Becoming Like God' in the *Timaeus* and Aristotle". In *Interpreting the "Timaeus–Critias": Proceedings of the Fourth Symposium Platonicum*, T. Calvo & L. Brisson (eds), 327–39. St Augustin: Academica.

Sedley, D. 2002. "The Origins of the Stoic God". In *Traditions of Theology: Studies in Hellenistic Theology*, D. Frede & A. Laks (eds), 41–83. Leiden: Brill.

Sedley, D. 2007. *Creationism and Its Critics in Antiquity*. Berkeley, CA: University of California Press.

Sextus Empiricus 1936. *Against the Physicists*, R. Bury (trans.) (Loeb Classical Library, vol. III of Sextus' complete works). Cambridge, MA: Harvard University Press.

Sextus Empiricus 1997. *Against the Ethicists*, R. Bett (trans.). Oxford: Oxford University Press.

Sextus Empiricus 2000. *Outlines of Scepticism*, 2nd edn, J. Annas & J. Barnes (eds). Cambridge: Cambridge University Press.

Sextus Empiricus 2005. *Against the Logicians*, R. Bett (ed. & trans.). Cambridge: Cambridge University Press.

Shaw, G. 1995. *Theurgy and the Soul: The Neoplatonism of Iamblichus*. University Park, PA: Pennsylvania State University Press.

Shayegan, Y. 1996. "The Transmission of Greek Philosophy in the Islamic World". In *History of Islamic Philosophy*, S. Nasr & O. Leaman (eds), 98–104. London: Routledge.

Siorvanes, L. 1996. *Proclus: Neo-Platonic Philosophy and Science*. New Haven, CT: Yale University Press.

Skinner, Q. 1969. "Meaning and Understanding in the History of Ideas". *History and Theory* **8**: 3–53.

Snell, B. 1953. *The Discovery of the Mind: The Greek Origins of European Thought*. Cambridge, MA: Harvard University Press.

Sorabji, R. 1983. *Time, Creation, and the Continuum*. Ithaca, NY: Cornell University Press.

Sorabji, R. 2005. *The Philosophy of the Commentators, 200–600 AD: A Sourcebook: Vol. 1, Psychology*. Ithaca, NY: Cornell University Press.

Staats, R. (ed.) 1984. *Makarios-Symoen, Epistola magna: Eine messalanische Mönchsregal und ihre Unschrift in Gregors von Nyssa "De instituto Christiano"*. Göttingen: Vandenhoeck & Ruprecht.

Stead, C. 1976. "Ontology and Terminology in Gregory of Nyssa". In *Gregor von Nyssa und die Philosophie*, H. Doerrie, M. Alternburger & U. Schramm (eds), 107–27. Leiden: Brill.

Steel, C. 2007. "Proclus on Divine Figures: An Essay on Pythagorean-Platonic Theology". In *A Platonic Pythagoras: Platonism and Pythagoreanism in the Imperial Age*, M. Bonazzi, C. Levy & C. Steel (eds), 215–42. Turnhout: Brepols Publishers.

Stiglmayr, J. 1895. "Der Neuplatoniker Proklus als Vorlage des sogenannten Dionysius Areopagita in der Lehre Übel". *Historisches Jahrbuch* **16**: 253–73, 721–48.

Stokes, M. 1971. *One and Many in Presocratic Philosophy*. Washington, DC: Center for Hellenic Studies.

Stokes, M. 1992. "Socrates' Mission". In *Socratic Questions: New Essays on the Philosophy of Socrates and Its Significance*, B. Gower & M. Stokes (eds), 26–81. London: Routledge.

Taran, L. 1987. "Cicero's Attitude towards Stoicism and Skepticism in the *De Natura Deorum*". In *Florilegium Columbianum: Essays in Honor of Paul Oskar Kristeller*, K.-L. Selig & R. Somerville (eds), 1–22. New York: Italica Press.

Tarrant, H. 2000. *Plato's First Interpreters*. London: Duckworth.

Tarrant, H. & D. Baltzly (eds) 2006. *Reading Plato in Antiquity*. London: Duckworth.

Thaumaturgus, G. 1998. *Address of Thanksgiving*. In *St. Gregory Thaumaturgus: Life and Works*, M. Slusser (trans.). Washington, DC: Catholic University of America Press.

Theophrastus 1929. *Metaphysics*, W. Ross & F. Fobes (trans.). Oxford: Clarendon Press.

Thom, J. 1995. *The Pythagorean "Golden Verses"*. Leiden: Brill.

Tigerstedt, E. 1974. *The Decline and Fall of the Neoplatonic Interpretation of Plato*. Helsinki: Societas Scientiarum Fennica.

Turner, D. 1995. *The Darkness of God: Negativity in Christian Mysticism*. Cambridge: Cambridge University Press.

Vanneste, J. 1959. *Le Mystère de Dieu*. Brussels: Desclée de Brouwer.

Varro 1976. *Marcus Terentius Varro*, Antiquitates Rerum Divinarum, vols 1 & 2, B. Cardauns (ed.). Mainz: Akademie der Wissenschaften und der Literatur.

Vernant, J-P. 1991. "*Psuche*: Simulacrum of the Body or Image of the Divine?". In his *Mortals and Immortals: Collected Essays*, F. Zeitlin (ed.), 186–92. Princeton, NJ: Princeton University Press.

Vlastos, G. 1975. *Plato's Universe*. Oxford: Oxford University Press.

Vlastos, G. 1989. "Socratic Piety". In *Proceedings of the Boston Area Colloquium in Ancient Philosophy*, vol. 5, J. Cleary & D. Shartin (eds), 213–38. Lanham, MD: University Press of America.

Vlastos, G. 1991. *Socrates, Ironist and Moral Philosopher*. Ithaca, NY: Cornell University Press.

Vlastos, G. 1994. "Socrates' Disavowal of Knowledge". In his *Socratic Studies*, M. Burnyeat (ed.), 39–66. Cambridge: Cambridge University Press.

Wallis, R. 1995. *Neoplatonism*, 2nd edn. London: Duckworth.

Wehrli, F. 1945. *Die Schule des Aristoteles: Texte und Kommentar*, vol. 2. Basel: Schwabe.

West, M. 1983. *The Orphic Poems*. Oxford: Oxford University Press.

Winston, D. 1985. *Logos and Mystical Theology in Philo of Alexandria*. Cincinnati, OH: Hebrew Union College Press.

Winston, D. 1989. "Two Types of Mosaic Prophecy according to Philo". *Journal for the Study of the Pseudepigrapha* **4**: 49–67.

Wolfson, H. 1947. *Philo: Foundations of Religious Philosophy in Judaism, Christianity, and Islam*, 2 vols. Cambridge, MA: Harvard University Press.

Wolinski, J. 1995. "Le Recours aux *epinoiai* du Christ dans le *Commentaire sur Jean d'Origène*". In *Origiana Sexta: Origène et la Bible*, G. Dorival & A. Le Boulluec (eds), 465–92. Leuven: Peeters.

Wyrwa, D. 1983. *Die christliche Platonaneignung in den Stromateis des Clemens von Alexandrien*. Berlin: De Gruyter.

Xenophanes of Colophon 1992. *Fragments*, J. Lesher (trans. & comm.). Toronto: University of Toronto Press.

Zaidman, L. & P. Pantel 1992. *Religion in the Ancient Greek City*, P. Cartledge (trans.). Cambridge: Cambridge University Press.

Zhmud, L. 1989. "Pythagoras as a Mathematician". *Historia Mathematica* **16**: 249–68.

Zhmud, L. 1997. *Wissenschaft, Philosophie und Religion im früher Pythagoreismus*. Berlin: Akademie.

INDEX